## DATE DUE

| | |
|---|---|
| JUN 1 2 1997 | |
| | |
| SEP 8 1997 | |
| JAN 4 1999 | |
| | |
| FEB 2 5 1999 | |
| | |
| | |
| | |
| | |
| | |
| | |
| | |
| | |
| | |
| | |
| GAYLORD | PRINTED IN U.S.A. |

# Cognitive
# Science
# and
# Clinical
# Disorders

# Cognitive Science and Clinical Disorders

Edited by

**Dan J. Stein**

*Department of Psychiatry*
*College of Physicians and Surgeons*
*Columbia University*
*and*
*New York State Psychiatric Institute*
*New York, New York*

**Jeffrey E. Young**

*Department of Psychiatry*
*College of Physicians and Surgeons*
*Columbia University*
*and*
*Cognitive Therapy Center of New York*
*New York, New York*

SETON HALL UNIVERSITY
WALSH LIBRARY
SO. ORANGE, N.J.

**Academic Press, Inc.**
Harcourt Brace Jovanovich, Publishers

San Diego   New York   Boston   London   Sydney   Tokyo   Toronto

*For our parents,*
*Solly and Fanny Stein,*
*and Manny and Ethel Young.*

This book is printed on acid-free paper. ∞

Copyright © 1992 by ACADEMIC PRESS, INC.

All Rights Reserved.
No part of this publication may be reproduced or transmitted in any form or by any
means, electronic or mechanical, including photocopy, recording, or any information
storage and retrieval system, without permission in writing from the publisher.

Academic Press, Inc.
1250 Sixth Avenue, San Diego, California 92101-4311

*United Kingdom Edition published by*
Academic Press Limited
24–28 Oval Road, London NW1 7DX

Library of Congress Cataloging-in-Publication Data

Cognitive science and clinical disorders / edited by Dan J. Stein,
Jeffrey E. Young.
    p.   cm.
  Includes bibliographical references and index.
  ISBN 0-12-664720-8
  1. Psychology, Pathological.   2. Cognitive science.   I. Stein,
Dan J.   II. Young, Jeffrey E., date.
  [DNLM: 1.Cognition.   2. Mental Disorders.   BF 311 C678475]
RC454.4.C615   1992
616.90–dc20
DNLM/DLC
for Library of Congress                                      92-11148
                                                                CIP

PRINTED IN THE UNITED STATES OF AMERICA
92  93  94  95  96  97    BB    9  8  7  6  5  4  3  2  1

# Contents

## PART II

# Clinical Disorders

# 16   Information Processing, Experience, and Reading Disability

**Louise C. Spear and Robert J. Sternberg**

# Contributors

Numbers in parentheses indicate the pages on which the authors' contributions begin.

**Patricia A. Carr** (79), Department of Psychology, University of Notre Dame, Notre Dame, Indiana 46556

**Marylene Cloitre** (19), Department of Psychology, New School for Social Research, New York, New York 10003, and Cornell Medical College, New York, New York 10021

**Jonathan D. Cohen** (99), Department of Psychology, Carnegie Mellon University, Pittsburgh, Pennsylvania 15213, and Department of Psychiatry, University of Pittsburgh, Pittsburgh, Pennsylvania 15260

**Vanessa C. Hayden** (211), Department of Psychology, University of Arizona, Tucson, Arizona 85721

**Eric Hollander** (235), Department of Psychiatry, College of Physicians and Surgeons, Columbia University, New York, New York 10032, and New York State Psychiatric Institute, New York, New York 10032

**Christian Holle** (187), Department of Psychology, State University of New York, Albany, Albany New York 12222

**Rick E. Ingram** (187), Department of Psychology, San Diego State University, San Diego, California 92182

**W. Jake Jacobs** (211), Department of Psychology, University of Arizona, Tucson, Arizona 85721

**Mark H. Johnson** (43), Department of Psychology, Carnegie Mellon University, Pittsburgh, Pennsylvania 15213

**John F. Kihlstrom** (247), Amnesia and Cognition Unit, Department of Psychology, University of Arizona, Tucson, Arizona 85721

**William J. Lyddon** (171), Department of Psychology, University of Southern Mississippi, Hattiesburg, Mississippi 39401

**George Mandler** (61), Department of Psychology, University of California, San Diego, La Jolla, California 92093, and University College London, London NW3 1QY, England

**Thomas V. Merluzzi** (79), Department of Psychology, University of Notre Dame, Notre Dame, Indiana 46556

**Lynn Nadel** (211), Department of Psychology, University of Arizona, Tucson, Arizona 85721

**Mike R. Oaksford** (129), Cognitive Neurocomputation Unit, University of Wales, Bangor, LL57 2DG, United Kingdom

**Keith Oatley** (151), Center for Applied Cognitive Science, Ontario Institute for Studies in Education, Toronto, M5S 1V6 Canada

**Marcus Richards** (289), Department of Neurology and Gertrude H. Sergievsky Center, College of Physicians and Surgeons, Columbia University, New York, New York 10032

**David Servan-Schreiber** (99), Department of Psychiatry, University of Pittsburgh, Pittsburgh, Pennsylvania 15260, and Department of Computer Science, Carnegie Mellon University, Pittsburgh, Pennsylvania 15213

**Louise C. Spear** (313), Department of Special Education, Southern Connecticut State University, New Haven, Connecticut 06515

**David Spiegel** (99), Department of Psychiatry and Behavioral Sciences, Stanford University, Stanford, California 94305

**Dan J. Stein** (3, 235, 271), Department of Psychiatry, College of Physicians and Surgeons, Columbia University, New York, New York 10032, and New York State Psychiatric Institute, New York, New York 10032

**Yaakov Stern** (289), Department of Neurology and Gertrude H. Sergievsky Center, College of Physicians and Surgeons, Columbia University, New York, New York 10032

**Robert J. Sternberg** (313), Department of Psychology, Yale University, New Haven, Connecticut 06520

**Elisabeth Targ** (99), Department of Psychiatry and Behavioral Sciences, University of California, Los Angeles, Los Angeles, California 90024

**J. M. G. Williams** (129), Department of Psychology, University of Wales, Bangor, LL57 2DG, United Kingdom

**Jeffrey E. Young** (271), Department of Psychiatry, College of Physicians and Surgeons, Columbia University, New York, New York 10032, and Cognitive Therapy Center of New York, New York, New York 10024

# Preface

As we enter the last decade of the century, it is tempting to try and view this volume from the perspective of the various developments that have taken place during this century both in general psychology and in clinical science. In general psychology, there has been a dramatic shift away from behavioral and phenomenological approaches toward a cognitivist paradigm. The emergence of the multidisciplinary field of cognitive science, including cognitive psychology, artificial intelligence, linguistics, and philosophy, epitomizes the success of cognitivist and computational models of the mind. However, in clinical science, in which psychoanalytic and community-based approaches were once central, biological psychiatry and cognitive–behavioral therapies now predominate.

In this volume we attempt to build bridges between current research in cognitive science and contemporary clinical theory and practice. Increasing contributions to this intersection of fields have been made in the past decade. Nevertheless, cognitive scientists have, by and large, ignored many phenomena that are well known to clinicians. Only recently have they begun to pay attention to emotion, and they continue to view emotional disorders as peripheral. Conversely, although clinicians have increasingly employed cognitivist constructs in their thinking and their work, the incorporation of cognitive science into the clinic has been incomplete. This volume begins with the idea that the intersection of cognitive and clinical science benefits both cognitive scientists and clinicians.

Cognitive science provides the clinician with complex multifaceted models of the mind and with a variety of methodologies for measuring and studying psychological phenomena. Few clinicians adhere any longer to the energy-based models of psychoanalysis or to the stimulus–response models of behaviorism. Nevertheless, it is unclear which model of the mind should replace them. Computational and cognitivist models form the basis of cognitive science, and increasingly they are employed by both clinical practitioners and clinical researchers.

**xiii**

Clinicians offer the cognitive scientist a realm of phenomena that is at the core of what the mind is and does. For example, everyday emotional experience, more subtle alterations in consciousness, and finally, severe depression, anxiety, dissociation, and psychosis are windows that may provide important views of the mind. The detailed descriptions of psychopathology or psychotherapy that clinicians provide may be far more significant than a particular laboratory finding. If the cognitivist approach is to advance, it must explain not only cognition but also an individual's affect and the various cognitive–affective alterations and disturbances.

Part I of this volume provides a theoretical background to the intersection of cognitive and clinical science. Stein begins with a general overview of this junction, including possible advantages and drawbacks of work in the area. Subsequent chapters investigate important topics within the intersection, or illustrate the role of particular branches of cognitive science in clinical studies.

Freud and Piaget exerted an influence on both cognitive science and clinical science. Freud's methods were primarily clinical; he focused on clinical disorders and the role of the unconscious. Piaget, whose methods were more laboratory oriented, focused on cognitive processes and their development. Both investigators noted the importance of processes that take place unconsciously, of developmental stages, and of cognitive–affective interactions. In Chapter 2, Cloitre explores current cognitive science theory and research on unconscious processes. Johnson (Chapter 3) describes a cognitivist approach to the development of visual attention and its possible clinical implications.

Central branches of cognitive science include cognitive psychology and artificial intelligence. The linear processing of digital computers provided early cognitive psychologists with various symbolic or representational constructs. The parallel processing done by distributed processors provided later cognitive psychologists with connectionist or network ideas. Mandler (Chapter 4) describes the role of certain representational constructs in understanding emotion, and he suggests that this work may be applicable to understanding emotional disorders. In Chapter 5, Merluzzi and Carr describe the role of similar constructs in clinical assessment and evaluation. Cohen, Servan-Schreiber, Targ, and Spiegel (Chapter 6) propose a connectionist model of schizophrenia, arguing that this model accounts not only for experimental findings on information processing in schizophrenia, but also incorporates our neurobiological knowledge of this disorder. Williams and Oaksford (Chapter 7) provide a connectionist model of anxiety and depression. Similarly, they propose that their model is consistent with both experimental cognitive psychology and contemporary neuroscience.

Other branches of cognitive science include linguistics and philosophy. In Chapter 8, Oatley focuses on language and narrative and argues that a cognitive view of narrative is helpful in understanding central aspects of clinical science. Lyddon (Chapter 9) uses philosophical notions to explore different kinds of cognitive psychotherapy, and he argues that different epistemological perspectives underlie these forms of psychotherapy.

Part II of this volume focuses on particular clinical disorders. Ingram and Holle (Chapter 10) discuss information–processing approaches to understanding and researching depression. Jacobs, Nadel, and Hayden (Chapter 11) propose an integrative cognitive science model of certain anxiety disorders. Stein and Hollander (Chapter 12) suggest that cybernetic constructs with a neurobiological underpinning may be useful in understanding and treating obsessive–compulsive disorder. In Chapter 13, Kihlstrom reviews early cognitivist theories of dissociation and conversion disorders, then he extends these to include more contemporary theory and research. Stein and Young (Chapter 14) focus on the role of schema theory in understanding and treating personality disorders. Richards and Stern (Chapter 15) review cognitive studies of disturbances of memory and other functions in Alzheimer's disease. Finally, Spear and Sternberg (Chapter 16) propose a model of the cognitive processes involved in reading disability.

I would like to close by acknowledging the guidance and support of mentors and colleagues. Anthony Starfield was my first teacher in computer studies, and his thinking was fundamentally important to the development of my interest in cognitive science. Eric Hollander mentored my neurobiologically focused research during the editing of this volume, and I am grateful to him for his superb teaching and ready encouragement. David Forrest and David Olds have always been willing to read preliminary drafts and have provided helpful and insightful criticisms and comments.

This volume would not have been possible without the love and support of my wife, Heather. My greatest happiness has been sharing my life with her.

My co-editor, Jeffrey Young, would like to acknowledge the inspiration and guidance of Aaron Beck.

*Dan J. Stein*

# Theoretical Frameworks

# 1

# Clinical Cognitive Science: Possibilities and Limitations

**Dan J. Stein**

*Department of Psychiatry*
*College of Physicians and Surgeons*
*Columbia University*
*and*
*New York State Psychiatric Institute*
*New York, New York*

Development of Cognitive Science
Cognitive Science Models
Clinical Cognitive Science
Advantages and Limitations

This chapter considers the intersection between cognitive and clinical science in general terms, sketching the theoretical background of the area, and considering some of its potentials and limitations. The chapter begins by considering the range of models of mind that cognitive science employs. The development of these cognitivist or computational models is described briefly, and they are compared and contrasted with other important models in general psychology. The question of whether these models are useful in the clinical context is raised, and early work at the juncture of cognitive and clinical science is discussed. Finally, some advantages and drawbacks of this convergence are presented.

## Development of Cognitive Science

Cognitive science has shown tremendous growth since its inception. The "cognitive revolution" now constitutes a predominant paradigm in general psychology. Cognitive science has developed into a multidisciplinary enterprise comprising cognitive psychology, artificial intelligence, linguistics, neuroscience, anthropology, and philosophy (Gardner, 1985).

Literature devoted to the subject continues to proliferate, and the number of university departments of cognitive science is increasing.

Various attempts have been made to provide a definition of cognitive science (Miller, 1979; Norman, 1980; Bruner, 1983). A cognitive information-processing account views the mind as an information processing system that selects, transforms, encodes, stores, retrieves, and generates information and behavior (Lachman, Lachman, & Butterfield, 1979). A computational view emphasizes that "cognitive science, sometimes explicitly and sometimes implicitly, tries to elucidate the workings of the mind by treating them as computations, not necessarily of the sort carried out by the digital computer, but of a sort that lies within [the] broader theory of computation" (Johnson-Laird, 1988, p. 9). A rigorous equation of mental and computational processes in turn raises a series of foundational debates about what a computational theory of mind entails, and whether such a theory can be accurate (Fodor, 1983; Pylyshyn, 1984; Dreyfus & Dreyfus, 1986; Harre, 1988; Searle, 1990).

From the clinical perspective of this volume, a defining formulation of mind in computational terms is not necessarily useful. Instead, we are interested in formulating a view of cognitive science that is broad, that is, that encompasses much of the work in cognitive science, but also specific, that is, that contrasts with noncognitive science approaches with which clinicians may be more familiar. Perhaps the best way to formulate such a view is to consider the particular models of mind that cognitive science employs. Cognitive scientists are interested in mental structures and processes, their representational significance, and their physical instantiation (Stillings et al., 1987). Their cognitivist or computational models range from symbolic and rule-based models that view human cognition as one instance of a universal science of representations (Fodor, 1983), to a variety of more ecological approaches that emphasize the embedding of the mind in environment (Lakoff, 1988; Neisser, 1988), to the connectionist paradigm, which sees cognition emerging from neural networks or parallel-processing systems (Rumelhart & McClelland, 1986a,b).

Perhaps the best way of introducing these cognitivist and computational models is in terms of their developmental origins. A number of factors, including the failure of behaviorism, the advent of computing machines, and various theoretical advances, led to the emergence of cognitive science (Gardner, 1985). One of the most important theoretical advances was the development of computer science. The father of this field was Turing (1936), a British mathematician who described a simple machine (the Turing machine) that executed instructions in binary code, and proposed that such a machine could, in principle, perform any computational task. He also suggested the notion of a universal Turing machine that would take a coded version of all other Turing machines as input and then emulate their behavior.

Computer science can be see immediately as relevant to psychology, since the question arises of whether the human mind can be instantiated on a universal Turing machine. Turing (1950) himself considered it possible to program a machine so a user communicating with the machine and with a person would be unable to differentiate between the two (the Turing machine test).

A number of other developments consolidated the importance of computational constructs for psychology. For example, it was proposed that certain concepts were useful in explaining both computing machines and human brains. This idea was clearly formulated at a seminal meeting in 1948, the Hixon Symposium on "Cerebral Mechanisms in Behavior" (Jeffress, 1951) at which Von Neumann and McCulloch were the opening speakers. The all-or-none property of neuronal activation could be compared to the determination of logical statements as either true or false. Further, neural networks and logical statements could be described in electrical terms as circuits through which current passed or failed to pass.

In addition, it was argued that certain constructs were useful in explaining both computing machines and human minds. Thus, Wiener (1961) proposed that machines and minds that had feedback mechanisms displayed purposefulness. Central to control and communication engineering was the notion of the message, whether it was transmitted by electrical, mechanical, or neural means. Information, Shannon (1938) showed, was independent of its physical representation.

The idea that mind and computer are in some way alike—that the mind is one particular system (carbon based) for processing information and the computer is another (silicon based)—is a powerful one. It may be seen as the nidus from which cognitive science developed. Miller has set the date of birth of cognitive science as September 11, 1956, at the Symposium on Information Theory at the Massachusetts Institute of Technology, a day on which a number of important papers were presented (Gardner, 1985). First, Miller himself gave an empirical paper on inherent constraints in short-term memory processes. Work by other psychologists in the 1950s, including Broadbent (1954) and Cherry (1953) in Britain and Bruner and colleagues at Harvard (Bruner, Goodnow, & Austin, 1956), gave further impetus to the development of cognitive psychology, and established the discipline and its empirical methodologies as a cornerstone of cognitive science. Second, Newell and Simon argued that artificial intelligence was possible and drew significant comparisons between artificial and human problem-solving processes. Along with computer scientists such as Minksy and McCarthy, they founded the field of artificial intelligence and helped establish a computational methodology for cognitive science. Finally, Chomsky developed his idea of a grammar based on linguistic transformations. This early work, coupled with his scathing review (Chomsky, 1959) of Skinner's work on verbal behavior (Skinner,

1957), supported the shift from behaviorism to cognitivism, and established linguistics as a framework in which the issues of cognitive science could be considered.

In addition to cognitive psychology, artificial intelligence, and linguistics, core branches of cognitive science include neuroscience, anthropology, and philosophy. Neuroscience provides the lower limit of cognitive science because, although cognitive processes may be theorized independent of their physical instantiation, cognitive processes in humans are underpinned by a particular neurobiological substrate. Anthropological studies set the upper limit of cognitive science because, although cognition takes place in individual persons, cognitive structures, processes, and products may differ from place to place and from time to time. Finally, many of the questions that cognitive scientists attempt to answer were raised first by philosophers. Philosophers also have addressed the founding principles of the discipline. As cognitive science has advanced, philosophers have been faced with the metacognitive question of the nature of the mind and the world that allowed this scientific advance to take place.

Cognitive science, in its short history, has evolved in a number of important ways. This development may be seen in the transformation of models of mind that cognitivists tend to employ. Early in the development of cognitive science, the standard model was of the mind as a sequential processor, similar to the early digital computer. The mind was a passive recipient of information that was registered in a short-term memory and perhaps encoded in a long-term memory. Subsequent models specified the structures that organize information and the controls that order its processing. Currently, this cognitive architecture is specified typically in either symbolic or connectionist terms. The elements of symbolic systems are symbols that are stored in associative structures. Symbolic systems include levels-of-processing models (Craik & Lockhart, 1972), spreading activation constructs (Collins & Loftus, 1975), and schema approaches (Neisser, 1967). The elements of connectionist systems are simplified and schematized neurons that are interconnected in a network. Again, a variety of these parallel-processing models have been developed (Rumelhart & McClelland, 1986a,b).

Although advances in computational science have provided an impetus toward more sophisticated cognitive science models, it also is notable that the cognitivist interest in mental structures and processes, their representational significance, and their physical instantiation can be seen in work that predates the invention of the computer. Important precognitivist work includes, for example, that of Helmholtz, Bartlett, and Piaget. Helmholtz developed the notion of unconscious inference to explain how the nervous system used past knowledge to interpret current perceptions. Barlett (1932) developed the notion of the schema, defined as an active organization of past reactions or experiences that operates in a well-adapted organic response, in order to explain his experimental findings on the memory of narratives. Finally, Piaget (1952) emphasized the biological basis of schemas and detailed their developmental transformation from sensorimotor reflexes to the operations of formal thought. The concepts of unconscious processing, and of schemas and their change, are important in contemporary clinical cognitive science.

## Cognitive Science Models

Further development of cognitivist and computational models of the mind is possible by comparing and contrasting them with other important models of the mind in general psychology. From a clinical viewpoint, perhaps the most important alternative models of the mind are the behaviorist, the psychoanalytic, and the biological models.

The behaviorist strategy of attempting to discover the laws of the relationship between stimuli and responses is well known. This strategy self-consciously makes the mind into a "black box," asserting that only the observable can be studied scientifically. In contrast, the cognitive model explicitly states that the mental structures in the "black box" and the processes whereby they generate cognitive products (thoughts and feelings) are of the greatest interest.

Nevertheless, it is possible to see a continuity between the behaviorist and the cognitive science models. Although the behaviorist model is limited to inputs (stimuli) and outputs (responses), the cognitivist model is concerned with inputs, processing, and outputs. Like behaviorists, cognitivists are concerned with empirical data and strict measurement, and with laboratory-based experimental proofs.

The classical psychoanalytic model of the mind was an energy-based one. For Freud (1894)

> in mental functions something is to be distinguished—a quota of affect or sum of excitation—which possesses all the characteristics of a quantity (though we have no means of measuring it), which is capable of increase, diminution, displacement and discharge, and which is spread over the memory-traces of ideas somewhat as an electric charge is spread over the surface of a body.

Freud described how the forces of the unconscious are expressed, transformed, or repressed, resulting in everyday behaviors and in psychopathology. During development these forces manifest in different configurations: developmental events therefore affect later dynamics in specific ways. Psychoanalysis leads to insight into such dynamics, and allows the patient to work through them.

Again, however, it is possible to demonstrate a continuity between psychoanalysis and cognitive science. Freud, for example, was a cognitivist insofar as he divided the mind into different mental structures, and provided a theory of how these structures process affects and symbols. His later work is even more cognitively oriented; for example, he describes anxiety not in terms of energy, but in terms of its role as a signal. In 1925, he wrote that

> at one time [I] attached some importance to the view that what was used as a discharge of anxiety was the cathexis which had been drawn in the process of repression. To-day this seems to [me] of scarcely any interest. The reason for this is that whereas [I] formerly believed that anxiety invariably arose automatically by an economic process [amount of energy], [my] present conception of anxiety as a signal given by the ego in order to affect the pleasure–unpleasure agency does away with the necessity of considering the economic factor.

Finally, post-Freudian psychoanalysts, including the self-psychologists, the object relations school, and the interpersonalists, increasingly have employed cognitively oriented constructs such as self and other representations (Stein, 1992a).

The biological model of the mind focuses on the neuroanatomical, neurochemical, and neurophysiological substrates of mental processes. Proponents of this model may state that all psychological explanations are reducible to neurobiological ones. This model contrasts with the cognitive science model, which contends that cognitive phenomena necessarily require psychological explanations. Psychological events are emergent phenomena, and psychological explanations are not reducible to biological ones.

Once again it is possible to see a continuity between the biological model and cognitive science. It has been mentioned that neuroscience provides the lower limit of cognitive science. Although some cognitivists are interested in information processing in only the most abstract sense, many others are interested specifically in how information processing occurs in the human neurobiological substrate.

## Clinical Cognitive Science

The psychoanalytic, behavioral, and biological models of the mind have, of course, all been employed in the clinical context. Psychoanalysis was developed to account for specific clinical phenomena and, during the first part of the century, constituted the predominant paradigm in American psychiatry. A behavioral model has been more popular in clinical psychology. In recent years, psychiatrists increasingly have asserted their role as physicians, and biological psychiatry has become central.

As cognitive constructs have become available, however, they have been used increasingly by clinical theorists and practitioners. Cognitive therapies constitute a central portion of psychotherapy today (Dobson, 1988). Although these therapies are not necessarily formal extensions of cognitive science, they nevertheless draw on many of its constructs and employ some of its methodologies. In addition, as has been indicated, psychoanalytic models have become increasingly cognitive. Behavioral therapists have adopted cognitive therapy techniques; the term "cognitive-behavioral" is popular. Finally, a biological perspective is not inconsistent with cognitive science; some theoretical work in clinical psychobiology has been informed by cognitive science (see Chapter 11).

The question then arises of a possible formal integration of cognitive and clinical science. Just as the work of precognitivists preceded the emergence of cognitive science, so the work of certain early clinicians may be seen as pioneering this integration. Perhaps the most important of these pioneers was Freud, whose cognitivist tendencies were described earlier. Theorizing in a way that was perhaps even more consonant with contemporary clinical science, Janet also described different components of the mind and their processing of symbols and affects. Like Freud, he believed that mental processes took place outside of awareness, and that the laws of this processing could explain clinical symptoms. In the years that have passed since the work of these men, a series of additional integrative developments has taken place in both cognitive and clinical science.

One important advance necessary for the development of clinical cognitive science has been an increasing emphasis in cognitive science on emotion. Humans are, after all, not only the most intelligent of the animals, but perhaps also the most emotional (Hebb, 1946). Moreover, it may be argued that this relationship between intelligence and emotionality is a necessary one. In a seminal paper, Simon (1967) argued that emotion in humans is comparable to the prioritized interruption of different processes by one another in complex artificial intelligence systems with multiple goals and limited resources. The idea that cognitive design problems are solved by emotional processes remains popular in attempts by contemporary cognitive scientists to theorize emotion (Oatley & Johnson-Laird, 1987; Sloman, 1987), and has helped generate a rapidly growing empirical literature on cognitive-affective processing. The cognitive study of emotion has immediate implications for the understanding of affective experience and change in the clinic (Greenberg and Safran, 1987; see Chapter 4).

Another important area in cognitive science that has clinical relevance is the study of unconscious processing. Early work by Helmholtz was followed by various empirical studies. For example, Poetzl (1917) demonstrated that subliminal tachistoscopic presentation of stimuli could influence dream content. It was not until the emergence of cognitive science, however, that the "cognitive unconscious" (Kihlstrom, 1987) became a respectable area of study. Research has focused on such areas as selective attention, subliminal perception, implicit memory, hypnotic suggestion, and dreaming (Erdelyi, 1985; Foulkes, 1985; Kihlstrom, 1987). Although this research immediately brings the work of Freud to mind, there appear to be important differences between the cognitive unconscious and the psychoanalytic unconscious (Shevrin, 1988). According to Freud, the unconscious is a set of drives, affects, and motives that has an organization and content more primitive than that of consciousness, but that nevertheless has latent potential for interacting with other elements of the psyche. According to cognitive science, the unconscious is a set of cognitive processes, including attitudes and dispositions, that act prior to consciousness, therefore actively organizing and ordering experience and behavior. Nevertheless, contemporary work on unconscious processing establishes a dialogue between cognitive and clinical scientists (Bowers & Meichenbaum, 1984; Uleman & Bargh, 1989; see Chapter 2).

A number of early cognitivists have been interested specifically in emotional disorders. Ruesch and Bateson (1968) were among the first to apply cybernetic notions to psychopathology and psychotherapy. In cognitive psychology, Hilgard (1986) built on early work by Janet on dissociation to develop a neodissociative model of the dissociative disorders. This work exemplified the potential utility of cognitive psychology constructs in conceptualizing emotional disorders.

In artificial intelligence, Colby pioneered the investigation of clinical phenomena. Colby (1963) developed a program, PARRY, that incorporated a model of paranoid processes, and succeeded in simulating a paranoid patient. The difficulty of such work and the magnitude of Colby's achievement are illustrated by the limited amount of subsequent research in this area (Tomkins, 1972; Clippinger, 1977). PARRY perhaps continues to constitute the best computer simulation of a psychopathological entity.

Linguists, neuroscientists, and social psychologists have long had strong interests in clinical phenomena. Some of this work has fallen into the realm of cognitive clinical science. Linguists have, for example, developed cognitive models of disorders such as aphasia and dyslexia (see Chapter 16). Cognitive approaches to narrative may contribute to the understanding of clinical dialogue and the mechanisms of the "talking cure" (see Chapter 8). Neuroscientists from Hebb (1946) to Edelman (1987) have attempted to incorporate cognitivist constructs to explain cognition and its disorders. Cognitively oriented work in social psychology has been particularly relevant to clinical science, and has tackled such important concerns as self and other representations and mood disorders (Cantor & Kihlstrom, 1981; Kuiper & Higgins, 1985; Markus & Wurf, 1987; Westen, 1988). Related literature that has explored these issues in their developmental context is also relevant to clinical science (Emde, 1983; Stern,

1985; see Chapter 3). Finally, it may be argued that philosophy, too, constitutes an important foundational discipline for clinical cognitive research (Mahoney, 1990; see Chapter 9).

A reciprocal interest by clinicians in cognitive science is clearly apparent. This interest may be seen in both the psychoanalytic and the cognitive-behavioral traditions. In the psychoanalytic literature, for example, there has been discussion of cognitive psychology and its experimental findings (Rapoport, 1951; Holt, 1964), information theory (Rosenblatt and Thickstun, 1977; Peterfreund, 1980), artificial intelligence (Galatzer-Levy, 1985), and computer modeling (Wegman, 1985). Extensive contributions have been made by writers interested in the juxtaposition of cognitive science and psychoanalysis (Eagle, 1986; Pfeifer & Leuzinger-Bohleber, 1986; Colby & Stoller, 1988; Dahl, Kachele, & Thoma, 1988; Horowitz, 1988, 1991). In the nonanalytic literature, several early authors developed cognitive approaches to clinical disorders (Kelly, 1955; Ellis, 1962; Bandura, 1969; Breger, 1969; Beck, 1974; Mahoney, 1974; Meichenbaum, 1977). More recently, several papers and volumes have contributed specifically to the development of a convergence of the clinical and cognitive sciences (Merluzzi, Rudy, & Glass, 1981; Ingram, 1986; Williams, Watts, MacLeod, & Matthews, 1988).

The intersection between clinical and cognitive science can be characterized in terms of the different cognitivist and computational models employed. Early cognitive therapists, for example, employed a model that was similar to the standard sequential processing model in cognitive science. Subsequent cognitive clinicians have employed more sophisticated symbolic and connectionist architectures. The employment of these cognitivist and computational models provides a nidus for a clinical cognitive science.

Schema theory, for example, is an important construct in both cognitive and clinical science (Stein, 1992; see Chapter 14). Earlier, the work of Bartlett and Piaget on schemas was mentioned. In subsequent cognitive science, schemas have been employed in work on memory, concept representation, problem solving, movement, and language. The schema concept has also taken root in clinical theory and research. This has happened in diverse schools. Several authors in the cognitive-behavioral tradition, including Beck (a founder of cognitive therapy), have employed the notion of schemas (Beck, 1964, 1967, 1990; Arnkoff, 1980; Goldfried & Robbins, 1983; Turk & Speer, 1983; Greenberg & Safran, 1984; Young, 1990). In the psychoanalytic tradition, the schema concept has also been used extensively (Wachtel, 1982; Slap & Saykin, 1983; Eagle, 1986), particularly by Horowitz (1988, 1991).

Schema theory provides a way to conceptualize how underlying nonobservable mental structures process representations and thereby generate observable mental events such as thoughts or feelings. In the clinical setting, schema theory allows exploration of such fundamental issues as how mental structures allow self and other representations, how they are based in neurobiology, how they develop and change, and how they generate various abnormal emotions, cognitions, and behaviors. Similarly, the construct may be employed to think through the etiology, assessment, and treatment of a particular disorder (see Chapter 5). The clinician can, for example, theorize the factors responsible for the development of a particular schema, develop measures to assess and evaluate the schema, and plan a strategy for coping with a schema or changing it (see Chapter 14).

The connectionist concept of a neural network is a more recent construct that is finding increasingly wide employment in the different cognitive sciences and in the clinical sciences. Connectionist models offer an important alternative to representational constructs and have been used to explain a variety of phenomena (Rumelhart & McClelland, 1986a,b). In clinical science, an early paper by Hoffman (1988) suggested that neural network theory can be used to differentiate between bipolar disorder and schizophrenia. Several subsequent papers have applied connectionist principles to clinical problems (Caspar, Rothenfluh, & Segal, 1991; Cohen & Servan-Schreiber, 1991; see Chapter 7).

Connectionist models again provide a way to conceptualize how underlying nonobservable mental structures generate observable mental phenomena. In addition, neural network theory has the promise of providing strong links between biological and psychological data. Not only can neural networks be designed to incorporate neurophysiological data, but the learning, changing, and parallel processing that they demonstrate are reminiscent of neurophysiological findings. Although neural networks may be less intuitively understandable than schemas, computer implementation of a network provides a rigorous methodology for hypothesis testing.

## Advantages and Limitations

Cognitive science has a prima facie appeal for the clinician who is interested in an integrative theoretical apparatus for studying the mind and its disorders. As a multidisciplinary arena, with different perspectives and fields, cognitive science appears to offer the clinician models of the mind that are complex and multifaceted. Whereas so much contemporary clinical science has been criticized for being either mindless or brainless (Lipowski, 1989), a broad cognitive approach is neither. The range of cognitive sciences allows a focus on both nature and nurture. Finally, cognitive science has important continuities with such divergent approaches as the psychoanalytic and the behaviorist schools of psychology, and therefore seems to allow incorporation of their discoveries.

The cognitive science approach also provides the clinical practitioner and researcher with a series of experimental methodologies and assessment techniques. It allows clinical phenomena to be measured outside the office and introduces various scales and measures into the clinic. These methodologies appear to go beyond the limitations of behavioral or self-report approaches (see Chapter 5). Cognitive science self-consciously views itself as compatible with important developments in contemporary natural and social science, as an enterprise that will result in further scientific discovery and progress. This view allows clinicians to move beyond the dilemma of choosing between studying the mind using outdated natural science metaphors or conceptualizing clinical work as hermeneutic rather than scientific (Stein, 1991b).

The development of a clinical cognitive science may be advantageous for cognitive science as a whole. From a theoretical viewpoint, it is likely that an understanding of pathological structures and processes will shed light on related normal structures and processes. Further, the clinician has access to a range of mental phenomena that is simply not available to many cognitive scientists. Psychopathology is exhibited in a variety of forms, from the psychopathology of everyday life to incapacitating mental disorder. In psychotherapy, individuals reveal themselves and their thoughts with a detail that is not encountered by many cognitive scientists. Psychopathology and psychotherapy involve a variety of mental structures (cognitive and affective), processes (top-down or molar and bottom-up or molecular), and events (dreams, fantasies, hypnotic recollections, hallucinations, and delusions.).

The development of clinical cognitive science also may counter important criticism of cognitive science as lacking ecological validity, that is, not being applicable to the everyday world. Neisser, who had published the pioneering and optimistic volume *Cognitive Psychology* in 1967, published *Cognition and Reality* a decade later; in that volume he called for an ecologically valid psychology that would deal with the kinds of problems humans encounter and solve in day-to-day life. Winograd, whose work on a limited-domain expert program had been pivotal for artificial intelligence in the years around 1970, wrote some years later that

> current systems, even the best ones, often resemble a house of cards. . . . The result is an extremely fragile structure which may reach impressive heights, but collapses immediately if swayed in the slightest domain (often even the specific examples) for which it was built. (Bobrow & Winograd, 1977)

Lakoff (1980), a former student of Chomsky, argued that meaning and use affect virtually every syntactical rule, so the demonstration by Chomsky of the autonomy of syntax from semantics and pragmatics could no longer be considered viable. It is important, then, that disease and healing are central aspects of human life. Psychopathology and psychotherapy necessitate an understanding of humans in all their biopsychosocial complexity. The multifaceted nature of the clinic has the potential of providing cognitive science with a paradigm that is not only theoretically productive but also ecologically valid.

Nevertheless, several possible criticisms of a clinical cognitive science can be mentioned. This chapter has focused on the particular models of mind that cognitive science offers to clinical theoreticians and practitioners; criticisms of clinical cognitive science will be discussed from this perspective. One possible argument is that clinical cognitive science merely translates the concepts of earlier clinical models into its own terms without adding anything of value. This argument is one that modern psychoanalysts might offer, claiming that they already employ cognitive science concepts, but simply use an older terminology. However, the energy model of the mind is a rudimentary one and cognitivist constructs provide greater sophistication, therefore holding promise of providing more explanatory power. Nevertheless, psychoanalysts may respond that the objections to Freud's energy model are well known, and that few clinicians continue to adhere to this model. Some analysts have, for example, argued that it is possible to discard Freud's biologically based metapsychology, but retain his concepts as useful psychological constructs (Brenner, 1976). Others have argued that psychoanalysis is a hermeneutic enterprise, and that different natural science models of the mind serve as narrative devices (Spence, 1982).

These options are problematic. Freud's metapsychology is connected intimately with his clinical observations and techniques. If the foundational constructs of a science are flawed, it is difficult to imagine how the science can progress without discarding the constructs. Similarly, a view of psychoanalysis as simply narrative is difficult to juxtapose with a view of psychoanalysis as offering a scientific model of the mind. Thus, although psychoanalysis certainly provides a detailed description of important clinical phenomena, as well as a number of seminal hypotheses regarding their underlying psychological structures, the progress of psychodynamic ideas seems to requires innovative theoretical constructs. In providing a possible theoretical conceptualization of psychodynamic work, cognitive science immediately supercedes mere translation of older terminology. Further, the work of Horowitz and other psychoanalysts who have used cognitivist models appears to demonstrate that they do provide good explanatory power for psychoanalytic phenomena. Finally, the introduction of cognitivist ideas and techniques into traditional psychoanalysis may foster certain technical advances (cf. Wachtel, 1987).

A second argument against a cognitive clinical science approach is that clinical work is primarily a pragmatic exercise and that it is unnecessary to introduce a range of theoretical baggage. This argument is one that certain cognitive therapists might offer. If cognitive therapy works, there is no need for its constructs to have a theoretical or experimental foundation in the cognitive sciences. This objection appears to be insubstantial. Distinctions between applied clinical and pure psychological knowledge, or between knowledge garnered in the office and that developed in the laboratory, are artificial. The different knowledge bases of the clinician and the cognitivist intersect, overlap, and make reciprocal contributions.

Another easily refuted argument is the antitechnology or moral one. Computers and people are often contrasted as cold science and technology on the one hand and warm artistry and creativity on the other. An interesting debate developed between Colby, the creator of PARRY, and Weizenbaum (1966, 1976), who developed a program called ELIZA that simulated a psychotherapy session. Colby is a strong supporter of cognitive science. However, when Weizenbaum noticed that people interpreted his program as an indication that psychotherapists could be replaced by computers, he emphasized the limitations of cognitive science, noting that computers should not be allowed to replace humans at certain tasks. However, despite the complex philosophical literature comparing computational and mental states, the issue is not whether computers can or should replace minds, but whether cognitivist and computational models can and ought to be used to conceptualize and investigate minds. It is noteworthy that, whereas PARRY was based on a specific model of paranoid processes (and therefore directly contributed to the science of psychopathology), ELIZA was not a model of psychotherapy per se (and did not make a direct contribution to the science of psychotherapy) but a study of the rules of dialogue.

Perhaps a stronger argument against clinical cognitive science is that, although it is laudable to attempt to strengthen cognitive science by moving its focus from the laboratory to the clinic, the models of cognitive science are insufficiently complex to permit this shift. If these models are limited in the laboratory then they will be limited in the clinic. It has been mentioned, for example, that early cognitivist clinicians employed a model that was similar to the standard sequential-processing model of the mind. They argued that psychopathology involves the distortion of information processing and psychotherapy involves the correction of such distortions. It is not difficult to fault this view for failing to account for the adaptive growth of psychological structures and processes in a particular environment or for the mind as structured in a particular context that it, in turn, structures. Nevertheless, the straightforward standard model may be useful in accounting for certain restricted processing deficits, such as those seen in schizophrenia or autism (Ingram, 1986). Further, as cognitive constructs have become more sophisticated, clinicians have deepened their cognitive approaches. Thus, more contemporary cognitivist clinicians have seen the mind not as a passive processor of information but as an active constructor of representations. Psychopathology has been seen as adaptive but also as inappropriate, and psychotherapy has been viewed as corrective but also as a meaningful process.

Clinicians with an experiential or phenomenological orientation are perhaps most likely to be distrustful of cognitive clinical science. What can a computational model tell us about the perceptions, feelings, and experiences of a patient? How can a cognitivist approach contribute to an understanding of the meaning of a symptom? First, it should be emphasized again that the goal of cognitive clinical science is not to replicate human experience on the computer, but to provide a computational account of the mechanisms that generate the phenomena of human experience. It cannot be objected that cognitivist constructs are, in principle, limited because humans and computers are different in important ways. Thus, although human minds are often irrational and computational processes are characterized by logical regularity, cognitive scientists have constructed important models of human irrationality (Johnson-Laird & Wason, 1970; Tversky & Kahneman, 1983). Still, despite work in cognitive science on phenomena such as affect and meaning, a great deal of work remains to be done before the production of the more subtle phenomena of human thinking and feeling is understood. The failure of other models to represent these phenomena fully should, however, provide perseverance in this task.

Clinicians with a strong biological or sociocultural orientation may ask whether a cognitive science approach to clinical phenomena will be able to include biological or sociocultural findings. Many cognitive scientists are uninterested in work at these levels. Nevertheless, cognitive science is presented in this chapter, and in this volume, as a multidisciplinary field that includes the biological and social levels as lower and upper limits of cognitive processing. Given the sometimes peripheral position of these perspectives in cognitive science, however, sustained work devoted to their incorporation into a clinical cognitive science is likely to be necessary.

One of the most important criticisms of clinical cognitive science involves questions of definitional precision. The term schema, for example, has been used by different clinicians in diverse ways. Whereas Horowitz (1988) developed a division of schemas into motivational, role, and value schemas that is consistent with Freud's division of the psyche into id, ego, and superego; Beck, Freeman, and associates (Beck et al., 1990) divided schemas into cognitive, affective, and action schemas, consistent with their view of the linear progression of thoughts, feelings, and behaviors. Further, a variety of related concepts such as scripts, self-systems, personal constructs, plans, and frames are popular in the cognitive and clinical literature. This diversity may reflect partially the theoretical fertility of cognitive science, and may be helpful in providing a range of ideas and models. Nevertheless, the diversity also reflects a lack of agreement on the taxonomy of representation, and a lack of detailed knowledge about the complexities of human cognitive architecture. Clearly, further work is necessary to clarify and consolidate the theoretical apparatus of cognitive science.

Theoretical diversity contributes to the difficulties that researchers have experienced in measuring constructs such as schemas. Problems in measurement are, however, expected in research on posited entities that underlie observable phenomena. Detailed clinical observation and advances in assessment techniques will be necessary to resolve these methodological difficulties (Rudy & Merluzzi, 1984; Segal, 1988).

In short, it is not clear that any a priori objections to cognitivist and computational models of clinical phenomena exist. By the same token, of course, it cannot be asserted that these models are the best possible models. Which models of clinical phenomena are best will have to be discovered empirically rather than by a priori argument. At present, cognitivist models clearly do not constitute the last word on clinical disorders. At this early stage, however, it is unwise to make final judgments. The subsequent chapters in this volume, each of which explores an aspect of current work at the interface of cognitive and clinical science, speak to the strength of this juncture.

# 2

# Avoidance of Emotional Processing: A Cognitive Science Perspective

**Marylene Cloitre**

*Department of Psychology*
*New School for Social Research*
*and*
*Cornell Medical College*
*New York, New York*

This chapter explores the empirical evidence for the notion that individuals can avoid attending to, analyzing, and remembering information that is painful or threatening. To clinicians from various traditions, the idea that clients avoid confronting painful experiences or memories seems self-evident. Similarly, our own judgments and actions as well as those we observe in others might indicate that the phenomenon is commonplace.

There has been increased interest among clinicians and cognitive psychologists in understanding the cognitive processes that guide these experiences. One of the goals of this chapter is to review processes such as selective attention, selective memory, and memory dissociations, and suggest that they provide plausible cognitive bases for the operation of emotionally driven avoidance strategies.

A second aim of the chapter is to provide an outline of a cognitive-affective model of functional amnesia and suggestions for ways in which this model might be tested. Much more research has been completed in the recent past on the phenomena of attentional biases than on memory biases for traumatic, threatening, or negative information. The chapter reviews the literature in both areas, making an effort to identify similarities between attentional strategies used to selectively search the external environment and potential search strategies used during memory scanning. It will be argued that functional amnesia and its associated symptom picture may be understood as a consequence of selective memory search and of the operation of selective strategies over two types of memory—implicit and explicit. Although the literature presentation is organized to facilitate the presentation of this model, the review includes a relatively complete and wide range of studies investigating attentional and memory biases in nonclinical populations. A review of studies concerning clinical populations will be presented in Chapter 13.

## Historical Overview

### Repression as a Precursor to the Concept of Cognitive Avoidance

> Repression . . . is, fundamentally, an attempt at flight.
>
> Freud, 1926
> Inhibitions, Symptoms, and Anxiety
> (*Standard Edition*, p. 153)

Little in the experimental literature supports the existence of repression and the unconscious as conceived in the psychoanalytic context. In the terms specified by drive theory, repression is defined descriptively as an unconscious mental force that actively inhibits threatening information of a sexual or aggressive nature from coming into awareness; the unconscious is viewed as the repository and generator of the sexual and aggressive impulses. To describe in this way and dismiss the concepts of repression and the unconscious, however, is unfair to Freud's original conceptualizations, which were of greater breadth and were derived from close observation of the behaviors of his patients.

Freud furnished detailed case histories that document the avoidance of emotionally painful ideas and memories and associated negative consequences (Breuer & Freud, 1893; Freud, 1894). He also provided provocative formulations concerning the nature of mental representation for emotional memories and the processes that govern them, many of which are surprisingly consistent with contemporary cognitive psychology (see Erdelyi, 1985; Caspar, Rothenfluh, & Segal, 1991). Thus, it seems fitting to begin the discussion with some of his observations.

Freud's initial characterization of the phenomenon of repression was based on the reports of patients who could recall explicitly conscious efforts to "push away," "not think about," or in some way "suppress" an idea, memory, or experience that was emotionally painful (Freud, 1894, pp. 69–70). As noted by Erdelyi and Goldberg (1979), Freud wrote of an exchange with one of his patients, Miss Lucy R., that supports this view. He queried his patient, ". . . if you knew you loved your employer, why didn't you tell me?" To this the patient responded, "I didn't know or rather I did not want to know. I wanted to drive it out of my head and not think of it again: and I believe lately I have succeeded" (Breuer & Freud, 1893, p. 117).

According to Freud, these intentional efforts of forgetting were the result not only of the patient's encounter with a painful idea but also of the patient's evaluation that he or she lacked the power to resolve the dilemma by the "processes of thought." (Freud, 1894, p. 69). Thus, repression appears essentially to be an effort to flee from psychic pain when other mental efforts are deemed unlikely to succeed in resolving the emotional disturbance. This type of response to the internal objects of the psychic world (ideas) can be viewed as parallel to the phenomenon observed in the external world—the fight/flight response in the face of an impending threat. Viewed in this way, the motivation for and function of repression has intuitive appeal, suggesting that the desire to avoid threat or pain cuts across both the cognitive and the behavioral domains of human experience.

In summary, the basic concept of repression as developed from Freud's early clinical observations can be defined as selective memory (and attention) motivated by a need to avoid painful affect associated with specific information (Holmes, 1974). This basic definition, as noted elsewhere (Erdelyi & Goldberg, 1979; Erdelyi, 1985), does not stipulate the affective nature of the painful idea, the mechanisms by which avoidance of the painful idea is achieved, or that the process be unconscious.

The view of repression as motivated selective attending and forgetting fits easily in the conceptual framework of cognitive psychology. One of the basic principles of the information processing perspective is that humans select and attend to only a subset of the rich and varied information available in the environment. This selective process is considered an adaption to the discrepancy between the finite capacity of humans to process information and the nearly infinite amount of information available in the environment. The basic purpose of the selection process is believed to be to organize information, make experience comprehensible, and thus facilitate goal-directed behavior.

Cognitive science traditionally has not included or considered the role of emotions in the operation of selective processing. However, it would not seem unreasonable that humans would enlist all resources at their disposal to aid in the selection of information that will maximize functioning in the environment. Repression, according to Freud's earliest formulation, occurred when an individual could not resolve a problem of strongly emotional and troubling force. With no other alternative available, avoiding the troubling memory or any information in the environment associated with the memory could minimize psychic distress or maximize psychic well-being and thus contribute to successful goal-directed functioning. This view of repression is compatible with a functional analysis of selective processing.

Some current data suggest that individuals who avoid assimilating or remembering negative information actually do function better and have a greater sense of psychological well-being than those who cannot or do not do this (e.g., Taylor & Brown, 1988). However, Freud's writings suggest that avoidance could prove to be an *unsatisfactory* coping response when, for any number of reasons, the affective strength of the memory was so powerful that complete forgetting of the memory could not be achieved.

Freud (Breuer & Freud, 1893; Freud, 1894) interpreted his early cases of hysteria as examples of individuals who had succeeded in forgetting a traumatic memory only partially and thus "suffered mainly from reminiscences." Although these patients were able to eliminate a threatening memory from conscious awareness, aspects of the memory remain in the form of "persistent motor innervation" or other types of sensory experience (Freud, 1894, p. 71). A common example of this phenomenon is provided in the report from one of my patients who had succeeded in forgetting an upsetting discussion that occurred over a dinner of lobster. Following this event, however, she became unable to swallow lobster meat and felt nauseated by the sight of lobster. Erdelyi (1985) describes this experience as a paradox in which "the memory is not remembered (consciously) but is remembered (somatically)" (p. 24).

This apparently paradoxical state of affairs is not foreign to cognitive psychologists who study memory functioning. A growing body of research indicates that there are at least two distinct memory processes or systems that are relatively dissociable—implicit and explicit memory. Explicit memory concerns the ability to consciously recollect information about an event, as exemplified during the activities of recall or recognition. Implicit memory, in contrast, is memory of an event that occurs without awareness and often is expressed through behaviors such as changes in perceptual or motor behaviors or affective responses when presented with contextual cues related to the event.

The implicit/explicit memory distinction and the dissociable character of the two memory processes provide a cognitive basis for Freud's observations of the hysteric, or functional amnesic. The paradoxical, and potentially illogical, circumstance of the functional amnesic who both remembers and does not remember the traumatic event is resolved when memory is understood to be composed of at least two relatively independent but simultaneously functioning processes or systems. Under this analysis, the amnesic can be understood as successfully having avoided coming into contact with any explicit memory (e.g., recall) of the traumatic event but, nevertheless, having failed to avoid experiencing the influence of implicit memory (a perceptual or motor response to a cue associated with the event). The mechanisms by which differential effects of the accessibility of implicit and explicit memories might occur are explored in the latter part of the chapter.

The author of this chapter takes the perspective that the desire to avoid painful knowledge and the efforts to satisfy that desire are relatively ubiquitous. The results of these efforts range from the relatively successful—in which there are no negative or even positive effects on psychological health—to the only partially successful such as those Freud described. The goal of this chapter is to describe cognitive mechanisms and processes, such as selective attention and selective memory, that might serve as the basis for the operation of emotionally driven avoidance strategies and to specify conditions for their operation. Descriptions of avoidance strategies are based on and integrated with current models of cognitive processing; empirical tests for the existence of these strategies are either explicitly formulated or described as having the potential to be.

## Selective Attention

### Perceptual Defense

The several hundred studies (see Erdelyi, 1974, for review) concerning the perceptual defense phenomenon constitute the first experimental efforts to evaluate whether or not individuals avoid potentially threatening information. In this paradigm, subjects are shown threatening and non-threatening stimuli words that are displayed very briefly in subliminal exposure and for progressively longer intervals until the subject can identify the word correctly. The expectation is that potentially threatening information processed at the subliminal level (registered without conscious awareness) will activate defensive strategies that will disrupt perceptual processing in a way that will prevent the threatening information from reaching consciousness. This disruption was believed to be manifest in the observation of higher recognition thresholds (markers of conscious awareness) for threat than for nonthreat stimuli. An early study by McGinnies (1949) that produced this effect showed that, when college students were presented with taboo words (e.g., Kotex, penis) and neutral words (e.g., house, apple), recognition thresholds were higher for the taboo words than for the neutral words. An important aspect of the paradigm was that, during the task, galvanic skin responses (GSR) of the subjects were obtained as an indicator of emotional reactivity to the stimuli. The GSRs for the subliminal stimuli were found to be higher for the threat than for the nonthreat words. This indicated that, although the subjects had no conscious awareness of the stimuli, they had, nevertheless, registered, understood, and reacted to the emotionally laden stimuli.

Although several criticisms have been made concerning the interpretation of this type of effect, it has been concluded in reviews of the literature that the effect is reliable and occurs consistently, even when studied under more experimentally rigorous conditions (Erdelyi, 1974; Dixon, 1981; Dixon & Henley, 1991). For example, the most compelling criticism has been that higher recognition thresholds for taboo words are the result of a response bias. That is, subjects may recognize taboo and neutral words equally but may delay reporting having seen the taboo word because they are embarrassed to do so. The problem of "response bias" has been resolved fairly well by adoption of signal detection approaches and other experimental paradigms. Some researchers prefer the paradigm in which subjects are asked to respond to a neutral stimulus (e.g., bright light or dot) that is yoked to or associated in some way with emotionally relevant stimuli (which the subject may or may not be aware of perceiving). The rationale is that responses to the neutral stimulus will be influenced by its association with a threat stimulus but, because the subjects are not aware of or required to respond to the threat information, the artifact of response bias is ruled out (Dixon & Henley, 1991). Effects consistent with a perceptual defense model have been obtained with this type of paradigm (Henley & Dixon, 1976; Henley, 1986).

### Biased Attentional Search

Experimental paradigms that center on subject responses to relatively brief exposures to threat or taboo information have limitations. The ecological validity of these studies is somewhat compromised because, in real life, individuals must respond not only to threats that appear for a fleeting interval but also to those that present themselves vividly and for some time (e.g., a robbery, a car accident). For this reason, we will turn to studies that focus on supraliminally and vividly presented emotional material.

One group of studies has presented subjects with pictorial representations of frightening or traumatic scenes and assessed attention to traumatic or threatening relative to less emotional or neutral material. Early studies evaluated attentional bias by measuring the length of time subjects chose to look at unpleasant (mutilated bodies, corpses) compared to pleasant and neutral slides (Carroll, 1972; Lewinsohn, Bergquist, & Brelje, 1972). Results showed little consistent evidence of differences in looking time for the different types of pictures.

Recent studies have used the more sensitive measures of eye movements and fixation to track attentional patterns to emotionally salient information. Loftus, Loftus, and Messo (1987), for example, showed college students a film of a customer waiting in line at a fast food store. The subjects saw one of two versions of the film. In one version, the customer hands a check to the cashier; in the other version, the customer points a gun at the cashier. The film clips were otherwise identical. Eye movements indicated that those students watching the gun version fixated on the gun longer than those students watching the check version fixated on the check. This finding was interpreted to suggest that attention, as measured by eye fixations, is greater for threatening than nonthreatening information. Further research (Christianson, Loftus, Hoffman, & Loftus, 1991) indicated that the preferential attention this type of stimulus elicited was related specifically to its threatening or negative quality rather than to its general salience as a novel or unusual stimulus in the environmental field (i.e., the von Restorff effect; see Detterman, 1975).

In a similar type of eye fixation study, the eye patterns of women judged to be "repressors," that is, individuals who tend to avoid threat, were compared to those of women who were judged to be "sensitizers," that is, individuals who tend to approach threatening information (see Luborsky, Crits-Cristoph, & Alexander, 1990). All subjects were shown a slide of a man reading a newspaper in the background, with the profile of a naked woman's head and breast in the foreground. As expected, the repressors showed few eye fixations on the breast and many more on the man and the newspaper; the sensitizers, in contrast, showed a greater number of fixations on the breast than on the background.

These results contradict the Loftus et al. (1987) and Christianson et al. (1991) studies, which showed that subjects consistently showed preferential attention to the emotional information. The divergence in these results can be explained by differences in subject populations or by the character of the emotional material. It may be that the Loftus subjects were predominantly sensitizers, thus making attention to the emotional stimulus the dominant pattern of response. It is also possible that stimuli referring to physical injury and blood may have a different significance to a viewer than sexual material has. Attention to physical threats might be a genetically encoded part of a survival surveillance mechanism, whereas sexual stimuli may affect individuals differently depending on the degree to which the stimuli are found socially threatening or disturbing.

These studies suggest that both personality factors and stimulus factors may interact to produce patterns of attentional approach or avoidance. An elegant study by MacLeod and Mathews (1988) evaluated the interaction of these effects. Medical students were asked to press a key when a dot probe appeared in various locations on a computer screen they were viewing. The dot probe sometimes followed presentation of generally threatening words (e.g., ill) and at other times followed presentation of exam-related threatening words (e.g., failure, exam). The subjects were tested at two intervals: once at the beginning of the semester and then 12 weeks later, preceding the exam period. As indicated by the relative speed of their responses, students with high trait anxiety were found to show preferential attention to exam-related words whereas low trait subjects did not. Interestingly, during the second testing period, high trait anxious subjects showed increasing bias *toward* the exam words whereas low trait subjects showed increasing bias *away from* the exam words. The authors suggest that high and low trait anxious individuals have different styles of responding to emotional information with increases in state anxiety; whereas high trait anxious subjects spiral into higher states of anxiety and show increased focus on exam-related stimuli, low trait anxious subjects may respond to the anxious state as a cue to reduce attention to the threatening information.

These results in particular and the complete set of studies discussed indicate that factors related to the individual (personality style, state, and trait anxiety) and to the nature (blood as opposed to nudity) and anxiety-eliciting charge of the stimulus all contribute to patterns of attention toward or away from potentially threatening information. The broader issue, not to be overlooked, is that selective attention to emotionally laden information is pervasive.

### Effects of Attentional Bias on Memory

A typical consequence of biased attention to emotionally salient information is that, whereas memory for the salient information is intact, memory for peripheral information is impaired.

In the study by Christianson et al. (1991), mentioned earlier, subjects were presented with neutral, emotional, or unusual sequence of slides with one critical slide in the middle. In the neutral condition, the critical slide showed a woman riding a bicycle; in the emotional condition, the woman was seen lying on the ground bleeding from her head; in the unusual condition, the woman was seen carrying the bicycle on her shoulder. The eye movement data indicated that attention to the blood-and-injury scene was greater than attention to the other two. In addition, consistent with the attention data, subjects presented with the emotional material showed better memory of a central detail associated with the woman (the color of her coat) and showed a trend toward poorer memory of the peripheral details (the color of the background car) than subjects exposed to the unusual or neutral slides. Several other studies with more limited designs (i.e., no attention measure and/or no memory measure of the emotionally salient information) have produced results consistent with the study above in that memory for information peripheral to an emotionally salient stimulus, compared with a nonemotional stimulus, is impaired (Christianson and Nilsson, 1989; Erdelyi & Appelbaum, 1973; Erdelyi & Blumenthal, 1973; Loftus & Burns, 1982).

The results of the Christianson et al. (1991) study are helpful in clarifying some aspects of cognitive processing that underlie emotional experiences. The attentional patterns obtained are consistent with Easter-brook's (1959) idea that an emotional event triggers attentional narrowing, so some information may be well attended to and remembered at the expense of other information. Christianson and Nilsson (1989) suggest that this mechanism may be helpful in explaining certain amnesias observed in individuals who have suffered a substantial traumatic event. They describe a woman who, after being raped, can remember only fragments of her experience: a red brick and the smell of alcohol on her attacker's breath. This fragmented memory may be the result of attentional narrowing activity that has been disrupted continuously during the overwhelming course of a violent attack.

An interesting aspect of additional studies conducted by Christianson et al. (1991) was that, when allocation of attention was limited to one eye fixation directed by a fixation point to a central detail, the subjects still showed better memory for the central detail (and somewhat poorer memory for the peripheral information) in the trauma scene than in the other scenes. Thus, although attention to all three scenes was equal, memory remained better for the traumatic scene. The authors suggest one explanation for this effect: better memory for the emotional information may come from greater poststimulus conceptual analysis. Emotional material may receive more elaborate assessment of its causes and consequences than neutral information. Another possibility mentioned is that emotional information is encoded, perceptually, differently than other types of information or is processed perceptually by a primitive memory system with a phylogenetically entrenched sensitivity to emotional information.

These observations and speculations are consistent with recent observations made in clinical populations. Christianson et al. (1991) suggest that emotional information may be processed in a different way to produce stronger encoding as a result of differences in either conceptual or perceptual processing. Although these two different stages or aspects of processing are well recognized (see Williams et al., 1988), the authors have no evidence of which of these aspects of processing might be sensitive to emotional information. In a study (Cloitre & Liebowitz, 1991) evaluating emotional processing in a clinically anxious group, individuals with panic disorder were given memory tasks that discriminated between conceptual and perceptual memory. It was found that clinically anxious subjects showed both enhanced perceptual and enhanced conceptual memory for threatening over positive and neutral information. These results indicate that both conceptual and perceptual processing systems respond more sensitively to threatening (at least negative) information, although the degree to which this occurs may be greater in clinically anxious than in healthy individuals.

## Selective Memory

The studies just discussed show that memory can be influenced by the emotional salience of the information. These memory effects, however, are derived from encoding processes that determine, in an absolute sense, the fundamental availability of the information for retrieval. Of even greater interest are the ways in which retrieval or search activities can be organized or manipulated so information that is known to be stored in memory becomes inaccessible.

### Shifts in Perspective

Anderson and Pichert (1978) showed that information that was inaccessible initially could be recalled after a shift in perspective. In this study, subjects read a short story about two boys playing hooky from school from the perspective of either a burglar or a person interested in buying a home. After recalling the story once, the subjects were asked to shift perspectives. During the second recall, information that had not been recalled before emerged. Subjects whose second recall was based on the perspective of the burglar recalled more features of the story, for example, the presence of jewels in the house, that were relevant to a burglar theme. In contrast, subjects whose second recall was based on the house-buyer's perspective remembered aspects of the house, such as the leaky roof and a damp basement, that had not been recalled at first.

These data show that a variety of information had been encoded initially but that instruction—or, more broadly, motivation to remember the material in a certain way—guided retrieval of a coherent but selected subset of information. When queried about the absence of information that later emerged, most subjects said they had simply forgotten the information or that it did not seem relevant despite the request to write down everything they had read. The study shows that individuals remember selectively according to themes or schemas of current interest and that a greater range of information can be elicited with shifts in perspective. This phenomenon is consistent with clinical observations that, during therapy, efforts between the therapist and patient to explore and shift perspective on issues may succeed in eliciting information that was not accessible previously.

### Directed Forgetting

Another well-known phenomenon of selective memory is "directed forgetting." It has been shown that subjects given explicit instructions to forget specific information will, on a later memory test, indeed show poor memory (both recall and recognition) of the "forget" material (e.g., Bjork & Woodward, 1973; MacLeod, 1975; Wetzel, 1975; Horton & Petruk, 1980). One common way to obtain this effect is to present subjects with a series of words and, after each word, indicate that it is to be remembered or forgotten. Generally the subjects are given an incentive to remember selected words and forget the other words by being told that they will later be tested on the "remember" words and not on the "forget" words. At test, however, subjects are tested on both types of words; they show much poorer memory of the "forget" words.

One obvious explanation for this effect is simply that the information that the person has been directed to forget has not been well rehearsed or elaborated during encoding, producing a relatively weak memory trace that is less likely to be retrieved successfully. The explanation has been supported by a few studies (e.g., Woodward, Bjork, & Jongeward, 1973; MacLeod, 1975). However, there is also evidence that, when efforts are made to insure that subjects have encoded test information satisfactorily, later instructions for subjects to forget or remember still produce memory decrements for the "forget" but not the "remember" material. In a study by Davidson and Bowers (1991), subjects studied to the point of perfect recall a list of 16 words falling into one of four categories (i.e., birds, flowers, alcoholic beverages, furniture). All subjects then were given the suggestion to forget one category of words (the category and all its items were named); half the subjects received the suggestion under hypnosis and the other half received the suggestion in a normal alert state. Results showed that both groups of subjects showed amnesia for the words falling in the targeted category but not for the nontargeted words.

Some investigators have suggested that the way in which directed forgetting is effected during retrieval processes may be through a global disabling (Davidson & Bowers, 1991) or a global inhibition (Bjork, 1989; MacLeod, 1989) of the retrieval mechanisms. The results just presented argue against these suggestions. Subjects recalled all categories of information but the targeted set, suggesting that retrieval mechanisms are intact but are operating selectively, guided by cues available during retrieval (e.g., retrieve all the birds and all the furniture, and forget about drinks).

Evidence from attention research has established firmly that individuals scan the external environment and select information for further processing. It does not seem unlikely that a search through memory can be similarly selective. Individuals may use certain cues to guide their memory search (cues associated with "remember" but not with "forget" instructions), enhancing retrieval for the "remember" but not the "forget" information. This suggestion is consistent with a line of research that has shown that when cues used during retrieval "match" very specific information of the stored memory (e.g., a word that rhymes with a target word or identifies the category of word), that information is more likely to be remembered than when a cue is not available or is in some way mismatched (Tulving & Thompson, 1973). Thus if subjects are, for example, using cues such as birds or furniture to guide their memory, they are less likely to recall information about drinks. To assume that affective state or the affective valence of a stimulus might be used as a retrieval cue during a directed memory search does not seem unreasonable. If an individual wishes to avoid recalling a negative or threatening memory, he or she might generate a positive state temporarily and use the affective state as a cue during a memory search. The individual would be more likely to find memories that match the positive affective state and less likely to retrieve a negative memory.

In summary, selective memory processes show flexibility in the range and specificity of stimuli to which they can be applied. Directed forgetting, for example, can occur with individual words (MacLeod, 1989; Paller, 1990), with a list of words (Bjork, 1989), or with a subset of individually presented words that share a common characteristic (Davidson & Bowers, 1991). This flexibility is consistent with clinical reports of amnesia for emotionally upsetting events: some clients have no memory of the entire event, whereas others forget only a selected portion.

Directed forgetting may operate in one of two ways. An event may be tagged immediately as an event to forget and, thus, may never be encoded well, leading to poorer memory. Alternatively, an event may be encoded well but poor memory of it might be a result of a mismatch between the information represented in memory and that given in a retrieval cue. Both formulations have merit and seem consistent with clinical observations. It is easy to imagine that some experiences (e.g., an embarrassing but not significant social encounter) may simply not be encoded well as a result of a self-instruction to forget that occurs almost simultaneously with the event. Alternatively, there may be events that are well processed at time of occurrence but, at some later point, a person acquires a motivation to forget. For example, Freud (1901), in *The Psychopathology of Everyday Life,* describes the writer who suddenly cannot find his pen and papers on an occasion when he would rather be out taking a stroll. Selective memory search in which the writer is scanning his memory for the location of his walking stick rather than that of his pen might make the retrieval of his pen a low probability event.

### Affective Specificity in Selective Memory Effects

The studies described present evidence that forgetting or selective memory occurs by several mechanisms. None of them attempts to assess whether directed forgetting can operate specifically over threatening compared with other affectively charged memories. Studies, however, have shown that impaired memory can be specified fairly well to threatening and negative information, at least among a certain set of individuals.

In a series of studies, Davis (1990) identified individuals who were characterized as "repressors" by virtue of specific personality traits as revealed by self-report inventories and compared their performance on a variety of memory tasks to that of "nonrepressors." Typically, subjects were asked to report personal memories elicited by the presentation of affectively laden cues. In one of her most carefully designed studies, Davis found that repressors, compared with other subjects, were slower to report memories when the cues referred to experiences of anger, fear, and self-consciousness, but not when the cues referred to experiences of happiness, sadness, or guilt. Davis suggests that anger, fear, and self-consciousness are all emotions related to circumstances under which "attention is focused on the self in a threatening, evaluative way." The other emotions, including the negative emotions of sadness and guilt, do not share this characteristic.

The memory patterns obtained in this study indicate that impaired retrieval does not occur across a variety of emotions or among a variety of individuals. Rather, diminished memory is associated specifically with threat or evaluation and with a certain type of "repressive" individual.

## Implicit Memory

The studies described in the previous section have shown that, under a variety of motivational conditions, recall and retrieval of specific information can be impaired significantly. These findings contributed to characterizing one aspect of repression. They offer no explanation, however, of the paradoxical nature of repression, namely that, although the individual does not consciously remember certain information, knowledge of this information is available and is expressed, without awareness, through various other behaviors. This section is devoted to a description of the evidence for memory without awareness; the following section will discuss the conditions under which memory without awareness can exist relatively independent of conscious memory.

In the past decade, evidence from cognitive studies has been accumulating that suggests that experiences not available to conscious recollection nevertheless influence judgment, learning, and action (Bowers, 1984; Khilstrom, 1987; Williams, Watts, MacLeod, & Mathews, 1988). This variety of phenomena can be represented as part of the implicit/explicit memory distinction. Schacter and colleagues have suggested that, whereas explicit memory refers to conscious recollection of information to which a person is exposed, implicit memory describes those situations in which information that "is encoded during a particular episode is subsequently expressed without conscious or deliberate recollection" (Schacter, 1987, p. 501).

## Subliminal Perception

The earliest studies demonstrating knowledge without awareness focused on the phenomenon of subliminal perception. In these studies, subjects were presented with stimuli below the range of consciousness, manipulated by means of tachistoscopic or dichotic listening presentations. Despite the absence of conscious awareness of these stimuli, behaviors of the subjects indicated that they had perceived, judged, and interpreted the given information. [See Dixon & Henley (1991), Erdelyi (1985), and Safran & Greenberg (1987) for reviews.] In one of the earliest dichotic listening studies, Corteen and Wood (1972) found that, when words that previously had been related to a shock experience were presented in the nonattending channel, subjects would produce skin conductance changes consistent with the registration of a shock event. It was also found that words that bore a semantic relationship to the shock words produced a similar skin response. The findings suggested that emotional or physiological responses could occur to stimuli and related information even when presented outside of conscious awareness.

This line of research has been criticized severely on methodological grounds concerning whether or not the presented stimuli are indeed out of conscious awareness (Erickson, 1960; Holender, 1986). Recent studies using new experimental techniques have demonstrated more convincingly the subliminal character of the presentation of stimuli and produced effects similar to those of the earlier studies (Marcel, 1983a,b; Cheeseman &

Merickle, 1986). Several studies using subliminal perception paradigms have shown the influences of nonconscious processes on affective judgments (Wilson, 1979; Kunst-Wilson & Zajonc, 1980), evaluative and social judgments (e.g., Bargh & Pietromonaco, 1982), and shifts in psychopathological states (see Silverman, 1983; Weinberger, 1991).

## Preference Judgments

The first assessment of implicit and explicit memory effects on judgments occurred in the context of the subliminal perception paradigm. In a study by Kunst-Wilson and Zajonc (1980), subjects were given subliminal presentations of geometric shapes. Explicit memory was evaluated by a forced choice recognition test in which the subject was presented with one new item and one old item. Subjects performed at chance level, which did not provide evidence for recollection of the previously seen stimuli. Nevertheless, when subjects were asked simply to judge which of a (old/new) stimulus pair they liked better, subjects consistently chose shapes they had seen before, suggesting the presence of implicit memory for the stimuli.

Another line of research indicates that preference judgments for clearly detectable stimuli are governed by rules of which there is no awareness. For example, Nisbett and Wilson (1977) found that, when consumers were asked to say which in an array of similar goods (e.g., stockings) was of the highest quality, they tended to choose the rightmost item. Although this effect was quite strong, an in-depth query indicated that the participants had no awareness of that selection criterion and, further, rather vigorously denied using it when it was raised as a possible explanation for their behavior.

## Rule Learning

In more recent studies, researchers have explored the range of potential rules that can be learned and applied without awareness. Lewicki (1986) showed that subjects rather easily learned covariations among certain stimulus characteristics of individuals shown in photographs (e.g., long/short hair) and particular personality traits given as descriptions of them (e.g., kind/persistent). Subjects' knowledge of the rule was evidenced by subsequent judgments consistent with the covariation rule; however, the subjects could not state the nature of the covariation explicitly. Similarly, Reber and his colleagues (Reber, 1976; Reber, Allen, & Regan, 1985; but see also Dulany, Carlson, & Dewey, 1985) have shown that subjects can learn artificial grammars, as evidenced by their ability to discriminate correctly between grammatical and ungrammatical sentences of a synthetic language, but cannot articulate the rules by which they are making their judgments.

## Priming Effects

Most of the research concerning implicit and explicit memory has used repetition priming effects and contrasted them with conventional tests of explicit memory such as recall and recognition. Unlike conventional memory tests, priming tasks do not involve explicit reference to any information to which the subject has been exposed; nevertheless, performance is influenced by such information. A priming effect is obtained when responses to a stimulus are facilitated as a result of recent exposure to that stimulus; this performance facilitation occurs without conscious recollection of the previous exposure. For example, in a word-stem completion task, subjects are asked to complete a 3-letter fragment (e.g., suff_) with the first word that comes to mind; a priming effect is obtained when subjects show a significant preference to complete the fragment to form a word recently seen in the experimental setting (e.g., suffuse) rather than a word that has a higher frequency in the language (e.g. suffer) (e.g., Warrington & Weiskranzt, 1974; Graf, Squire, & Mandler, 1984; Danion, Willard-Schroeder, Zimmermann, Grange, Schlienger, & Singer, 1991). Tasks used to assess priming effects are word fragment completion (e.g., Tulving, Schacter, & Stark, 1982), word identification (e.g., Jacoby & Dallas, 1981), lexical decision (e.g., Scarborough, Gerard, & Cortese, 1979), and reading a transformed script (Kolers, 1975, 1976; Masson, 1984).

One interesting aspect of priming effects is that, compared with explicit memory effects, they rely more heavily on the re-experiencing of the specific sensory and perceptual, rather than on the semantic or meaningful aspects of the previous exposure. There are various lines of evidence for this view.

First, priming effects can be obtained using stimuli that have only sensory or perceptual features and no inherent meaning, for example, dots and line patterns (Musen & Treisman, 1990). Second, priming effects are diminished when the words in the initial exposure phase and the implicit memory phase are mismatched in presentation modality (e.g., visual–auditory) over when they are matched (e.g. visual–visual or auditory–auditory); this discrepancy does not occur in explicit memory tasks (see MacLeod & Bassilli, 1989; Roediger, Weldon, & Challis, 1989). A smaller subset of studies has obtained *no* priming effects when modalities were mismatched, whereas explicit memory effects were obtained regardless of presentation modality (Graf, Shimamura, & Squire, 1975; Kirsner, Milech, & Standen, 1983; Roediger & Blaxton, 1987a,b). These data suggest that priming effects are significantly, if not primarily, influenced by the perceptual and sensory characteristics of the stimuli or of the associated processing events.

## Perceptual/Motor Patterns

Implicit memory for routinized perceptual/motor skills has been demonstrated rather ingeniously in studies with normal subjects. These studies suggest that motor patterns and their sensory consequences are represented cognitively. Such routines are believed to be accessible to conscious awareness, for example, when an individual is planning an act or evaluating its possible consequences. However, it is clear that these routines often become cognitively activated and influence behavior without conscious awareness.

In an example of this type of research, Van den Bergh, Vrana, and Eelen (1990) showed typists and nontypists pairs of letters and asked which of two combinations they liked better. One category of letter combinations was letter pairs that would be typed (according to touch typing rules) with the same finger; the other, with different fingers. Compared with nontypists, the typists preferred the different-finger letter combinations. The researchers suggest the typists' preference arose from well-encoded motor rules for touch typing in which different-finger letter combinations allow for cooperative motor actions, whereas same-finger letter combinations produce competitive motor responses. Nevertheless, when subjects were shown separate lists of all the same-finger combinations and all the different-finger combinations, not one subject was able to identify the categorical difference between the two sets of letters.

Klatzky, Pellegrino, McClosky, and Doherty (1989, Exp. 4) evaluated the extent to which engaging in a motor movement would facilitate sensibility judgments about sentences concerning the movement. Subjects learned and practiced handshapes (e.g., clench, poke) in association with an iconic cue that bore some visual relationship to the motor movement (e.g., clench = > > > >). Judgment time for phrases such as "clench the newspaper" (as opposed to "clench the window") was found to be facilitated when preceded by a relevant iconic prime. Presumably, the presentation of the icon primed the memory representation of the motor movement and the associated information about its interaction with objects, facilitating judgments about these movements. Although this study did not investigate the relationship between implicit and explicit memory, the obtained priming effect suggests the presence of implicit memory for the functional aspects of certain sensory or motor patterns.

A further set of observations about implicit memory for sensory or motor routines concerns cases of neurological amnesia. Although the memory capacities in these individuals will be described later in greater depth, one remarkable characteristic of these people is that, despite a striking inability to recall or report any number of experiences consciously, they still are able to perform well on sensory or motor tasks, benefit from practice on sensory or motor skills, and learn new ones. Schacter (1983), for example, describes playing a game of golf with an amnesic individual who showed extremely poor ability to remember such things as whether he had taken a shot recently and the location of his tee shots (as evidenced by his inability to locate and retrieve the balls). Nevertheless, he was able to execute complex perceptual–motor behaviors involved in skillful playing in a fluid and untroubled way.

In summary, a review of the studies described in this section suggests that memory without awareness influences a wide range of cognitive processes and activities (judgment, learning, action). Further, there is a growing body of evidence that implicit memory is exhibited primarily in memory of stimuli or processes that involve evaluative/affective or perceptual–motor aspects of experience.

## Dissociative Aspects of Implicit and Explicit Memory

The previous section described the numerous ways in which memory of experiences occurs outside of phenomenal awareness. Another line of research has focused on direct comparisons between implicit and explicit memory and on the ways in which they can be distinguished. Although several theoretical models of implicit and explicit memory are available (see Schacter, 1987; Richardson-Klavehn & Bjork, 1988), the common belief is that implicit memory is expressed most often through tasks that depend on exposure to and processing of sensory (perceptual) or motor aspects of experience (i.e., "data driven") whereas explicit memory is formed by and relies on the meaningful elaboration of events and their relationship to other information (i.e., "conceptually driven") (see Roediger, Weldon, & Challis, 1989).

Several studies have shown that factors that influence explicit memory performance are quite different from those influencing implicit memory. The dissociation in performances on these two types of memory tasks led to the suggestion that implicit and explicit memory are distinct and relatively independent memory systems or processes. The most typical dissociation observed is the ease with which, and various means by which, explicit memory for an event becomes impaired, while under the same conditions implicit memory remains intact.

### Neurological Amnesia

The earliest known description of an implicit/explicit memory dissociation was reported by Claparède concerning a neurological case of amnesia (see Schacter, 1987). Claparède (1911/1951) described an amnesic woman who hesitated to shake hands with him after he had pricked her with a pin during a handshake, although she had no recollection of him or the handshake. The memory dissociation is shown by the fact that, although the woman's behavior was influenced by the event, she had no conscious recollection of it.

Schacter and his colleagues have engaged in a systematic investigation of memory in neurological amnesia and have found consistently that amnesic individuals are impaired seriously on standard tests of explicit memory but perform at normal levels on a variety of implicit memory tasks.

Amnesiacs show intact implicit memory for many tasks that depend on the perceptual–motor (sensory) aspects of their experience. Despite their inability to recall ever having performed certain tasks, amnesiacs show exposure-related performance facilitation in activities such as perceptual identification of briefly flashed or degraded words, reading mirror-inverted script, serial pattern learning, and puzzle solving (see Schacter, 1987). Another interesting characteristic of the dissociation observed in amnesiacs is that implicit (but not explicit) memory persists for the evaluative or affective aspects of their experience. Johnson, Kim, and Risse (1985) found that amnesiacs produced positive or negative evaluations of men shown in photographs consistent with the evaluatively loaded biographies they had heard about the men earlier, although they did not recognize the men nor have any conscious recollection of having seen the photographs.

Dissociation of implicit and explicit memory also is obtained among individuals without neurological impairment using experimental and pharmacological manipulations. Variations in the degree of elaborative or meaningful analysis of the event consistently have been found to have a significant effect on explicit memory tasks but do not influence implicit memory performance. For instance, if an individual is discouraged from engaging rather than encouraged to engage in a meaningful analysis of a stimulus, recall of that stimulus will be impaired but implicit memory, as exhibited by performance on a word completion task, will not (e.g., Jacoby & Dallas, 1981; Schacter & Graf, 1986).

More recent studies have found that changes in state, such as the presence of clinical depression (Danion et al., 1991) or the administration of alcohol (Hashtroudi, Parker, Delisi, Wyatt, & Mutter, 1984) or benzodiazepines (Fang, Hinrichs, & Ghoneim, 1987; Danion, Zimmerman, Willard-Schroeder, Grange, & Singer, 1989), produce dissociations in which explicit but not implicit memory is impaired.

### Dissociation in Functional Amnesia

Hysterical or functional amnesia, from a behavioral perspective, can be characterized as an instance of dissociation of implicit and explicit memory in which conscious recollection is impaired but implicit memory remains intact. Schacter (1987) summarizes the report of Pierre Janet (1893) that describes a woman who

> became amnesic after being mistakenly informed by a man who appeared suddenly in her doorway that her husband had died. Even though she subsequently could not consciously remember this incident, she "froze with terror" whenever she passed the door that the man had entered. (p. 504)

The impaired explicit memory is reflected by the fact that the woman has no conscious recollection of the upsetting episode by the doorway. Implicit memory is exhibited by her emotion-laden behavior (fear and terror) when presented with a visual cue (the doorway) that represents one aspect of the initial experience. This dissociation is similar to that obtained in the Johnson et al. (1985) study in which neurologically impaired subjects could not remember ever having been shown certain photographs, yet produced affective/evaluative responses consistent with their earlier exposure to the photographs. In both cases, an emotional response was elicited by the presence of a visual cue associated with the affectively laden memory, despite the absence of any conscious recollection of the event.

Thus, the experience of repression, descriptively defined as the paradoxical experience of both "not knowing" and "knowing" (Erdelyi, 1985), can be viewed as one example of the dissociation between an impaired explicit memory (absence of conscious knowledge) and an intact implicit memory (knowledge expressed through affective or behavioral response).

## Implicit/Explicit Distinction and Selective Processing

There are no ready explanations of how the dissociation between implicit and explicit memory occurs in functional amnesia. However, this type of dissociation is consistent with a range of other observations that indicates that explicit memory is susceptible to disruption though a variety of agents and manipulations that do not affect implicit memory. Implicit memory remains unperturbed despite neurological damage, the administration of alcohol or benzodiazapines, and the presence of clinical depression. Thus, manipulations described earlier, for example, shifts in perspective and directed forgetting, may be effective in producing impaired recollection of a specific event but leave untouched the "memories" of the experience that are expressions of the relatively imperturbable implicit memory.

At least one study, using a directed forgetting paradigm, has shown that such a strategy influences explicit memory but has no effect on implicit memory. In this study (Paller, 1990), subjects were asked to evaluate semantically a series of words that was presented in one of two colors. In a counterbalanced design, subjects were told that one color indicated the word should be forgotten and the other that the word should be remembered. Performance on two explicit memory tasks was influenced by the forgetting instruction, with poorer performance on the forget words; in contrast, implicit memory was equivalent for the forget and remember words.

In this study, the motivation to remember or forget a particular word derived from the subject's desire or willingness to follow the experimenter's instruction. This type of strategy, however, might be applied under conditions in which the motivation to forget is prompted by a desire to avoid painful or negative memories. An individual may be motivated to forget an upsetting event such as overhearing a negative personally directed comment. If the individual were to engage in a process such as directed forgetting we might expect that the technique would succeed in minimizing conscious recollection of the episode but would not exert any influence over the expressions of implicit memory. When presented with any salient stimulus that represented characteristics of the forgotten event, for example, the voice of the person who spoke ill of the individual, the individual might experience a feeling of upset or discomfort without understanding its source.

In order to evaluate this possibility, future studies should investigate the contribution of personality and the emotional characteristics of the information to memory performance observed in directed forgetting or other paradigms. Individuals who are predisposed to avoiding the processing of painful information may be more skilled than others at following "forget" instructions or may show greater ability to follow "forget" instructions for threatening than for nonthreatening information.

We have compared directed forgetting skills in individuals who have a history of childhood sexual abuse to those of individuals without a history of any abuse and have found that, although the groups do not differ in their performance on an implicit memory task for a series of words to which they were exposed, the sexually abused group tended to show greater ability to forget words designated for "forgetting" (Cloitre, Brodsky, & Cancienne, 1991). These results test and support a specific model of the way in which cognitive avoidance might operate in a population, those sexually abused in childhood, that has been suggested to develop skills at avoiding or ignoring information to maximize survival in a situation from which escape is not possible (Miller, 1984; Freyd, 1991). This is one example of the type of research that can be conducted to test a model of cognitive avoidance and to provide, potentially, some understanding of the cognitive-affective processing style of a population about which little is known.

## Summary and Future Directions

Research on attentional processes has shown consistently that emotionally directed selective attention does exist. Whether attention is biased toward or away from an affectively charged stimulus depends on the basic character of the stimulus (e.g., blood as opposed to nudity), its relevance as a threat stimulus (e.g., exam words during an exam study period), the context of stimulus presentation (what other information is in the field), and the characteristics, both state and trait, of the individuals responding to the stimulus.

The research as a whole suggests, first, that certain individuals (alternatively "high trait anxious" or "repressors") may be predisposed to avoiding information as a way of diffusing threat and, second, that an avoidance response seems to require that the threat stimulus pass a certain threshold of intensity or relevance. An interesting anomaly to this general description, deriving from the work of Loftus, Christianson, and colleagues, is the possibility that there are certain types of information relevant to physical survival (e.g., blood, injuries) to which there is an inborn tendency to attend and that are easily encoded and remembered.

Much less is known about the mechanisms underlying memory for emotional information. Nevertheless, converging lines of research suggest that memory, like attention, can be subjected to selective processes for the purposes of avoiding emotional pain. The studies by Davis have shown that a specific type of personality ("repressor") seems to have difficulty retrieving personally threatening, as opposed to neutral or other negatively valenced, information. These studies, however, evaluate the retrieval of information in a very general way and leave unexamined the mental operations that might be involved in these emotionally based effects.

Other studies have focused on memory search and retrieval processes, suggesting ways in which selective memory operates, but have not investigated the contribution of personality and the emotional characteristics of the information targeted for retrieval. Thus, future studies might adopt cognitive science paradigms to assess the ease with which individuals who seem to avoid emotional processing will adopt strategies, such as shifts in perspective or directed forgetting, to minimize recollection of potentially painful information.

The implicit/explicit memory distinction and associated differential effects of selective memory processes have been presented as providing the basis for a cognitive-affective model of hysterical or functional amnesia. This distinction has been shown to have the necessary features to provide a satisfactory description of functional amnesia. First, implicit and explicit memory have been shown to be dissociable in a way that is applicable to the amnesiac's experience; the dissociation allows for the absence of conscious awareness of an event and the simultaneous expression of knowledge of the event through some other behavior. Second, the amnesiac "remembers" the event somatically; fittingly, memory without awareness has been shown to have predominantly motor or sensory (perceptual) characteristics. Finally it has been shown that some differences in the mechanisms or processes that operate over the two types of memory exist, so conscious memory can be eliminated relatively successfully (almost at will) whereas implicit memory remains untouched by these strategies.

The application of cognitive processing paradigms can help explain a variety of clinical phenomena. For example, the implicit/explicit memory distinction can be extended to help explain the apparent paradox in the therapy session in which an individual at once has no ability to describe or recall any important interpersonal events, yet acts in a systematic way (toward therapist or others) that indicates the presence of some memory or guiding principle about interpersonal relating. It has been suggested further that more dramatic phenomena, such as the capacity of individuals to experience multiple personalties, might be associated with a fragmentation of explicit memory and an intact implicit memory, in which the latter might provided a substrate of personal coherence (i.e., a common knowledge base for all the personalities) (Nissen, Ross, Willingham, Mackenzie, & Schacter, 1988). These final remarks are speculative. Nevertheless, they indicate the ways in which conceptual and methodological advances in cognitive science may bring us closer to explaining and clarifying important clinical realities.

Conversely, it is clear that clinical phenomena such as functional amnesia, fugue states, dissociative states, depersonalization, and multiple personality disorders can be useful in testing the assumptions made about the basic operating principles of models of memory and cognition. In summary, the collaboration between cognitive science and clinical psychology, which has just begun, shows promise of being fruitful in developing more sophisticated and inclusive models of affective-cognitive functioning in both healthy and pathological states.

# 3

# Cognition and Development: Four Contentions about the Role of Visual Attention

**Mark H. Johnson**

*Department of Psychology*
*Carnegie Mellon University*
*Pittsburgh, Pennsylvania*

The crucial importance for cognitive science of studying development has been pointed out by several authors (e.g., Karmiloff-Smith, 1990, 1992; Melzoff, 1990). In this chapter, I choose to focus on a particular area of cognitive development during infancy that is of critical importance to our understanding of both normal cognitive functioning in adults and some types of clinical disorders. Discussion of this area, visual attention, also will allow some more general points to be made about the nature of cognitive development, and its importance to our understanding of adult cognitive processing and its breakdown. I begin by reviewing why I have chosen to focus this chapter, as well as most of my recent work, on the development of visual attention.

First, most of what we know about the cognitive abilities of human infants comes from studies in which the extent of looking toward visual stimuli is measured in various ways, for example, habituation, simultaneous choice preference, visual tracking of a moving object, and infant control procedures. Although we have learned much about the representations present in the infant mind at various ages using these techniques (e.g., Baillergeon, 1986; Spelke, 1988), we still know very little about the control mechanisms that underlie these looking behaviors.

A second reason for focusing on the development of visual attention concerns the significant correlations that have been reported between components of visual attention in early infancy and subsequent measures of temperament and intelligence. Several laboratories have reported significant correlations between measures such as novelty preference (the extent to which an infant looks toward novel stimuli) and subsequent measures of IQ at school age (Fagan & McGrath, 1981; Fagan, 1984). Similar correlations have been reported for aspects of temperament. If temperament is defined in terms of individual differences in emotional and motor reactivity and self-regulation (Rothbart & Derryberry, 1981), the attentional control gained in early infancy may serve an important regulatory function over the emotions. In addition to being able to initiate positive interactions, the child should be able to avoid the distress that often has been reported to accompany obligatory attention (Stechler and Latz, 1966; Tennes, Emde, Kisley, & Metcalf, 1972). With this in mind, Johnson, Posner, and Rothbart (1991a) predicted that children who can better disengage attention from one visual location to another would be less susceptible to distress from novelty and intensity, and would be more soothable. By administering a measure of temperamental individual differences, these investigators were able to relate the development of orienting to the control of negative emotion. They reported that those 4-month-olds who were able to disengage from a visual stimulus more easily were less susceptible to distress and more easily soothed. Relationships were found also between contingency learning and visual anticipations and soothability; infants who anticipated more tended to be less soothable and those who showed greater contingency learning tended to be more soothable. These correlations suggest an intimate relationship between components of attention in early infancy and aspects of subsequent cognitive functioning.

Developments in the orienting capacities of infants are also interesting because they may be related to developmental changes in early social interaction and in the self-regulation of the infant. For example, periods of extended orienting to the mother at 6 and 13 weeks are followed by decreases in orienting by 26 weeks (Kaye and Fogel, 1980). At the older age, infants are less likely to wait to respond to the mother's greeting, instead initiating the interchange themselves. During the period of early face-to-face interaction, the caregiver is also likely to look at the infant for very long periods (see review by Schaffer, 1984) and to maintain the infant in the face-to-face position. At about 4 months, there is a shift of infant attention to foci other than the mother (Brazelton, Krslowski, & Main, 1974; Kaye and Fogel, 1980; Cohn and Tronick, 1987) that often is associated with the mother turning the infant so that s/he can easily look around. Numerous hypotheses have been put forward to explain this developmental shift, including improvements in the child's ability to differentiate people from objects, improvements in reaching for objects that are followed by increased visual attention to objects, and improvements in the self-regulation of emotion (see review by Fogel and Walker, 1989). It is possible, however, that the observed shift may be related to basic changes in the child's ability to disengage from a visual location and to anticipate events at different spatial locations.

A fourth reason for interest in the development of visual attention concerns the role of attention in the acquisition of knowledge during development. In other words, what the young infant attends to may determine the subsequent specialization of the adult mind. Later in this chapter, I will illustrate this point more fully with respect to the example of face recognition. Eye movements are the first means by which young infants can manipulate the external world. Moving their eyes alters the portion of the external world to which they are exposed. This ability precedes developments in other aspects of motor output, such as walking and the ability to pick up and manipulate objects, that also allow the child to explore particular aspects of the external world.

Finally, visual attention is a topic about which there is a comparatively large body of information regarding its neural basis from adult clinical studies, brain imaging studies, and single-cell recording from nonhuman primates. It is thus a promising area for which to map cognitive changes onto their neural substrate. Further, it is an aspect of cognitive functioning that seems to be particularly sensitive to clinical disorders in both the adult and the child. Clinical disorders such as schizophrenia seem to be associated with specific deficits in components of visual attention (e.g., Cohen & Servan-Schreiber, 1992). Some childhood developmental problems, such as Attention Deficit Disorder and possibly autism (discussed later), may, at least partially, result from underlying deficits in particular components of visual attention.

## What Is Visual Attention?

Visual attention may be dissociated broadly into two types: *overt* and *covert* (Posner, 1980). Overt visual attention refers to shifts of attention, often called orienting, that involve head and eye movements. In contrast, shifts of covert attention can occur in the absence of head or eye movements. One metaphor that has been invoked to describe this latter mechanism is that of a "spotlight" or "beam" that illuminates particular parts of the visual field. (See Allport, 1989, for a review of attention processes.)

In recent years it has been suggested that attention is not a unitary phenomenon, but that it can be dissociated into a variety of component functions (Posner, 1980). Further, some of these functions may be subserved by particular brain regions or pathways (e.g., Posner & Peterson, 1990). This view is also adopted in this chapter; particular components of attention are proposed to develop at different ages.

## Four Contentions about the Development of Visual Attention

In this chapter, four contentions about the role of attention in development are put forward and defended. The first contention is that the development of attention follows a maturational sequence in early infancy. Thus, although the exact age at which a particular change takes place may vary, the developmental sequence of changes will be consistent across all normal infants. I argue for this contention on the basis of evidence from developmental neuroanatomy. The second contention is that later developing attention systems have a hierarchical relationship with earlier developing ones. I present some cognitive evidence in support of this contention. The tendency is most evident in the greater predictive, anticipatory, or "top-down" nature of subsequently developing attention systems compared with earlier ones. I suggest that the tendency for integration over wider temporal intervals is common to many developmental systems. The third contention is that the plasticity of cortical circuits, or what the infant learns about, is constrained at least partially by what she attends to during early life. In other words, biases to attend to particular classes of stimuli during early infancy insure that the range of input to cortical circuits in a plastic state is constrained. I will discuss examples that relate to species-specific information, for example, recognizing faces. The fourth contention puts forward a particular view about the relationship between developing attentional mechanisms and the development of systems involved in the processing and manipulation of representations. This view states that, in development, there is a "bootstrapping" relationship between the two components of cognitive architecture. To illustrate this contention, I discuss some evidence of the development of conspecifics and their behavior and communications. Finally, the possible application of these four contentions to clinical disorders is illustrated in the rare but devastating developmental disorder, autism.

## Development of Attention Systems Follows
## a Predictable Maturational Sequence

Visual attention has several components that may be supported by particular neural pathways. With this in mind, I have provided a theoretical account of how the maturation of certain pathways in the cerebral cortex determines the components of visual attention that are operating in the human infant at various ages. Since this contention has been discussed in detail elsewhere (Johnson, 1990a,b, in press), I will provide only a brief outline here. The hypothesis specifies the extent of cortical functioning in the human newborn, and accounts for changes in the development of visual orienting over the first few months in terms of the maturation of three cortical pathways (see Fig. 1). These three pathways and a fourth, the subcortical pathway, are derived from proposals that accounted for adult primate electrophysiological and lesion data by Schiller (1985).

The specific proposal here is that, first, the characteristics of visually guided behavior in the infant at a particular age are determined by which of these pathways is functional and, second, which of these pathways is functional is determined in turn by the maturational state of the visual cortex, the structure through which all pathways receive their input. For example, by 2 months of age, infants begin to be able to track moving objects smoothly and are more sensitive to stimuli placed in the nasal visual field (Aslin, 1981). The onset of these behaviors coincides with maturation of upper layer 4 of the primary visual cortex and the consequent "enabling" of the middle temporal pathway (see Fig. 1). This pathway provides the cortical magnocellular stream with control over the superior colliculus. After 3 months of age, the frontal eye field pathway is proposed to be enabled by maturation of layers 2 and 3 of primary visual cortex.

Thus, from the patterns of postnatal growth in the cortex, we are able to predict the sequence of development of certain cortical pathways and, hence, the sequence of development of the components of attention that the pathways are thought to subserve. What are the information-processing consequences of these neural pathways coming "on-line" at particular ages? This question may be addressed by focusing on the transitions in orienting behavior that occur between 2 and 4 months of age in the human infant.

## Later Developing Attention Systems Are More Predictive than
## Earlier Developing Ones

Over the first month or so of the infant's life, its visually guided behavior is very "input driven." For example, in a task in which an infant is required to track a moving object with its eyes, the eye movements never

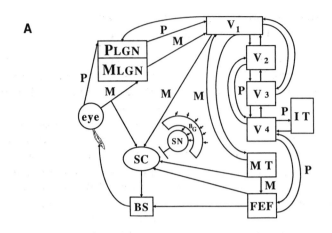

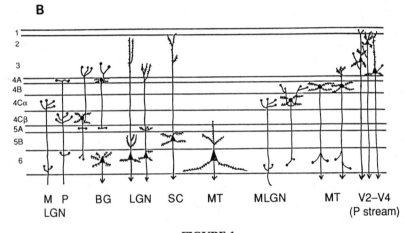

## FIGURE 1

(A) The four pathways proposed by Schiller (1985) to underlie oculomotor control. (1) A pathway from the retina to the superior colliculus (SC), the SC pathway is thought to be involved in the generation of eye movements toward simple, easily discriminable stimuli, and fed mainly by the peripheral visual field. (2) A cortical pathway goes both directly to the SC from the primary visual cortex (V1) and also via the middle temporal area (MT) to the SC (the MT pathway). This pathway is driven exclusively by the broad-band or magnocellular system (M). (3) A cortical pathway converges both broad-band and color-opponent (P) streams of processing in the frontal eye fields (the FEF pathway) and is involved in the detailed and complex analysis of visual stimuli, for example, the temporal sequencing of eye movements in complex arrays. (4) The final pathway for the control of eye movements, the inhibitory pathway, is an inhibitory input to the colliculus from several cortical areas via the substantia nigra (SN) and basal ganglia (BG). Schiller proposes that this final pathway insures that the activity of the colliculus can be regulated. LGN, lateral geniculate nucleus; BS, brain stem. Reprinted with permission from Johnson (1990a). (B) A schematic representation of primary visual cortex adapted from a diagram of the macaque visual cortex (Johnson, 1990a). Not all cell types or connections are shown.

anticipate the movement of the stimulus, even when they are first able to follow it smoothly (see Aslin, 1981). Simultaneously with the onset of development of the latest of the pathways controlling overt orienting (the FEF pathway; Fig. 1), the eye movements of the infant begin to reach the target of the moving stimulus before the stimulus itself does. That is, both saccades and smooth tracking begin to become anticipatory.

Evidence from other tasks supports the idea that only by 3 or 4 months can infants make such anticipatory eye movements. For example, Haith and his collaborators conducted a study in which 3.5-month-old infants viewed one of two series of slides that appeared either on the right or on the left of the infant alternating with either regular interstimulus intervals (ISI) or irregular alternation pattern and ISI (Haith, Hazan, & Goodman, 1988). The regular ISI generated more stimulus anticipations, and reaction times to make an eye movement were reliably faster than in the irregular series. The authors argue that infants of this age are able to develop expectancies for noncontrollable spatiotemporal events. Robinson, McCarty, and Haith (1988) report that they were unable to obtain these effects strongly in infants 6 and 9 weeks old. Thus, these results are consistent with the idea that, between 9 and 15 weeks, the ability to make anticipatory eye movements may emerge.

This conclusion is reinforced by the results of a recent study in which 2-, 3-, and 4-month-old infants were exposed to a number of trials in which a centrally presented stimulus predicted the location at which a target stimulus would appear (Johnson et al., 1991a). In each trial, one of two different fixation patterns would appear on a central monitor screen (see Fig. 2). After a short delay, a target stimulus would appear either on a right-hand side screen or on a left-hand side screen, depending on which of the two fixation stimuli had preceded it. After a number of such training trials, the infants were exposed to a small number of test trials in which the target stimulus came on in both possible locations, regardless of what the central fixation stimulus had been. Although infants of all ages studied showed low rates of anticipatory looking throughout the training period, only in the 4-month-old group did the percentage of anticipatory looking increase until almost one in three saccades was of this type. If the infants had learned to use the cue stimuli to predict the location of the reward stimulus, they should orient preferentially toward the appropriate location during the test trials. This turned out to be the case in the 4-month-old group, but not in the younger age groups. However, although anticipatory looking and the ability to use the central cue develop at about the same age, we should not assume that both are reflections of the same underlying process. Indeed, performance in these two measures turns out not to be correlated positively, suggesting different underlying mechanisms (Johnson et al., 1991a).

**Training trials**            **Test trials**

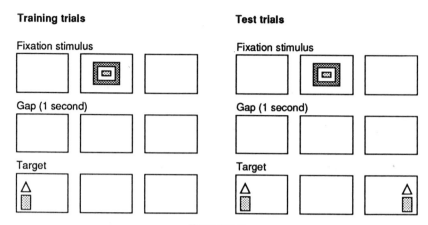

**FIGURE 2**

The three types of trials in the experiment of Johnson, Posner, and Rothbart (1991). The infant faced three monitor screens on which colored moving stimuli appeared in certain sequences.

It has been argued that the development of anticipatory looking is due to maturational events allowing the functioning of the frontal eye field pathway (see Fig. 1). What mechanisms underlie the ability to use a central cue in a predictive way? Success in using a central cue to predict the location of a target can be considered a marker for the existence of covert attention processes. If this is the case, then we are seeing a shift in the control of the infant's orienting behavior to a system that is more concerned with anticipating future events and less input driven. Concordant with this proposal is the suggestion by Posner and Rothbart (1990) that an even later developing attention system, the anterior attention system, influences changes in the infant's behavior toward the end of the first year of life. Orienting behavior in the infant thus may be characterized in terms of the emergence of successively more predictive stages of hierarchical control. First, we see a transition from a purely input-driven system to a system capable of making some anticipatory eye movements. Then, a further transition is made to a system that is capable of making higher order predictions about stimuli and that can be dissociated from eye movements. Finally, there may be a further transition of control to an attention system solely focused on internal processes.

## Learning Is Constrained by Attention during Development

In this section I argue for the importance of visual attention to determining the class of stimuli about which infants learn. In other words, what the young infant attends to is also what it learns most about. To illustrate this point, I will discuss some evidence on the development of face recognition.

When I began my work in this field, the existing literature appeared to be somewhat contradictory. Although the prevailing view, and most of the evidence, supported the contention that the infant requires 2 or 3 months to learn about the arrangement of features that compose a face, one study suggested that newborns 10 minutes old would track (by means of head and eye movements) a face-like pattern further than various scrambled face patterns (Goren, Sarty, & Wu, 1975). My colleagues and I began our investigations by attempting to replicate the claims made by Goren and co-workers. As in the original study, newborn infants (30 minutes old) were required to track different stimuli. This procedure differs markedly from that employed by other investigators. Instead of having the infant view one or more stimuli in static locations and measuring the length of time spent looking at the stimuli, in the Goren procedure the dependent measure is how far the infant will turn its head and eyes to keep a moving stimulus in view. The stimulus is moved slowly away from the midline and the angle at which the infant disengages its eyes from the stimulus is recorded. In the first study, we used three of the four stimuli used in the original study: a schematic face pattern, a symmetric scrambled face, and a blank face out-line stimulus. Although we and others (Maurer & Young, 1983) were un-able to replicate preferential head turning to follow the face pattern, we entirely replicated the effect using an eye movements measure (Johnson, Dziurawiec, Ellis, & Morton, 1991b; Experiment 1).

The replication of the Goren effect raised two questions. First, how specifically facelike is the stimulus required to be to elicit the preferential tracking? Second, what is the developmental time course of this prefer-ential tracking response? In an attempt to begin to address the first of these two questions, we performed an experiment identical to the one just mentioned except that we expanded the set of stimuli to include a pattern that possessed the configuration (arrangement) of high contrast areas that compose a face but lacked the features of a face, as well as a pat-tern that had facial features in the wrong arrangement. The former pattern might be effective if the tracking response was triggered by the ap-propriate spatial arrangement of high contrast "blobs" (somewhat similar to an unfocused image of a face). The results indicated that the face pat-tern was tracked further than all the other stimuli except the configura-tion stimulus (Fig. 3), suggesting that the correct arrangement of high contrast areas may be important for the preferential tracking. Of course much work remains to be done in defining the exact characteristics of the facelike patterns that are important, although unidimensional properties of the stimulus, for example, spatial frequency, cannot account for the preference.

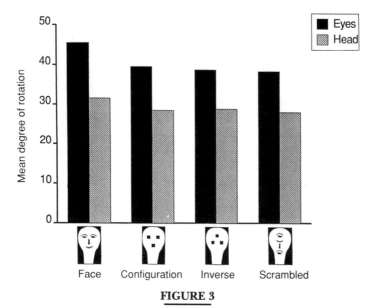

**FIGURE 3**

The mean extent of tracking facelike and non-facelike stimuli in experiment 2 of Johnson, Dziurawiec, Ellis, and Morton (1991). The face was tracked significantly further than all other stimuli except configuration.

The second question relates to the time course of the preferential tracking response. Although it is not feasible to test older infants with exactly the same procedure that we used with newborns, we devised an equivalent situation in which the infant was still required to track, by means of head and eye turning, similar stimuli. In this procedure, the infant was rotated with respect to the stimulus. (For details of the procedure, see Johnson et al., 1991b, Experiment 3.) Using this procedure, we tested groups of 4-week-olds, 6-week-olds, 3-month-olds, and 5-month-olds with stimuli similar to those discussed earlier. The results obtained indicate that, whereas the older three age groups show no significant preferential tracking of the face, the 4-week-old group does (Johnson et al., 1991b). Thus, it appears that the preferential tracking of facelike patterns disappears between 4 and 6 weeks after birth.

Why should this decline occur at this age? Morton and I have proposed that the preferential tracking response in newborns is mediated primarily by the subcortical visual pathway (Johnson, 1988; Johnson & Morton, 1991; Morton & Johnson, 1991). The time course of this response is similar to that of other newborn responses thought to be mediated by subcortical circuits, for example, the imitation of facial gestures (Maratos, 1982; Vinter, 1986) or prereaching (von Hofsten, 1984). The disappearance of these early reflex-like behaviors in the second month of life has been suggested to be due to inhibition by developing cortical circuits (e.g., see Muir, Clifton, & Clarkson, 1989). Another reason to suppose that the response of very young infants to faces is not mediated cortically is the absence of any of the hemispheric differences characteristic of adult face recognition (see DeSchonen & Mathivet, 1989).

Why should the tracking task be so sensitive to newborn preferences when standard testing procedures with static stimuli are ineffective? The peripheral visual field feeds more directly into the subcortical pathway, whereas the fovea feeds mainly into the cortical pathway. In a tracking task such as that described, the stimulus is moving continually out of the central visual field and toward the periphery. I have suggested that this movement into the temporal field initiates a saccade to refoveate the stimulus in newborns (for details, see Bronson, 1974; Johnson, 1990a). This consistent movement toward the periphery would not necessarily arise with static presentations; therefore, preferences will be elicited rarely. Thus, the tracking task may tap effectively into the capacities of subcortical structures such as the superior colliculus.

How can evidence in support of the claim that infants will not attend faces preferentially until 2 or 3 months of age be explained? One of the most cited studies supporting this view is that of Maurer and Barrera (1981). These authors used a sensitive infant control procedure, in which the infant viewed a series of individually presented static stimuli, to establish that, whereas 2-month-olds looked significantly longer at a facelike pattern than at various scrambled face patterns, 1-month-olds had no such preference. We (Johnson, Dziurawiec, Bartrip, & Morton, 1992) have attempted to replicate this result and to extend the original findings in two ways—by including in the stimulus set the defocused stimulus mentioned earlier and by also testing a 5-month-old group of infants. The results of the younger two age groups replicated the previous findings entirely: the face was looked at longer than any of the other stimuli by 10-week-olds but 5-week-olds showed no preferences. Initially, the result of the 5-month-old group was somewhat surprising: there was no significant preference for the face over the other stimuli. However, with increasing experience of faces, facelike stimuli may be required to be increasingly realistic to elicit preferential attention. If this is the case, another characteristic of real faces to our simple schematic face may restore the preference found at the younger age. We decided to test this hypothesis by adding the characteristic of internal feature movement. This was done using computer-generated stimuli similar to those used in earlier studies, except that one set of stimuli exhibited subtle facelike movement of the internal features. The results indicated that, although internal feature movement did not give rise to a face preference in 1-month-olds and did not alter the preference for a facelike pattern in 10-week-olds, it restored the preference for a facelike pattern in the 5-month-old infants.

It appears, then, that the development of face recognition in human infants can be accounted for in terms of two mechanisms with independent time courses. First, there is a system accessed via the subcortical visual pathway that underlies the preferential tracking in newborns, but loses influence by 6 weeks of age. Second, there is a system dependent on cortical maturity that requires exposure to faces and appears at 8 weeks of age. Increasing exposure to faces increases the specificity of input required to activate this second system. The primary function of the system present in newborns is to insure that the cortically mediated system is exposed to the appropriate class of stimuli, that is, faces, early in life. Simply put, since infants attend more to faces, they learn more about them.

Similar general arguments may be applied to the auditory domain and the subsequent acquisition of language. Jusczyk and Bertoncini (1988) have interpreted the literature on infant discrimination of components of speech sounds in terms of how these innate preferences might guide subsequent learning about speech. For example, infants are sensitive to the acoustic correlates of clausal units by at least 6 months of age (Hirsh-Pasek, Kemler Nelson, Jusczyk, Wright, Druss, & Kennedy, 1987). This ability is proposed to be critical for language acquisition, because determining the grammatical relationships among words requires grouping them according to what clause they appear in. Thus, early attentional preferences may select the appropriate components of acoustical input essential for language acquisition.

### Attentional Systems "Bootstrap" Representational Systems during Development

In the previous section, I discussed how learning is constrained by attention during development. In particular, I focused on the role of attentional biases present in the newborn. These orienting mechanisms have some preferences among the stimuli to which they are exposed. This information about the characteristics of stimuli arises independent of specific experience.[1] A number of such *primitive* representations exist, including some that are relevant to the structure of faces and to speech sounds. Only further experimentation will determine the exact nature and number of such primitive representations.

Most cortically mediated representations are assumed to be acquired through interaction with the external environment; thus, they may be

---

[1]More specifically, these representations are present in the infant's mind without any influence from the individual specific environment (see Johnson & Morton, 1991).

thought of as *acquired* representations. A key proposal of this chapter is that the neural circuitry supporting these representational systems is configured in response to a range of inputs constrained by attention systems (recall that in the first contention we discussed a number of cortical attention circuits). The contention put forward in this section states that once the neural circuitry underlying a particular representational system has been configured, it influences subsequently developing cortical attention systems. Development thus can be characterized as a bootstrapping process: lower level attention systems bias the input to higher level representational systems. These representational systems subsequently influence an attention system at their own level, and the process continues.

As a particular example of this contention, I shall return to the example of face recognition from the previous section. Earlier in this chapter it was argued that hierarchically arranged attention mechanisms possess a number of properties essential to constraining neural plasticity, so specialization for processing and manipulating particular classes of representations results. These properties include a more rigid maturational timetable for attention mechanisms than for the representational systems that are dependent on them (first contention) and their hierarchical arrangement (second contention). The latter property has the consequence that such systems become less input driven and more "top down" as development proceeds. Neurocognitive development thus may be viewed as a bootstrapping process. Lower order orienting systems constrain the input to representational systems that, in turn, will select, *even more restrictively*, the input for later developing higher order attention systems. With this viewpoint in mind, a particular example of an interaction between attention and representational systems during development will be outlined. This example concerns how information about the visual characteristics and behavior of conspecifics may be coded at levels that give the individual increasing ability to predict future events.

As discussed earlier, newborn human infants are predisposed to orient preferentially toward stimuli that possess some of the structural characteristics of human faces (see Johnson & Morton, 1991; Morton & Johnson, 1991), that is, infants have a primitive representation related to faces that influences a (subcortical) orienting mechanism. It was also pointed out earlier that this predisposition would insure that developing cortical circuits are exposed to faces rather than to other stimuli that commonly appear in the infant's visual environment. However, this is not the limit to how particular cortical circuits and pathways become specialized for processing information about the visual characteristics of conspecifics.

After the maturation of the cortical pathways subserving overt visual attention (see Fig. 1), the range of facelike stimuli to which infants will attend becomes greatly reduced. For example, a simple static schematic face is no longer sufficient to attract preferential looking in infants of 5 months of age. If the internal features of the face pattern move in a facelike manner, however, the preference for the face over other stimuli is restored (Johnson et al., 1992), that is, a higher order temporal component of the stimulus has been extracted. According to the contentions of this chapter, this result occurs because, at each level of attentional control, higher order invariants are extracted from the input, enabling greater predictive (anticipatory) abilities.

This increasing emphasis on the prediction of future events also can be seen in the results of studies designed to investigate the properties of single cells responsive to conspecifics. In a particular area of the macaque temporal lobe, the superior temporal sulcus (STS), there are cells responsive to faces, hands, and biological movement (Perrett, Rolls, & Caan, 1982). Whereas some cells respond only to components of a face or to a wide variety of face patterns, others are more selective still. These cells only respond to faces in particular views. More recent evidence, however, suggests that these cells encode face views in relation to the viewer, that is, they encode the direction of another's attention, not a characteristic of the face (Perrett et al., 1989). Encoding the direction of another's attention is likely to be a better predictor of subsequent behavior than encoding particular views of a face.

The same general argument may be applied to the perception of biological movement. Although cells in the temporal lobe may be tuned to orient the infant toward conspecific movement from an early age, other cells only respond to particular classes of goal-directed movements. One example of such cell responsiveness follows. This cell responds to whole body movement, in particular, to a person walking from different starting positions, but *only* when the direction of walking leads the person to the threshold of the laboratory door. Directions of walking that do not take the person straight to this door are less effective in provoking a response from the cell. Perrett and colleagues (Perrett et al., 1989) have argued that such cells encode higher order invariants of biological motion, those that have an intention behind them.

Information about the visual characteristics of conspecifics thus appears to go through a number of transitions. In the newborn, primitive representations concerned with the characteristics of faces and biological motion influence the activity of input-driven (subcortical) orienting circuits. As discussed earlier, this behavior insures that information about the characteristics of conspecifics enters developing cortical circuits. A result of this process may be that temporal and dynamic characteristics of the input are extracted, for example, those properties found in Perrett's goal-directed cells.

In terms of the testing of cognitive capacities, successful or unsuccessful performance in any particular task may be subserved by different neural circuits at different ages according to the framework presented in this chapter. Performance normally would be regulated by the highest level system available. With this in mind, we can make some sense of findings such as those of Goldman (1971) that, although prefrontal ablation impairs performance in spatial-delay tasks in adult monkeys, it does not impair the performance of infant monkeys. In the framework presented in this chapter, developmental shifts in the neural circuits that are crucial for particular tasks would be attributable to movement of the control of that behavior to a hierarchically higher level.

## Implications for Clinical Issues

The viewpoint proposed in the previous sections has implications for our understanding of clinical issues, as well as for our understanding of cognitive science. As an illustration of this point, I will discuss evidence relating to one rare but devastating developmental disorder, autism.

There have been persistent reports of abnormalities of attention in autistic individuals. For example, it was thought that autistic children were unable to attend to stimuli presented simultaneously and that they could only respond to a very restricted range of available environmental stimuli (Lovaas, Schreibman, Roegel, & Rehm, 1971). It is now clear, however, that some of the putative attentional deficits identified earlier may be attributed not to the specific diagnosis of autism, but to mental age (Lovaas, Koegel, & Schreibman, 1979) or motivational factors (Bray Garretson, Fein, & Waterhouse, 1990). Further, Frith (1989) points out that a more central cognitive deficit, such as a lack of "central coherence," would result in autistic children having relatively normal attentional abilities, but directing them toward inappropriate stimuli. Thus, attention could be odd without being impaired. An example of this concept is seen in an experiment by Weeks and Hobson (1987). These authors asked children to sort pictures of people. It was possible for the pictures to be sorted according to whether the expression on the face was happy or sad, or according to whether the person did or did not wear a hat. Whereas normal children tended initially to sort according to facial expression, autistic children tended initially to sort according to the presence or absence of a hat. On a second attempt, both groups easily could sort according to the other dimension. Thus, whereas the autistic group could discriminate and categorize as well as the normal group, autistic individuals chose to attend to a different feature of the stimuli.

Despite these results, there are still two reasons to consider the presence of abnormalities in attention in autistic children. First, most standard paradigms for studying visual attention, such as those developed by Posner and others (e.g., Posner, 1980; Posner & Peterson, 1990), have yet to be run on autistic populations. These experimental paradigms have the advantage that they are comparatively well understood in terms of the cognitive mechanisms and neural pathways that underlie them. Second, even when autistics perform similarly to normal subjects in attentional tasks, the neurophysiological mechanisms underlying that performance may be quite different. For example, Ciesielski, Courchesne, and Elmasian (1990) report that autistic subjects who perform as well as normal subjects on a rare stimulus identification task still show substantially different patterns of event related potentials. The investigators suggest that autistic individuals may use different attentional mechanisms than the normal subjects to compensate for deficits in other aspects of attention.

Although most researchers are happy to acknowledge that attention is abnormal in autistic populations, many, like Frith (1989), believe these abnormalities to be symptoms of a more central cognitive deficit. By adopting the contentions outlined earlier in this chapter, however, one can see that attention is intimately entwined with the development of representational systems during development. An early deficit in attention would thus give rise to subsequent abnormalities in certain classes of representational systems.

Baron-Cohen, Leslie, and Frith (1985) originally put forward the idea that the core cognitive deficit in autism may be the lack of a "theory of mind." "Theory of mind" is the term coined by Premack and Woodruff (1978) to refer to the ability to comprehend that others of your own species possess minds similar to your own, and are capable of having beliefs, desires, and other feelings. One way in which this deficit in autistic children can be demonstrated is by "false-belief" tasks. For example, Sally has a marble that she puts in a basket. Sally then goes away for a walk. While Sally is away, Anne comes in and moves the marble from the basket to a box. The autistic child is asked some questions to establish that she understands and remembers this sequence of events. Then she is asked, "When Sally returns, where will she look for her marble?" If the child simply tries to predict Sally's behavior in a physical way or according to personal knowledge, then she will attend to where the marble really is. If she predicts Sally's behavior in terms of Sally's (false) belief, then she will predict correctly that Sally will look in the basket.

Another false-belief scenario involves showing the child a container that normally contains a candy well known to the child (e.g., "Smarties") and asking the child what the container holds (Perner, Leekam, & Wimmer, 1987). The child replies, "Smarties." Then the box is opened and the child is shown that, alas, the box contains not Smarties but a pencil. Now the child is told that a friend will come in a minute and be shown the closed box, just as she was. The friend will be asked, "What's in here?", again, just as she was. The child is then asked what the friend will say. Again, only if the child can infer the friend's inevitable false belief will she reply, "Smarties."

Numerous studies, using these scenarios or variants thereof, have shown that most normally developing children at 4 years of age can infer and predict behavior on the basis of other people's beliefs. Autistic children, in contrast, perform poorly on these and related tasks, well out of line even with their own general intellectual level. Other clinical groups, such as Down's syndrome or specific language impaired children, perform roughly in line with their mental age (see Frith, 1989, for review). At the same time, autistic children appear to be relatively unimpaired in their understanding of social events that do not require an understanding of mental states but simply of behavioral dispositions (Baron-Cohen, Leslie, & Frith, 1986). Autistic children also show characteristic abnormalities in communication, for example, they have difficulties understanding noninstrumental communicative gestures and pragmatic aspects of language use (see Frith, 1989, for review). Finally, autistic children show abnormalities in their development of pretense, and do not exhibit spontaneous pretend play (e.g., Baron-Cohen, 1987).

The "theory of mind" deficit account of autism assumes a deficit in the child's ability to manipulate a particular class of representations, metarepresentations.[2] Although these authors maintain that a specific deficit of this kind can account for many of the behavioral deficits found in autistic children (Frith, 1989), the question of the developmental cause of the deficit is still open. One possibility is that there is a failure of maturation of the neural circuitry that supports the manipulation of metarepresentations associated with theory of mind (Leslie, 1987). Evidence consistent with this suggestion comes from a study in which the infant screening records of children subsequently diagnosed as autistic were examined (Johnson, Siddons, Frith, & Morton, 1992). Only at 18 months of age did the autistic sample become dissociable from a group of normal records and a group with non-specific developmental delay. This dissociation was apparent in a sudden increase in reports of social abnormalities.

Note, however, that in the framework presented in this chapter it is equally plausible that a deficit in some component of attention early in life may give rise to subsequent deficits, including those in the metarepresentations that support theory of mind. For example, a deficit in the newborn orienting toward faces described earlier would give rise to inadequate learning about faces over the first few months of life. This may have the consequence that the older infant fails to attend to (and therefore learn

---

[2]Whether or not these metarepresentations are specific to theory of mind is the subject of some debate (see Karmiloff-Smith, 1992).

about) biological motion, the actions of others, shared attention, and so forth. Since attending to these latter stimuli may be an essential prerequisite for developing an adequate theory of mind (Johnson & Leslie, 1992), it is possible that deficits in theory-of-mind representations would result.

Such an account of the autistic deficit would predict that an autistic child could acquire other classes of representations, but the lack of an appropriate attentional bias early on would mean that the specialized representational systems that developed could be very different from those of a normal child. Perhaps this accounts for the idiot savant phenomenon closely associated with autism. Such cases have extraordinary abilities in a particular domain such as drawing, music, or calendrical calculations (e.g., O'Conner & Hermelin, 1984). [The reader is referred to Karmiloff-Smith (1992) and Johnson and Leslie (1992) for expanded accounts of the same general arguments.] Regardless of whether or not the epigenetic account of autism just outlined is correct, it serves to illustrate the potential value of a developmental cognitive science perspective for our understanding of at least some clinical disorders.

In this chapter, I have argued for the importance of considering evidence from early infancy in understanding the normal and abnormal cognitive architecture of the adult mind. I also have given examples of how apparently minor deviations from normal functioning in early infancy might have profound and widespread consequences later in development.

## Acknowledgments

Portions of this chapter were written while I was a research fellow at the McDonnell–Pew Center for Cognitive Neuroscience at the University of Oregon. I thank Mike Posner and Mary Rothbart for their hospitality, generosity, and stimulating discussion during that time, and the Human Frontiers Scientific Foundation for financial support. Leslie Tucker assisted in the preparation of the chapter.

# 4

# Cognition and Emotion: Extensions and Clinical Applications

**George Mandler**

*Department of Psychology*
*University of California, San Diego*
*La Jolla, California*
*and*
*University College London*
*London, England*

Cognition
Emotion
Consciousness
Applications
    Stress and Anxiety
    Psychoanalysis

The importance of the emotions and the relationship between emotion and cognition pervades most clinical concerns. A mere chapter cannot do justice to the full panoply implied by the title, and therefore must restrict its domain. I begin with an introduction to cognition and cognitive science, and their role in contemporary theory. A consideration of the special role of cognitive science in the interpretation and analysis of human emotion follows, succeeded by a presentation of emotional phenomena in terms of autonomic arousal and evaluative cognitions. The central importance of conscious and unconscious processes is acknowledged by a discussion of the function of constructive consciousness. I then discuss a limited number of applications of these concepts, first in an exploration of stress and anxiety and their psychological causes and symptoms, and finally in an appreciation of the cognitive nature of psychoanalytic theory and psychodynamic therapy.

*Preparation of this chapter was supported in part by a grant from the Spencer Foundation.

## Cognition

Cognitive science, as a discipline, is heir to cognitive psychology, an area of theoretical psychology that has dominated psychological thinking for the past 30 years. Cognitive psychology was marked by a commitment to a psychological language and an acceptance of the complexity of human thought and action. Cognitive psychology—and subsequently, cognitive science—arose out of a fundamental shift in emphasis and theory in the late 1950s and the subsequent decade. These changes not only permitted psychology to free itself of the strictures of behaviorism, but also affected such diverse areas as anthropology, linguistics, and neuroscience (cf. Mandler, 1985). The major cultural change that apparently motivated these shifts was an attention to new ways of looking at the acquisition, storage, and transmission of information and knowledge. Most of these changes were in place by the late 1960s, when new ways of dealing with human memory, language, thought, and perception were firmly established. The new theory-rich psychology soon was able to build bridges to other disciplines, a connection that had been dormant or absent in previous decades. Perhaps most important was the development of neuropsychology, in part generated by the development in the psychology of memory and perception of observations and theories that were accessible to neurophysiological translations (cf. Shallice, 1988). In the 1980s, there followed an increasing realization that the neurosciences, cognitive psychology, linguistics, and the increasingly relevant developments in artificial intelligence, as well as new analyses of social interactions, were developing common interests and intersecting in research and theoretical endeavors. The budding coalition of these cognitive sciences led to the current establishment of cognitive science as a significant area of interlocking phenomena and theories.

"Cognition" sometimes means different things to different people in the field. In one usage, it refers to "thinking" broadly conceived; in another, it refers to any and all mental operations, including simulated mental processes; in a third usage, it refers to a representational system that incorporates "knowledge," again broadly conceived. In this chapter, the reader will find reference, at various times, to all three of these cognate interpretations, with some emphasis on the third one.

During the earlier development of the cognitive sciences, attention was paid primarily to purely "cognitive" (knowledge-related) phenomena, primarily memory, thought, and perception. Not until the 1970s did the new look penetrate into theory and research in areas not generally considered "cognitive." Among these areas was the analysis of emotional phenomena. However, the convergence of cognitive theories and emotion has not been complete. Most treatments are phrased in terms of emotion *and* cognition; it is symptomatic that this chapter title also uses that locution. The reasons for this continuing disjunction are largely historical. Emotion as an object of study has a long history; however, in contrast to other mental phenomena, it displayed a dearth of significant theoretical developments. Apart from the ideas of Descartes and his intellectual heirs, not until the time of William James and Sigmund Freud did the emotions receive significant analytic attention; even then, another six decades passed until new ideas emerged. In contrast, perception and memory have been in continuous construction and reconstruction up to the present. Finally, the apparent involuntary and inevitable nature of emotional experience seems to make it opaque to the kind of analytic endeavor that a constructive and representational cognitive approach demands.

The most widely accepted current representational approach involves the notion of cognitive schemas (cf. Mandler, 1985). A schema is a coherent unit of structured representation that organizes experience. Schemas are not carbon copies of experience, but abstract representations of experiential regularities. They range from the very concrete, involving the most primitive categorization of perceptual experience, to the very abstract, representing general levels of meaning such as "love" or "justice." Schemas are built up in the course of experience and interaction with the social and physical environment. They organize and interpret our world, and organize experience by defining and interpreting current encounters in terms of the schemas laid down by past similar and related experiences. Currently active schemas define what we are likely to see, hear, and remember, and also determine what we are unlikely to hear or see. Thus, we note the "time" when looking at a clock in a public square, but are unlikely to see (process) the precise form of the numerals. New information activates and constructs relevant schemas that in turn organize our experience of the world.

The activation of schemas proceeds automatically from the most concrete to the most abstract relevant schemas (bottom-up processing). At the same time, and also automatically, activated high-level schemas pass activation to lower schemas (top-down processing) and change or constrain subsequent thought and perception. Features that make up a schema may be wholly, partially, or not activated; activated schemas are similar to the preconscious entities of psychoanalytic theory (see subsequent text). Expectations develop as a consequence of activated schemas; they define what the world should look like. Expectations also are involved for those elements of schemas activated by top-down processing that are not supported directly by input evidence. Expectations are not met when evidence for all or part of an activated schema is missing; the result is a lack of congruity in schematic processing. This discrepancy is one of the causes of autonomic (sympathetic) nervous system arousal, in part to prepare the organism to cope with a changing environment (see subsequent text).

It is useful not to conceptualize schemas as neurophysiologically localized entities. Rather, they are constructed of distributed features (Rumelhart & McClelland, 1985) that are available for a variety of different schematic structures. Schemas also are not rigidly bounded representations but dispositional entities. Currently available information constructs (of distributed features) a particular representation that responds both to the immediate information and to the regularities (schemas) generated by past events.

Since schemas develop through experience, it is important to consider how they change. The single most important description of such a development has been provided by Jean Piaget, who analyzed the process of schema development in terms of *assimilation*, the integration of new elements or input into existing schemas, and *accommodation*, the change in schemas caused by input that cannot be assimilated.

In the following discussion, I first present an overview of an approach to emotion that makes cognitive processes central to the appearance of emotional experience. After discussing some problems of consciousness, I apply the emotion–cognition interaction to problems of clinical relevance, such as stress, anxiety, and psychoanalytic or psychotherapeutic issues. The confines of this chapter do not permit a full exploration of the relationship between cognitive science and emotional disorders. I will restrict my discussion to those aspects that are relevant to my cognitive explorations of emotion. [For an overview of the relevance of cognitive psychology to emotional disorders, see Williams, Watts, MacLeod, & Mathews (1988).]

## Emotion

The approach presented in this chapter stresses arousal and evaluation, as exemplified in discrepancy/evaluation theory that has been documented extensively (Mandler, 1975, 1984, 1990; see also Mook, 1987; Strongman, 1987). This approach views emotion as a combination of cognitive evaluative schemas with visceral arousal (which is perceived as emotional intensity). Together these components create a holistic conscious event, the experience of emotion.

The two dimensions of arousal and evaluation respond to the use of "emotion" in common language: emotions represent evaluative cognitions and emotions are "hot", that is, they imply a gut reaction or visceral response. Evaluative cognitions—what is good or bad, pleasant or unpleasant, noxious or desirable—provide the quality of the emotional experience, whereas visceral reactions generate its quantitative aspect. This approach to an analysis of emotion does not attempt to address all possible aspects of the concept of "emotion," but it is a necessary first step in developing a system that produces at least some of the observations that are subsumed under the common language notions of emotion (Mandler, 1975). To rephrase,

> We allow any and every meaning of the word emotion (without worrying about the exact nature of the meanings) to outline an approximate area of observation and experiment. We then attempt to account for as much of the data as possible with some small number of assumptions. (McNaughton, 1989, p. 4)

Regularities in human thought and action produce general categories of emotions, categories that have family resemblances and overlap in the features that are selected for analysis (for example, the simple dichotomy of good and bad, the appreciation of beauty, or the perception of evil). The source of the categories of emotion varies from case to case, and different emotional categories may be based on different experiential or environmental factors. For example, an emotional category may be based on the similarity of external conditions (in the case of some fears and environmental threats) on a collection of similar behaviors (in the subjective feelings of fear related to avoidance and flight). Other emotional categories, such as guilt and grief, depend on individual evaluations of having committed undesirable acts or trying to recover the presence or comfort of a lost person or object. All these emotional states involve evaluative cognitions; the features common to any particular category give rise to the appearance of discrete categories of emotions. On the other hand, the fact that classes of evaluative cognitions are very large, and variations within them practically infinite, insures that there will be an equally large, and practically infinite, number of different emotional experiences.

Evaluative cognitions provide the quality of an emotional experience, and visceral activity provides its intensity and peculiar "emotional" and passionate characteristics. Sympathetic nervous system (SNS) arousal not only insures the "hot" quality of the emotions, but also controls the felt intensity. Recent experimental evidence has shown that the degree of autonomic (sympathetic) arousal can be mapped to the felt intensity of an emotion (MacDowell, 1991).

A majority of occasions for visceral (SNS) arousal follows the occurrence of some perceptual or cognitive discrepancy, or the interruption or blocking of some ongoing action. Discrepancies are only a sufficient, not a necessary, condition for sympathetic arousal. Other sources of SNS arousal can and do play a role in emotional experience.

Discrepancies and interruptions depend, to a large extent, on the organization of the mental representations of thought and action. In schema theory, these discrepancies occur when the expectations generated by schemas are violated. This is true whether the violating event is worse or better than the expected one, and accounts for visceral arousal on both unhappy and joyful occasions. Usually, discrepancies are involved also in cases of conflict, that is, situations in which more than one possible action or thought is possible in response to situational or intrapsychic demands. Pursuing one or the other alternatives means abandoning some others; the general ambivalence displayed in conflicts generates arousal and emotional reactions. Most emotions follow such discrepancies, simply because the discrepancy produces visceral arousal.

In summary, interruptions, discrepancies, blocks, frustrations, novelties, and conflicts are occasions for SNS activity (cf. Mandler, 1964; Mac-Dowell & Mandler, 1989). All are occasions when the world is different than what usually has been experienced. It is reasonable to postulate such a "difference detector" (Mandler, 1992b) from an adaptive, evolutionary point of view. This attribute prepares the organism for the demands of the new situation, both cognitively and physiologically. Cannon (1930) approached such an extension of the functions of the autonomic nervous system when he argued that the homeostatic mechanism responds to changes in the external world.

## Consciousness

The holistic experience of emotion derives from the concatenation of arousal and evaluative cognitions into a unified experience. This process needs some further exposition, as does the role of unconscious processes. As in the case of emotion theory, the last 15 years have seen a revival of theoretical concerns with the role, uses, and functions of consciousness, and its place in contemporary cognitive psychology (Mandler, 1975a, 1992a; Miller, 1985). In contrast to the psychologies of the 19th century, cognitive psychology has relied primarily on unconscious processes in the explanation of thought and action. Locutions such as mental structures, representations, processes, and schemas imply a vast armamentarium of unconscious functions, only some of which may be directly evident in consciousness. An excellent example can be found in modern linguistics, which assumes vast unconscious structures that generate syntactically and semantically proper constructions; however, none of these mechanisms and processes ever appear in the conscious life of the linguistically competent individual.

Once theoretical arguments assign major functions to unconscious mechanisms, questions about what the functions of consciousness might be arise naturally. What is the process by which unconscious mechanisms affect conscious ones? How does information pass from the unconscious to the conscious? Such questions are fundamentally different from questions raised in the 19th century when Hartmann (1869) and Freud were vilified for even suggesting unconscious processes. It is not surprising that discussions about the usefulness of consciousness are prevalent among cognitive scientists, whereas discussions about the functions of the unconscious are dominant among clinical and personality theorists. The latter are, in the tradition of psychodynamic theories, concerned with the fine structure of unconscious motivational mechanisms, whereas the cognitive enterprise focuses on the fine structure of unconscious knowledge structures. However, the experimental and cognitive tradition has been to question the transition from unconscious to conscious to uncover the function of consciousness.

The quest for theories of consciousness—how unconscious processes generate or determine conscious states—is diagnostic of the major change in our view of consciousness. Whereas the dominant belief prior to the 20th century was in rational conscious humanity (and the notion of unconscious forces was an unlikely proposition), psychologists in the 20th century have concentrated most, if not all, determinants of behavior in hypothetical or at least unconscious forces. What needs to be explained is how those unconscious events interact with the subjective reality of consciousness.

Conscious contents are constructed from previously activated unconscious structures. Such a constructivist interpretation of consciousness responds to the appearance of unitary conscious contents that summarize and represent the most salient aspects of the current extra- and intrapsychic world. Conscious constructions represent the most general interpretation that is appropriate to the *current* needs and scene, in keeping with both the intentions of the individual and the demands of the environment. In the absence of any specific requirements (internally or externally generated), the current construction will be the most general (or abstract) available. Thus, we are aware of a landscape when viewing the land from a mountaintop, but become aware of a particular road when asked how we might get down, or of an approaching storm when some dark clouds "demand" inclusion in the current construction. In a problem-solving task, we will be conscious of those current mental products that are closest to the subjectively most likely solution to the problem. When a discrepancy occurs, the mental system easily may find some way to assimilate it; if this does not occur, a number of different consequences may follow. In particular, when current activations from the environment, the causes of the disruption, do not find readily an appropriate structure that accommodates their characteristics, then spreading activation will generate alternative ones that provide support for the new evidence generated by the world. In emotional experience, conscious constructions incorporate arousal and evaluative cognitions into unitary experiential "emotions."

Constructive consciousness is a complement to an underlying representational system that is characterized by schemas represented by distributed features. Such a system is relatively large (i.e., it represents the accumulated experiences of the individual), is relatively fast in accessing information, and operates in a parallel fashion (i.e., a large number of relevant features and schemas is accessed and activated at the same time). These characteristics would, without an additional buffer, make action and thought difficult if not impossible. The individual would be overwhelmed by information rapidly emerging in parallel fashion; action decisions in particular and decision processes in general would be overwhelmed by the amount and speed of the information produced. Consciousness is, among other things, the buffer that solves this problem. First of all, it is serial, that is, only one (small) cluster of information is accessed at any one time; it is also relatively slow and limited in capacity to a few items or events. From this perspective, consciousness is not an independently active "executive" system, but a mechanism that provides limited, but adaptively focused, access to the underlying unconscious cognitive machinery. The window into unconscious processes, information, and knowledge is small, and sometimes permanently closed, but it provides us with the only view of our intra- and extrapsychic world.

## Applications

### Stress and Anxiety

Because of the similarity in their precipitating factors and organic reactions, stress and anxiety are covered in a single section. They share general SNS arousal states. However, the difference between the two concepts will be shown to reside in the definition of stress as based on both situational and organismic states and the definition of anxiety as based on cognitive evaluative reactions of the individual.

### Stress

Definitions of stress in the experimental as well as the clinical literature usually are phrased in terms of the organism's *reaction* to some extra- or intrapsychic event. The use of the term normally includes both the event that gives rise to it and the individual's autonomic and cognitive reactions. The causal agent is assumed, sometimes listed, but rarely defined in any principled theoretical account. Typical is the definition used by Hans Selye, one of the foremost investigators of the concept. Selye defines stress as the result of any demand on the body, using "objective indicators such as bodily and chemical changes that appear after any demand" (Selye, 1982, p. 7).

What are the kinds of demands that typically are present in situations considered to be stressful? The usual listing of such "situations," such as bereavement, divorce, depression, or job loss, does not by itself provide a guide to preventive measures, except on a case by case basis. However, interruptions and discrepancies are a major source of stress, that is, situations that are defined as stressful frequently are marked by such discrepancies. Thus, a consideration of discrepancies and interruptions in daily life is helpful in understanding stress as well as in an analysis of both precipitating and ameliorative conditions. In short, the occasions when the world is not as we expect it to be cause stress. If our life proceeds as expected, if home and work situations change little, we do not experience stress. If, however, a spouse behaves in ways different from the expected, if a person close to us leaves or dies, or if demands at work are different from what they have been in the past, discrepancies occur, SNS reactions are triggered, and "stress" is experienced. Examine the person who states "I have been under a lot of stress lately" and you will find an individual who is faced with a lot of unexpected, surprising, and discrepant events. Needless to say, discrepancies do not define all stressful events; there are other "demands" (such as excessive exercise, lack of sleep, or unusual energy demands) that will define "stress," but a consideration of discrepancies will cover a large portion of the stress dimension.

Stressful experiences are marked not only by autonomic arousal, but by emotional evaluations that accompany them. Most, if not all, cases of stress will be marked by negative evaluations. Loss of a loved one, unexpected interruptions of relationships, unwanted divorces, and unreasonable work demands are all examples of situations that will be evaluated negatively. However, there will also be cases in which stress occurs in situations that are evaluated positively. For example, a planned change of residence, a separation that is desirable, and a job change all may be evaluated positively, but may lead to other negative effects of stress.

The more such discrepancies occur, the more one would expect them to affect the life and adaptability of the individual, as well as the likelihood of lowered resistance to illness (see subsequent text). Past research on life stresses has shown this to be the case. Surveys of life stresses (e.g., Holmes & Rahe, 1967; Dohrenwend, Krasnoff, Askenasy, & Dohrenwend, 1978; Rahe, 1979) have shown that the frequency of life discrepancies tends to be associated with frequency of illness. What is important to note is that discrepancies described in these surveys are not confined to negative or unpleasant situations, but also include such events as marriage, moving, and changing to a new job or occupation.

Consistent with our discussion of the emotional variables, the bodily symptoms used as indices of stress are associated with SNS arousal, as well as with attempts to deal with the stress stimulus or situation. Earlier extensive work by Frankenhaeuser and her colleagues has shown that "[n]ovelty, change, challenge, and anticipation may be considered key components in the psychosocial conditions triggering the adrenal-medullary response" (Frankenhaeuser, 1979). SNS arousal is important since it affects both current perceptions and interactions with other bodily processes. The phenomenal experience of stress consists in part of the experience of visceral arousal and consequently may interfere with thought and action. Central to this effect is the fact that the perception of arousal as well as the preoccupation with the stressing occasion interferes with ongoing conscious processing (Mandler, 1979, 1984). Autonomic arousal narrows attention in at least two ways. First, attention narrows automatically by the direct action of the autonomic nervous system; there is evidence that the autonomic nervous system acts as a signal to the organism that the world is different from what is expected (cf. Mandler, 1975). Second, autonomic arousal acts indirectly by occupying some of the limited capacity of attention or consciousness and thereby limits the attentional capacity that remains available to those events or stimuli that the individual considers important.

Current approaches to the effects of SNS arousal are influenced strongly by Easterbrook's (1959) hypothesis that increased arousal (emotion) reduces the number of cues used in a situation. This suggestion also reflected psychiatric concerns (Callaway & Dembo, 1958), and often was coupled with the notion that arousal (e.g., indexed by anxiety or panic) frequently produced task-irrelevant behavior (Mandler & Sarason, 1952; Bachrach, 1970). The task-irrelevant behavior noticed during periods of stress or panic is related to the observation that cognitive and behavioral efficiency differ for the central and the peripheral aspects of a stressful situation. The evidence for the central/peripheral distinction comes from research with auditory noise (Hockey, 1970), simulated danger situations (Weltman, Smith, & Egstrom, 1971), experimental studies (Bacon, 1974), and studies of memory under stress (Christianson & Loftus, 1991). What is considered "central" or "peripheral" depends, of course, on the idiosyncratic perception of the situation by the stressed person. Thus the restriction of attention to important or central events frequently may produce behavior that would be considered irrelevant or irrational from an objective point of view. As a consequence, situations of high stress may generate inappropriate and unadaptive behavior. On the other hand, a large variety of coping mechanisms can develop under stress. These mechanisms, discussed extensively by Lazarus (1991), may be successful or not; if they are, they ameliorate the deleterious effects of stress.

The effects of stress on health, that is, the impact of social events on illness, currently generally are considered under the rubric of "psychoneuroimmunology" (PNI). The notion that social events affect disease processes is well established in folk culture and has been investigated systematically for some time. (See Rogers, Dubey, & Reich, 1979, for an early review.) This chapter is concerned primarily with the effect of sympathetic arousal on the immune system and subsequent susceptibility to illness and disease. The notion that andrenergic processes reduce the effectiveness of the immune system has been demonstrated for some time (e.g., Bourne, Lichtenstein, Melmon, Henney, Weinstein, & Shearer, 1974). Individuals preoccupied with power relationships, who frequently encounter stress, have been shown to have low concentrations of immunoglobulin A and high adrenalin excretion rates (McClelland & Jemmott, 1980). Similarly, research on so-called Type A individuals, who tend to perceive their task performance as less than required and discrepant with their expectations and who are at risk for coronary heart disease, demonstrates that they show "greater cardiovascular changes indicative of sympathetic [autonomic nervous system] arousal" than individuals who do not exhibit Type A behavior (see, for example, Dembroski, MacDougall, Shields, Pettito, & Lushene, 1978; Jorgensen & Houston, 1981).

It is beyond the scope of this chapter to discuss at length the physiological mechanisms responsible for the stress–disease conjunction. Suffice it to say that SNS discharge affects lymphocyte action by a variety of possible peripheral and central mechanisms. These mechanisms are discussed at length in the most recent compendium on psychoneuroimmunology (Ader, Felten, & Cohen, 1991). Among the demonstrations most relevant to the present discussion is the work on bereavement and divorce (Kiecolt-Glaser & Glaser, 1991), on depression (Stein, Miller, & Trestman, 1991), and on psychosocial interventions (Hall & O'Grady, 1991).

### Anxiety

In contrast to stress, which is defined by situational variables as well as by individual reactions, anxiety is marked by the characteristics of the anxious individual, as well as by significant individual differences in susceptibility to its symptoms. Anxiety is also characterized by a specific class of evaluations—feelings of helplessness.

The appearance of anxiety is probably the most widely encountered and most widely discussed emotional phenomenon. Anxiety has been subject to a variety of different behavioral, existential, and psychoanalytic interpretations, and has received a host of experimental and physiological analyses. This chapter is restricted to an overview of anxiety in the context of the analysis of emotion described earlier, with special reference to human experimental investigations.

Given that any emotion involves arousal and evaluation, what are the relevant conditions in anxiety? The one description that applies to both the arousal and the evaluation dimensions is best termed "helplessness." Anxiety is characterized by situations in which the individual is unable to find, know, or execute thoughts or actions that are appropriate to the demands of the environment, thus giving rise to discrepancies, that is, wanting to act but being unable to do so. If helplessness produces arousal, it also characterizes the evaluation of the situation—not knowing what to do, how to act, or how to proceed. One of the major consequences of anxiety will be similar to one of those eventuated by stress, that is, the interference with ongoing thought processes because of a restriction of the limited capacity of consciousness, and the intruding action of trying to remove the internal or external causes of the anxious reaction. In the case of anxiety, in which the danger that is envisioned is not accessible to intervention, the latter efforts are likely to be even more deleterious and long lasting. Subsequent text returns to the problem of anxiety and cognitive efficiency.

In contrast to views that make sharp distinctions between fear and anxiety, usually in terms of "real" as opposed to potential danger, it is probably preferable to see fear and anxiety along a rather poorly defined continuum. Bowlby (1969, 1973) has noted that attempts to distinguish "real" from "neurotic" anxiety involve definitions of reality, but the reality of danger is usually in the perception of the anxious person. Bowlby saw the principal source of fear as the strangeness of a situation. Such a definition is, of course, consistent with the notion of helplessness, since what makes a situation strange is that we do not know how to deal with it.[1]

Sigmund Freud spent much of his life trying to disentangle the problem of anxiety. In the final version of his theory of anxiety (Freud, 1926/1975), Freud described three aspects of anxiety that are consonant with the view presented here. They are efferent or discharge phenomena (arousal), perception of these discharge phenomena (perception of arousal incorporated in emotional consciousness) and feelings of unpleasantness (evaluative cognitions). Similar to the notion of discrepancy is the statement that anxiety "seems to be a reaction to the perception of the absence of the object (Freud, 1926/1975)." The various primitive sources of anxiety, for example, the birth trauma, all point to an inability to cope with internal or external events that threaten to overwhelm the individual. As Karen Horney stated, basic anxiety is "the feeling a child has of being isolated and helpless in a potentially hostile world" (Horney, 1945).

Guilt and grief are tied closely to problems of anxiety. In anxious guilt, the individual is anxious about some past action or thought, real or imagined. It is impossible to undo the action, since the event is in the past, so the result is another variation of helplessness. In grief, the individual is faced with the absence of desirable interactions with a lost person. Again, it is impossible to reinstate that person, so the individual is again helpless

---

[1]For a discussion of the ontogeny of anxiety, see Kessen & Mandler (1961) and Mandler (1984).

in the face of trying to reactivate the lost person or interactions with them. Grief, in particular, is a good example of interruption and discrepancy; imagined and desired thoughts and actions are interrupted and hopes and wishes about certain individuals are discrepant with the reality of their permanent absence.

One of the central effects of anxiety is its interference with ongoing thought processes. Most of the work on the effects of anxiety on cognitive efficiency, that is, its direct effect on thought processes, has been done in the context of test-taking. The question generally asked is how the effect of interpreted or anticipated threat influence the efficiency of performance on complex intellectual tasks. Specifically, we are concerned with the effect of anticipated danger or threat on the performance of intellectual tasks.

The major research strategy has been to select individuals who report (on paper-and-pencil tests) high and low degrees of anxiety or concern about test situations. Items include reports of internal visceral events, attitudes toward tests, and reported thought processes about tests. The most accepted interpretation is that people who score high on such a test tell themselves that appropriate behavior in a test situation consists of observing their own behavior and examining their failures, whereas low anxious individuals orient their behavior and cognitions toward the specific requirements of the task (Mandler, 1972). Factor analyses of these test anxiety questionnaires reveal two factors consistent with this interpretation and with the two-factor approach to emotion discussed earlier. The factors are reported symptoms of bodily arousal and concerns with self-evaluation, that is, SNS arousal and evaluative cognitions (Morris, Davis, & Hutchins, 1981).

High anxious individuals perform worse on intellective tasks than do low anxious people; additionally, the absence of any further instructions (further reference to the test aspects of the situation) is most beneficial for high anxious people. On the other hand, instructions telling subjects that they failed are helpful for low anxious individuals (Mandler and Sarason, 1952). Similarly, high anxious subjects solve anagrams more efficiently than do low anxious individuals when the situation is nonthreatening, that is, when they are instructed that they are not expected to finish all the anagrams. When the subjects are told that the task is directly related to intelligence level and that they should finish easily if they are of average intelligence, the low anxious individuals perform significantly better than the high anxious ones (Sarason, 1961).

Similar preoccupations with indications of danger or threat have been found with clinically anxious patients (MacLeod, Mathews, & Tata, 1986). Mathews (1991) reports on a number of studies that find the deleterious effects of anxiety primarily under conditions in which the anxious individual is faced with choices, that is, in which a complex decision process is involved. Such observations further support the notion that helplessness, the inability to make choices, and the uncertainty of one's choice behaviors mark the evaluative cognitions of the anxious individual. Mathews (1990) notes that "worry" is the primary diagnostic criterion for generalized anxiety disorders, and argues that worry may be seen as "unsuccessful attempts at problem solving" (p. 457). Such lack of success at problem solving maps exactly to the helplessness that marks anxiety.

The situational discrepant events and the data provided by anxiety scales show that many people bring stress or anxiety into a situation, just as the situation brings out their stress potential. Both a potentially threatened individual and a properly interpretable situation are usually at work in producing stress and anxiety reactions.

### Ameliorations

What kind of ameliorative treatment is available for stress and anxiety reactions? The framework presented here identifies several treatment foci: discrepant situations, physiological response, and evaluative predispositions. Discrepant and interruptive situations can be identified for particular individuals, then they and the significant people in their world can be encouraged to change or avoid such situations. Ancient and contemporary recommendations for rest cures or changes of environment tend to address such variables. It should be remembered, however, that many stressful situations are stressful specifically for the individual involved. Such reactions will depend, to a large extent, on the way the person views the world and, particularly, on the expectations engendered by such perceptions.[2] Given the appropriate explorations of the perceptions and expectations, appropriate changes in the environment can be designed.

Without making any changes in the environment, the intensity of the stress and anxiety reactions can be manipulated by reducing the *intensity of the autonomic response*. A variety of centrally and peripherally acting drugs is available for such interventions.

Finally, the *evaluative cognitions* are subject to change. In the case of anxiety, such change involves either general or specific interventions. In the general case, the interpretation of "helplessness" that some individuals give to most, if not all, conflictful situations must change. A sense of competence and efficacy, generated in therapy, as well as by testing in the real world, reduces the tendency to interpret conflictful situations negatively. The specific cases involve a reinterpretation of idiosyncratic negative interpretations of social and personal settings, such as family relationships or professional adequacy.

---

[2]See, for example, Mandler (1989) for a discussion of how the expectation of errors can be beneficial in simple learning situations.

## Psychoanalysis

Psychoanalytic theory deserves special treatment in a discussion of cognitive science not only because Freud was one of the first to develop a psychological language *sui generis*, but also because many of his theoretical accounts foreshadowed the cognitivism of the second half of the 20th century.[3]

With respect to emotion, Freud's analysis of the experience of anxiety is very similar to a contemporary cognitive position. With respect to the visceral and evaluative dimensions of emotion in general, Freud stressed the importance of bodily functions in the generation of affect, which is a "process of discharge, a final expression of which is perceived as feeling." Further, "affectivity manifests itself essentially in motor (i.e., secretory and circulatory) discharge resulting in an (internal) alteration of the subject's own body" (Freud, 1915/1925).

Freud's description of the conscious and unconscious domain maps directly to contemporary conceptions. He distinguished between current limited conscious contents and the unconscious which he divided into two parts: the preconscious "which is only latent, and thus easily becomes conscious" and the "unconscious proper" where the transformation "is difficult and takes place only subject to a considerable expenditure of effort or possibly never at all." This division is consistent with the distinction between unactivated unconscious contents and activated ones, "latent" and preconscious, respectively. Just as unactivated unconscious material is not consciously accessible, so do unconscious contents have "no access to consciousness except via the preconscious" (Freud, 1900/1975). The additional distinction that needs to be made is that Freud's unconscious proper may need a further division. On the one hand is the psychoanalytic "dynamic" unconscious and on the other are unconscious mechanisms that may not, in principle, be amenable to conscious construction, for example, the structures that determine syntactic rules, perceptual mechanisms, and others. In general, modern cognitive psychologists would agree with Freud's statement that the unconscious (broadly speaking) "is as much unknown to us as the reality of the external world, and . . . is as incompletely presented by the data of consciousness as is the external world by the communications of our sense organs" (Freud, 1900/1975).

Interactions of the external world, the world of consciousness, and the operations of the unconscious are well demonstrated in dreaming. In the waking state, the stimulation and evidence from the external world structures our perception; schemas and their features are constrained by that evidence and stimulation. The world demands attention; thought and

---

[3]For a comprehensive treatment of psychoanalytic theory in terms of contemporary cognitive concepts, see Erdelyi (1985).

action and our conscious constructions respond to those imperatives. During sleep, the majority of these external influences is absent. However, activated schemas remain from the experiences of the day. These schemas are a relatively haphazard collection, and are not constrained by the structure of the external world. Conscious constructions, as in the waking state, are built out of activated schemas and features, but the activated structures are relatively "free," that is, unconstrained by the stimulation of the external world. However, they do not occur randomly in dreams; they too are organized, although often in unexpected and bizarre fashion. The remaining activations of driving a car, correcting proofs, or talking to a friend all may be organized into a new conscious content, however weird. Dreams are not random collections of these remaining activations; they are subject to higher order structures that "make sense" of these otherwise random remainders. Presumably such higher order structures represent the themes that we find to be the meaning imposed on dreams. It will be obvious that this account is a translation of Freud's discussion of dreams, daily residues, manifest contents, and the intrusion of the unconscious (Freud, 1900/1975). Manifest content of dreams is represented by the activated remains from waking activity, but the organization of that content into important themes that are idiosyncratic to the dreamer shows the influence of unconscious structures. These later schemas may have been activated but not used in conscious constructions, possibly because of their aversive character, that is, they were repressed.

Psychoanalytic treatment, whether orthodox or modified, including most current forms of psychotherapy, involves the exploration and restructuring of the cognitive map. Whether the procedure involves free association or directed "talking therapy," the aim is the same—to explore the associative network of the patient's thoughts and problem-solving procedures. "Associative" is used not in a theoretical, but in a generally descriptive, sense; free association is used to determine "what leads to what." This exploration makes it possible for the patient and therapist to determine categories of thought, connections that make neurotic symptoms and unadaptive actions and thoughts comprehensible.

The "associative" method of discovery of unconscious structures must be, and frequently is not, distinguished from any therapeutic efforts and effects. The latter occur when the existing semantic networks, the meanings imposed on the world, have been changed, amended, and restructured. A variety of procedures is available for such restructuring, including behavior therapy, which establishes new structures that circumvent maladaptive ones. The major road to such changes in cognition is usually a reinterpretation of existing concepts. Thus, such phenomena as transference reveal structures that are changed as a result of new experiences with the therapist and "acting out" in the "external" world. Therapy also involves making underlying nonverbal concepts and associations available to verbal expressions, which in turn are more accessible to interpretation and reinterpretation.

The usefulness of dreams to discover underlying "associations" and networks presumably arises from the fact that access to unpleasant thought processes may be facilitated because thought and imagined actions become less dangerous, simply because they do not (cannot?) lead to action in the world. Because of the haphazard choice of manifest contents for dreams, such interpretations are, of course, difficult and often misleading.

The restructuring of the underlying cognitive map of thoughts and actions results in the avoidance of negative, unpleasant emotional experiences, if for no other reason than that cognitions that lead to ambivalences, discrepancies, and conflicts are replaced by new perceptions and realizations that are adaptive or "reality oriented." One of the processes that is involved in such a restructuring is the ability to delay or avoid actions that would otherwise lead to aversive consequences. Actions that seem to produce undesirable (neurotic) consequences are delayed and newly discovered adaptations may be substituted. Freud (1911/1975) argued that the ability to delay gratification marked the triumph of the reality principle, the psychoanalytic equivalent of rationality.

Free or directed association is most successful when the patient is able to let the associative processes "flow freely." Obviously, current directive thoughts that avoid unpleasant associations or that direct current cognitions to irrelevant and nonthreatening ones would interfere with an exploration of the underlying "spreading activation." Brenner (1976, p. 191) has put it concisely: ". . . To the extent that anyone renounces conscious control over his thoughts, to the degree that he ignores his customary conscious interests, unconscious stimuli take over and control his thoughts."

Another approach to provide access to unconscious associations is apparently the very opposite of passive associations, that is, the initiation of emotional conflict. The notion that interruptions and discrepancies are often desirable for artistic creativity has been explored (Mandler, in press). The ability to create interruptions, new ways of seeing the world out of joint, seems to be necessary for scientific as well as aesthetic creations. A similar approach may provide access to dynamic unconscious processes. An interesting example is found in the French psychoanalyst Lacan's use of the totally unexpected shortening and interruption of his sessions with clients. One participant reports his personal experience with one of Lacan's unexpected short sessions: "The ending of the session, unexpected and unwanted, was like a rude awakening, like being torn out of a dream by a loud alarm." (One patient likened it to coitus interruptus). These short sessions seem to facilitate access to the unconscious and "[t]he combined pressure of the shortness of the sessions and the unpredictability of their stops creates a condition that greatly enhances one's tendencies to free-associate . . ." (Schneiderman, 1983). It is obvious from previous discussion that these unpredictable interruptions also will produce SNS arousal. It is possible that the emotional reaction to the interruption produces not only emotionally relevant associations, but also focuses current consciousness on idiosyncratically important thoughts and associations.

Contemporary cognitive psychology, in particular its analytic approach to separable components and mechanisms, has generated an objective and fruitful understanding of a variety of clinical phenomena. More specifically, the concepts of discrepancy and evaluation make possible the analysis and synthesis of cognitive processes that provide an important access to the sometimes opaque world of the emotions and stress.

# 5

# Cognitive Science and Assessment: Paradigmatic and Methodological Perspectives

**Thomas V. Merluzzi and Patricia A. Carr**

*Department of Psychology*
*University of Notre Dame*
*Notre Dame, Indiana*

Paradigmatic Perspectives
Cognitive Taxonomy
Methodological Perspectives
    Attentional Processes
    Retrieval and Recollection
    Schema and the Categorization of Information
    Scripts
    Hypothesis Testing, Judgment, and Decision Making
    Metacognition
Conclusion

## Paradigmatic Perspectives

Different perspectives on assessment are based on different assumptions that guide the assessment process. For example, the projective hypothesis that personality and psychopathology are caused by unconscious forces is based on the assumption that assessment data cannot be obtained directly because of defensive processes. Mischel (1968) referred to this method of assessment as a *sign* approach, that is, the information obtained from a projective test is used by the assessor to infer intrapsychic conflicts. In contrast, the assumption guiding the behavioral approach is that the assessment process represents a sample of that particular person's behavior in that situation. No deep inferences are made, that is, the behavior, and its antecedents and consequences, are assumed to be sufficient to account for maladaptive

# TABLE 1

## Overview of Projective, Trait, Behavioral, and Cognitive Approaches to Assessment

|  | Projective | Trait | Behavioral | Cognitive |
|---|---|---|---|---|
| Aims/goals | Identify dynamics of personality by inferring unconscious processes and issues from personal symbols | Identify a constellation or configuration of personality characteristics | Identify behaviors and the antecedents and reinforcers of those particular behaviors | Identify cognitive processes that interact with affect and influence behavior |
| Scope of assessment | Assess intrapsychic functioning to provide a broadbased description of personality | Assess many or few stable traits to provide a broad or narrow description of personality | Assess particular behaviors and provide specific information about the antecedents and reinforcers that may provoke and maintain the behaviors | Assess various aspects of information processing and their relationship to affective and behavioral states; may be broad or narrow in scope |
| Assumptions about methods | Information (symbols) is derived by methods that bypass defenses and is used to infer intrapsychic processes not readily available for conscious examination; idiographic, sign approach; emphasis on person factors | Personality constructs are accessible by self-report using instruments that are reliable and valid; nomothetic approach; emphasis on stable person factors | Direct observation in situations provides adequate information about behavior and the antecedents and reinforcers; idiographic, sample approach; emphasis on situational factors | Cognitive processes can be inferred from cognitive products, affective responses and motoric responses; idiographic and nomethetic, sample and sign approach; emphasis on person and situational factors |
| Conceptualization of clinical problems | Intrapsychic unconscious conflict is responsible for maladaptive affect and behaviors | Extreme scores on certain traits or on unusual configuration of traits may be associated with maladaptive affect and behavior | Environmental variables such as aspects of the situation and/or specific reinforcement contingencies cause or maintain maladaptive behaviors | Dysfunctional information processing or cognitive processes cause maladaptive affect or behavior |
| Uses of assessment results | Assessment results provide descriptive information that may be used to diagnose or to devise goals for therapy; global predictions regarding prognosis; conflicts may be identified that may be dealt with in therapy; may not be a sensitive process or outcome measure because of reliability problems | Assessment results are used to classify and diagnose or to imply broad goals that relate to changes in the structure, level, or configuration of traits; global predictors regarding prognosis; may not be a sensitive process or outcome measure to assess treatment effects | Assessment results and treatment are closely connected; assessment used to select treatments and document the effectiveness of treatment; sensitive outcome measure but not useful as process measure | Assessment results may be used to devise goals for treatment; changes in dysfunctional cognitive processes may be part of treatment; may be useful process and outcome measure |

behavior. Trait approaches assume that some stable constellation of personality characteristics can be accessed by directly asking the person. These traits are based on extensive sampling and are distributed normally; thus, any person's score on a trait dimension can be compared to a population. Cognitive assessment (from an information processing perspective) is based on the assumption that cognitive processes have an impact on affective and behavioral responses. This approach views cognitive processes as the causes of behavior; however, the environment also is viewed as a critical component in the assessment process. It is assumed that transformations of the stimulus (whether internal or external) by the individual are a function of the cognitive structures, propositions, and processes.

Table 1 summarizes some of the assumptions of four approaches to assessment. In contrast to previous attempts to compare major approaches to assessment (Barrios, 1989), we have chosen to separate traditional assessment into projective and trait because the assumptions underlying each of those approaches are quite different. Collapsing those approaches into one category seems to reflect the fact that, in practice, the paradigmatic assumptions may be ignored, that is, clinical assessors may use projective tests (e.g., Rorschach Inkblot Test) and trait tests (e.g., Minnesota Multiphasic Personality Inventory) to arrive at a description of the person that may not include information about intrapsychic conflict or actuarial predictions. In practice, these methods of assessment are used to describe the person in order to arrive at a clinical diagnosis.

Just as projective and trait methods have been combined under the label "traditional assessment," behavioral and cognitive assessment methods have been "lumped" together. (Parks & Hollon, 1989; Groth-Marnat, 1990). One might assume that because cognitive assessment is included under the behavioral assessment label that the paradigmatic assumptions that underpin these approaches are similar. They are not! Merluzzi and Boltwood (1990) and Merluzzi, Rudy, and Glass (1981) have contrasted the paradigmatic assumptions for each of these models of assessment. On virtually all the important paradigmatic dimensions, the two approaches differ. For example, behavioral approaches assume that cognitive activity is rather passive and irrelevant to either assessment or intervention. Behavior is seen as a function of the environment. The cognitive perspective, on the other hand, assumes that cognitive activity is active and dynamic, and that behavior is a product of this activity. It follows from those differences that, in contrast with the behavioral perspective, the cognitive perspective assumes that cognitive processes transform input and construct "reality" (Merluzzi & Boltwood, 1990).

Combining behavioral and cognitive approaches is based on the emergence of cognitive therapy as a phenomenon that was not well connected to information processing or cognitive science. The inclusion of cognitive components in traditionally behavioral treatments, as exemplified by the

pioneering work of Meichenbaum and Mahoney, seemed to stretch the parameters of behavioral approaches rather than create a new paradigm. This
approach to treatment and assessment has been referred to as cognitive-
behavioral, reflecting assessment methods that tap thoughts or treatments
that change thoughts. Ellis' Rational Emotive Therapy and Beck's Cognitive Therapy for depression are more cognitive than cognitive-behavioral;
however, those approaches are based only peripherally on cognitive science. Eventually, the cognitive revolution did have a more profound effect
on clinical science, as exemplified in Ingram (1986), Horowitz (1991), and
this volume. These works represent an attempt to integrate the clinical and
cognitive sciences.

## Cognitive Taxonomy

The assimilation of cognitive assessment by behavioral assessment is
based also on the fact that cognitive assessment has, to a great degree, focused on cognitive products. Kendall and Ingram (1987) have proposed a
broader taxonomic system for cognitive assessment that contains four
major components: (1) cognitive structures, (2) cognitive propositions (or
content), (3) cognitive operations (or processes), and (4) cognitive products (pp. 91–92). Cognitive structures refer to the organization of information or how the information is stored and organized by the individual.
Structural aspects include concepts such as long- and short-term memory
(Ingram & Wisnicki, 1991). Cognitive propositions (or content) refer to
the information that is stored in the cognitive structures. Included in this
component of the taxonomy are abstract semantic knowledge and concrete episodic knowledge. Cognitive operations refer to procedural knowledge or the mechanisms by which information is encoded, stored, and
retrieved. Finally, cognitive products are the outputs from the system. For
the most part, cognitive assessment has focused on cognitive products or the
thoughts, ideas, and beliefs of which the person is consciously aware (Nasby
& Kihlstrom, 1986).
    The first three components of Kendall and Ingram's taxonomy have
been the subject of research in psychopathology that describes particular
disorders, but these components have received little attention in the literature on assessment.

## Methodological Perspectives

In the rest of the chapter, we will present a perspective on clinical assessment that is based on cognitive psychology. This presentation will not

be technical instruction but an attempt to introduce the concepts and parlance of cognitive psychology into the clinical assessment process. Much of what we do as clinicians is based on the conceptual framework to which we adhere. In clinical training, the conceptual frameworks for assessment are based primarily on the projective, trait, or behavioral perspectives. Even if formal testing is not used, clinical judgments that provide us with a working description of the client, and our approach to diagnosis, may be based on our theoretical framework. Thus, our intent is to introduce constructs from cognitive psychology that may be useful in the assessment process.

In the following sections, we will present several components of cognitive information processing. Although the distinction between these components may give the impression that each is a separate entity in the cognitive processing of information, in fact, all are components that interact in human cognitive processes that operate on information. However, we present them separately to facilitate an understanding of each component. The goal of the presentation of methodological perspectives is to make the language of cognitive psychology more applicable to clinical assessment. As we conceptualize our client's problems, the language and terminology of cognitive psychology and cognitive science may contribute to a more complete picture of psychopathology as well as have implications for treatment.

As opposed to the dominant trend in cognitive assessment, the focus of this section will not be on cognitive products but on cognitive structures, propositions, and processes. For each of the components of cognitive processing, there will be a presentation of the component from the perspective of cognitive psychology followed by a discussion of the implications of that component for clinical assessment.

### Attentional Processes

In the course of processing information, a large amount of information appears to enter the sensory apparatus (Anderson, 1990); however, the information that is retained for processing is a function of attentional processes. Prevalent models of attention consider that process to have limited capacity (Kahneman, 1973). Thus, during any moment in time we may deploy our attention to a variety of tasks or stimuli. Further, that deployment policy may change from moment to moment as we adjust to the demands of the tasks or stimuli. Attention may be deployed successfully to several tasks or to one task, as long as the total attention deployed is less than a person's total attentional supply (Merluzzi et al., 1981).

Selective attention, or the ability to attend to some things and not attend to others, is a critical skill; without this capacity we would be overwhelmed with information constantly. On the other hand, if our attentional capacity is very narrow, we may not be able to process information efficiently enough to learn new tasks that may be adaptive or important for our well-being. In addition, attention is a critical aspect of processing because only information that is attended to is passed on to other systems in memory for storage in a more enduring form.

Competition for attention is reduced in those instances in which one task (of several that the person may need to attend to) is overlearned. For example, when first learning to drive a car with standard shift, one may need to deploy all available attention to the task of driving. Conversing in that instance may tax the attentional capacity of the driver. However, an experienced driver has little difficulty talking and negotiating the many subroutines necessary to keep the car on the road. The tendency for overlearned tasks "to take less and less attentional resources, and to interfere less and less with other concurrent tasks . . . is usually termed automaticity" (Baddeley, 1990, p. 124). As opposed to automatic processes, controlled responses require conscious control.

A study by Granholm, Asarnow, and Marder (1991) tested the assumption that schizophrenics have a lower capacity for processing resources than do normal individuals. Some literature suggests that schizophrenics have normal automatic processing capacity but are deficient in controlled processing. The subjects (chronic schizophrenics and controls) were given a large number of trials on a high speed visual search task (multiple frame search task; Shiffrin & Schneider, 1977) that constituted the automatic processing task. After that task was practiced to the point that it was considered to be a "resource-free" automatic process, the authors introduced a second task, an auditory shadowing task. Thus, after 320 trials on the visual search task, subjects had to repeat letters that were presented aurally. The results indicated that, at higher processing loads, that is, when the auditory task competed with the visual task, the schizophrenics' performance on the auditory task was impaired significantly compared with that of the normal controls. Although these findings do not eliminate the possibility that schizophrenics may have abnormal automation processes, they do illustrate the importance of attention deployment and attentional capacity in controlled processing of information. Although the literature on schizophrenia does indicate that there are some deficiencies in attentional processes, the allocation of attention is also an issue for persons with less severe problems.

Problems in attention deployment may be caused by the competing demands of anxiety, depression, and fear. For example, Wine (1980) has conceptualized anxiety as a problem of attention control. Wine's direction-of-attention hypothesis states that differences in the performances of high and low anxious individuals may be a function of the attentional focus of those individuals. High anxious persons allocate proportionally more of their attention to self-preoccupied worry than do low anxious subjects. Therefore, high anxious persons might deploy less attention to the demands of the task than would low anxious persons. Thus, if a task is difficult, a high anxious person may devote some attention to the task but also devote a great deal of attention to worry-oriented thoughts, limiting the attention available for the task.

The direction-of-attention hypothesis is also consistent with the notion that anxious persons may not be sensitive to some cues because of a reduced attentional capacity or may attend selectively and be hypersensitive to other cues that are consistent with their fear. In addition, that hypersensitivity and vigilance may interfere with the effective processing of information. For example, McNally, Kaspi, Riemann, and Zeitlin (1990) presented to Vietnam combat veterans with posttraumatic stress disorder (PTSD) a series of words that were neutral (e.g., INPUT), positive (e.g., LOVE), obsessive compulsive (e.g., GERMS), and posttraumatic (e.g., BODYBAGS) in a Stroop task. In the Stroop task, words printed in varying colors are presented, and the subject must name the color of the letters while attempting to ignore word content. Compared with a group of Vietnam combat veterans without PTSD, the PTSD group had more Stroop interference for the posttraumatic words; there were no differences between the groups on the other words. Similar findings were reported for persons with high trait anxiety (Richards & Millwood, 1989), social phobia (Hope, Rapee, Heimberg, & Dombeck, 1990), and other anxiety problems. The Stroop task in these studies illustrates the interference of processing as a result of what may be an automatic attentional bias, that is, in the brief period of processing the words in the McNally study and in similar studies, cognitive interference and arousal provokes selective attention and, therefore, selective processing of information.

In the literature on depression, it appears that attentional processes also play a role. Beck, Rush, Shaw, and Emery (1979) have described automatic thoughts that depressed individuals engage in often. Further, Ingram, Lumry, Cruet, and Sieber (1987) have noted that depressed individuals may be more chronically self-focused in terms of their attention deployment than nondepressed individuals, and that there may not be much flexibility in that deployment policy. Thus, the negative view of self that is characteristic of depressives would be enhanced by this attentional perspective because self-focused attention enhances the salience of current thoughts and affect. Further, the automaticity of the thoughts may mean that control processes may not operate on that self-referent information; thus, some of the automatic thoughts, although salient, may not be readily available for examination. However, the impact of those automatic processes is quite apparent, since depressives attend selectively and process information in a fashion consistent with the negative depressive schema.

In summary, the role of attention may be a key element in assessment from a cognitive perspective. The attention deployment policy of an individual may affect the information he or she attends to and the selective nature of the cues used to guide behavior. Attention deployment may limit the capacity of the individual to take into account relevant information that may be useful in successfully coping with life tasks. A key to understanding further information processing is knowing what is attended to and what is not, and what biases might interfere with attention to relevant information.

## Retrieval and Recollection

For the most part, the clinical assessment process is concerned with the retrieval of episodic and autobiographical memory. Episodic information is stored with concrete referents that include affect, time, and space; autobiographical information is a more elaborate form of episodic memory that has an emphasis on the self. Moreover, it has been suggested that autobiographical memory is stored in a domain in long-term memory that may be separate from other domains (De Renzi, Liotti, & Nichelli, 1987).

Retrieval can be tested by a recognition method in which the person is given an extensive list of items and is asked to indicate the items that were presented previously or the incidents or events that occurred in the past. The recall method, on the other hand, requires the person to generate (in writing or orally) the items that had been presented previously or information about events that occurred in the past. Generally, recognition is superior to recall and illustrates the retrieval problem: we learn and know more than we can freely recall, that is, the information may be available as evidenced by the superiority of recognition but may not be readily accessible (Baddeley, 1990).

Retrieval cues and context may enhance recall, that is, some of the limitations of retrieval may be overcome by giving cues that prompt recall or some context that is compatible with the original learning. The context-dependent nature of learning and retrieval gives us some guidelines for enhancing the recall of clinically relevant information. In order to encourage clients to recall clinically relevant information, it is helpful to have the client describe the surroundings first. The context provides cues that will prompt more accurate and elaborate recall. Based on a study by Wagenaar (1986) that is reviewed later in this section, a number of cues might be used to prompt the retrieval of autobiographical information. Also, the process of retrieval enhances the probability that the information will be accessed more easily in subsequent attempts to retrieve the information.

In addition to being context dependent, retrieval also may be state dependent. Theories that account for the relationship between affect and cognition have proposed that mood affects memory in both the encoding and retrieval stages of information processing. Generally, those theories assume that memory operates as an associative network in which affect primes memories that are associated with that particular mood. Thus, if one is in a depressed mood, the recall of negative events that were learned in that state will be enhanced. In addition, if the connections between events are strong, then the recall of one event may enhance the recall of other related events in the associative network. Conversely, the strength of one associative network actually may inhibit recall of other information in networks that are not compatible with the activated network. In essence, the activation of one network may inhibit the accessibility of information in another network (Stinson & Palmer, 1991).

Research also indicates that people may engage in mood incongruent recall, that is, they may try to inhibit the active network and willfully activate the competing network. In an interesting series of studies, Parrott and Sabini (1990) presented evidence that people in natural settings engage in mood incongruent recall of autobiographical memories. The authors speculate that people may regulate their mood states by "recalling material incongruent with their present mood, particularly when in bad moods" (p. 321). Although their evidence does not apply directly to depression or other clinical disorders, we can speculate that depressives may not engage in mood incongruent recall to manage affect as often as normal individuals do, that is, the associative network for negative affect and content may be better developed in depressives than in normals. Therefore, the initiation of a mood incongruent network may be more difficult.

There has been increasing interest in autobiographical memory or what Baddeley (1990) has termed recollection. Recollection may probe general semantic memory for items such as the names of teachers for a particular grade and then ask for episodic memories such as an incident that happened during that period of time. In a fascinating case study, Wagenaar (1986) studied his own autobiographical memory over a period of several years by writing information about daily incidents. He included information about the people involved, the incident, where it occurred, and when it occurred. He also noted the personal salience of the event, as well as how emotionally involving it was, and how pleasant it was. He later prompted recall (2 to 5 years later) of these events by giving himself one, two, or three cues for recall that consisted of one item or a random combination of items of the *who, what, where,* and *when* information. Retention for all incidents did deteriorate over time and resembled a typical forgetting curve, with more material lost over time. However, he noted a few general tendencies: the more cues given the better the recall; *when* information was not an effective cue alone but was very useful in combination with other cues; and the more salient the item, the more emotional involvement, and the more pleasant, the better the recall of the incident.

The study by Wagenaar (1986), as well as other studies, seems to indicate that cueing is critical in the accurate recall of autobiographical memories. However, it is not uncommon to find that people forget and distort autobiographical information. It appears that, although the retrieval of a broad outline of events is reasonably accurate, if there are no contextual and affective cues, forgetting and distortions are to be expected. One approach to the collection of autobiographical information in memory research is the autobiographical memory schedule, which systematically questions subjects about both personal information and events from different periods of their lives (Baddeley, 1990, p. 294).

## Schema and the Categorization of Information

Schemas and categorization concepts are interrelated so closely that it may be useful to consider their properties and clinical implications together. Of the constructs that bridge the domains of cognitive and counseling or clinical psychology, schemas are among the most widely researched and accepted. They offer a flexible heuristic for a cognitive approach to both assessment and clinical intervention. Categorization may be seen either as a subprocess embedded within schemas or as a distinct process that serves a distinct function. However, the latter conceptualization has limited clinical applicability. Winfrey and Goldfried (1986) note five major functions of schemas; there is certainly some overlap with the categorization functions. These functions are (1) to facilitate recognition, recall, and comprehension; (2) to influence the speed of information processing and problem solving; (3) to gather information into meaningful and more easily retrieved units; (4) to enable the individual to fill in missing information; and (5) to provide greater confidence in prediction and decision making.

Schemas may be thought of, in terms of both content and structure, as organized representations of conceptually related information that serve to guide the processing of new information. Because schemas tend to be prototypical, or generalized, representations of more complex concepts, they often serve to facilitate information processing and problem solving by allowing us to conserve attentional capacities and to infer from incomplete information. However, these functions that, ideally, serve us well also may contribute to the development and maintenance of psychopathology through distortions in the content of the schemas or through the application of inappropriate schemas.

The role of categorization processes in dysfunctional behaviors or affective states is less clear. The determination of category membership may be the first step in the activation of a specific schema. It has been demonstrated that both schema-congruent and schema-incongruent information is processed more quickly than information that is only partially schema-relevant (Kuiper & Rogers, 1981). In addition, a recent study by Mathews, Mogg, and Eysenck (1990) found evidence that anxious subjects use a selective search based on the category to which a stimulus belongs, which in this case was threat cues. Because categories do not have fixed boundaries, individuals have difficulty judging whether items at the periphery are actually members of that category. For example, in a person's "authority figure" category, a policeman may be classified quite easily as such whereas a librarian, on the periphery of that category, may be classified less readily as an authority figure. These types of indeterminance may contribute to the hypervalence of particular schemas.

Beck and Freeman (1990) note that highly personalized idiosyncratic schemas are activated during disorders such as depression or anxiety, and that these schemas become prepotent, inhibiting other more adaptive or appropriate schemas. In ambiguous situations or in those that require a judgment at the periphery, one could assume the likelihood of activation of a hypervalent schema. Thus, if authority figures are anxiety evoking for a particular person, the hypervalent anxious schema is likely to be activated even when cued by the presence of someone peripheral to that category, for example, the librarian.

In the assessment of schemas, it is useful to distinguish between cognitive propositions, or content, and cognitive structures, or the organization, arrangement, and representation of that content (Ingram & Kendall, 1987). In a sense, the content determines the domain and related beliefs and the process or structure determines how new information and experiences will be perceived and integrated. Most researchers attempting to verify the existence of schemas or examining content have focused on adjectives or descriptors. The seminal work of Markus (1977) attempted to address both content and process. Stating that the influence of cognitive structures on the selection and organization of information is probably most apparent when we process information about ourselves," her studies examined the influence of self-schemas on the speed of processing information about the self. Preliminary schemas were determined through the use of adjective checklists and semantic differential scales; the self-information presented to the subjects consisted of adjectives to be judged as "me" or "not me." Many subsequent researchers have followed this model, with the assumption that schema content is available to consciousness. This may be the case in particular domains, but those schemas below the level of conscious awareness in both content and process would seem to be more liable to distortion and, therefore, more clinically relevant.

Kendall and Ingram's use of the term "propositions" is useful because schemas may also involve if–then statements. Information undergoing schematic processing is subject to "if–then" propositions, presenting the possibility of bias at two levels. During a selective search (Mathews et al., 1990), an individual may filter information in a search for specific ifs, such as anxiety-evoking stimuli. The "then" portion of the proposition is likely to be a result of schematic completion effects, thus compounding and reinforcing the systematic bias.

Research paradigms and assessment techniques, such as reaction times with a modification of the Stroop task (e.g., Segal, Hood, Shaw, & Higgins, 1988; Hope et al., 1990; Segal & Vella, 1990) or the use of speeded classification and verification, are not practical in a clinical assessment situation, although both have been used widely to examine both schemas and categories. Greenberg and Beck's (1989) endorsement of trait adjectives can produce global self- and worldview schemas but, as Nasby and Kihlstrom (1986) point out, most clients' problems are related to a specific domain of content. It may be more useful to think of self-schemas as domain, or context, specific. The set of self-schemas could be seen, then, as a whole that constitutes the self-concept. In this way, not only would the individual self-schemas be clinically relevant but the discrepancies among the schemas in varying contexts would be relevant as well.

Higgins' (1987) self-discrepancy theory predicts the types of emotional vulnerabilities associated with specific combinations of discrepancies between what he refers to as self-state representations. These self-states appear to be very similar to self-schemas but, instead of specifying contexts, Higgins identifies two underlying cognitive dimensions: domains of the self (actual, ideal, and ought) and standpoints on the self (own and other). The combinations of actual/own and actual/other can be seen to constitute a person's self-concept; the other four combinations can be seen as self-guides. The greater the discrepancy between an individual's self-concept and his or her self-guides, the greater the discomfort the person is likely to experience. It is important, too, to bear in mind with Greenberg and Beck's approach that, although a portion of the content of a schema is available to consciousness, some of the content is not, and the process, or structural organization, normally is not conceptualized as falling within the domain of procedural knowledge, or as being a process that can be monitored via metacognition (Dohr, Rush, & Bernstein, 1989).

To assess a client's schemas, one must begin with the assumption that certain schematic distortions are operating; then one can determine the domain of the schema or schemas contributing to the client's distress. It may also be useful to address questions such as: In what ways is information distorted? Do the conclusions fit the incoming information? What assumptions does the client present repeatedly? What is the relationship between affect and information processing abilities? In traditional counseling situations, this information is readily available by observing how the client reports events and related affective states, by noting what information the client has "filled in," by noting and discussing the client's reaction to feedback, or, perhaps most valuable, by processing the therapeutic relationship.

The therapist then can use this information to determine the most effective means of intervention. The information obtained not only describes the client's current state, but also prescribes ways of presenting information and feedback so the client will be able to integrate the information and minimize dysfunctional processing. One cannot be sure whether, through cognitive therapy, the client is "correcting" the distortions in existing schemas or creating new schemas and reducing the applicability of dysfunctional ones.

A few clinical assessment procedures have been developed. Kihlstrom and Cunningham (1991) have developed, for clinical use, a computer program, PERSPACE, for assessing schemas of self and others. The multivariate analysis of information obtained by free-generation and probe response options yields dimensions, factors, and clusters that "reflect the way the subjects perceive themselves and the social world around them" (Kihlstrom & Cunningham, 1991, p. 324). The authors propose that PERSPACE be used as part of a routine clinical assessment, that the results be shared and discussed with the client, and that it also be administered on completion of therapy to determine if changes are consistent with the goals of treatment.

Two other methods of assessment involve the analysis of clinical interviews or therapy sessions. Horowitz, Merluzzi, Ewert, Ghannam, Hartley, and Stinson (1991) discuss the application of Role–Relationship Models Configuration, to inferring concepts of self and others, as well as of scripted transactions related to a central theme or supraordinate self-schema. Hartley (1991) illustrates the use of the Structural Analysis of Social Behavior to infer person schemas from interpersonal interactions, with the assumption that person schemas are generalized from past relationships and will be used to guide current behaviors.

## Scripts

The concept of the schema just discussed also may be extended to include the schematic representation of events. Scripts are the conceptual representations of stereotyped event sequences that are highly predictable (Schank & Abelson, 1977). Scripts may be used to plan everyday situations in which we may depend on a sequence of events to occur in a fashion that leads to specific goals. Essentially, we may use scripts to guide our behavior and to fill in information in the context of interactions with other people. Thus, with a minimum amount of information, we are able to anticipate a sequence of events and detect aberrations in that sequence to move toward some goal. For example, Bower, Black, and Turner (1979) studied a restaurant script that had four scenes (entering, ordering, eating, and exiting) and a number of sequential steps in each of the four scenes. Events were expected to unfold in a predictable sequence, in which one event could cause the next to occur.

We can assume that individuals acquire a large number of scripts by direct experience and by vicarious means. Also, in many situations, several scripts may be relevant; however, according to Abelson (1981), we choose the most "available" one, that is, we choose the most salient script that is cued by the situation. Finally, some scripts may be stronger than others. A strong script is one in which the orderly sequence of events is linked causally, that is, in which one event literally triggers the next in a sequence that is fixed.

Scripts also can be applied to social situations, that is, social scripts can be viewed as consensual sets of behaviors and expectancies that allow individuals to interact smoothly (Merluzzi, Rudy, & Krejci, 1986) and accomplish some social goal. For example, Pryor and Merluzzi (1985) studied differences between expert and novice daters in processing "getting a date" and "going on a first date" scripts. Essentially, Pryor and Merluzzi found that, with respect to the content, meaning, and organization of the scripts, novices and experts did not differ. However, experts were able to order events in the script significantly faster than novices when the events were presented in a random order. Thus, compared with novices, experts may have a more cognitively cohesive script that may suggest that they have overlearned the sequence through practice.

Expertness in the scripted sequence may enhance "availability" and promote "chunking" of the information into units that are easier to construct and retrieve. Thus, we would expect experts to devote less time than novices to the controlled processing of the scripted information. Another consequence of expertness is that the person may devote less working memory and attention than a novice to the processing of script-consistent behaviors and, therefore, have more "residual on-line capacity for dealing with inconsistent or unexpected events" (Pryor & Merluzzi, 1985, p. 377).

Shank (1982) expanded on the original notion of the script to include what he has termed memory organization packets (MOPs) and thematic organization points (TOPs). Each MOP contains scenes that comprise a setting and a goal. A particular script may have several MOPs that constitute coherent subcomponents in the script. MOPs may overlap in a script and may be common across a number of scripts that share similar features. At a more abstract level is the TOP, which organizes the MOPs into groups that may be different in some concrete detail but similar in content or structure.

From an assessment perspective, the clinician may want to probe into the client's idiosyncratic conception of the sequence of events for a particular situation. Each MOP sequence can be analyzed for the appropriateness of the order of and relationship among events in that sequence as well as for the relevance and appropriateness of the goal. Scripts can be elicited by having clients write or describe the sequence of events in problematic and nonproblematic situations. The evaluation of scenes and goals for each sub-component or MOP may unveil a pattern in the scripted materials. For example, socially anxious individuals may have some rejection patterns in the scripts and may perceive their actions as causing the rejection.

A more elaborate assessment scheme might have information for particular scripts from a large sample, so the client's script may be compared to a normative sample. The compilation of several scripts may lead to some organization of the scripts according to the thematic nature of the scripts (TOPs).

## Hypothesis Testing, Judgment, and Decision Making

The area of hypothesis testing, judgment, and decision making involves a variety of cognitive processes, from attention to metacognition, but is included as a separate entity because an awareness and understanding of the systematic and tenacious biases and "errors" may prove useful to the clinician when distinguishing between "normal" maladaptive distortions in cognitive processes and "abnormal" maladaptive ones.

Hypothesis formation and hypothesis evaluation are components of inductive reasoning, in which one moves from the specific to the general. In order for an argument to be inductively valid, the conclusions must be probable if the premises are true, so probability estimation plays a part in our evaluation of a given hypothesis or of a broader inference drawn from specific information—a fundamental aspect of learning and decision making in novel situations.

Bayes' Theorem is a mathematical formula that prescribes a means of hypothesis evaluation based on probability theory. A prior probability is the probability before evidence that a hypothesis is true; a posterior probability is the probability after some evidence that a hypothesis is true. Bayes' Theorem provides a formula for adjusting posterior probabilities when new information is presented. For example, the probability of a student failing an exam, given no other information, is 1 in 5 or .20. However, posterior probability estimates would include probabilities based on past test performance by the student. This posterior probability would be altered with additional information, such as the history of the professor in failing students or the amount of time spent studying. Much of the research in decision theory has focused on how individuals deviate from this logical prescription and which factors influence and maintain what has been termed the "illusion of validity," wherein we not only violate the logic of probability theory, but maintain confidence in our judgments despite much evidence to the contrary (Einhorn & Hogarth, 1978; Kahneman & Tversky, 1982). Thus, a student with test anxiety would continue to believe that his or her chances of failure were 1 in 5 (or worse), in spite of additional evidence that would suggest that the probability was much less.

Einhorn and Hogarth (1981) note the importance of causality in human inference as well as the fact that causality has no role in probability theory. The calculation of probabilities is based on relative frequencies of occurrence and, even in the determination of conditional probabilities, no causality is implied. The authors postulate that a causal schema may be the basis for the observed biases, in which information that supports a causal inference is processed selectively. This bias may be even more apparent in the analysis of past events. Fischoff (1973) used the term "creeping determinism" to describe the effects of outcome knowledge on individuals' probability judgments as well as their apparent lack of awareness of these effects. Van den Bout, Cohen, Groen, and Kramer (1987) examined the search for causes of negative events in depressed individuals and found that greater depression was related to greater concern with causality and avoidability. Predictability and control are both factors that long have been accepted to be related to affective states and psychological functioning. It is not surprising, albeit often frustrating, that we search for and even impose causal explanations on seemingly random events.

Fischoff and his colleagues also examined the "overconfidence" subjects had about their knowledge (Koriat, Lichtenstein, & Fischoff, 1980), and found evidence for confirmatory bias, or the selective focusing on evidence that supports a chosen answer while ignoring evidence to the contrary. In a more recent study by Golin (1989), depressed and nondepressed subjects were presented with a series of vignettes and conclusions. Subjects were to assume either that they had drawn the conclusion or that someone else had. When asked to rate the plausibility of the conclusions, depressed subjects judged positive inferences by others as less plausible than did nondepressed subjects. Golin concludes by stating that "cognitive psychotherapy aims to remedy this loss of objectivity by training such persons to regard as 'hypotheses' what they presume to be facts" (p. 497). Such a change would seem to be a monumental task, at times.

In their examination of the persistence of the illusion of validity, Einhorn and Hogarth (1978) applied signal detection theory to account for both errors in probability judgment and the difficulty that individuals have in making use of disconfirming information. These investigators posit that frequencies are coded in memory more easily than probabilities. As a result, individuals use the frequency of positive hits in their judgments and generally ignore information in other cells (false negatives, negative hits, false positives). In part, this may be because the determination of probabilities also requires the coding of nonoccurrence of an action or prediction, which is often difficult to conceptualize and may be difficult to represent in memory. A socially anxious individual, for example, may predict consistently that he or she will behave ineptly at parties. Given Einhorn and Hogarth's rationale, this individual will have difficulty encoding times at which he or she was not inept (false negative) but will encode quite readily the frequency of ineptness or predicted behavior (positive hits). In addition, the salience of the unpleasant experiences will be greater given the relatively greater level of affect, thus contributing to the ease of encoding and retrieval or availability.

The authors also note that presenting individuals with statistical or correlational feedback is unlikely to correct the illusion, because the contingency judgments are not made on the basis of statistical theory in the first place. The implications for intervention are, indeed, complex.

### Metacognition

The term metacognition refers to cognition about cognition, or an individual's knowledge, understanding, and awareness of cognitive processes and states, or mental activity. From a cognitive perspective, an individual's metacognitive abilities will determine, to a great degree, the current level of functioning as well as the individual's capacity to benefit from therapy or to understand, monitor, and alter dysfunctional cognitive processes and products. More than just in terms of executive functions, as Wellman (1985) notes, ". . . development of an understanding of mind and an understanding of reality are intertwined" (p. 29).

Flavell's (1979) distinction between metacognitive knowledge, both declarative and procedural, and metacognitive experience, or immediate thoughts, judgments, and feelings about ongoing mental activity, is clinically relevant. Metacognitive knowledge includes an understanding of one's cognitive resources and skills as well as a basis for understanding the social world of self and others and the physical world of objects. This aspect of metacognition may provide the basis for self-reflection and self-analysis, but metacognitive experience is necessary for any alterations in knowledge. The metacognitive experience can increase awareness and invoke metacognitive knowledge. Flavell's conceptualization of metacognitive experience allows, too, for the influence of affective states on the instantiation of metacognitive knowledge.

Yussen (1985) expands on Flavell's classes of metacognitive knowledge to include (1) tasks, or the knowledge of influences on performance; (2) self, or knowledge of one's own skills and abilities; (3) strategies, or the value of various strategies; and (4) interactions, or knowledge of how other classes interact. When thought of in this way, the assessment of metacognitive processes, of both knowledge and experience, becomes a useful tool in determining both the basis and domain of deficiencies or distortions in cognitive and metacognitive processes, and provides information useful in the development of a hierarchy of intervention strategies. For example, a depressed individual's knowledge of his or her abilities may be distorted so strengths are discounted and weaknesses are exaggerated across tasks. Tasks, strategies, and interactions would then likely appear to the individual to be inconsequential and, thus, would not be monitored; the probability of a negative outcome for a given situation or task would be increased. The assessment question would, then, become one of determining the most efficacious balance between addressing the client's metacognitive experience of self and increasing his or her metacognitive knowledge of tasks and strategies.

If, as Yussen asserts, ". . . cognitive phenomena express themselves in the solution of problems" (p. 274), then one could infer that metacognitive phenomena express themselves in the solution of problems, the analysis of outcomes through the monitoring of performance, and the subsequent alterations of these problem-solving strategies. All these processes fall within the domain of psychotherapy; an individual's abilities to effectively carry out these processes are important considerations in assessment, with respect to both current levels of functioning and, to some degree, prognosis.

The bulk of research in metacognition is found in the developmental literature. Day, French, and Hall (1985), in their description of the development of metacognitive abilities in children, make the process sound strikingly like a therapeutic relationship. An initial assumption, taking Vygotsky's view, is that these functions develop through social interaction. The "expert" initially and temporarily assumes metacognitive control of the situation while the learner focuses on a subcomponent; eventually, the learner gains awareness and control over mental processes, both problem solving and self-regulation, through practice and prompting. Especially interesting is their observation that ". . . children may not realize that directions . . . in the form of questions can provide information about the task solution" (p. 39).

One can draw parallels between this process and a hypothetical therapeutic process, beginning with the assumption that change is an interactive process. Returning to the example of the depressed client with a distorted knowledge of self, or of his or her abilities, the therapist at first assumes metacognitive control through the acquisition of accurate (and more objective) knowledge of the client's skills, as well as of an understanding of the client's metacognitive knowledge and abilities. Then, while focusing on one aspect of functioning, the therapist may provide feedback or guide the client to monitor feedback on that aspect more accurately. In our example, the therapist may choose to focus on improving the client's metacognitive knowledge of self to reduce or eliminate distortions. This process may be accomplished by eliciting information about self-talk or filtered data, examining with the client the basis for his or her conclusions, or discussing the client's judgments and affect related to performance. In addition to acquiring more accurate knowledge of self, the client acquires metacognitive experience that is more salient and more functional, allowing the client eventually to reassume control for both the knowledge and the experience aspects of metacognition.

As Wellman (1985) notes, ". . . an understanding of one's own and others' cognition is instrumental both in certain cognitive performances and in a further understanding of the social world of self and others" (p. 2). As the name given to the concept implies, an understanding of metacognitive processes is fundamental to accurate assessment and effective intervention. The more conscious this understanding is, the more effective the cognitively oriented therapist may be.

## Conclusion

The construction of information that is used in clinical assessment is derived from many sources, including test data and interviewing. Although instruments are available to assess cognitive products, the description of clinical problems, from a cognitive perspective, usually does not refer to cognitive structures, content, and operations. Our intention was to present some perspectives on information processing and their implications for clinical assessment.

The perspectives chosen—attention, retrieval, schemas, scripts, hypothesis testing, and metacognition—represent, for the most part, higher order processing, that is, each of these perspectives on information processing involves some complex processes that may have relevance for the analysis of clinical problems. In essence, our goal in this chapter was to foster a conceptual shift in clinical assessment to integrate basic conceptual areas of cognitive science with the process of clinical assessment. In doing so, we hope that the description of clients' problems may reflect the cognitive processes that underlie the disorder as well as suggest treatment strategies that are derived from the assessment process.

# 6

# The Fabric of Thought Disorder: A Cognitive Neuroscience Approach to Disturbances in the Processing of Context in Schizophrenia

**Jonathan D. Cohen**
*Department of Psychology*
*Carnegie Mellon University*
*and*
*Department of Psychiatry*
*University of Pittsburgh*
*Pittsburgh, Pennsylvania*

**Elisabeth Targ**
*Department of Psychiatry and*
*Behavioral Sciences,*
*University of California, Los Angeles*
*Los Angeles, California*

**David Servan-Schreiber**
*Department of Psychiatry*
*University of Pittsburgh*
*and*
*Department of Computer Science*
*Carnegie Mellon University*
*Pittsburgh, Pennsylvania*

**David Spiegel**
*Department of Psychiatry and*
*Behavioral Sciences*
*Stanford University*
*Stanford, California*

The word "context" comes from the Latin words "com" and "texere," which mean "to weave together." In all domains of human information processing—from visual pattern recognition to language and problem solving—appropriate behavior relies on the correct interpretation of intricate contextual interactions. Even the simplest and most commonplace acts involve the processing of contextual information. For example, deciding what shirt to put on in the morning can be influenced by the weather, the activities planned for the day, which shirts are clean, one's mood, or a number of other factors.

The importance of contextual information long has been recognized in a variety of fields, including philosophy (Wittgenstein, 1953), linguistics (Carnap, 1947), computer science, and psychology (Wertheimer, 1938). With Shakow's theory of segmental set (Shakow, 1962) this concept first found application in schizophrenia research. In remarking on his findings concerning schizophrenic reaction times, Shakow commented that "here we see particularly the various difficulties created by *context* [sic] . . . It is as if, in the scanning process which takes place before the response to a stimulus is made, the schizophrenic is unable to select out the material relevant for optimal response" (Shakow, 1962, p. 25). Although Shakow was referring to the behavior of schizophrenics in a specific experimental paradigm, schizophrenics appear to have difficulty using context in a variety of cognitive domains.

The recognition that schizophrenics have difficulty processing context may help us understand why they behave the way they do. However, this explanation lacks a description of the actual mechanisms—cognitive or biological—that underlie this behavior. How does the processing of context actually occur, and how is this disturbed in schizophrenia? Further, how can these processes, and disturbances of them, be related to the growing number of findings concerning neurobiological abnormalities in schizophrenia? Despite the longstanding knowledge that schizophrenics suffer from information processing deficits, and the more recent consensus that these result from underlying biological abnormalities, there has been little success in identifying the specific cognitive processes that are impaired in schizophrenia, and in relating these to biological mechanisms.

In this chapter, we will review our recent work on how developments in cognitive science can be used to address these issues. The body of this work is presented in detail elsewhere (Cohen & Servan-Schreiber, 1992a,b). Here, we will provide an overview that is intended to give the reader a sense of our approach. In particular, we will draw on computer simulation models developed in the connectionist framework. This framework provides theoretical concepts that are intermediate between the details of neuroscientific observations and the box-and-arrow diagrams of traditional information processing or neuropsychological theories. We will show how connectionist models can be used to explain aspects of schizophrenic behavior in terms of specific underlying biological disturbances. At the behavioral level, we will focus on schizophrenic disturbances of attention and language by describing a set of connectionist models that simulate both normal and schizophrenic patterns of performance in three experimental tasks, two that tap attentional performance (the Stroop task and the continuous performance test) and one that measures language processing abilities (a lexical disambiguation task). The models specify the mechanisms that underlie the processing of context in these various tasks, and show how a disturbance in these mechanisms can give rise to schizophrenic patterns of performance in these tasks.

The models also show us how biological variables that are relevant to schizophrenia may be involved in cognitive performance. In particular, they suggest that schizophrenic cognitive deficits may be explained by a specific biological disturbance, a reduction in the effects of the neurotransmitter dopamine in prefrontal cortex (PFC). To illustrate this, we will show first how a particular parameter of the models can be used to simulate the neuromodulatory effects of dopamine at the neuronal level. Then we will describe simulations in which this parameter is disturbed in a component of the models corresponding to the function of PFC. In the case of each of the behavioral tasks simulated, this disturbance leads to changes in performance that quantitatively match those observed for schizophrenics in those tasks. Thus, the models provide a set of mechanisms that can account for both cognitive performance, and its relationship to underlying biological processes.

## Cognitive and Biological Disturbances Associated with Schizophrenia

The set of phenomena to be addressed by the models spans a large and diverse literature concerning cognitive deficits in schizophrenia, the anatomy and physiology of dopamine systems, the neurophysiology and neuropsychology of frontal cortex, and the involvement of these biological systems in schizophrenia. A full review of these areas is beyond the scope of this chapter. (See Cohen & Servan-Schreiber, 1992a, for a more comprehensive review.) In the sections that follow, we highlight the findings concerning information processing and biological deficits in schizophrenia that serve as the focus of the models. These findings can be organized into four basic observations or arguments. (1) Schizophrenics' performance on a variety of cognitive tasks indicates a decreased ability to use context information to select appropriate behavior. (2) PFC is involved directly in, and is necessary for, the representation and maintenance of context information; the normal function of PFC relies on the activity of the mesocortical dopamine system. (3) Dopamine has a modulatory effect on the activity of PFC by influencing the responsivity, or *gain*, of cells in this brain region. (4) Schizophrenia is associated with abnormalities of both frontal cortex and dopamine activity.

## Disturbances in the Processing of Context in Schizophrenia

We suggest that schizophrenics make inadequate use of context in a variety of cognitive domains. What precisely is meant by context? Webster's dictionary defines context as "the parts of discourse that surround a word or passage and can throw light on its meaning." Although this definition captures the meaning of context as it applies to language, a broader definition is needed for our purposes. We think of context as any information held in mind in such a form that it can be used to mediate an appropriate behavioral response. For example, this information can be a set of task instructions, a specific prior stimulus, or a set of prior stimuli (such as the sequence of words in a sentence). By this definition, context information is relevant to, but does not form part of, the content of the actual response. This characteristic distinguishes context information from the kind of information traditionally thought to be stored in short-term memory. We usually think of short-term memory as storing recently presented information, the identity of which must later be retrieved, or "declarative" information, in the sense used by many psychologists (e.g., Anderson, 1983).

In contrast, we think of memory for context as information stored in a form that allows it to mediate a response to the stimulus other than the simple reporting of its identity. This distinction is important because it suggests that disturbances of context can be dissociated from disturbances in short-term memory. Indeed, we believe that this is the case in schizophrenia. For example, schizophrenics show normal performance on a number of short-term memory tasks (e.g., Oltmanns & Neale, 1975; Larsen & Fromhold, 1976). However, they consistently show deficits in tasks that rely on the processing of context. To illustrate this, we will consider three different tasks: a selective attention task, a sustained attention task, and a lexical disambiguation task. In each case, we will see that the processing of context plays an important role, and that schizophrenic deficits, in both attention and language tasks, can be related to a degradation in the processing of context.

### Stroop Task

The Stroop task (Stroop, 1935) taps a fundamental attentional phenomenon: the ability to respond to one set of stimuli, even when other more compelling stimuli are available. The paradigm consists of two sub-

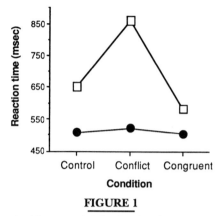

**FIGURE 1**

Performance in the standard Stroop task (after Dunbar & MacLeod, 1984). Data are average reaction times to stimuli in each of the three conditions of the two tasks, color naming (□) and word reading (●).

tasks. In one, subjects name the color of the ink in which a word is printed. In the other, subjects read the word aloud while ignoring ink color. Three types of stimuli are used: conflict stimuli, in which the word and the ink color are different (e.g., the word RED in green ink); congruent stimuli, in which they are the same (e.g., the word RED in red ink); and control stimuli. The control stimuli for word reading are typically color words printed in black ink; for color naming they are usually rows of Xs printed in a particular color. The subjective experience of performing this task is that word reading is much easier, and there is no difficulty in ignoring the color of the ink. In contrast, it is much harder to ignore the word when the task is to name ink color.

These experiences are reflected in the time it takes for subjects to respond to stimuli of each type (see Fig. 1). Three basic effects are observed: (1) word reading is faster than color naming; (2) ink color has no effect on the speed of word reading; and (3) words have a large effect on color naming. For example, subjects are slower to respond to the color red when the word GREEN is written in red ink than when the word RED or a series of Xs appears in red ink. Thus, normal subjects have a harder time selectively attending to colors and ignoring words than doing the reverse. This result is referred to commonly as the Stroop effect. If schizophrenics suffer from an attentional deficit then this effect should be exacerbated, that is, they should be less able to ignore word information, and should show a greater interference effect. Reaction time studies of schizophrenic performance in the Stroop task demonstrate such an increase in interference effects (Wapner & Krus, 1960; Abramczyk, Jordan, & Hegel, 1983; Wysocki & Sweet, 1985).

However, because an overall slowing of reaction time is also observed, the significance of this increase in interference is not clear. It simply may reflect an unanticipated effect of general slowing of performance rather than a specific attentional deficit (See Chapman & Chapman, 1978, for a discussion of differential and generalized deficits.) This issue has not been resolved in the literature. In subsequent text, we will discuss how a simulation model of this task can help distinguish the effects of a general slowing from those of a specific attentional deficit.

Considerations of the Stroop effect typically focus on the role of selective attention. However, the processing of context is also central to this task. The conflict stimuli are ambiguous (e.g., the word RED in green ink); without knowledge of the task instructions, it is not clear to which dimension of the stimulus the individual should respond. In other words, the task instructions provide the necessary context for interpreting the stimulus and generating the correct response. In Stroop experiments, trials typically are blocked by task (e.g., all color naming or all word reading), so that the proper context is consistent and regularly reinforced. However, in other attentional tasks, such as the continuous performance test, this is not the case.

### Continuous Performance Test

In the continuous performance test (CPT; Rosvold, Mirsky, Sarason, Bransome, & Beck, 1956), subjects are asked to detect a target event among a sequence of briefly presented stimuli, and to avoid responding to distractor stimuli. The target event may be the appearance of a single stimulus (e.g, detect the letter X appearing in a stream of other letters) or the appearance of a stimulus in a particular context (e.g, respond to X preceded by A). The percentage of correctly reported targets (hits) and erroneous responses to distractors (false alarms) is used to compute a measure of the ability to discriminate target from nontarget events (d'), independent of response criteria. Schizophrenics (and often their biological relatives) show a decrease in d' (lower hit rates and similar or higher false alarm rates) compared with normal and nonschizophrenic patient controls (e.g., Kornetsky, 1972; Rutschmann, Cornblatt, & Erlenmeyer-Kimling, 1977; Spohn, Lacoursiere, Thomson, & Coyne, 1977; Erlenmeyer-Kimling & Cornblatt, 1978; Nuechterlein, 1983,1984). This deficit is most apparent in versions of the task that make high processing demands, that is, when stimuli are degraded or when memory of the previous stimulus is necessary. For example, in the CPT-double, a target event consists of two consecutive identical letters. In this version, memory of the previous letter provides the context necessary to evaluate the significance of the current letter; inability to use this context would impair performance. Schizophrenics perform especially poorly on this and similar versions of the task (Nuechterlein, 1984).

### Schizophrenic Language Deficits

Impaired use of context has been observed in schizophrenic language processing using a variety of experimental methods, including speech reconstruction (ordering sentences that have been randomly rearranged; Rutter, 1979), cohesion analysis (examining the types of references used in speech; e.g., Rochester & Martin, 1979; Harvey, 1983), and the cloze technique (guessing the words deleted from a transcript of speech; e.g., Salzinger, Portnoy, & Feldman, 1964; Salzinger, Portnoy, Pisoni, & Feldman, 1970). (For reviews of this literature see Maher, 1972; Schwartz, 1982; Cozolino, 1983.) The clearest evidence for a disturbance in the processing of context, however, comes from a classic study conducted by Chapman, Chapman, and Miller (1964). They examined schizophrenics' interpretation of lexical ambiguities and found that schizophrenics tended to interpret the strong (dominant) meaning of a homonym used in a sentence, even when context suggested the weaker (subordinate) meaning. For example, given the sentence "The farmer needed a new *pen* for his cattle," schizophrenics interpreted the word "pen" to mean writing implement more frequently than did control subjects. Schizophrenics did not differ from control subjects in the number of unrelated meaning responses that were made (e.g., interpreting "pen" to mean "fire truck"), nor did they differ in the number of errors made when the strong meaning was correct. These findings were corroborated in a number of subsequent studies (Benjamin & Watt, 1969; Blanley, 1974; Strauss, 1975). One possible basis for this deficit is that schizophrenics fail to maintain adequate representations of prior stimuli for use as context when interpreting subsequent ones. However, this conclusion cannot be substantiated by the early studies, since they were conducted with paper and pencil, thus failing to control for temporal parameters of performance (e.g., subjects ability to look back to earlier parts of the sentence). However, we conducted a study to test this idea more directly. We designed a lexical ambiguity task, similar to the one used by Chapman and his colleagues, in which we could manipulate the temporal parameters of performance in the task.

Subjects were presented with sentences that consisted of two clauses; each clause appeared individually on a computer screen. One clause contained an ambiguous word in neutral context (e.g., "you need a PEN"), whereas the other clause provided disambiguating context (e.g., "in order to keep chickens" or "in order to sign a check"). Clauses were designed so they could be presented in either order: context first or context last. The ambiguity in each sentence always appeared in capital letters so it could be identified by the subject. Subjects were presented with the sentences and, after each presentation, were asked to interpret the meaning of the ambiguity as it was used in the sentence. Sentences were distributed across three conditions: (1) weak meaning correct, context last; (2) weak meaning correct, context first; (3) strong meaning correct, context first. For example, a given subject would have seen the ambiguous word "pen" under one of the three following conditions, and then would have chosen a response from the list of possible meanings.

(1) without a PEN [*clear screen, pause*] you can't keep chickens

*or*

(2) you can't keep chickens [*clear screen, pause*] without a PEN

*or*

(3) you can't sign a check [*clear screen, pause*] without a PEN
[*clear screen, pause*]

The meaning of the word in capital letters is:

a writing implement (*dominant meaning*)
a fenced enclosure (*subordinate meaning*)
a kind of truck (*unrelated meaning*)

The results of this study (see Fig. 2) corroborated the Chapman's original findings: schizophrenics made significantly more dominant meaning errors than did controls when the weak meaning was correct. However, the findings also provide support for an explanation in terms of a restriction in the temporal range over which schizophrenics are able to use context. A dominant response bias occurred only when the context came first (2); when context came last, schizophrenics correctly chose the weak meaning. Further, this error was the only type that reliably distinguishes schizophrenics from controls. Thus, schizophrenics appear to have had difficulty using context, but only when it was temporally remote (i.e., came first), not when it was more recently available (i.e., came last). Further, schizophrenics appear to suffer specifically from a deficit in memory for context, not in short-term memory in general. Schizophrenics had no trouble remembering the ambiguity, even when it came first and did not appear again in the trial. These findings suggest that the impairment observed in language tasks may be similar in nature to the impairments observed in attentional tasks; that is, a difficulty in remembering and using context to control action.

### Prefrontal Cortex, Dopamine, and the Processing of Context

Intensive research on biological abnormalities in schizophrenia has paralleled research on schizophrenic information processing deficits. Some of these abnormalities involve systems that are believed to play a central role in the construction and maintenance of internal representations of context—prefrontal cortex and the mesocortical dopamine system.

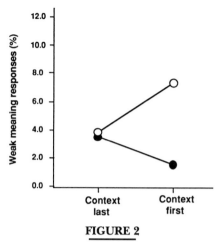

**FIGURE 2**

Medians for the rates of strong meaning responses for schizophrenics (○) and patient controls (●) when the weak meaning was correct. Because of the low overall rate of weak meaning responses when the strong meaning was correct, and of unrelated responses in all conditions, as well as the lack of any significant differences between groups in these types of errors, these data are not shown.

Several studies suggest that frontal areas are involved specifically in maintaining context information for the control of action. For example, at the neurophysiological level, Fuster (1980) and Goldman-Rakic (1987) have observed cells in PFC that are specific to a particular stimulus and response, and remain active during a delay between these. These investigators have argued that neural patterns of activity are maintained in PFC that encode the temporary information needed to guide a response. At the behavioral level, these authors and others (e.g., Mishkin & Pribram, 1955; Rosvold, Szwarcbart, Mirsky, & Mishkin, 1961; Damasio, 1979; Rosenkilde, 1979; Stuss & Benson, 1986) have reported data suggesting that PFC is needed to perform tasks involving delayed responses to ambiguous stimuli. Diamond and Goldman-Rakic (1989) have emphasized that prefrontal representations are required, in particular, to overcome reflexive or previously reinforced response tendencies in order to mediate a contextually relevant, but otherwise weaker, response (see also Diamond, 1985,1990a,b; Diamond & Doar, 1989).

Physiological measures in humans have begun to provide converging evidence for this role of PFC. Studies using measures of regional cerebral blood flow (e.g., Berman, Illowsky, & Weinberger, 1988; Weinberger, Berman, & Zec, 1986; Weinberger, Berman, & Chase, 1988) as well as regional cerebral metabolism (e.g., Cohen et al., 1987; Cohen, Semple, Gross, Holcomb, Dowling, & Nordahl, 1988) have shown that, in normal subjects, prefrontal activity correlates with performance in tasks that rely on internal representations of context.

Data from both laboratory and clinical studies indicate that dopaminergic innervation of PFC (part of the mesocortical dopamine projections from the brain stem nuclei) is necessary for this brain region to maintain internal representations of context. For example, in one study, Rhesus monkeys were unable to perform a delayed response task following selective destruction of dopamine terminals in PFC (Brozoski, Brown, Rosvold, & Goldman, 1979). This deficit was as severe as that following full surgical ablation of the same area of cortex. Moreover, performance recovered almost entirely with dopamine agonists such as L-DOPA and apomorphine. Similar findings have been reported with respect to attentional impairments (e.g., Corwin, Kanter, Watson, Heilman, Valenstein, & Hashimoto, 1986) and, more recently, working memory deficits (Sawaguchi & Goldman-Rakic, 1991).

## Neuromodulatory Effects of Dopamine

Dopamine seems to be crucial to the function of PFC. However, what are the mechanisms by which it exerts its influence on PFC function? Several observations suggest that catecholamines, such as dopamine and norepinephrine, have a modulatory influence on information processing in the brain. Dopamine and norepinephrine neurons originate in discrete nuclei localized in the brain stem; their fibers project radially to several functionally different areas of the central nervous system. The baseline firing rate of these neurons is low and stable, and the conduction velocity along their fibers is slow. These characteristics result in a steady state of transmitter release and relatively long-lasting postsynaptic effects that are consistent with a modulatory role. Most importantly, recent evidence suggests that the effect of dopamine release is not to increase or reduce the firing frequency of target cells directly (e.g., Schneider, Levine, Hull, & Buchwald 1984; Chiodo & Berger, 1986). Instead, like norepinephrine, dopamine seems to modulate the response properties of postsynaptic cells so both inhibitory and excitatory responses to other afferent inputs are potentiated. Some investigators have described this effect as an increase in the signal-to-noise ratio of cell behavior (Foote, Freedman, & Oliver, 1975) or an enabling of its response (Bloom, Schulman, & Koob, 1989).

## Prefrontal Cortex and Dopamine in Schizophrenia

The behavioral data reviewed earlier concerning schizophrenic performance deficits indicate an insensitivity to context and a dominant response tendency. These deficits are consistent with evidence that schizophrenia is associated with frontal lobe impairment. Schizophrenics show typical frontal lobe deficits on standard neuropsychological tests, including the Wisconsin Card Sort Test (e.g., Malmo, 1974; Kolb & Whishaw, 1983) and the Stroop task (as described earlier). In addition, imaging and electrophysiological studies suggest an atrophy and abnormal metabolism in the frontal lobes of schizophrenics (e.g., Ingvar and Franzen, 1974; Weinberger, Bigelow, Kleinman, Klein, Rosenblatt, & Wyatt, 1980; Buchsbaum, et al., 1982). Recent studies have demonstrated abnormal metabolism in the PFC of schizophrenics specifically during performance on tasks requiring memory for context such as the Wisconsin Card Sort Task and a variant of the CPT (Weinberger et al., 1986; Cohen et al., 1987,1988). This work strongly suggests that anatomical and physiological deficits of frontal cortex indeed may be associated with some behavioral deficits observed in schizophrenics.

The hypothesis that frontal lobe dysfunction is involved in schizophrenia fits well with the prevailing neurochemical and psychopharmacological data concerning this illness. The PFC is a primary projection area for the mesocortical dopamine system, a disturbance of which has been implicated consistently in schizophrenia (e.g., Meltzer & Stahl, 1976; Nauta & Domesick, 1981). In view of these findings, several authors have proposed that reduced dopaminergic tone in PFC may be associated with hypofrontality in schizophrenia, and may be responsible for several of the cognitive deficits that have been observed (e.g., Levin, 1984; Geraud, Arne-Bes, Guell, & Bes, 1987; Weinberger et al., 1988).

## Connectionist Simulations

We have reviewed evidence suggesting that schizophrenics suffer from an inability to construct and maintain internal representations of context for the control of action; that PFC plays a role in maintaining such representations; that an intact mesocortical dopamine system is necessary for the normal function of PFC; and that disturbances of both PFC and the mesocortical dopamine system appear to be involved in schizophrenia. However, despite a growing recognition that these findings are related, no theory has been proposed yet that answers the following question. How does a disturbance of dopamine activity in PFC lead to the pattern of cognitive deficits observed in schizophrenia? Recent developments in cognitive science offer a new approach to answering this kind of question. In the remaining sections of this chapter, we will present a set of computer simulation models, developed within the connectionist framework, that simulate human performance in the behavioral tasks described earlier and can explain how schizophrenic deficits in these tasks can arise from a disturbance of dopamine in PFC. As background, however, let us briefly review the principles that define the connectionist modeling framework.

## Connectionist Framework

The principles of connectionism, or parallel distributed processing (McClelland & Rumelhart, 1986; Rumelhart & McClelland, 1986a), provide a framework for building computer models that can simulate cognitive phenomena. At the same time, these principles are meant to capture the salient details of the mechanisms underlying information processing in the brain. The principles can be divided, approximately, into those relating to processing and those relating to training.

### Processing

Each unit in a connectionist network is a simple summing device. It accumulates inputs from other units and adjusts its output in response to these inputs (see Fig. 3). Typically, units are grouped into modules, and modules are connected into pathways. Information is represented as the pattern of activation over the units in a module. The activation of each unit is a real valued number varying continuously between a minimum and a maximum value, that can be thought of as the unit's probability of firing. The responsiveness of each unit is scaled by its gain parameter, which serves as a multiplier for the effects of excitatory and inhibitory inputs to the unit. Processing occurs by the propagation of signals (spread of activation) among units within and between modules. This occurs via the connections that exist between units. The connections between the units of different modules constitute processing pathways.

### Training

The ability of this type of system to perform a given task depends on its having an appropriate set of connection weights in the pathway that runs from the input module(s) to the output module(s) relevant to the task. The connections in a pathway are set by learning. Although several different connectionist learning techniques have been described, the generalized delta rule or back-propagation algorithm (Rumelhart, Hinton, & Williams, 1986) is in widest use. In brief, this algorithm involves the following series of operations. (1) Present an input pattern to the network; (2) allow activation to spread to the output level; (3) compute the difference (error) for each output unit between its current activation and the one desired (i.e., the one specified by the target, or teaching pattern); (4) "back propagate" these error signals to the input units. The back-propagation algorithm provides a way for each unit in a pathway to

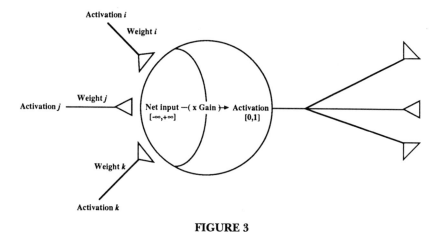

**FIGURE 3**

Schematic representation of a typical unit in a connectionist system

compute the adjustment it must make to its connection weights to best reduce the error at the output level. A common criticism of this algorithm is that it is not biologically plausible, that is, it is difficult to imagine that real neural systems rely on the back propagation of error signals for learning. However, back propagation implements the general phenomenon of "gradient descent," the gradual reduction of error by incremental adjustments in connection weights. Gradient descent has proven to be a powerful concept for describing many of the details concerning human learning behavior (e.g., Cohen, Dunbar, & McClelland, 1990). Thus, back propagation may offer a reasonable approximation of the type of learning that occurs in neural systems, even if the actual algorithm is different.

It is important to recognize, also, that most connectionist models are not intended to be detailed circuit diagrams of actual neural networks. Rather, like statistical mechanical models in physics and chemistry, connectionist models are designed to capture those features of a lower level system (information processing mechanisms in the brain) that are most relevant at a higher level of analysis (cognition and behavior). Thus, an important goal of such models is to examine the effects of biological variables on behavior without having to reproduce the entire brain to do so.

Our purpose in developing biologically plausible models of information processing is that we believe (1) this will lead to more realistic models of cognitive phenomena, and (2) it will be possible to relate behavior directly to biological processes. (For an in-depth discussion, see Rumelhart & McClelland, 1986b.) Connectionist models have begun to show promise along these lines in their ability to explain a variety of phenomena at both biological and behavioral levels. These phenomena include the computation of spatial orientation from retinal and eye-position information (Zipser & Andersen, 1988), the computation of object shape from shading information (Lehky & Sejnowski, 1988), the acquisition of regular and irregular verb forms in English (Rumelhart & McClelland, 1986c), text to speech translation and disturbances of this phenomenon in surface dyslexia (Seidenberg & McClelland, 1989), and access to word meaning from word form in deep dyslexia (Hinton & Shallice, 1991).

Using the connectionist framework, we have developed simulation models of three tasks relevant to research on schizophrenia: the Stroop task, the CPT, and the lexical disambiguation task earlier. Each model was designed to simulate normal performance on one of these tasks. Although the models differ in the details necessary to capture differences between these tasks, all three rely on a common set of information processing principles (as described earlier) and, in particular, share a mechanism for representing and maintaining context. In each case, this mechanism relies on a specific module that we identify with the function of the PFC. Having established the ability of each model to capture normal performance in the corresponding task, we then examined the effects that reducing the gain of units in the context module had on performance, in order to explore the hypothesis that such a disturbance can account for schizophrenic deficits in these tasks. We begin our description of the models by showing how the physiological influence of dopamine can be simulated by changes in the gain parameter of individual units. We then describe simulations that show that a change in gain in the module used to represent context can account for differences between normal and schizophrenic performance in the Stroop, CPT, and lexical disambiguation tasks.

## Simulation of the Physiological Effects of Dopamine

The action of dopamine can be simulated in connectionist models as a change in the sensitivity of processing units to their input. First, however, let us consider the relationship between the input to a unit (i.e., the signals it receives from the other units to which it is connected) and that unit's activation (corresponding to the firing rate of neurons). In general, we assume that units respond to their input in a nonlinear, or saturating, fashion, that is, the unit's activation is driven toward a maximum value by excitatory input and toward a minimum value by inhibitory input. Physiological experiments suggest that, in biological systems, the shape of this function is sigmoid, with its steepest slope around the baseline firing rate (e.g., Freeman, 1979; Burnod & Korn, 1989). The same experiments also indicate that small increments in excitatory drive result in greater changes in firing frequency than equivalent increments in inhibitory input. These properties can be captured by the logistic function with a constant negative bias:

$$activation = \frac{1}{1 + e^{-\,(gain*net)\,+\,bias}}$$

(See Fig. 4; gain = 1.0.)

In this function, the sensitivity of the unit's activation to the net input is determined by the gain parameter; the potentiating effects of dopamine can be simulated by increasing this parameter. As Fig. 4 (gain = 2.0) illustrates, with an increase in gain, the unit becomes more sensitive to afferent signals while its baseline activation (net input = 0) remains the same. Elsewhere we have shown that such a change in gain can simulate a number of different catecholaminergic effects at both biological and behavioral levels (e.g., the influence of catecholamines on the receptive field of individual units, the influence of amphetamines on stimulus detection in humans, and stimulus response generalization in both humans and rats; Servan-Schreiber, 1990; Servan-Schreiber, Printz, & Cohen, 1990).

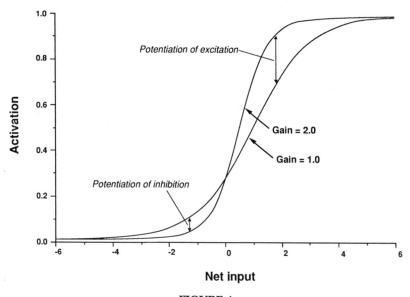

**Net input**

**FIGURE 4**

The influence of the gain parameter on the logistic activation function of an individual unit. Note that, with an increase in gain, the effect of the net input on the unit's activation is increased, whereas the reverse is true with a decrease in the gain. These effects simulate the consequences of dopamine release on target neurons in the central nervous system.

To simulate the neuromodulatory effects of dopamine in a particular brain area, we change gain equally for all units in the module that corresponds to the area that are assumed to be influenced by the neuromodulator. For example, the mesocortical dopamine system has extensive projections to PFC. To model the action of dopamine in this brain area, we change the gain of all units in the module that corresponds to this PFC. In the models described next, our interest is in the effects that a *reduction* of dopaminergic tone in PFC has on behavior. We simulated this situation by reducing the gain of the units in the module used to represent and maintain context. In all three models, simulation of schizophrenic performance was conducted by decreasing gain from a normal value of 1.0 to the reduced value of 0.6.

### Simulation of the Stroop Effect

Cohen and colleagues described a connectionist model of selective attention that simulates human performance in the Stroop task. In brief, this model consists of two processing pathways, one for color naming and one for word reading, and a task demand module that can facilitate processing selectively in either pathway (see Fig. 5). Simulations are conducted by activating input units corresponding to stimuli used in an actual experiment (e.g., the input unit in the color naming pathway representing the color red) and the appropriate task demand unit. Activation is then allowed to spread through the network. This spread leads to activation of the output unit corresponding to the appropriate response (e.g., "red"). Reaction time is considered to be linearly related to the number of cycles it takes for an output unit to accumulate a specified amount of activation.

The model was trained to perform the word reading and color naming tasks by presenting it with the input patterns for each of the responses it is expected to make, and using a standard connectionist learning algorithm (back propagation) to adjust the connection weights accordingly. During training, the model was given more experience with (i.e., a greater number of training trials on) the word reading task than the color naming task. This corresponded to the common assumption that human adults have had more experience generating a verbal response to written words than to colors they see. Because of this aspect of training, connection weights in the word reading pathway developed larger values than did those in the color naming pathway. As a result, when the network is presented with conflicting inputs in the two pathways (e.g., the word RED and the color green), it responds preferentially to the word input. Of course, human subjects are able to overcome this tendency and respond to the color instead of the word when requested to do so. To capture this effect in the model, a set of "task demand" units is included that represent the in-

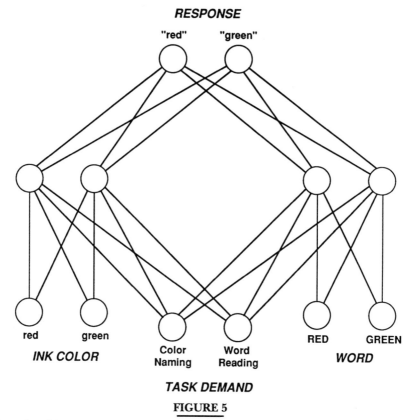

**RESPONSE**

"red"    "green"

red    green
**INK COLOR**

Color    Word
Naming   Reading

RED    GREEN
**WORD**

**TASK DEMAND**

**FIGURE 5**

Network architecture for the Stroop model. Units at the bottom are input units and units at the top are the output (response) units.

tended behavior (i.e., color naming or word reading). The specification of a particular task is represented by the appropriate pattern of activation over these units.

The task demand units are connected to the intermediate units in the two pathways and modulate their responsiveness. For example, when the pattern corresponding to "color naming" is activated over the task demand units, activation spreading from these units has a sensitizing effect on processing units in the color pathway but a "desensitizing" effect on units in the word pathway. This response modulates the flow of information in the two pathways to favor the color pathway. The result is that, although the connection strengths in the color pathway are weaker, a signal presented to this pathway is able to overcome the otherwise dominant response mediated by the word pathway. In other words, the model is able to attend selectively to information in the task-relevant pathway. Note that spreading activation and attentional modulation are not different processes. Attentional modulation of both pathways is a consequence of activation spreading from the task demand units to the intermediate units in each pathway. Thus, both the "direct processing" of information and its attentional modulation rely on the same mechanisms of processing. (See Cohen et al., 1990, for a more detailed discussion.)

This simple model is able to simulate a wide variety of empirical phenomena associated with the Stroop task. It captures all the phenomena depicted in Fig. 1 (asymmetry in speed of processing between word reading and color naming, the immunity of word reading to the effects of color, the susceptibility of color naming to interference and facilitation from words, and greater interference than facilitation effects). It also captures the influence of practice of interference and facilitation effects, the relative nature of these effects (i.e., their dependence on the nature of a competing process), stimulus onset asynchrony effects, and response set effects (see Cohen et al., 1990).

The model also clarifies the relationship between attention and the internal representation of context. Stimuli that vary in more than one dimension are inherently ambiguous (e.g., "Should I respond to the word or the color?"). Task instructions provide the context necessary to disambiguate the stimulus and choose the appropriate response. Further, task instructions must be represented internally since, as we have said, the stimuli themselves do not indicate which task to perform. In the model, this internal representation was captured as a pattern of activation in the task demand module. This pattern had a direct attentional effect: it was responsible for selecting one pathway for the processing of information and not the other. Thus, the model suggests that attentional selection can be thought of as the mediating effects that the internal representation of context has on processing.

These ideas are directly relevant to schizophrenic deficits. If PFC is responsible for maintaining the internal representation of context, and if schizophrenia involves a disturbance of frontal lobe function, then we should be able to simulate schizophrenic deficits in the Stroop task by disturbing processing in the task demand module. More specifically, if frontal lobe dysfunction in schizophrenia is due to a reduction in the activity of its dopaminergic supply, then we should be able to simulate this by reducing the gain of units in the task demand module.

Figure 6 shows the results of this simulation, in which the gain of only the task demand units was reduced; all other units were unperturbed. This change in the context (i.e., task demand) module produces effects similar to those observed for schizophrenics: an increase in overall response time, with a disproportionate increase on color naming conflict trials. It is im-

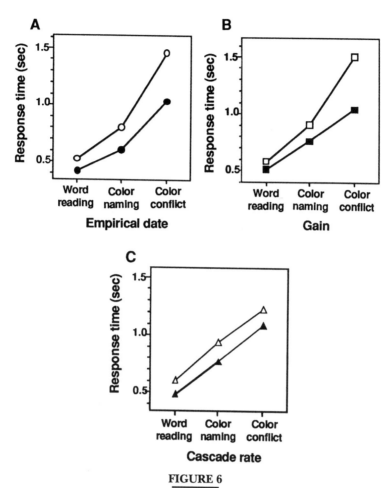

**FIGURE 6**

(A) Stroop task performance for normal (●) and schizophrenic (○) subjects, and results from simulations manipulating (B) the gain parameter (task demand units only) and (C) cascade rate (all units) in the network. Empirical data are the response times (in seconds) for stimuli in each condition of the Stroop task, averaged over the three empirical studies referred to earlier in this chapter. Simulation data are the number of cycles required for processing stimuli of each type, averaged over 1000 trials of each type, and scaled by a constant (0.02) to facilitate comparison between these and the empirical data. The 5% confidence intervals for all simulation data are all less than 0.02. Open symbols represent reduced gain (0.6) and reduced cascade rate (0.065). Closed symbols represent normal gain (1.0) and normal cascade rate (0.01).

portant to emphasize here that this simulation was conducted without making any changes to the original Stroop model (Cohen et al., 1990), other than manipulating the gain of units in the task demand module as motivated by our hypothesis. Thus, the model shows that a lesion restricted to the mechanism for processing context can produce both an overall degradation in performance and the expected attentional deficit.

The model also allows us to address a problem that frequently besets the interpretation of schizophrenic deficits. Recall the argument that, given an overall degradation of performance, it is difficult to know whether poor performance in a particular experimental condition is due to a specific deficit or to a more generalized one responsible for the *overall* degradation. This difficulty reflects a limitation in our ability to attribute cause when the information we have about a system is restricted to its behavior and we lack any knowledge about underlying mechanisms. However, the model provides us with a tool for specifying possible mechanisms, and studying the behavior they produce. We described a mechanism for a specific attentional deficit, a disturbance in the context module. We can compare this deficit to a more generalized deficit—one that produces an overall slowing of response—by decreasing the rate at which information accumulates for units in the network. This accumulation is determined by a parameter called the cascade rate. We tested for the effects of a generalized deficit of this sort by reducing the cascade rate for all units in the network. The reduction in cascade rate was selected by matching the degree of slowing in the word reading condition of the simulation to the degree of slowing observed for schizophrenics relative to control subjects in the empirical data. The results of this manipulation are shown in Fig. 6C. An overall slowing of response is seen, but no disproportionate slowing in the interference condition is apparent. Thus, slowing the processing rate of units throughout the network is unable to account for schizophrenic performance in the interference condition of the task. We have explored other deficits that produce an overall slowing of response (e.g., an increase in the response threshold) with similar results. In contrast, as we noted earlier, impairment of the context module produces both effects: slowing occurs in all conditions, but is most pronounced in the interference condition.

Chapman and Chapman (1978) have pointed out the danger in assuming that degraded performance in a particular task condition necessarily reflects a deficit in processes related to that condition. If the condition is also the hardest one for normals (as is the case for the interference condition of the color naming task), then even a disproportionate degradation of performance in that condition could be caused by a generalized deficit (i.e., one that is not specific to any particular processing component). We have tried to show how a simulation model can help us deal with this problem. Our model demonstrates that a specific attentional deficit provides a better account of the data than a number of possible generalized deficits. Further, the model provides a new interpretation of the data, reversing the typical view; it shows how a *general* degradation in performance can arise from a *specific* deficit, rather than the other way around. To our knowledge, this possibility has not been considered in the literature. Of course, our results do not preclude the possibility that some other model could account for the findings in terms of a different deficit, specific or generalized. However, by providing an explanation of the findings in terms of an explicit set of information processing mechanisms, we have set a threshold for explanation that must be met by competing alternatives. Further, we have shown how simulation models can be used to deal with the problem of differential deficits described by Chapman and Chapman. When tasks (or conditions) differ in difficulty, it is still possible to compare competing hypotheses by specifying the mechanisms believed to underlie the deficit, and comparing their ability to account for the empirical data.

Finally, as discussed earlier, the model relates a disturbance in selective attention directly to the processing of context. Selective attention is viewed as the effect that context has on processing; a failure to maintain an appropriate contextual representation (e.g., the task demand specification) leads directly to a failure in selective attention. In the Stroop task, this failure manifests as an increased susceptibility to interference in the color naming task. This interference, in turn, reflects the increased influence of dominant response processes (e.g., word reading) that occurs with the weakening of attention. Schizophrenic performance often has been characterized as reflecting a dominant response tendency (e.g., Chapman et al., 1964; Maher, 1972), although no specific mechanism has been proposed for this effect previously. We will return to this issue in our discussion of schizophrenic language performance.

### Simulation of the Continuous Performance Test

The Stroop model shows how contextual information and its attentional effects can be represented in a connectionist model, and how a specific biologically relevant disturbance in this mechanism can explain aspects of schizophrenic performance. One question we might ask is, How general are these findings? In the following simulation, we extend the principles applied in the Stroop model to account for performance in the CPT.

As discussed earlier, schizophrenics show consistent deficits in the CPT. This is particularly true for variants in which a demand is placed on memory for context. For example, in the CPT-double, a target consists of any consecutive recurrence of a letter (e.g., a B immediately following a B). Thus, subjects must remember the previous letter, which provides the necessary context for responding to the subsequent one. Schizophrenics perform poorly in this task. This may be because of an impairment in the processing of context that, like deficits in the Stroop task, might be explained by a reduction of dopaminergic tone in PFC. If this is so, then we

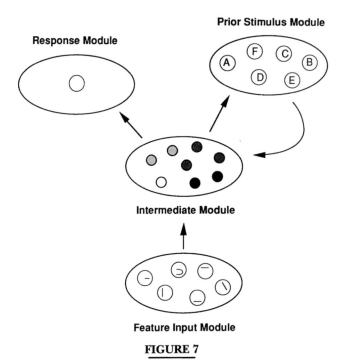

**FIGURE 7**

Network used to simulate the CPT-double. Note the bidirectional connections between units in the intermediate and prior stimulus modules.

should be able to simulate schizophrenic deficits in the CPT-double using the same manipulation used to produce deficits in the Stroop task: a reduction of gain in the module responsible for representing and, in this case, maintaining context. To test this, we constructed a network to perform the CPT-double.

The network consisted of four modules: an input module, an intermediate (associative) module, a letter identification module, and a response module (see Fig. 7). The input module was used to represent the visual features of individual letters. Stimulus presentation was simulated by activating the input units corresponding to the features of the stimulus letter. The network was trained to associate these input patterns with the corresponding letter units in the letter identification module. In addition, the network was trained to activate the unit in the response module whenever a stimulus letter appeared consecutively two or more times. This response was made possible by introducing a set of connections from the letter units back to the intermediate units. This allowed the network to store and use information about the previous as well as the current stimulus. (See Cohen

& Servan-Schreiber, in press, for a more complete description of training and processing in this model.) Note that there is a direct analogy between the role played by the letter units in this model and the role played by the task demand units in the Stroop model. The representation over the letter units in the CPT model provided the context for disambiguating the response to a particular pattern of input, just as the task demand units did in the Stroop model. In the CPT model, however, context was determined by the previous input, and therefore changed from trial to trial.

Following training, the network was able to perform the CPT-double task perfectly for a set of 26 different stimuli. To simulate the performance of normal subjects, who typically miss on 13% of trials and false alarm on 1% of trials (see Fig. 8A), noise was added to the net input, with the amount adjusted to match the performance of the network with that of human subjects. The results of this simulation appear in Fig. 8B (gain = 1.0). Then, to simulate schizophrenic performance, we disturbed processing in the letter module, which was responsible for representing and maintaining context, by decreasing the gain of these units by an amount comparable to the amount used in the Stroop simulation (0.66). The percentage of misses increased to 20%, whereas false alarms increased slightly to 1.1%. These numbers closely match the results of empirical observations of schizophrenic subjects (see Fig. 8A).

Although some authors have interpreted schizophrenic performance in the CPT in terms of a deficit in sensory processing, our model suggests an alternative hypothesis. Performance deficits are due to a degradation in the memory trace required, as context, for processing the current stimulus. We assume that this memory trace is maintained in PFC and is influenced directly by changes in the dopaminergic supply to this area. This hypothesis is consistent with our account of Stroop performance and with disturbances of language processing.

### Simulation of Context-Dependent Lexical Disambiguation

The language model (Fig. 9) incorporated elements of the two previous simulations. The network was similar to the CPT model (Fig. 7). It was trained to associate input patterns representing lexical stimuli (e.g., the word PEN) to patterns in two output modules: a response module and a discourse module. Patterns in the response module specified the meaning of the input words (e.g., "writing implement"), whereas the discourse module represented the topic of the current sequence of inputs (i.e., the meaning of the sentence, rather than the meaning of individual words). As in the CPT model, there were two-way connections between the intermediate module and the context (discourse) module. Thus, once a discourse representation had been activated by an input pattern, it could be used to

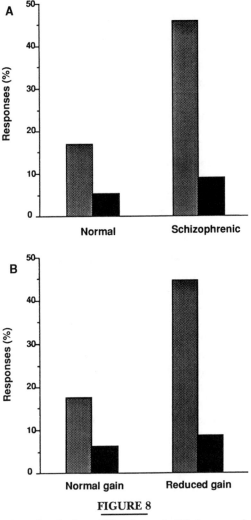

**FIGURE 8**

(A) Percentage of misses (hatched) and false alarms (solid) for normal and schizophrenic subjects in the CPT task. (B) The simulation run with normal and reduced gain on units in the prior stimulus module. Empirical data are from Cornblatt, Lenzenmeyer, & Erlenmeyer-Kimling (1989). This article reports d′ and ln beta values; we obtained the values for misses and false alarms directly (B. Cornblatt, personal communication). In addition, Cornblatt et al. (1989) distinguished between "false alarms" (responses to stimuli similar to the target) and "random errors;" since both types of errors consist of responses to nontarget stimuli, we have combined these and considered them together as false alarms. Simulation data are based on 1000 trials run in each condition. The 5% confidence intervals for the normal gain condition were ±2.3% for misses and ±1.7% for false alarms; for the reduced gain condition, they were ±3.1% for misses and ±1.8% for false alarms.

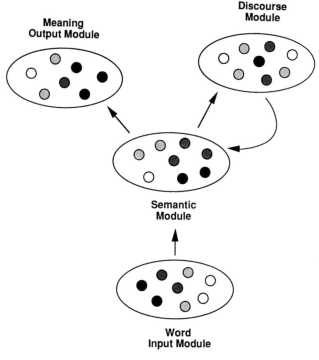

**FIGURE 9**

Schematic diagram of the language processing model. Patterns of activation over the units in the input module are assumed to represent the current sensory stimulus (e.g., the orthographic code for a written word), whereas the output module is assumed to represent the information necessary to generate an overt response (e.g., the phonological code needed to pronounce the meaning of the word). Note that the connections between the semantic and discourse modules are bidirectional.

influence the processing of subsequent stimuli in the semantic module. This set-up provided the mechanism by which context could be used to resolve lexical ambiguity.

The model was trained to produce an output and discourse representation for 30 different input words, some of which were ambiguous. In the case of ambiguous words, the model was trained to produce the response and discourse patterns related to one meaning (e.g., PEN → "WRITING IMPLEMENT" and *WRITING*) more frequently than those related to the other (e.g., PEN → "FENCED ENCLOSURE" and *FARMING*).[1] This asym-

---

[1]We refer to input words in upper case, to output responses in quotation marks, and to discourse representations in italics.

metry of training was similar to that in the Stroop model (trained on words more than colors), with a comparable result. When presented with an ambiguous input word, the network preferentially activated the strong (more frequently trained) response and discourse representations. To permit access to the weaker meaning, the network was sometimes presented with an ambiguous word as input along with one of its associated discourse representations (e.g., PEN and *WRITING*), and trained to generate the appropriate response (i.e., "WRITING IMPLEMENT"). Finally, the network was trained on a set of context words, each of which was related to one meaning of an ambiguity; these words (e.g., CHICKEN) were trained to produce their own meaning as the response ("FOWL") as well as a discourse representation that was identical to the corresponding meaning of the related ambiguity (*FARMING*).

To simulate performance in our experiment, the model was presented with pairs of context and ambiguous words (representing the clauses used in the experiment) in either order. After presentation of each pair, the network was probed with the ambiguous word, simulating the subjects' process of reminding themselves of the ambiguity and choosing its meaning. At each time step of processing, a small amount of noise was added to the activation of every unit. The amount of noise was adjusted so the simulation produced an overall error rate comparable to that of control subjects. The model's response on each trial was considered to be the meaning that was most active over the output units after the probe was presented. To simulate schizophrenic performance, we introduced a disturbance analogous to the one in the CPT model: a reduction in gain of units in the context module. The results of this simulation (shown in Fig. 10, along with the results of the empirical study) show a strong resemblance to the empirical data. They demonstrate both significant effects. In the low gain mode, the simulation makes about as many more dominant response errors as do the schizophrenic subjects. However, as with the human subjects, this only occurs when context comes first. (The number of unrelated errors, not shown in Fig. 10, was approximately the same in both the low gain and the normal gain mode.) The model provides a clear view of this relationship between dominant response bias and memory. When gain is reduced in the context module, the representation of context is degraded; as a consequence, the model is more susceptible to the cumulative effects of noise. If a contextual representation is used quickly, these effects are less, and the representation is sufficient to overcome a dominant response bias. However, if time passes (for example, when context is presented first), the effects of noise accumulate, and the representation is no longer strong enough to mediate the weaker of two competing responses.

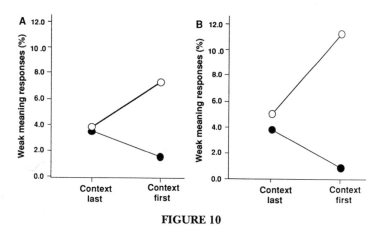

**FIGURE 10**

(A) Percentage of strong meaning responses when the weak meaning was correct for schizophrenic (○) and control (●) subjects in the empirical study and for the simulation. (B) The rate of unrelated errors (not shown) and of weak meaning responses, when the strong meaning was correct, were the same in the normal (1.0) and reduced gain (0.6) conditions of the simulation, and were of the same magnitude as those observed for human subjects (about 1–2%). The 5% confidence intervals for the simulation data are ±1.1% for context last and ±0.6% for context first in the normal gain condition, and ±1.3% for context last and ±2.0% for context first in the reduced gain condition.

## Conclusion

We began by reviewing behavioral data concerning deficits of selective attention and language processing in schizophrenia. We also reviewed data that indicate that PFC and its dopaminergic supply are important for the construction and maintenance of internal representations of context, and that disturbances in these systems are involved in schizophrenia. We then showed how the connectionist framework can be used to relate these findings to one another. We presented three models that (1) simulated quantitative aspects of performance in the Stroop task, the CPT, and a lexical disambiguation task; (2) elucidated the role of the internal representation of context, and its relationship to attention, in these various tasks; (3) related behavior in these tasks to biological processes; and (4) identified a specific disturbance in these processes that could account for schizophrenic patterns of performance.

At this point, one might ask, What have we really learned from the simulation models themselves? After all, the data already exist, and the principles or ideas captured by the models usually can be expressed more simply without the use of a computer program (indeed, one might argue that this is precisely what we have done in this chapter). McClelland (1988) has provided an articulate reply to this question, in describing the relevance of models to empirical investigations in psychology. He points out that models can (1) bring seemingly disparate empirical phenomena together under a single explanation; (2) provide new interpretations of existing findings; (3) reconcile contradictory evidence; and (4) lead to new predictions. We have tried to show how our models realize these different goals. For example, by showing that a disturbance in the internal representation of context can explain impairments of selective attention, language processing, and overall reaction time in schizophrenia, the models bring these seemingly disparate phenomena together under a single unifying explanation. By revealing that an overall increase in reaction time could arise from a specific rather than a generalized information processing deficit, they provide a reinterpretation of the data. Cohen & Servan-Schreiber (1992a) argue that the models also suggest a reconciliation of contradictory findings with respect to the CPT and prefrontal activation, and that they lead to new predictions concerning normal and schizophrenic performance on behavioral tasks, as well as predictions about dopamine effects on prefrontal metabolism.

McClelland also emphasizes the role that models play in formalizing theoretical concepts. By committing a set of ideas to a computer program, and examining their ability to account for quantitative data, the ideas are put to a rigorous test of both internal coherence and resolution of their explanatory power.

Most important, however, is the role that modeling plays in the discovery process. At times the insights provided by a model may seem, in retrospect, to be obvious or not to have required the effort involved in constructing a computer simulation. On other occasions, one may be concerned with the possible circularity of a theory based on a model that presumably has been designed with the theory in mind. Usually, however, such perceptions fail to recognize that the insight and the emerging theory came from the process of developing the model itself. The three models we described here actually were developed independently, and for different purposes. The Stroop model was developed to account for normal performance in this task (Cohen et al., 1990); the CPT simulation was developed to explore gain as a model of catecholaminergic effects on behavior (Servan-Schreiber et al., 1990); and the language model was inspired by our work on the processing of ambiguous stimuli in recurrent networks (Cleeremans, Servan-Schreiber, & McClelland, 1989; Servan-Schreiber, Cleeremans, & McClelland, 1991). Only when we compared the mechanisms at work in these different models did we realize how all relied on common principles of processing. This suggested a hypothesis about the relationship between biological and behavioral factors in schizophrenia. In this way, the models provided an important vehicle for the *discovery*, not just the *testing*, of new ideas.

Of course, in their present form, the models leave many issues unresolved. For example, they focus on a circumscribed set of laboratory findings concerning schizophrenic behavior. How do we explain the more obvious, and tragic, sequelae of schizophrenia, such as hallucinations, delusions, and disturbances of affect? The models also leave many biological issues unaddressed. For example, it is frequently argued that schizophrenia is associated with an *increase*, not a decrease, in dopamine function. Can the models address this? Also, how specific are the mechanisms and processes that we have described to schizophrenia? What other biological factors are involved in schizophrenia? The answers to these questions are beyond the scope of this discussion. We have begun to address some of these in our work. (See Cohen & Servan-Schreiber, 1992a,b, for a full discussion.) However, most issues will require additional research. Nevertheless, we hope to have shown, in this chapter, how we can begin to use connectionist models to integrate findings at the behavioral and biological levels, and to advance our understanding of the interactions that can occur between processes at each of these levels. In doing so, we hope to provoke further exploration of these exciting new methods from cognitive science in the study of psychopathology.

## Acknowledgments

Preliminary versions of this work were presented at the 142nd annual meeting of the American Psychiatric Association, May, 1989, and at the annual meeting of the Cognitive Science Society, July, 1990.

We gratefully acknowledge the helpful suggestions made by David Galin, Steve Matthysse, James McClelland, Benoit Mulsant, and David Plaut during the development of this work. In addition, John Csernansky, Len Horowitz, Roy King, Tracy Kristoffersen, and Sue Theimann participated in the design and implementation of the experimental study of schizophrenic language performance that we reported.

This work was supported by a National Institutes of Mental Health (NIMH) Physician Scientist Award (MH00673) to J. D. Cohen and a NIMH Individual Fellow Award (MH09696) to D. Servan-Schreiber. Part of this work was supported also by a research grant from the Scottish Rite Schizophrenia Research Program, N.M.J., U.S.A., to J. D. Cohen, and a research fellowship from Western Psychiatric Institute and Clinic to D. Servan-Schreiber.

# 7

# Cognitive Science, Anxiety, and Depression: From Experiments to Connectionism

**J. M. G. Williams**
*Department of Psychology*
*University of Wales*
*Bangor, United Kingdom*

**Mike R. Oaksford**
*Cognitive Neurocomputation Unit*
*University of Wales*
*Bangor, United Kingdom*

## Cognitive Psychology and Psychopathology

In this chapter we will focus on two aspects of cognitive science: experimental studies of cognitive processes and computational modeling. We will show how each can be applied to studies of emotional disorders. In particular, a recent model of emotion that distinguishes two stages of processing (priming as opposed to elaboration) and two types of processing (affective decision as opposed to resource allocation) will be outlined. We shall show how this model, arising from the experimental literature, could be implemented in a neural network. Finally, we discuss the implications for the study and treatment of psychopathology.

The psychopathologies we wish to understand are emotional disorders, particularly anxiety and depression. The Diagnostic and Statistical

Manual DSM-III (R) defines General Anxiety Disorder by the presence of unrealistic or excessive anxiety about two or more life circumstances (e.g., possible misfortune to one's child who is in no actual danger) over a period of 6 months. During this period, the person is bothered on "more days than not." The anxiety is not associated with panic, embarrassment in public, or being contaminated, or other diagnoses would be appropriate (panic disorder, social phobia, and obsessive–compulsive disorder, respectively). Neither is the anxiety secondary to a Mood Disorder (e.g., Major Depression). Additionally, patients must have six or more of the following symptoms in the absence of any organic cause: trembling, muscle tension, restlessness, easy fatigability, shortness of breath, palpitations, sweating, dry mouth, dizziness, nausea or diarrhea, flushes or chills, frequent urination, trouble swallowing or lump in throat, feeling keyed up or on edge, exaggerated startle response, difficulty concentrating or mind going blank, trouble falling asleep or staying asleep, and irritability.

The DSM-III(R) defines Major Depression in more "episodic" terms. Patients must have five or more of a number of symptoms occurring during the same 2-week period. This list of symptoms must include either depressed mood (most of the day, nearly every day) or a markedly diminished interest or pleasure in virtually all activities. Other signs or symptoms a person may have are weight gain or weight loss (more than 5% of body weight in one month) or increased or decreased appetite nearly every day; insomnia or hypersomnia; psychomotor agitation or retardation (observed); fatigability or loss of energy; feelings of worthlessness or excessive or inappropriate guilt; a diminished ability to think or concentrate, or indecisiveness; and recurrent thoughts of death (not just fear of dying), recurrent suicidal ideas, or some actual or planned suicidal behavior.

Diagnostic systems such as DSM-III(R) aim to be theory-neutral. They attempt to define signs and symptoms that cluster together, are relatively easily quantifiable, and are able to be assessed reliably by clinicians across different cultures. (Whether they succeed or fail in this enterprise is not our concern.) They try to avoid committing themselves to particular theories, whether dynamic, biological, cognitive, or other. Their aim is differentiation—separating different disorders as clearly as possible.

In an interesting way, information processing accounts of emotions have taken the converse position. They have produced general purpose models of emotion and emotional disorder without taking account of diagnostic differences. This is caused, possibly, by the use of nonclinical subjects in much of the model development (e.g., Bower, Gilligan, & Monteiro, 1981), but also by the nature of information processing models to be generic higher order frameworks of people in general. The most common information processing frameworks used to explain emotions were those of associative network theory (Bower & Cohen, 1981) and schema theory (Neisser, 1976; Taylor & Crocker, 1981). Neither of these frameworks gives different explanations or makes different predictions about the cognitive *structures* underlying different patterns of emotion, nor about the different *processes* involved in encoding or retrieving from the structures. The only differences were at the level of cognitive *products*, the content of the thoughts and images. However, knowledge of the distinction between anxiety and depression in terms of the content, or themes, associated with each (danger in anxiety, loss in depression) has been available for years. Such knowledge was central to Freud's account of the emotions, for example. If information processing models can distinguish different emotional states only in terms of the contents of their conscious mental representations, they are in danger of failing to add any value to previous explanations.

## Distinctions between Anxiety and Depression in Information Processing

Experimental cognitive psychology set out to explain the biases that characterized emotionally disordered individuals, particularly biases in attention, memory, and judgment. About the basic phenomena to be explained, there seemed (and seems still) to be little doubt. Anxious and depressed patients appear to attend selectively to negative material. Someone who is anxious may attend to noises in the house at night, believing them to be caused by burglars, or attend to their own heartbeat, believing it to be irregular or abnormal and to signal an impending heart attack. Someone who is clinically depressed appears to attend to negative events. A remark made by a co-worker about people being late for work is noticed and interpreted as a reference to the patient. A group of people laughing among themselves is noticed and interpreted to mean that they are deliberately excluding the individual. It also appears characteristic of these clinical states that such negative biases come and go as anxiety or depression rises and falls (Teasdale and Fogarty, 1979; Clarke and Teasdale, 1982; Richards and Whitaker, 1990).

How are such biases to be understood? The first task for cognitive psychology was to bring the phenomena under experimental control, to demonstrate them in the laboratory. Only then could further work be done on the underlying processes. At first this task seemed quite straightforward. A considerable number of studies found biases in attention in highly anxious people. For example, Burgess et al. (1981) used a dichotic listening paradigm in which patients had to shadow (repeat out loud) one of two messages played, one to each ear. The investigators found that socially anxious and agoraphobic subjects were more likely to notice anxious words or phrases embedded out of context in the message that was not being shadowed. Foa and McNally (1986) replicated the effect with obsessive–compulsive patients. Words such as "urine," "cancer," and "rabies" were embedded in the nonshadowed message. Patients showed a greater sensitivity to these stimuli, both on measures of skin conductance and on their ability to react by pressing a button whenever they became aware of one of the words in the unattended channel. Although each of these experiments has been criticized (see Williams, Watts, MacLeod, & Mathews, 1988), later experiments have confirmed that perceptual sensitivity is greater for threatening stimuli in anxious patients, and is not merely caused by response biases.

One of the most careful demonstrations of this tendency of anxious patients to orient toward threat in such a perceptual paradigm was the visual dot-probe experiments of MacLeod, Mathews, and Tata (1986). The investigators presented anxious and control patients with pairs of words. The words appeared simultaneously on a visual display unit (VDU) screen, one above the other and 3 cm apart. The patients read the top word aloud, and also pressed a button as fast as possible whenever they detected a dot on the screen. The dot appeared in the place where a word had been, but it only appeared on some trials. Sometimes it replaced a top word, sometimes, a bottom word. The words could either be neutral or threatening, with either type of word appearing in either location. The important dependent variable was the speed with which patients pressed the button when the dot appeared where a threat word had been compared with the speed of reaction when (a) the dot appeared in place of a neutral word, or (b) a threat word appeared at the alternative location. (Other researchers found that subjects detect such a dot-probe more quickly if they are attending to the location at which the dot appears; Navon & Margolit, 1983).

Anxious patients and controls showed different response patterns. The pattern of results for anxious patients suggested that they oriented attention toward the location of threat (they were quicker to respond when a dot replaced a threat word). The pattern for controls suggested the opposite. They oriented attention away from the location of threat (they tended to be quicker to respond to the probe when it replaced a nonthreat word). On this and other perceptual tasks, anxious patients have been found to be more likely to "pick up" threatening material. In the 1980s literature, explanations in terms of schema theory were typical, for example, anxious patients had "danger schemata" that were overactive (Mathews & MacLeod, 1985,1986; MacLeod et al., 1986).

However, schema theory also had been used to explain biases in memory in depressed patients (e.g., Bradley & Mathews, 1983). Despite these explanations, attempts to find biases on perceptual tasks that were associated with depression had not paralleled the success of the experiments in anxious patients. Gerrig and Bower (1982) had found that experimentally induced depressed mood did not affect perceptual threshold. Powell and Hemsley (1984) conducted a similar study of visual threshold with depressed patients, but only found trends toward significant results. MacLeod and colleagues (1986) gave depressed patients their visual dot-probe task. They found no evidence of bias on this task in depressed patients. If schema theory predicted attentional bias in anxiety, and such bias was found, why should it be difficult to find such bias in depressed patients who also had been suggested to have biased schemata?

Had this been the only difficulty for this generic model of information processing, then the impulse to modify the theory would not have been very compelling. However, a similar dissociation started to appear for the field of memory bias. A large number of studies had found a memory bias in depressed subjects; whether the memory tasks were word list (e.g., Clarke & Teasdale 1985), stories (Bower, 1981; Cohen, 1981), or the person's own autobiographical memory (Lloyd & Lishman, 1975; Teasdale & Fogarty, 1979; Moore, Watts, & Williams, 1988; Williams & Scott, 1988). Of particular interest is the highly reliable finding that, if depressed patients are shown a list of positive, negative, and neutral words, they will later tend to show preferential recall of the negative words. (See Williams et al., 1988, for review.) However, use of similar memory paradigms using threat words with anxious patients failed to show a selective memory bias (Mogg, Mathews, & Weinman, 1987).

Another generic cognitive framework, the associative network theory, was cited most often as guiding the search for explanations of these memory data (Bower, 1983; Teasdale, 1983). Network theory, like schema theory, made no differential predictions for anxious and depressed moods. According to network theory, each emotion has a specific node in memory that collects many other aspects of the emotion that are connected to it by associative pointers. Any mood at recall is assumed to have an effect if it matches mood at encoding, or is congruent with the material to be recalled. If such congruency occurs, the memory search is biased to proceed along the same associative pathways set up at encoding. The combination of the activity of "emotion nodes" and the activation of other associative nodes, coupled with the biased search that such activation produces, is considered to account for perceptual biases, priming in lexical decision experiments, state-dependent learning, and mood-congruent encoding and retrieval phenomena. Nothing in the theory predicted the emerging dissociations that were being observed between perceptual and memory paradigms and between anxiety and depression. How could these results be explained?

Williams and colleagues (1988) begin their explanation with the distinction made by many information-processing theories between automatic and strategic processing. They suggest that the dissociation just discussed can be accommodated best by distinguishing not between perceptual and memory processes, but between passive automatic aspects and active strategic aspects of both encoding and retrieval. A bias in the passive automatic aspect of processing need not entail a bias in active strategic aspect of processing, and vice versa.

Evidence that it is necessary to assume two independent aspects of processing arises from many sources. Among the most compelling sources are results from perceptual memory tests (sometimes referred to as implicit memory or indirect tests of memory). In one such paradigm, subjects are presented with a list of words, and later given a threshold test in which they have to identify a larger set of words, each presented for 35 msec. They find it easier to identify words they have seen before, even if they cannot pick out which words were "old" in a conventional recognition test. Similarly, if presented with the first few letters of a word and asked to use the letters to think of any word that could complete it, subjects tend to complete it with a word they have seen recently. Once again, this bias is independent of the subjects' ability to recognize which words they have been shown previously.

Tests of implicit and explicit memory have shown that they react differently to depth of processing manipulations. Graf and Mandler (1984) presented a list of words to subjects who were asked a question of each word, either about the structure ("How many T junctions are there in the word?") or about the meaning ("Is it a pleasant word?"). Normally, such an encoding manipulation has a large effect on later retrieval. Subjects can recall many more of the words that were processed semantically. Graf and Mandler (1984) replicated this "depth of processing" phenomenon, but found that the depth to which a word had been processed made little difference in the implicit memory performance (subjects were given the first three letters of some six-letter words and asked to complete them). Both structural and semantic encoding were equally likely to bias the subject's later word completion. (See Chapter 2 for a discussion of the theoretical issues involved in the field of implicit memory.)

Williams and co-workers (1988) used the distinction that emerged from experiments such as these to explain the dissociations that were arising in anxious and depressed patients' performance on different types of tasks. The attentional tasks that had been used to study anxiety were similar to the perceptual threshold tasks that had been used to study implicit (perceptual) memory. The memory tasks that had been used to study depression were similar to the depth of processing paradigms that were used to study explicit memory. Following Graf and Mandler (1984), Williams and his group distinguished between two processes that operate on mental representations—*priming* and *elaboration*. *Priming* is automatic, occurring because the processing of a stimulus involves automatic activation of the multiple subcomponents involved in the representation of that stimulus. The result is strengthening of the internal organization of the representation, making the word more accessible, that is, the word will come to mind more readily when only some of its features or components (e.g., initial letters) are presented. *Elaboration,* a more strategic process, consists of the activation of a representation in relationship to other associative representations to form new relationships between them and to activate old relationships. The result of the spread of activation to associates produced by this process of elaboration is to make the word more retrievable, because such elaboration generates new and reinstates old paths for retrieving the word (Williams *et al.,* 1988). This dual process account allows the following prediction to be made: anxiety makes certain items more accessible, whereas depression makes certain items more retrievable. Accessibility and retrievability may be uncorrelated because they depend on these different processes. Biases in anxiety and depression may be independent because anxiety primarily reflects differences in priming processes and depression primarily reflects differences in elaboration processes.

Whether one is trying to explain bias in priming or in elaboration, each stage of processing needs to (a) be able to assess the affective salience of an item and (b) be able to allocate the resources toward (or away from) the item for extra (or less) processing of it on the next perceptual encoding cycle (Neisser, 1976). Williams and associates (1988) distinguished such *affective decision* from *resource allocation* (see Fig. 2). Directed allocation of resources at the priming stage of processing can be assessed by such tasks as the visual dot-probe, in which attention seemed to have been pulled toward or away from the location of threat. Directed allocation of resources at the elaboration stage can be seen in free recall tasks, in which the number of negative words recalled reflects the ease with which mnemonic structures were available or constructible at encoding and retrieval to help or hinder the elaboration processes.

One advantage of a model that differentiates between initial priming and subsequent elaboration is that it maps onto the clinical distinction between anxiety (largely characterized by hypervigilance) and depression (largely characterized by rumination about losses, procrastination, and inertia). Anxiety, in everyday living, helps a person anticipate and avoid danger. It makes sense that the system underlying anxiety should include, as one component, a mechanism that reacts rapidly to even a partial representation of a possibly threatening stimulus. On a busy road, it makes sense that part of a car seen on a blind corner activates the representation of the whole vehicle. In the wild, it is adaptive that the tail of a snake or the ear of a tiger should represent the whole. The organism may need to take quick avoidance action, so there is little reason (at that time) to recruit a further strategic system that would elaborate the stimulus. Such elaboration might interfere with the actions necessary for escape.

In contrast, the problems that cause or maintain depression do not require quick avoidance or escape. Depression represents the maladaptive end of a continuum, the adaptive end of which is concerned with helping individuals come to terms with losses, disengage from past sources of reward, and gradually re-engage in alternatives. Depression is therefore a response to an event or a series of events that, in the long term, will require strategic problem-solving behavior rather than immediate escape or avoidance. It is not surprising, then, to find that depressed people do not show enhanced "pick up" of negative information. It is more adaptive for depression to involve a system that allows for strategic retrieval of previous problem-solving attempts and their outcomes.

We now turn to the question of how to model, computationally, these processes underlying anxiety and depression. First, however, we introduce the general concepts of modeling in general and connectionist modeling in particular.

## Connectionism and Psychopathology

In this section we look at how the behavioral data reviewed in the last section could be simulated within the framework of parallel distributed processing (PDP) or connectionism (McClelland & Rumelhart, 1986; Rumelhart & McClelland, 1986). (See Chapter 6 for detail on the parallel distributed processing framework.) We shall introduce briefly those concepts that will be central to our discussion of how to model emotional disorders. After some brief comments on modeling dysfunctional behavior, we will suggest how the approach of Cohen and Servan-Schreiber (1989) may be extended to provide an implementation of the functional level model of depression and anxiety proposed by Williams et al. (1988).

### Parallel Distributed Processing

Connectionist models can be described in terms of the processing units they employ, how the units are put together to make a network (i.e., their topology), and how or whether the models learn (Hanson & Burr, 1990).

#### Units

A connectionist unit is an idealization of the way an individual neuron functions (see Fig. 1). A unit has input lines (the dendritic arbor) that carry information from other units, and output lines (axonal tree) that convey information to other units. Input lines carry weights (synapses) that modulate the inputs. An input line carrying a positive weight is said

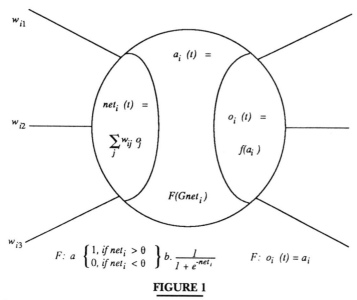

$w_{i1}$

$w_{i2}$

$w_{i3}$

$a_i\ (t)\ =$

$net_i\ (t)\ =$

$\sum_j w_{ij}\ o_j$

$F(Gnet_i)$

$o_i\ (t)\ =$

$f(a_i)$

$F\colon a\ \begin{cases} 1, \ if\ net_i\ >\ \theta \\ 0, \ if\ net_i\ <\ \theta \end{cases}\ b.\ \dfrac{1}{1+e^{-net_i}}$  $F\colon o_i\ (t) = a_i$

**FIGURE 1**

A standard connectionist unit. $w_{ij}$, Weight from unit $j$ to unit $i$; $net_i(t)$, net input to unit $i$ at time $t$; $o_j$, output from unit $j$; $o_i(t)$, activation of unit $i$ at time $t$; $F$, activation function, $a$, binary threshold, or $b$, sigmoid function; $G$, gain parameter; $o_i(t)$, output of unit $i$ at time $t$; $f$, output function (simplest is output = activation).

to be excitatory. An input line carrying a negative weight is said to be inhibitory. Whether a unit is active depends on its net input (a weighted sum of the inputs) and the unit's activation function. Different models may employ different activation functions. Perhaps the simplest activation function is a binary threshold. If the net input exceeds the threshold, the unit turns on (activation 1); if not, it stays off (activation 0). More complicated functions include the sigmoid function that produces a continuous output between 0 and 1. In summary, connectionist units are very simple processors. They achieve their computational power by working collectively. The kinds of collective computations they can perform depend on how they are connected to form a network, that is, on the topology of the network.

### Topology

Network topology or connectivity describes which units are connected to which other units. For some applications, this description will include a specification of which units are able to take inputs from outside the network and which produce the output of the network. All units can be connected to each other, in which case the network is totally connected. Total connection allows activation to flow through the network in arbitrary directions. Perhaps the most frequently used structure, however, is the feedforward network, which only allows information to flow in one direction. Two distinct pools of units are recognized in these networks: input units and output units. Any other units in the network are called hidden units. When hidden units are present, the networks are known as multilayer networks. These networks are especially important, since development of learning algorithms for such networks (Rumelhart, Hinton, & Williams, 1986a,b) enabled PDP to transcend the limitations of an earlier period of connectionist research (Rosenblatt, 1962; Minksy & Papert, 1969).

### Learning

The memory of a network is embodied in its synaptic weights. Learning therefore involves the modification of these weights. In every network, the weights (along with the activation function and the network topology) determine the outputs that are produced by the inputs. In some applications, we want to teach the network to produce a particular output. In other applications, we simply want to store information about an input. In yet others, we may want to classify inputs without any prior conception of how the classification should be achieved. In all cases, during the training phase, on being presented with an input, the weights on the connections between units are modified in accordance with a learning rule. The principle advantage of connectionist models is their ability to program themselves to perform a variety of tasks without the intervention of a programmer.

Connectionist models, although highly idealized, nonetheless may capture important aspects of biological reality, thus providing the possibility of modeling the interface between cognition and its biological substrate. In the next section, we describe how the functional level model of the effects of emotional disorders on cognitive processes just reviewed (Williams et al., 1988) may be implemented in a connectionist framework. A functional level "model" specifies what the mechanism ought to do, without indicating how it should be done. The possibility provided by PDP for building a bridge between functional level description and biological hardware is one of the most exciting aspects of the approach.

### Modeling Dysfunctional Behavior

Modeling dysfunctional behavior has pursued a particular methodology. A model of normal function on a particular task is constructed first. Then some intervention is carried out and the effects on the network's subsequent performance is observed. For example, in Hinton and Shallice's (1991) model of acquired deep dyslexia, a network was constructed first that successfully maps words to their meanings. This model then was "lesioned" selectively to mimic the damage found in neuropsychological patients. The performance of the lesioned network then was compared with that of the unlesioned network. A similar methodology was adopted in Cohen and Servan-Schreiber's (1989) model of cognitive deficits in schizophrenia. Rather than lesion the network, however, the gain parameter was turned down in a subset of units in the model. The gain parameter multiplies the net input, either increasing (gain > 1) or decreasing (gain < 1) the chance of firing. This intervention was treated as analogous to the biological effects of dopamine deficiency.

We approach the modeling of depression and anxiety in a manner similar to that of Cohen and Servan-Schreiber (1989). We will identify various unit parameters that, when varied, may emulate the effects of depression and anxiety in the performance of various tasks. However, in this brief chapter our concerns will be more with general design principles than with modeling particular task performances. We will present a general outline of how cognitive deficits in depression and anxiety may be implemented. We begin by outlining the functional level analysis of depression and anxiety put forward by Williams and colleagues (1988).

### Functional Level Analysis

Figure 2 summarizes the functional level model of the relationship between cognition and emotion (Williams et al., 1988). The model concentrates on the differential effects of anxiety (Fig. 2A) and depression (Fig. 2B). In both cases, the model also distinguishes between the effects of transient mood states and more enduring emotional traits. Anxiety and depression reflect affective decision making and resource allocation processes that operate at different processing stages in the cognitive system. Thus, the main components of the model are, at each processing stage, an affective decision mechanism (ADM) and a resource allocation mechanism (RAM). Anxiety operates at the preattentive stage whereas depression acts at the elaborative stage. At each stage, a decision is reached concerning the threat or negativity value of an event, which in turn affects the way resources are allocated to processing that event. The relationship between high and low threat or negativity and resource allocation at either stage depends on the individual. In "normal" individuals, it is assumed that the affective decision matches the threat value or negativity value of the stimulus. However, in individuals suffering from a state disorder, the affective decision mechanisms are biased so the outputs from the ADMs are abnormally high, mimicking the effects of either a high threat or a highly negative stimulus. Trait effects are explained in terms of enduring tendencies to react to the output of the ADMs in particular ways. In response to negative or high threat output, an individual may direct attention

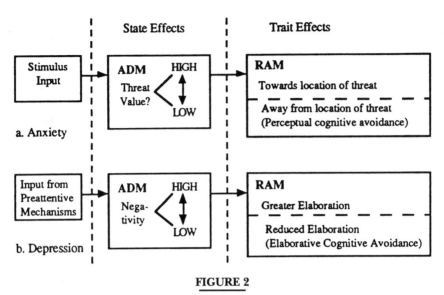

**FIGURE 2**

The Williams et al. (1987) model of state and trait effects in anxiety (A) and depression (B).

toward or away from the threat. Trait anxiety is associated with an enduring tendency to allocate excessive resources to processing a perceived source of threat. Similar effects occur at the elaborative stage with high negativity items leading to either increased or reduced resource allocation. Clinical depression may be associated with an enduring tendency toward greater elaboration of negatively perceived stimuli, and reduced elaboration of neutral or positive stimuli.

The principal aim of the Williams group model was to provide a general framework in which to understand emotional effects on cognitive processes. It does so mainly by showing how the emotions, particularly emotional disorders, may affect the ability to access and retrieve information from memory. Note that the model describes how these disorders may best be viewed in terms of the inappropriate biasing of mechanisms that normally perform important adaptive functions. In the following sections, our aim will be to arrive at a biologically principled account of how such biases emerge. We now discuss how the Williams group model could be implemented in a neural network.

## Connectionist Implementation

We begin with the assumption that the dual processes of the Williams group model can be captured by two separate theoretical neurotransmitter systems. The two theoretical neurotransmitter systems we describe are not intended to map directly onto known biological systems. Thus we will be working on an idealization of biological reality, but nonetheless with building blocks that have known biological correlates.

### Dissociation and Modulation

We suggest that emotions have their effects through a system secondary to the primary systems responsible for learning and memory. Neurotransmitters can have primary effects in synaptic transmission but also can have a variety of secondary modulatory effects on a neuron. (See Shepard, 1988, for a review.) In accounting for the pattern of dissociation observed in anxiety and depression, we will invoke two theoretical secondary messenger systems that serve to modulate individual neurons. We suggest that anxiety is due to abnormalities in the F system (F represents the three Fs: fear, flight, and fight), whereas depression is due to abnormalities in the H system (H represents hedonic). Each system possesses associated theoretical neurotransmitters. The F system involves a single neurotransmitter, which we label $T_f$; the H system involves two complementary neurotransmitters, $T_{h+}$ and $T_{h-}$ (positive and negative hedonic tone, respectively). We propose that release of $T_f$ is implicated not only in, for example, initiating rapid avoidance action, but also in suppressing the plasticity of surrounding synaptic connections, that is, it serves to suppress learning. Therefore, although a given unit may be "on," associations will be less well learned. Distributions of $T_{h+}$ and $T_{h-}$ modulate the likelihood that given units will come on. For example, neurons that have many receptor sites for $T_{h+}$ participate in encoding positively hedonically toned objects or events. These neurons also release $T_{h+}$ when active, thus increasing the probability of other positively toned items being activated.

The core idea behind the implementation is that the modulatory function of neurotransmitter systems can be modeled in terms of the effects these substances have on the parameters of individual units. As Cohen and Servan-Schreiber described (1989; see also Servan-Schreiber, Printz, & Cohen, 1990), these parameters have the effect of potentiating or depotentiating certain subsets of units, that is, making them more likely to turn on. The main distinction between the F and the H systems is determined by the timescale on which they work. We will discuss the H system first.

### The H System

We will discuss the operation of the H system in the context of a standard constraint satisfaction network of the type used in Rumelhart, Smolensky, McClelland, & Hinton's (1986c) on-line schema model. Such models encode the likelihood of features co-occurring in the weights connecting the units. When a unit encoding a feature is clamped on, those feature units that are most likely to co-occur with it will gradually switch on in accordance with the units' activation function. At the same time, those units that are most unlikely to co-occur with the original unit will switch off gradually.

Such a network typically encodes semantic knowledge, for example, that bathrooms contain baths, sinks, and toilets. However, we also want to encode the hedonic relationships between contents. Such relationships may cross-cut semantic relationships. For example, "table" and "chair" are semantically related structurally because they can be subsumed under the superordinate category "furniture" and lexically because they share many prototypical features, for example, made of wood, has legs, and so on. However, "table" and "moon" may become positively hedonically related because an innately pleasurable experience was had at the table under the moonlight. Although semantically unrelated either structurally or lexically, these contents may be related by such an experience in such a way that, in some circumstances, one may become an effective retrieval cue for the other.

As we have suggested, in the brain these hedonic processes may be implemented by the neuromodulatory functions of neurotransmitters. In a model, they can be conceived of best in terms of a secondary "hedonic" network that interacts with the primary "semantic" network. An additional set of connections reflects the hedonic relationships between units (see Fig. 3). Hedonic inputs to each unit are grouped into two pools: negative tone inputs ($T_{h-}$) and positive tone inputs ($T_{h+}$). The net hedonic input is the difference between the sum of the weighted inputs to each pool

$$net_h = |\alpha \Sigma h+_i - \beta \Sigma h-_i| \tag{1}$$

where $h_i = w_{ij}(h) o_j$, $w_{ij}(h)$ is the weight on the hedonic connection from the $j$th to the $i$th unit, and $o_j$ is the output of the $j$th unit. $\alpha$ and $\beta$ are parameters that reflect the concentrations of $T_{h+}$ and $T_{h-}$.

The time course of activity in the hedonic connections is slower than in the semantic connections. This can be modeled by making the hedonic outputs of a unit less responsive than the semantic outputs. The following output function makes the responsiveness of the network dependent on the parameter $\epsilon$:

$$o_i(t) = o_i(t-1) + \epsilon[a_i(t) - o_i(t-1)] \tag{2}$$

Equation 2 says that the current output at time $t$ [$o_i(t)$] depends on the previous output [$o_i(t-1)$] and the difference (positive or negative) between the current activation [$a_i(t)$] and the previous output weighted by $\epsilon$. If $\epsilon$ is less than 1, then changes in activation from $t-1$ to $t$ will be less than perfectly mirrored in the output. In other words, the hedonic outputs would react more slowly to changes in activation than the semantic outputs for

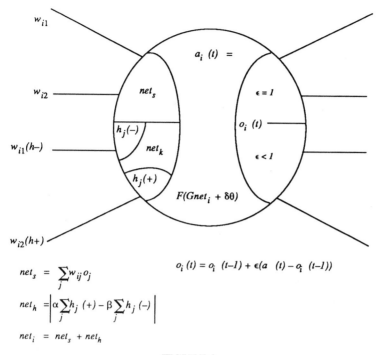

$$net_s = \sum_j w_{ij} o_j$$

$$net_h = \left| \alpha \sum_j h_j(+) - \beta \sum_j h_j(-) \right|$$

$$net_i = net_s + net_h$$

$$o_i(t) = o_i(t-1) + \epsilon(a_i(t) - o_i(t-1))$$

**FIGURE 3**

A connectionist unit modified to incorporate the modulatory effects observed in anxiety and depression. $w_{ij}(h-)$. Weight on the negatively hedonically toned connection from unit $j$ to unit $i$; $w_{ij}(h+)$; weight on the positively hedonically toned connection from unit $j$ to unit $i$; $h_j(-)$; weighted negatively hedonically toned input from unit $j$; $h_j(+)$; weighted positively hedonically toned input from unit $j$; $net_s$, net semantic input; $net_h$, net hedonic input; $\epsilon$, responsivity parameter; $\delta$, attention parameter.

which $o_t = a_t$, that is, $\epsilon = 1$. In consequence, affective signals could endure longer than normal activation in order to influence subsequent processing when a stimulus is removed, so potentiating effects will endure longer for units that are related hedonically also.

The parameters $\alpha$ and $\beta$ are central to our account of depression. They reflect the concentrations of $T_{h+}$ and $T_{h-}$. High levels of $T_{h+}$ ($\alpha > 1$) will lead to the greater potentiation of units that are positively hedonically related. High levels of $T_{h-}$ ($\beta > 1$) will lead to the greater potentiation of units that are negatively hedonically related. Normal subjects, if anything, tend to be biased toward the retrieval of positively hedonically toned material. In this model, this is reflected by an $\alpha$ value normally greater than 1 and a $\beta$ value normally less than 1.

## F System

In a network, recognition and recall involve the same basic processes of content addressability, whereby the activation of a subset of features representing an object or event will be sufficient to retrieve the whole representation. That neural networks provide content addressable memory systems always has been one of the psychologically most appealing properties (see Rumelhart & McClelland, 1986). The distinction between recognition and recall depends only on the source of the partial memory probe, that is perceptual systems (recognition) or some other part of the cognitive system (recall).

As we have defined it, priming is simply content addressability. Priming is therefore a part of the normal function of network memories. Priming, however, could not occur equally for all stimuli in the environment. Stimuli that are in focal attention demand more priming. Similarly, those events that, for one reason or another, need attention also will require more priming than events that are not or need not be attended to currently. One reason an object or event would need to be attended to is that it is a potential source of threat. Thus, anxiety may be regarded as part of normal attentional mechanisms with certain physiological side effects.

Some work has been done on attention in neural networks (Grossberg, 1982,1987; Spitzer, Desimone, & Moran, 1988; Phaf, Van der Heijden, & Hudson, 1990). Generally, it is agreed that specific representations are, in some way, potentiated so they are more likely to be instantiated than other representations. We can see how such a system should work by considering a search problem. In your work room you are searching for the stubby, cross-headed, red-handled screwdriver. It would assist in this search if the units representing these features (and whose conjoint activity forms the distributed representation of this object) were potentiated relative to the representation of, for example, the small, round, green-topped jar containing the hand cleanser. If this were not the case then, on scanning the room, picking up the features green-top and round would be as likely to instantiate the representation of the jar as picking up the features stubby and red-handled would be to instantiate the representation of the screwdriver. Clearly, for attentional purposes, a semantically selective potentiation is required so, for example, the representation of the screwdriver is given a selective advantage over the representations of the other items in the room.

Three other factors should be noted. First, especially in a search problem, it is important to encode the physical location of the object, once detected. The point of the search is rarely simply to confirm that, for example, the screwdriver is in the work room. The point is to locate it, pick it up, and use it. Second, the potentiation of the representation of the screwdriver need not endure much beyond successful location. Thus, the time course of attentional potentiation is likely to be rapid, so control can pass quickly to subsequent actions, for example, finding the 1-inch, cross-headed, steel screws. Third, since the goal is to locate an object, there is no need to establish further associations between the object and its surroundings. It is, for example, beside the point that the screwdriver is sitting next to the glue pot. Hence the representation of the screwdriver need not be elaborated, that is, new associations concerning its co-occurrence with other objects need not be encoded.

In anxiety, the locus of semantic selectivity will be determined by associations with physiological factors involved in avoidance behavior. This determination may be mediated by lower brain centers. However, for our current purposes, how the units making up a representation of an object or event are selected for potentiation will be ignored, not because these processes are deemed unimportant, but because, in network terms, it is a hard problem for which we currently do not have a solution. We concentrate instead on what occurs after selection.

As we have suggested, anxiety is mediated by the modulatory effects of a specific neuromodulator we have designated $T_f$. In other accounts, attentional processes also are mediated by the neuromodulators (Phaf et al., 1990). To account for the effects of $T_f$ concentrations, we choose to parameterize the bias term. The input to the activation function is as follows:

$$G net_i + \delta\theta \qquad (3)$$

G is the gain parameter that multiplies the net input ($net_i$). [This parameter was varied by Cohen and Servan-Schreiber (1989) in their model of schizophrenia.] $\theta$ is the bias term. The parameter $\delta$ captures the effects of $T_f$ concentrations. We could have allowed $T_f$ to affect G, as Cohen and Servan-Schreiber did. However, this would have meant that a unit could not be potentiated in the absence of other inputs. To capture attentional processes seems to require that units can be biased to come on, even with minimal inputs or, indeed, with none. When concentrations of $T_f$ are high, $\delta$ is greater than 1. As we will suggest, the tendency of normal individuals to avoid anxiety-evoking stimuli indicates that equilibrium levels of $T_f$ lead to $\delta < 1$. This would have the consequence that representations of anxiety-evoking stimuli are biased against coming on compared with nonanxiety-provoking stimuli (where $\delta = 1$). The time course of changes in $\delta$ depends on concentrations of $T_f$, which reduce rapidly when a stimulus is located.

$T_f$ also affects learning. In this brief proposal for how depression and anxiety may be accounted for in network terms, we have no specific learning rule in mind. However, all learning rules have the basic form

$$\Delta w_{ij} = \eta y \qquad (4)$$

where $y$ is the learning rule and $\eta$ is the learning rate parameter. We suggest that a side effect of high concentrations of $T_f$ is to turn down $\eta$, thereby suppressing the learning of new associations. Since only the units in the representation of selected objects or events are potentiated, these within-representation connections will be enhanced more than elaborative connections to other active representations. Thus, a stimulus representation may be primed without necessarily leading to enhanced elaboration.

### Return to the Functional Level

The unit and network properties outlined capture the essential characteristics of the Williams group's ADMs and RAMs at the two levels of processing they propose. We look at anxiety first.

Threat value assignment is determined by $T_f$ levels that in turn affect $\delta$ and $\eta$. High levels of $T_f$ lead to $\delta > 1$, which leads to potentiation and attention being directed toward the location of threat. Normal levels of $T_f$ lead to $\delta < 1$ for anxiety-provoking stimuli and, hence, to a lower likelihood of a unit coming on. When other stimuli are available, this will lead to attention directed elsewhere, that is, away from a source of threat. Location is a within-representation feature that also is potentiated strongly. However, associations with other aspects of the environment are less well learned because of suppression of the learning rate parameter $\eta$.

In depression, the situation is rather different. Representations of objects and events are related hedonically as well as semantically. Increased levels of $T_{h-}$, that is, high negativity value, leads to $\alpha > 1$ and, hence, to the potentiation of hedonically associated representations. This occurs over an extended time frame, because $\varepsilon < 1$. Thus, more negative items will be recalled to elaborate negative inputs. The normal bias of $\alpha < 1$ and $\beta > 1$ leads to less elaboration of negative stimuli in normal individuals (a self-serving bias).

In this framework, the distinction between automatic and strategic processes is reflected in the time course of potentiation. Priming acts rapidly to ensure that objects are recognized and located as quickly as possible. However, once located, attention must pass equally rapidly to appropriate action. In contrast to these rapid processes, the hedonic relationships between contents slowly create a hedonic context that biases retrieval toward hedonically related material over an extended period.

## Clinical Implications

We have, in this chapter, presented experimental evidence that the cognitive biases evident in anxiety and in depression arise from different aspects of the information processing system. Anxiety is associated with hypervigilance to some aspects of the environment, a phenomenon that can be modeled experimentally using the emotional Stroop test (e.g., Watts, &

Sharrock, 1985) or the visual dot-probe task (MacLeod et al., 1986). Depression does not seem to be associated with such attentional bias but with bias in recollection. Whereas anxiety biases the automatic processing or priming of stimuli, depression appears to bias strategic aspects of processing, that is, elaboration. Also, this chapter has shown how such systems may be realized in an artificial neural network. Finally, we have shown how the mechanisms outlined could, in principle, account for the pattern of dissociation observed between anxiety and depression.

To see how a connectionist model of these cognitive processes could be implemented, we proposed two separate theoretical neurotransmitter systems, specifically, theoretical secondary messenger systems that act to modulate individual neurons. These systems were not intended to map directly onto known systems, but it is interesting to note how much actual biological systems do correspond to these theoretical constructs. The evidence for the role of neurotransmitters in depression and anxiety derives largely from work on the influence of drug treatments. (For a review, see Lickey & Gordon, 1983; for less detailed overviews, see Bridgeman, 1988; Kolb & Wishaw, 1990.) Looking at depression first, antidepressant drugs (mostly tricyclics, tetracyclics, and monoamine oxidase inhibitors) both remediate the symptoms of depression and affect neurotransmitter systems. However, it remains unclear which system is responsible for which effects. The neurotransmitters dopamine, serotonin, and norepinephrine each have been implicated and, although most recent antidepressants have attempted specifically to target one system, there are complex interactions between systems that remain to be mapped. In this respect, it is interesting that our theoretical systems assume the interaction of a system concerned with negative hedonic tone with another concerned with positive tone. The model suggests that the degree of negative and positive mood may not always correlate in depression and is consistent with the clinical observation that anhedonia may not always be present in depression. It is more certain that there exists a dissociation between anxiety and depression at the neurobiological level.

In anxiety, different transmitter systems have been implicated. For example, anxiety has been associated with the inhibitory neurotransmitter gamma-aminobutyric acid (GABA). The molecular structure of benzodiazepines is very similar to that of GABA. Benzodiazepines appear to enhance the inhibitory effects of GABA (Gavish & Snyder, 1980). Thus, anxiety may be due to a release from inhibition by lowered concentrations of GABA. Also, the role of norepinephrine in anxiety has long been suspected. (Crow, 1968; for a brief overview, see Munro, 1986). This neurotransmitter is distributed throughout the brain from a local site called the locus coeruleus. Lesions at this site lead to decreased levels of norepinephrine and impair a number of tasks that depend on the organism's sensitivity to punishment or nonreward

(Gray, 1990). Moreover, neurophysiological evidence has shown that norepinephrine modulates neuronal plasticity in the rat hippocampus (Hopkins & Johnston, 1984). Munro (1986) simulated the effects of changes in neuronal plasticity by varying the learning rate parameter $\eta$. Similarly, we have suggested that the learning rate parameter $\eta$ is affected by varying concentrations of $T_f$.

In summary, there is evidence to show that the behavioral dissociation between anxiety and depression is reflected rather directly at the neurobiological level, and that the neurotransmitters that are implicated have the effects that the model requires.

Note that the computational modeling of these processes is still in its very early stages. We have not implemented particular tasks in which anxiety and depression reveal their opposite effects. Neither have we validated the model by showing that it behaves in a "human-like" way on these tasks when we vary the parameters to simulate anxiety or depression.

As Williams and associates (1988) indicate, it is most unlikely that anxiety never affects elaborative processes and depression never affects priming. There are many subtypes of anxiety and depression; the cognitive performance of each of these must be examined to define the limits of the model. The advantage of the model is that it allows for dissociation to occur, but does not require it. This gives us a framework within which other forms of psychopathology may be examined. For example, people who suffer paranoid states may be biased in both priming and elaboration. They are hypersensitive to signs of external hostility, and elaborate this hypervigilance into complex accounts involving the mafia, police, or CIA. Although a dual-process account seems irrelevant in a case in which both processes are biased, it may nevertheless be helpful for therapy to work on the assumption that bringing about debiasing in one aspect of processing may not affect the other aspect. Priming and elaboration processes may need to be addressed independently. This need to address both components of the cognitive system constitute one of the main therapeutic implications of the disassociation between priming and elaboration. A similar distinction has been made by others. For example, Brewin (1989) distinguishes between "situationally accessible" and "verbally accessible" emotional memories in his account of how psychotherapy has its effects. His "situationally accessible" memory maps closely onto our account of automatic priming and his "verbally accessible" memory maps onto our account of elaboration.

The aim of computational modeling is to make cognitive models more precise, not to derive clinical implications directly. The clinic is too complex an environment to be captured by models of the emotional states of the individual anxious or depressed patient who attends. Let us consider one example. Equation 1 for determining the net input to a unit indicates that the potentiation due to negative hedonic tone may be counterbalanced by the association of positively toned material. At this level, it would suggest that attempting to associate positive events with events that presently elicit a depressive response may serve to reduce the negative event's potentiating effects for depressive material. Does this occur clinically? It can, and is built into therapy techniques such as coverant control and systematic resensitization (see Williams, 1992). However, the approach must be graded carefully so the amount of negative material is not so great that it swamps the mood and the amount of positive material is not so great that it appears implausible or too effortful for the patient to imagine.

A core feature of cognitive behavior therapy with depressed patients is the teaching of skills to help distance themselves from their negative thoughts and interpretations long enough to reevaluate the objective evidence. Sometimes the objective evidence will be very negative. Reality is often bad for many people who come for help with emotional problems. Even then, however, the emotional disturbance itself usually affects the individual's judgment in such a way that their problem-solving skills are reduced, and the extent to which they blame themselves unfairly for their predicament is increased. Cognitive therapy has an important role in allowing people to see even a bad reality more clearly.

For example, a woman with few opportunities to go out because of her poverty and child rearing responsibilities is very likely to become depressed when further negative events arise. The effect of a depression will be to cause catastrophization and overgeneralization in thinking patterns. This means that she is very likely to interpret the fact that a friend has not been in contact for a while to mean that the friend is sick of her, and that *all* her friends are probably sick of her. Cognitive therapy does not deny the importance of the poverty and child rearing responsibilities in the onset of her depression, and will try to increase her coping skills by helping her "hear" when the depression is "talking" and set up experiments to test the belief that her friends have deserted her. Should this prove to be the case, the focus of therapy can become that of making new friends. Should the experiment show that the friends are still available, the patient will have learned something about how the plausibility of the negative self-talk in depression can be undermined. In the terms of our model, the ability of one negatively termed event to activate other associated negative events will have been reduced.

Further, the effect of negative mood to potentiate all negative memories also will have been reduced by such procedures. This may prove to be the critical difference between antidepressant treatment and psychological treatment for depression. Antidepressant treatment alters the amount of neurotransmitters available at synapses, altering the balance of positive and negative tone, but antidepressants do not affect the topology of the network unless the individual takes advantage of the improved mood to engage in pleasurable activities despite their previous negative associations. If the individual does not take such advantage, the result will be that, when the antidepressants are withdrawn, relapse or recurrence will be very probable. In fact, this is precisely what occurs in a large proportion of depressed patients. In contrast, relapse rates following treatment with cognitive behavior therapy are significantly lower (see Williams, 1992). Future work will need to examine how relapse prevention measures may be added to antidepressant treatments. The advantage of having a model that attempts to make precise predictions about such manipulations is that we will be able to simulate the interaction of drug treatments and therapies that change other parameters of the model prior to such clinical work. It is the interaction of these two domains which remain one of the most exciting areas of contemporary cognitive science.

# 8

# Integrative Action of Narrative

**Keith Oatley**

*Center for Applied Cognitive Science*
*Ontario Institute for Studies in Education*
*Toronto, Canada*

## Introduction

The narrative form is used frequently in neurology and psychiatry, when physicians take histories, when psychoanalyses unfold, and as epidemiological studies are undertaken. The common element is that narrative is the principal vehicle that people use to explain action, its reasons, and its consequences. In cognitive science, narratives have been treated as goal-based and as having problem-solving motifs. Emotions tend to occur at junctures—when problems arise and the protagonist does not know how to act. Neurology and psychiatry can be seen properly in a similar way, not simply in terms of the determinism of mechanisms of neural functioning or early upbringing, but in terms of how intentions are formed, how actions are taken, and how consequences occur. In this interpretation, narrative has a force not of mere story telling, but of the means by which reasons, actions, and consequences are related and understood, by oneself or by others. In this chapter, three types of study are considered. One of Freud's psychoanalytic cases provides the first example, one of the studies of Brown and his colleagues on the epidemiology of depression provides the second, and some of the cases and conclusions of Sacks' neurological work, the third. The conclusion is that narrative is not just a vehicle by which a patient may address a clinician, or a clinician address a readership. It nearly defines what neurology and psychiatry are principally about, namely, the problematics of action in a world in which voluntariness is constrained by limited resources and the outcomes of action are uncertain.

## Narrative and Problem Solving

Narrative has been important in clinical practice since early times. Here, for instance, are the first sentences of a case history from a physician's notes from classical Greece

"A woman at Thasos became morose as the result of a justifiable grief, and although she did not take to her bed, she suffered from insomnia, loss of appetite, thirst and nausea. She lived on the level ground near Pylades' place." (Chadwick & Mann, 1978, p. 134)

Like other stories, this one begins with a setting, Thasos, and the habitation near Pylades' place. The central character, a woman, is introduced. She encounters vicissitudes: a justifiable grief and falling into moroseness. This history goes on to describe how she suffered convulsions and a fever before reaching a crisis. The series in which this case occurs is called *Epidemics Book III*. It is believed to have been written in the fifth century BCE (before the Common Era) and is in the Hippocratic body of writings. The stories in *Epidemics Book III* are about the courses of individual cases of infectious diseases. As stories they leave something to be desired, because there are only two plots. One is exemplified by the case history of the woman from Thasos. The patient recovers following a *krisis*, which had the ordinary Greek meaning of a point of judgment or decision and the technical medical meaning of a turning point at which a fever may resolve. In the other plot, the patient dies.

One can assume that physicians 2400 years ago, as now, found that the story form was a natural means of representation. No doubt they first heard what had happened in this same form. In this form, too, they recorded and published their own accounts. In modern clinical practice, narrative remains a medium in diagnosis, in publication, and in teaching medical knowledge.

In cognitive science there has emerged a theory of what narrative is and how it is understood. One of the first theories (Rumelhart, 1975) remains one of the best. Rumelhart suggested that stories have a structure, and can be analyzed in terms of a schema or as a kind of grammar. Stories do not have syntax in the same way that sentences do; a number of people have objected to the idea of story grammars on these grounds (e.g., Johnson-Laird, 1983). However, most agree that stories typically have recognizable constituents and constraints. Many narratives start with a setting and a central character whose actions and experiences will constitute the main plot. Actions are connected by a plan with a goal. Rumelhart points out that stories tend to have a problem-solving motif, that is, the central character's plan meets vicissitudes. These vicissitudes often give rise to emotions. The resolution of a story then consists of solving or transforming the problem, ideally in a way that is not obvious to the reader. In a short story, there may be one episode of this kind; in a novel, there are usually many, with each problem being transformed to give rise to another. Problem solving has been a central concern in cognitive science, so the problem-solving motif connects story understanding to this concern.

Clearly, case histories of the kind that the Hippocratic physician wrote in *Epidemics Book III* conform to the pattern described by Rumelhart, although they lack the literary element of subtlety of plot. This same pattern has been maintained in the more recent clinical applications of narrative. The question I will address in this chapter is, "What are we to make of this story form?"

Is the story form merely a convenient vehicle for conveying information in which first something happens, then something else, then something else that is problematic? Is it merely a means for conveying temporal sequence in a way that is well understood by clinicians and lay people alike and carries, in addition, the idea of problem solving of the kind that occurs in diagnosis? If this were so, we would conclude that stories are sometimes convenient but scarcely of theoretical importance in understanding clinical disorders. The important focus would be on mechanisms of healthy functioning and of disease. As the understanding of these mechanisms improved, we would find the story form replaced in medicine by writing of a kind suitable for communicating scientific and technical knowledge. For such purposes, stories would become not only old fashioned, but perhaps actively detrimental to scientific thinking (cf. Nisbett & Ross, 1980).

The displacement of stories by technical writing has indeed occurred in descriptions of diseases and in the contents of textbooks. We might conclude that narrative form may have some mild historical interest, or even that it may still be useful for purposes of communication with lay people or neophytes. The inclinations of scientists, however, are to take mechanisms seriously but discount mere stories. If practitioners in psychiatry and clinical psychology still traffic in stories, it is because the scientific principles of their disciplines are not as advanced as those in microbiology, oncology, or immunology.

## Stories and Mechanisms in Psychiatry

In psychiatry, the narrative form takes on other functions in addition to communication of the sequence of events in an illness. Ever since Freud asked each patient in analysis "to give [him] the whole story of his life and illness" (Freud, 1905/1953, p. 16), narrative has become an essential element in many forms of psychotherapy.

Freud was explicit about the relationship of his accounts of cases to fiction. He said, "It still strikes me myself as strange that the case histories I write should read like short stories and that, as one might say, they lack the serious stamp of science" (Freud & Breuer, 1893,1895/1955, p. 160).

Freud seems to be expressing the common intuition that, whereas explanations of how mechanisms work are serious, stories are not. My proposal in this chapter is that something is awry in this intuition. If in psychiatry and clinical psychology we regard stories not merely as makeshift, it is because something other than mechanism is at issue, and it too must be taken seriously. Narrative is the means by which we can understand human action in a way that is not captured in analysis of mechanisms.

Twenty years after his confession of unease with the story form, Freud was more confident and put forth the following argument, that is, told an allegorical story, in a passage from the *Introductory Lectures*:

> Suppose that one dark night I went to a lonely spot and was there attacked by a rough who took away my watch and purse. Since I did not see the robber's face clearly, I laid my complaint at the nearest police station with the words: "Loneliness and darkness have just robbed me of my valuables." The police officer might then say to me: "In what you say you seem to be unjustifiably adopting an extreme mechanistic view. It would be better to represent the facts in this way: 'Under the shield of darkness and favoured by loneliness an unknown thief robbed you of your valuables.' In your case the essential task seems to me to be that we should find the thief. Perhaps we shall then be able to recover the booty." (Freud, 1915,1916/1963, pp. 45–46)

In this passage, Freud points to a conception that is different from the mechanistic. In psychiatric cases, he proposes, what is wrong does not have much to do with mechanistic events such as darkness. The problems of psychiatry are better analyzed in terms of a deliberate agency of a human kind, for example, a thief. Psychiatric complaints are about the vicissitudes of voluntary agency, of other people treating patients in ways they resent, of experiences that they did not wish for, of being unable to cope however much they try, or of finding themselves acting repetitively but in ways inconsistent with their view of themselves. For voluntary human agency and its vicissitudes, it is arguable that narrative points to a proper means of understanding, not just until neurobiology has advanced a bit further, but permanently. In this case, we may look to cognitive science and ask what is understood about narrative and its implications in diagnosis, epidemiology, and psychotherapy.

To approach these questions I will first address plans, why they are problematic for humans, and how problems are the central pivots around which plots turn. Then I shall introduce and employ some cognitive scientific understandings of narrative, discussing examples from each of three areas in which narrative form is of continuing importance—psychotherapy, epidemiological studies of life events causing psychiatric breakdowns, and neurological disease.

## Plans and Plots

If plots in stories derive their coherence from plans of one or more characters, what is known in cognitive science about such plans? A plan is a sequence of actions to achieve a goal. It usually is assembled symbolically using some kind of simulation procedure. If human beings were gods, with perfect knowledge, unlimited power, and infinite resources, there would be no narratives, although there might be technical descriptions of how to assemble such plans. Artificial intelligence provides glimpses of what such descriptions might be like for the actions of robots in limited domains (e.g., Fikes & Nielson, 1971). For gods and properly functioning robots, plans run as anticipated. Only among humans is action taken apparently voluntarily, but with resources and knowledge that are so limited that the outcome is often unpredictable (cf. Simon, 1967; De Sousa, 1987).

In the human case, plans do not always achieve the desired goal. Human plans meet problems that often elicit emotions. Variations on the sequence "plan–vicissitude–emotion–problem-soving attempt" are the stuff of stories. We can imagine that the human fascination with narrative occurs partly because the problems involved are just beyond the capacity of our cognitive systems. Stories are about things happening that were not foreseen or could not be controlled, of people who may or may not be trustworthy, or of irreconcilable conflicts of goals. As we read or listen, we think about how we would approach these problems, and we look forward to seeing how the person with whom we have identified in the story is going to act.

Perhaps the first insight of cognitive science in this area is that, when we understand a story and its world, we create a mental simulation. We run the character's plan in the simulation space of our own mind. Our ability to do this speaks to the existence of mental planning structures, and the ability of mental schemata to construct possible worlds.

Our abilities to plan can thus be used in two ways. When we wish to act, we run our planning routines in a forward direction, imagining a sequence of actions that will achieve a goal. When we understand a story, we can run these routines in reverse (cf. Wilensky, 1983). We take a sequence of actions as described in a story, infer which plan could connect them meaningfully, and consider which goals were achieved. More remarkable yet, when we do this, we use ourselves to simulate the character whose actions are being described. We personally experience emotions resulting from the plan and the events that result.

An early version of this idea was proposed by Aristotle in his *Poetics*, in which he described a play as a simulation (*mimesis*) of actions. We can make a good case that Aristotle was an early cognitive scientist; certainly he was moved by many of the same concerns that inspire modern cognitive scientists. He formulated some of the basic ideas, notably the idea of functionalism, that the same function could be achieved in different embodiments. If this seems an anachronism, we could certainly maintain that notions of *mimesis*, of tragedies having narrative structure, and of the audience being moved by emotions derived from plots, were conceived by Aristotle and followed up in the cognitive revolution. As a result of the invention of computers, the functionalist idea could be explored. We can see that the problem solving that is inherent in action perhaps can be done by silicon-based machines as well as carbon-based ones.

For an Aristotelian or a cognitive scientist, the issues for understanding action and the portrayal of action in story form are the same. Human plans are limited by human knowledge and resources, and these limitations set the problems that we struggle to understand. For clinicians, such problems are also those for which people make consultations.

In addition to the consequences of action being beyond human capacity to foresee or control, another problem is familiar to clinicians and novelists. Human goals may sometimes be unconscious. To act with full conscious intention means that one has a conscious goal, and enacts a plan calculated to achieve that goal, knowing that one has the necessary resources. In ordinary life, able-bodied adults can speak correctly of intending to make an omelet but not of taking a round-trip to Saturn. Sometimes in clinical disorders, people intend things they cannot achieve or seem to act with only partial intent, achieving some outcome without a conscious goal. These, too, are among the traditional concerns of fictional narrative.

The contribution of cognitive science to these problems has not been simply to assert that psychiatric syndromes often can be understood in terms of the goals and plans of a protagonist, although this idea is important (cf. also Schafer, 1976). It has been to show what is involved in understanding a plan as a narrative. I shall illustrate this concept with one of Freud's early case histories, the case of Miss Lucy R. (Freud & Breuer, 1895) and with Wegman's (1985) cognitive analysis of the case.

## Freud: The Case of Miss Lucy R.

Miss Lucy R. was a British governess. For several years she had looked after the two daughters of a wealthy widower, the managing director of a factory in outer Vienna. Freud begins his story by saying that this woman was referred to him by a colleague who had been treating her for a recurrent infection of the nose. At the end of 1892, new symptoms appeared. Freud's colleague surmised that these were not due to her infection.

Freud takes over. He diagnoses depression. Most strikingly, he describes an unusual and unmistakably psychiatric symptom. In addition to a loss of the sense of smell, which seemed to be hysterical, the woman suffered from an olfactory hallucination that tormented her—the smell of burned pudding.

Freud engages the reader with a problem to solve, a problem of the kind that physicians confront many times each working day, but Freud, the consummate storyteller, also confronts the reader with a mystery. What are we to make of a 30-year-old governess, of somewhat delicate constitution, suffering from a hallucination of burned pudding?

Miss Lucy told Freud her story over a period of therapy that lasted, intermittently, for 9 weeks. Freud retells it to his readers. He has his own story to tell, and he interweaves it with Miss Lucy's. Freud's story is that he was not very good at hypnosis, and often could not get it to work. For his purposes, he decided that he could get along without it. One means he used was to allow his patient to maintain her ordinary waking state. Then, if there was something missing from her story that was essential to understanding it, something that she claimed not to know, he would place his hand on her forehead. Then he would say that when he released his hand an idea or image would come to the patient's mind. This image would restore a forgotten memory, and fill a gap in the narrative.

After trying hypnosis with Miss Lucy to no avail, Freud tried his method of pressing and releasing pressure on her forehead. He did this as he asked her to say what was associated with the smell of burnt pudding. A memory emerged of a scene in which she was playing at cooking with the two little girls who were her charges, and the postman arrived bearing a letter. She was in time to recognize the handwriting of her mother and the postmark from Glasgow, before her two charges playfully snatched the letter, saying that she was not to have it until her birthday, in two days time. While the children were playing this game, there occurred a strong smell. The pudding they had been making was burning. "Ever since this," said Miss Lucy, "I have been pursued by the smell. It is there all the time and becomes stronger when I am agitated" (Freud & Breuer, 1895/1957, p. 114).

In stories, protagonists encounter problems about how to act, and readers encounter problems in trying to understand the narrative in terms of a coherent plan of the protagonist. In Freud's cases, there are additional problems of understanding because the patient leaves gaps in the story. Freud had discovered a wonderful method. A patient who is, at the same time, the protagonist tells her story; understanding her problems of action converges with the problem of understanding the narrative. With his method of asking for associations, with or without pressure on the forehead, Freud could ask the patient for memories or images of events that might fill those gaps that were simultaneously making the person's life problematic and making the story difficult for Freud to understand.

Freud questioned Miss Lucy, "What could it be about [the scene of cooking pudding] that made it so agitating?" (p. 114) Miss Lucy said she was moved by the children's affection. Ill feeling had begun in the house when the housekeeper, the cook, and the French governess intrigued against Miss Lucy for having ideas above her station, and they had made allegations to the children's grandfather. Miss Lucy did not receive as much support as she expected when she complained to her employer and the children's grandfather. So she had given notice. Her employer had urged her to take several weeks before finally deciding, and it was in this state of uncertainty that the incident had occurred.

The children's mother had been a distant relative. Miss Lucy said, "I had promised her on her death-bed that I would devote myself with all my power to the children, that I would not leave them, and that I would take their mother's place with them. In giving notice I had broken this promise" (p. 115). This agitated her when she thought of leaving her position.

Freud talked about the progress made by this clarification, and the way in which the unusual choice of the olfactory system as a vehicle for a hysterical hallucination perhaps was prompted by her infection of the nose. As yet, however, the understanding was incomplete. Moreover, the symptoms remained. Other than some slight remission in the intensity of her hallucinations, Miss Lucy's problems remained unresolved, and her depression was unabated.

Next, Freud gives us a brief tutorial about what to do when, in therapy, something still seems missing from a full understanding. He says that when a hysterical symptom is acquired for the first time, some idea is intentionally repressed from consciousness. What was this idea in Miss Lucy's case?

As in a good detective story, all the clues are available, although their significance is not understood. However, they are present in the analysis. They are present, too, in Freud's case history, and I have been careful to include them in my abbreviated account. To be more explicit, here is a list of the significant clues. A 30-year-old woman supports herself as a governess in a foreign city away from her close relatives; a wealthy man is widowed and has two affectionate children; an unpleasant intrigue concerning the governess getting above herself was mounted by colleagues; a vow not to leave the children but to take their mother's place and a decision to leave were made.

How do we interpret these clues? What Freud decided was this: "I believe that really you are in love with your employer, the Director, though perhaps without being aware of it yourself, and that you have a secret hope of taking [the children's] mother's place in actual fact. And then . . . ," added Freud, "You're afraid of [the servants] having some inkling of your hopes and making fun of you" (p. 117).

With no ado, Miss Lucy said, "Yes, I think that's true." When asked why she had left such a significant gap in the narrative, since this would have made sense of it, she said, "I didn't know, or rather I didn't want to know. I wanted to drive it out of my head and not think of it again; and I believe latterly I have succeeded" (p. 117). Freud says approvingly in a footnote to this page that he never managed to give a better description than this of the strange state of both knowing and not knowing something, and that one cannot understand it unless one has experienced such a state oneself.

Miss Lucy explained how impossible it would be for a poor girl such as herself to marry a rich man of good family. She explained that she had lived in the house happily for several years, free from unattainable desires, but her love began when one day her employer, who had always been a reserved man, had said to her how much he depended on her for looking after the children, and looked at her meaningfully. She allowed herself to dwell on hopes, but when there was no further development she decided to banish the whole idea from her mind.

Freud said that he had expected that now that the roots of her trauma had been exposed, there would be an improvement. There was none. So, as in the best stories, we find ourselves again in uncertainty.

Freud's argument was that hysterics leave gaps in their stories because of repression. Something must be kept out of mind; therefore, it does not appear in the story. To make sense of the story, the omitted material must be discovered and, in its discovery, not just the story but the patient is made whole. She or he can again act with a unity of intention and self-understanding.

Still, Miss Lucy's symptoms did not clear up, and Freud expressed dissatisfaction. Then, after an interruption of treatment due to a recurrence of Miss Lucy's nasal infection, she returned to say that the smell of burned pudding had disappeared to be replaced by another smell, of cigar smoke, which she thought also might have been there previously, although masked by the pudding smell. Again Freud applied his mnemonic hand to Miss Lucy's forehead. The scene she recalled, dating from 2 months before the scene of the burned pudding, was of a family meal at which she and the

French governess were present, as well as the two children, the Director, and the children's grandfather, with a guest and old family friend, the firm's chief accountant. When the accountant rose to leave, he went to kiss the children, and the Director flared up and shouted, "Don't kiss the children" (p. 120). Miss Lucy said she felt a stab at her heart. The smell that now afflicted her was the smell of the cigars that the gentlemen had been smoking after dinner.

Freud applied his hand once again to Miss Lucy's forehead, and at last the mystery was solved. In a scene yet earlier than the meal with the accountant, Miss Lucy remembered a lady who had come to visit her employer. As she was leaving, the lady had kissed the two children on the mouth. After the lady left, Miss Lucy's employer flew into a rage and threatened to dismiss her if ever she let anyone kiss them again.

It was this, proposed Freud, that had been the traumatic moment at which her hopes of a development in her relations with her employer had been crushed. She had been longing for more tender intimations. Instead she suffered a humiliating threat of dismissal at a trivial incident for which she was not even responsible. The memory of the scene with the accountant was a repeated stab at her heart, because her employer's shouting at the accountant so closely matched the outburst at herself when the lady visitor had left.

Wegman's (1985) contribution has been to show how, in order to understand the episode of the lady visitor, some of the processes of computational story understanding proposed by Schank and Abelson (1978) can be employed.

Schank and Abelson describe a representation called a script, a structure of a temporal sequence of actions and events. The idea of a script often is introduced using the example of what happens at a restaurant: one enters, orders food, eats it, pays, and leaves. In Western culture, a storyteller need merely mention going to a restaurant, and the reader mentally summons his or her restaurant script and will be able to make inferences based on it. (See also Bower & Morrow, 1990, for the kinds of inferences that come automatically to mind during understanding.) If, in a story, a character is described as eating in a restaurant and finding that she has no money, we will infer that a serious situation has arisen, because in the restaurant script the knowledge is represented that a bill will be produced that the character has a legal obligation to pay.

Much cultural knowledge, we can argue, is represented in terms of scripts. These structures allow inferences that are essential for understanding, but do not have to be described in detail by the storyteller. Part of the pleasure of reading is to make such inferences from the barely necessary clues given by the author. If the author were to indicate all possible implications of every situation and action, then stories would be impossibly tedious.

To create a program for story understanding would involve using ideas of universal story structure and formalizing some specific cultural knowledge about the world in which the story takes place. A computer program in which this was done would then become a simplified paradigm of the ordinary understanding process, although within a limited domain. Wegman points out that Freud's activities in understanding Miss Lucy's story are not different from this generalized understanding process. They are similar to what would occur in a computer program for narrative comprehension. The task for any understanding is that of using representations of knowledge to make necessary inferences from barely sufficient clues in the narrative.

For the visit of the lady to Miss Lucy's employer, for instance, Wegman points out that a visit script would be invoked. What do we know about visits? They involve arrival, conversation, and a parting. Could kissing the children at the end of the lady's visit be interpreted as a parting ceremony? Scarcely, says Wegman, because, if so, the storyteller would not mention it: We know that some ceremony ends nearly all visits. If the storyteller mentions kissing, we know it must be significant in some other way. To find out how it might be significant, a story understanding program based on Schank and Abelson's work would mark this incident as "weird," and look for other information about kissing to explain why it was mentioned. It might find that kissing could be a mild health threat, a means of affirming an affectionate relationship, or an erotic action. Without further evidence, however, understanding would be suspended at this point, awaiting some later clarification.

Then, says Wegman, a story understanding program would try to make sense of Lucy's employer becoming angry. Again, it would search in the narrative for a goal of the angry person that had been violated. A well-constructed program would also have some stored knowledge about emotions, for example, the person at whom anger is directed is likely to be responsible for a goal violation that has caused the anger.

Freud's contention was that hysterics left gaps in their narratives, and that his principal job as analyst was to make inferences about what might fill them. What emerges from cognitive analyses of narrative, such as Wegman's, is that any understanding of a narrative involves inferences based on cultural knowledge. The step taken in computational story understanding is making certain pieces of cultural knowledge explicit, but this same kind of knowledge and comparable inferences are needed for any kind of story understanding.

All stories have gaps. All stories require readers constantly to make inferences. Freud's claim amounts to saying that the gaps left by hysterics are larger than usual, because hysterics are unconscious of some of their goals. These hysterical gaps are the ones he would fill, but his methods were entirely similar to those later formalized by Schank and Abelson as being necessary for any kind of story understanding.

Freud wrote that, after Miss Lucy had recalled the lady's visit, the moment when her hopes had been extinguished and she tried to put the whole idea out of mind, her condition improved. Two days after she had recalled this scene and Freud had made his interpretation of it, she appeared at the consulting room smiling, with her head held high. Freud asked whether the Director had asked her to marry him. She said nothing had happened, that she was normally a cheerful person, and she had awoken the day before with a weight lifted from her mind. "And are you still in love with your employer?" asked Freud. "Yes, certainly I am," she replied, "but that makes no difference. After all, I can have thoughts and feelings to myself" (p. 121). Freud reported that 4 months later he met her by chance, at "one of our Summer resorts," and found her in good spirits with her recovery maintained.

As we try to understand Miss Lucy's story, we can infer that a reason that the wealthy widower may have become angry at the lady for kissing his children was that he thought that the lady might have matrimonial plans aimed at him and his fortune, and that she might see a relationship with his children as helpful in fulfilling her goal. The mystery of Miss Lucy's depression, Freud guessed, was connected to this same idea. Her employer's rage had crushed her. Freud filled a gap by inferring that her response might have been because she had started to entertain affectionate longings toward her employer. When something quite the opposite of affection occurred in her employer's angry outburst, we can search our representations for what we know about the predicament of governesses in the 1890s, and see how the employer might have guessed at the intention of his lady visitor, and might easily have become angry at Miss Lucy as well, obliquely letting her know that he would not allow her any approach through his children. We can only speculate about whether he wanted also to remind Miss Lucy of her subordinate position on which he wanted to depend without any reciprocal demands or implications, or whether he was unaware of how his previous confiding in her could have been experienced as encouraging.

What is achieved by a cognitive, or knowledge-based, approach to such cases, is the realization that a general theory of narrative understanding is possible (cf. Oatley, 1990). Analyses, whether by literary critic, by psychotherapist, or by cognitive scientist, have certain features in common. These features include the idea of plots as the plans of the story's characters that readers or hearers simulate in their own minds, of the inferences that are the bases of understanding, and of the vicissitudes in a plot as problems that are just beyond ordinary human resources to foresee and, in tragedies, beyond any solution whatever.

The suggestion of psychoanalysis is that much of what people consult psychiatrists and psychologists about is not disorder of mechanism but, as one analyst (Szasz, 1961) has stated, problems in living. For such problems, we can argue, the narrative form based on goals, plans, and problem solving as explicated in cognitive science is an appropriate representation. In contrast, the graphs, equations, diagrams, and technical recipes of natural science are appropriate to understanding mechanisms.

## Clinical Depression and Problems in Living

One of the pathologies of clinical psychology is overgeneralization. For instance, Szasz (1961) claimed that not only some but all psychiatric syndromes are problems in living. This idea is balanced only by the opposing overgeneralization by some neuroscientists that all mental illnesses are primarily disorders of mechanism. An unaddressed issue is what syndromes, and with what kinds of prevalence, might be primarily problems in living, and what proportion is primarily disorders of mechanism. This question is epidemiological. It is unanswerable from either the couch or the neurochemical laboratory.

A large step in understanding the epidemiology of psychiatric disorders was taken when research diagnostic interviews of adequate reliability were developed (e.g., Wing, Cooper, & Sartorius, 1974). For the first time, these interviews allowed estimates of prevalence of psychiatric syndromes in the community. For instance, the lifetime prevalence of schizophrenia, which many believe to include a disorder of neural mechanisms although not exclusively dependent on such a disorder, is on the order of 1% worldwide, with no large differences as a function of culture or sex. For depression, however, the prevalence in Western industrialized societies is on the order of 10% in any given year, and women are about twice as likely as men to be at the case level. In addition to international differences in prevalence of depression, there are large differences in prevalence as a function of social class (Brown & Harris, 1978) and of living in cities as opposed to rural areas (Brown, Davidson, Harris, Maclean, Pollock, & Prudo, 1977). Perhaps most striking are the threefold differences in the prevalence of nonpsychotic psychiatric disorder (largely depression) as a function of being married as opposed to unmarried. Men are about three times more likely to be depressed if unmarried than if married. For women, the pattern is reversed; they are three times more likely to be depressed if married than if unmarried (Bebbington, Hurry, Tenant, Sturt, & Wing, 1981). These large differences suggest that depression is more affected by the way in which people live than by some primary dysfunction of neural mechanisms.

The work that established a social origin of most cases of depression was that of Brown and Harris (1978). They found, in a community survey of 458 women in Camberwell in London, that 8% had an onset of depression within the year prior to interview. A further 7% had been depressed for more than a year, 1% had a chronic anxiety syndrome, and 0.5% had some other chronic nonpsychotic psychiatric condition. Of the onset cases of depression, 89% had suffered a serious problem within 38 weeks before symptoms occurred. Among women who were not depressed, only 30% had experienced serious problems.

Brown and Harris defined two kinds of problem capable of provoking depression: acute events that were severely threatening and chronic difficulties of a major kind. Acute problems included bereavements, life-threatening illnesses to someone close, separations, and losses of employment when prospects of re-employment were minimal. Major chronic problems, which had lasted at least 2 years in order to be categorized as such, included living in squalid and cramped accommodation, coping with a violent husband or a chronically sick child, or having children constantly in trouble with the police.

Brown and Harris found, however, that not everyone who suffered such a problem became depressed. Some women had protective factors in their lives that included having the social support of someone, typically a spouse or a lover, in whom the woman could confide and having a job outside the home. Only women who suffered a severe problem and were without a protective factor had depressive breakdowns. Oatley and Bolton (1985) reviewed nine other cross-sectional studies with adequate methodology conducted in England, Canada, and the United States. With some variation of the factors that were protective, all studies confirmed that severe events and major difficulties can cause depression.

From the work of Brown, Harris, and others who have used similar methodologies, we can begin to answer the question about the proportion of depressive breakdowns due to problems of living in the following way. Psychotic breakdowns are rare, and happen to only about 1% of the people at any time in their lives. Nonpsychotic breakdowns are common. At any one time, about 10% of an urban population has a nonpsychotic psychiatric syndrome. Although many of these syndromes include anxiety symptoms, virtually all involve depression when they begin. About 90% of such syndromes are precipitated by a problem in living. The other 10%, then, are possibly due to a primary disorder of mechanism. Although lack of some factors that are protective against the impact of life problems could also be due to mechanisms, and perhaps be genetically based, a large majority of people who suffer psychiatric breakdown would not have broken down if a problem in living, a severe event or major chronic difficulty, had not occurred.

The use of the narrative form has made this work on etiology in terms of problems in living possible. For each potentially severe event or difficulty, the interviewer collects information from the sufferer about what occurred and when. This biographical information is termed the "context." This context is read to a group of researchers, who are blind to the diagnosis and who rate the severity of the event or difficulty. For each event, a rating of "long-term contextual threat" is made on a 4-point scale of severity of the threat, lasting more than a week, that would accrue to an average woman in that context, from such an event. For each difficulty, a similar rating is made on a 6-point scale. The ratings are made by consensus, using a set of principles evolved during the research and ratings of comparable incidents that have been collected previously and rated by the team.

The best analogy for this procedure is the action of the chorus in a Greek play, externalizing and discussing societal intuitions about the significance of what has happened. The procedure embodies the notion of *Verstehen*, understanding gained by entering imaginatively into the life of another person as one does when listening to a story. In Brown and Harris's version, since the ratings are blind to the interviewees' diagnoses, understandings are reached without contamination from any theory of the relationship of events and difficulties at breakdowns.

## Life Histories

The solutions that are possible for clinical problems are many. With ordinary medical histories, the problem is presented by the patient to the physician, who harnesses technology to provide a cure or a palliative. Psychoanalytic histories typically show how the psychotherapist allows patients to discover that the cure is largely in their own hands as they reappropriate a part of their life from which they had become alienated. From epidemiological psychiatry, we see that amelioration of some problems may require societal change, for example, in the relationships between men and women or between social classes. A further problem arises in the cases treated by the neurologist Sacks. With neurological illness, there is often no cure. If a medical intervention is available, it perhaps alters the balance between conflicting forces and leaves the question of amelioration open.

Sacks has shown how narrative is primary, even when neurological mechanism is at stake. Here, for instance, is a case from Sacks on migraine.

> This 32-year-old man was an ambitious and creative mathematician whose life was geared to a weekly psychophysiological cycle. Toward the end of the working week, he would become fretful, irritable, and distractable, "useless" at anything save the simplest routine tasks. He would have difficulty sleeping on

Friday nights, and on Saturdays would be unbearable. On Sunday mornings he would awaken with violent migraine, and would be forced to remain in bed for the greater part of the day. Toward evening, he would break out in a gentle sweat and pass many pints of pale urine. The fury of his sufferings would melt away with the passage of these secretions. Following the attack, he would feel a profound refreshment, a tranquility, and a surge of creative energy which would carry him to the middle of the following week. (Sacks, 1971, p. 47)

Sacks creates for the resolution of the migraine a new term, comparable to the Hippocratic "crisis," designating a more gradual resolution, with cathartic properties—"lysis." The course of this disease provides another plot in the book of medical narratives.

More significant however, is a growing recognition of a different kind of relationship between mechanism and narrative. Sacks expounded this in a recent article 20 years after his first publication of this case.

When I "cured" this man of his migraines, I also "cured" him of his mathematics. Along with the pathology, the creativity also disappeared, and this made it clear that one had to inspect the economy of the person . . . One has to inquire into the entire human drama that surrounds the attacks, to explore what they might mean in a particular person. One has to take not just a "medical" history, but to try to construct a complete human narrative. (Sacks, 1990, p. 45)

Sacks (1976) went on from his book on migraine to *Awakenings*, the moving stories of a few survivors of the epidemic of *Encephalitis lethargica* that occurred between 1917 and 1927. Following their infection these people had fallen into a suspended state with a Parkinsonian postencephalitic syndrome. In 1969 Sacks, using the dopamine precursor L-DOPA, was able to afford an awakening to some of these people whom he found languishing in a chronic hospital where he was working. What is made clear in *Awakenings* is that, in this kind of neurological syndrome, there are no drugs that cure. It is a deep misunderstanding of neurological, physiological, and psychological principles that L-DOPA or any other drug acting on neural transmitter systems has a specific curative action and regrettable side effects that will be fixed by a little more research in neuropharmacology. Thus, for instance, the mechanism of neuroleptic drugs used in the treatment of schizophrenia is thought to involve dopamine antagonism (Crow, 1985), but this assumption carries a risk, frequently realized in long-term treatment of schizophrenia, of inducing motor disorders of a Parkinsonian kind. L-DOPA is a drug with an opposite effect. A potentiation of dopamine action occurs that is capable of augmenting the action of a depleted number of cells in certain parts of the extrapyramidal motor system, hence waking patients out of frozen immobility. This therapy, however, also stimulates propensities to tics and unwanted actions of all kinds, to compulsions, to hallucinations and delusions, and even to frenzies of uncontrolled and discoordinated movements.

To suffer neurological damage is an accident of fortune that profoundly affects one's embodiment. It is an accident, like the accident of birth. It confers certain abilities and disabilities. It is like a hand of cards, predisposing toward some possibilities and blocking off others. A neurological illness or accident diminishes resources; however, at the same time the sufferer must shape his or her personhood and create a life from the embodiment that is left. What a drug does in such circumstances, and what Sacks presumably did for the mathematician with migraine, is to change the balance of resources. By rearranging resources, the drug sets a new problem to the patient, of how to shape personhood from a somewhat different endowment, one that is pharmacologically supported.

Some diseases now can be made to retreat entirely. No doubt many of the infections described by the Hippocratic doctor would now be cured by antibiotics. Even now, however, cures are not available for some viral illnesses, such as HIV. Sacks has shown that when disease cannot be abolished, what is at issue often is not simply the causal processes of mechanism, and not entirely the intentions that can be related in narrative form in psychotherapy. At issue is a rapprochement, an accommodation between the constraints of mechanism and the infinities of what can wished for or intended. In *Awakenings*, Sacks quotes Leibnitz:

> I find indeed that many of the effects of nature can be accounted for in a twofold way, that is to say, by a consideration of efficient causes and again independently by a consideration of final causes. Both explanations are good . . . for the discovery of useful facts in Physics and Medicine. And writers who take these diverse routes should not speak ill of each other . . . The best plan would be to join the two ways of thinking. (Sacks, 1976, p. 264)

Mechanism and narrative may require quite different mental operations to understand them (Bruner, 1986). Narrative is our way of accounting for effects "by a consideration of final causes," that is, of purposes and intentions. It is the joining of "the two ways of thinking" to which Sacks has been led to understand what goes on in his patients, as they, in the struggle with their disease, encounter the necessity of making some similar rapprochement between mechanical causes and personal intentions. The question for the patient is how to create a self from the resources available. The problem for the physician is to understand this, and perhaps help rearrange these resources, be they pharmacological, environmental, or personal. As soon as Sacks has pointed it out, it becomes obvious that this rearrangement, or something like it, must be at the center in every neurological case, whether treated by drugs or not.

Here is another of Sacks's descriptions, of a patient Rose R., with a postencephalitic syndrome dating from 1926. She was awakened by L-DOPA in 1969, and found the augmentation of her dopamine mechanisms intolerable.

"I can't bear it," she said, "everything is gone." And her "awakening" had a deeply anachronistic quality: she spoke of figures from the 1920s as if they were still alive; she had mannerisms, turns of phrase, that had been obsolete for 40 years, but still seemed entirely current to her. She said, "I *know* it's 1969, but I *feel* it's '26. I *know* I'm sixty-four, but I *feel* I'm twenty-one." And she added, "I can't bear the present time—all this television, trash, nonsense. None of it means anything to me." And, perhaps in accordance with this state of mind, she suddenly ceased to respond to L-DOPA, and reverted again to the catatonic state she had been in for forty years; nor were we ever able again, by chemical means, to make any change in her condition. (Sacks, 1990, p. 46)

For most of Sacks's patients, a period of awakening and return to health was followed by tribulation, as aspects of disease asserted or reasserted themselves. For some, health was sustained although never by means of the drug alone. One patient (Miron V.) at first did very badly on L-DOPA, with violent oscillations between frenzy and stupor, but when Sacks was able to set up for him a cobbler's bench in the hospital, so that he could again do the work he had once loved, and when he was again reunited with his family, this "gave him back a firm base of identity and health, and alleviated the violent physiological oscillations he had been having" (Sacks, 1990, p. 46).

Sacks went on in his 1990 article to explain that one way of seeing neurological syndromes is that a symptom such as a catatonia, a compulsion, an inhibition, or a tic is an unintegrated element in the person's life. It has no place in the person's sense of voluntariness or self. Often symptoms such as Parkinsonism, multiple sclerosis, dementia, or the effects of accidental brain damage can take over the larger part of a person's life. "Health," says Sacks, "is infinite and expansive in mode, and reaches out to be filled with the fullness of the world, whereas disease is finite and reductive in mode, and endeavors to reduce the world to itself" (1976, p. 272). The effects of a malfunctioning mechanism squeeze out, as it were, the person, but in certain kinds of activity health is restored, as if the personal is reasserted. The person reaches out to the world and embraces it. This can occur when a person becomes centered in a way of life and can integrate neurological resources into a larger scheme, as occurred with Miron V. This can also occur by domesticating a symptom, which another of Sacks's patients, Miriam H., showed. She was able, at one point, as she struggled to contain the effects of L-DOPA treatment, to convert a tic into a movement to adjust her spectacles. Integration may come from art—from music, painting, literature—or from play, or from ritual or drama. One patient, Leonard L., who, at 27, had been prevented by the effects of his disease from finishing his Ph.D. at Harvard, experienced under L-DOPA a joyful awakening from an almost complete catatonia. The awakening lasted just a few weeks and gave way to an accelerating plethora of needs, compulsions, hallucinations, manic impulses, and motor symptoms that all fell into obeyance when for 3 weeks, for 12 or 15 hours a day, he typed almost ceaselessly with two dystrophic fingers a 50,000-word autobiography, a narrative of his life and tribulations, showing "for the most part an extraordinary humor, detachment, and passion for accuracy" (Sacks, 1976, p. 250).

For the person who becomes engaged in them, work, art, play, and ritual can take an individual up into the activity. Perhaps people can become fully themselves when engaged in some such activity. Interacting creatively with a medium, attending at some performance, and engaging with other people involve the self. This interacting self also shapes the activity of the brain. It becomes the integrating center. Symptoms become peripheral or may recede altogether.

To make sense of these phenomena, Sacks rejects the Cartesian dualism of the purposeful mind steering a mechanistic body. Rather, the mind and body are one, which helps explain how, in the postencephalitic patients with extensive damage to extrapyramidal neurons, an activity that involves the self could act just as powerfully as a drug, more powerfully, in a sense, because selfhood is the creation of meaningful organization. A drug merely affects some neurons but not others. It is unregulated by the usual homeostatic processes and it is not subject to the usual adjustments or specificities of naturally released transmitter substances.

The self is created from embodiment and the surrounding world. Sacks draws his theory from a number of sources, including the work of Bartlett, who showed that remembering, including the remembering on which one's sense of self is based, is not simply

> the re-excitation of innumerable fixed, lifeless, and fragmentary traces. It is an imaginative reconstruction, or construction, built out of the relation of our attitude towards a whole active mass of organized past reactions or experience, and to a little outstanding detail which commonly appears in image or in language form. (Bartlett, 1932, p. 213)

This structuring of remembering and acting is based on schemata, which are active organizations "of past reactions, or of past experiences, which must always be supposed to be operating in any well-adapted organic response" (Bartlett, 1932, p. 201).

As Sacks proposes, "schemata," perhaps the central concept of cognitive science, also should be the central concept in neurology. Not only do schemata organize experience but, as Sacks found in his neurological patients, they organize the brain and are capable of so doing even when terrible neurological damage has occurred. Without such organization, the responses of postencephalitic patients to L-DOPA were merely chaotic movements.

Sacks draws on the theory of Edelman (1987) that groups of neurons become organized during development to create structures, categories, and abstractions. Neurophysiological evidence, from Gray and Singer (1989) among others, is consistent with this view. This work, although very new, provides a link between clinical observations, cognitive theory, and neurophysiology. As we create the structure of a life, and as we take part in an engaging activity of art or interaction, the structuring that the brain accomplishes also can come to integrate those parts or modes of brain activity that are liable to fragmentation or disintegration.

Of course, a person's life is not a narrative, but narrative is the way in which we can describe to ourselves and to others the idea of personal coherence in the worlds of love, work, accomplishments, and disappointments. Without such a sense of coherence, a life can become "a tale told by an idiot, full of sound and fury, signifying nothing" (Shakespeare, *Macbeth*, 5, 5).

Narrative is *the* primary model that we have of the integration of human action. As Aristotle remarked in the *Poetics*, in a well-constructed drama all the parts fit together in such a way that if one is removed or dislocated, the whole suffers. By relating a series of actions to intentions, by tracing the results of an intention to an outcome, by understanding an emotion that may result and the resolutions that may occur, narrative becomes the means by which we can begin to glimpse the possibilities of wholeness in human life.

In psychotherapy, and in ordinary life, narrating one's story to another person may itself be the means of healing or attaining integration. In epidemiological psychiatry, narrative has become the means by which we begin to understand the etiology of the most prevalent psychiatric syndromes, and can perhaps begin to integrate individual plights with the need for social change. In neurology, it is narrative, of the kind that Sacks has written, of people with damaged brains, that begins to allow glimpses of the situation of all of us, embodied in a neurological mechanism. In health, this mechanism is one that we ourselves partially shape, like a narrative, by our intentions, the actions we undertake, and the lives we create, but in disease, this mechanism is subject also to limitations and malfunctions that can threaten the integrative effects and draw off action into symptoms.

# 9

# Cognitive Science and Psychotherapy: An Epistemic Framework

**William J. Lyddon**

*Department of Psychology*
*University of Southern Mississippi*
*Hattiesburg, Mississippi*

Epistemic Contexts
Cognitive Psychotherapy and Epistemology
    Rationalist Approach
    Empiricist Approach
    Constructivist Approach
Role of Epistemology in Psychotherapy
Implications and Future Directions
Concluding Remarks

The cognitive revolution and its sequelae constitute one of the most significant conceptual shifts in late 20th-century psychological science (Weimer & Palermo, 1973; Dember, 1974; Gardner, 1985; Baars, 1986). Not only have cognitive theories come to pervade psychological research on learning, memory, motivation, personality, and social psychology, but the recent emergence of the field of cognitive science underscores a common interest in cognitive constructs among such diverse disciplines as linguistics, anthropology, philosophy, computer science, and psychobiology (Zimbardo, 1985; Posner, 1990). Paralleling these general intradisciplinary and interdisciplinary trends, the impact of "cognitivism" on the domain of psychotherapy has been particularly dramatic. During the past decade, a myriad of cognitively oriented theories and therapies has become a prominent feature of the psychotherapeutic landscape (Kendall,

1983; Cormier & Cormier, 1985; Dryden & Golden, 1986; Ingram, 1986; Dobson, 1988; Freeman, Simon, Beutler, & Arkowitz, 1989).

Although the relatively brief history of cognition in psychotherapy has been characterized by significant conceptual development and differentiation, relatively little consideration has been given to the role of epistemology in contemporary cognitive approaches to change. Epistemology is the study of knowledge and knowing (Mahoney, 1991) and seeks to address fundamental questions related to the sources, nature, and validity of knowledge. In spite of the fact that epistemology traditionally has been under the purview of philosophical rather than psychological inquiry, the emergence of the cognitive perspective in psychology and the evolution of the interdisciplinary field of cognitive science have contributed to a greater convergence of philosophical and psychological thought (cf. Weimer, 1977; Flanagan, 1984; Gardner, 1985; Baars, 1986). Not only is philosophy the oldest of the cognitive sciences, but its epistemological branch has helped identify some of the fundamental issues studied by empirically oriented cognitive scientists. Gardner (1985), for example, contends that the field of cognitive science reflects

> ... a contemporary, empirically-based effort to answer long-standing epistemological questions—particularly those concerned with the nature of knowledge, its components, its sources, its development, and its deployment. (p. 6)

An important consequence of the significance of epistemology in cognitive science is an acknowledgment among cognitive scientists that their explicit cognitive theories and models of mind are anchored by a host of implicit epistemological assumptions about the human knower, knowledge, and knowing processes (cf. Weimer, 1979; Fodor, 1983; Simon, 1983; Mahoney, 1991). Fodor (1983), for example, uses the term "epistemic boundedness" to underscore the idea that our epistemic assumptions constrain the kinds of things we can know and the beliefs we can entertain.

The notion that there is an inherent interdependence between epistemological commitment and scientific theory has led a number of biological, physical, and social scientists to examine critically the epistemic assumptions associated with contemporary scientific knowledge and methods of inquiry (Sampson, 1978; Koch, 1981; Gergen, 1982; Capra, 1983; Polkinghorne, 1983,1986; Howard, 1986,1991; Varela, 1986; Lakoff, 1987; Stam, Rogers, & Gergen, 1987; Lyddon, 1991a). The domains of psychotherapy and counseling have not been immune to such examination. Psychologists in these specialities have also begun to explore the philosophical commitments that may undergird their theories and therapeutic efforts (cf. Lyddon, 1988,1989a, 1990,1991b; Mahoney, 1991; Neimeyer, in press) as well as study individual variation in basic philosophical assumptions and how these differences may covary meaningfully with other cognitive, personal, and clinically relevant variables (Schacht & Black, 1985;

Johnson, Germer, Efran, & Overton, 1988; Lyddon, 1989b; Neimeyer, Prichard, Lyddon, & Sherrard, in press; Lyddon & Adamson, in press). Consistent with this trend, the primary purpose of this chapter is to provide an epistemic framework for understanding recent developments in the evolving intersection between the cognitive and clinical sciences. The guiding assumption throughout is that current cognitive approaches to change are epistemologically bounded in a specifiable manner. In particular, the suggestion will be made that contemporary cognitive psychotherapies may be differentiated with respect to their dominant epistemic commitments to rationalism, empiricism, or constructivism. To illustrate this point, the epistemic assumptions, cognitive emphases, and criteria for evaluating knowledge validity associated with these three epistemologies are outlined first. Then, paralleling these epistemic contrasts, three forms of cognitive therapy (rationalist, empiricist, and constructivist) are described with representative examples of each form evident in current theory and practice. The final section of this chapter will describe a number of implications of this framework for future research and theory building within the domain of cognitive psychotherapy.

## Epistemic Contexts

Central questions in the study of human knowledge and knowing include (1) Where does genuine knowledge come from? (the question of origins); (2) Is there a real world outside the mind and, if so, can we know it? (the question of appearance versus reality); and (3) How is truth distinguished from error? (the question of validity). Although philosophers historically have been divided on these issues, at least three prominent epistemic traditions may be identified: rationalism, empiricism, and constructivism.

### Rationalism and Empiricism

Disagreement over the relative importance of thought and experience in our ability to know has fueled a fundamental controversy in epistemology—the great debate between rationalism and empiricism (Gardner, 1985; Mahoney, 1991). Rationalism is based on the belief that knowledge emerges from self-evident a priori truths that are independent of experience. With conceptual roots in the classic Greek philosophies of Pythagoras, Plato, and Aristotle and in the 17th- and 18th-century philosophies of Descartes, Spinoza, and Leibniz, rationalism embraces the doctrine of rational supremacy, that is, the doctrine that reason and the "higher" intellectual processes should rule over feelings and actions (Mahoney & Lyddon, 1988). From a rationalist perspective, knowing is a deductive process in which ideas of reason and logic intrinsic to the mind are the primary sources of objective knowledge. Reality, the unchanging order behind the flux of everyday appearances, is only accessible by means of universal truths that are themselves unchanging and absolute. As a result, valid knowledge is that which is logically consistent and corresponds to authorized standards of truth and rationality.

In contrast, empiricism has its roots in the philosophies of Locke, Berkeley, and Hume and is a theory of knowledge based on the thesis that all knowing emanates from experience or through the senses. Empiricism presumes the existence of a single relatively stable external reality and characterizes knowledge acquisition as a gradual process of induction. According to this "received view," knowing involves a process of discovering and internalizing an external reality (Mahoney, 1991), a process limited only by the possibilities of experiment and careful observation. As a result, knowledge is deemed valid (or justified) by the degree to which it reliably maps the real world of verifiable observations.

## Constructivism

In contrast to the justificational claims of rationalism and empiricism, constructivism is a nonjustificational epistemic position based on the assertion that humans actively create their personal and social realities (Mahoney & Lyddon, 1988). Associated with a philosophical lineage that includes Vico's (1725/1948) *New Science* and concept of "imaginative universals," Kant's (1791/1969) treatise on the limits of derived knowledge, and Vaihinger's (1911/1924) neo-Kantian philosophy of "As If" (see Mahoney, 1988, for a detailed historical review), constructivism also is identified with the views of various contemporary psychologists, "experientialist" linguists, sociologists of knowledge, and symbolic anthropologists (Anderson, 1990). From a constructivist perspective, the primary source of knowledge is the human capacity for creative and imaginative thought, the ability to construct reality through symbolic means (language, myth, metaphor, or narrative). By suggesting that human knowledge, to a large extent, is invented rather than revealed through rational analysis or sense experience, constructivism presents a challenge to rationalist and empiricist claims about the attainability of objective and valid knowledge. More specifically, instead of establishing various validity criteria for objective knowledge, constructivists tend to view knowledge as inherently fallible. As a result, constructivists suggest that knowledge should be evaluated in terms of its current functional and adaptive value, that is, in terms of how well knowledge structures "fit" their changing contexts rather than how well they perfectly "match" (correspond to) either authorized rational standards or objectivist notions of external reality.

# Cognitive Psychotherapy and Epistemology

As previously noted, a primary purpose of this chapter is to suggest that recent trends of development in the cognitive therapies may be differentiated in terms of their dominant epistemic commitments. Paralleling the foregoing discussion on epistemology, rationalist, empiricist, and constructivist forms of cognitive psychotherapy are described in this section, along with representative examples of each form evident in current theory and practice.

## Rationalist Approach

Mahoney (1991) suggests that rational supremacy, the foundational doctrine of rationalism, lies at the core of the rationalist approach to cognitive psychotherapy and involves the following contentions:

> (1) thinking and reasoning can and should control or guide one's life; (2) irrational thought is dysfunctional; (3) psychological disorders are the expression, among other things, of irrational or unreasonable beliefs and images; and (4) effective therapy requires the identification and "correction" (for example, by rote substitution or reasoned argument) of irrational beliefs. (p. 132)

As previously noted, an epistemic commitment to rationalism presumes that valid knowledge is that which is logically consistent with authorized principles or "truths." In a similar fashion, rationalist approaches to cognitive psychotherapy assume that psychological adjustment is a function of the degree to which persons' beliefs are consistent with warranted criteria for "rational thinking." Although a listing of contemporary rationalist cognitive therapies would include cognitive appraisal therapy (Wessler & Hankin-Wessler, 1986), rational behavior therapy (Maultsby, 1984), rational stage-directed therapy (Tosi & Eshbaugh, 1980), and systematic rational restructuring (Goldfried, 1988), Ellis' rational-emotive therapy (RET; Ellis, 1962; Ellis & Dryden, 1987) is presented as an exemplar of a rationalist cognitive approach.

### Rational-Emotive Therapy

RET, especially in its "elegant" form (Ellis, 1980,1984a), is based on the assumption that at the root of many emotional and behavioral disturbances are evaluative cognitions that are fundamentally irrational. As Ellis (1989) states:

> the basic tenet of RET is that emotional upsets as distinguished from feelings of sorrow, regret, annoyance, and frustrations, *are caused* by irrational beliefs. (p. 207; emphasis added)

The RET standard for determining a rational or an irrational belief involves two interrelated criteria: (1) the *content* of one's thinking and

(2) the *style* of one's thinking. The content-based criterion defines irrational thinking by various lists of specific or general irrational beliefs (cf. Ellis, 1962,1979,1984b; Ellis & Harper, 1975; Ellis & Bernard, 1985), whereas the stylistic criterion defines irrational thinking in terms of its absolute and dogmatic qualities (Dryden & Ellis, 1988). In either case, these are not empirically derived criteria (cf. Sutton-Simon, 1980; Arnkoff & Glass, 1982) but have been set forth by Ellis and others as warranted standards for defining irrational (and, by implication, rational) thought.

Following from the presumed etiological relationship between irrational cognitions and emotional disturbance, one of the primary tasks of the rational-emotive therapist is to use reason and logical persuasion to demonstrate to clients how their irrational cognitions "create" or "cause" their emotional difficulties. Within a deductive framework, the rational-emotive therapeutic focus is on the correction of various irrational, dogmatic, and absolute premises that clients bring to and add to their interpretations of life events. The RET practice of critically challenging and reformulating these premises into new evaluative criteria, criteria that are consistent with authorized notions of rationality, underscores the epistemic commitment to rationalism of RET (Mahoney, Lyddon, & Alford, 1989; Lyddon, 1992).

## Empiricist Approach

As previously noted, an epistemic commitment to empiricism assumes that valid knowledge is a function of the accuracy of perception, that is, of the extent to which inductively derived observations correspond to external reality. In a similar vein, empiricist approaches to cognitive therapy tend to construe emotional and behavioral problems as directly related to the degree to which persons accurately perceive and interpret their experience. Salient examples of an empiricist approach to cognitive therapy include Beck's cognitive therapy (Beck, 1976; Beck & Weishaar, 1989) and contemporary information-processing models (Ingram, 1986; Winfrey & Goldfried, 1986).

### Beck's Cognitive Therapy

Cognitive therapy as conceptualized by Beck and his colleagues is founded on the premise that emotional and behavioral problems, particularly depression and anxiety disorders, stem from a person's inaccurate perceptions and "distortions of reality" (Beck, 1976; Beck & Emery, 1985). Recent conceptualizations of the model suggest that the human cognitive apparatus is composed of several interrelated coding systems that have adaptive and survival value. Beck and Weishaar (1989), for example, suggest that these systems

. . . are designed by evolutionary and developmental (learning) processes to select specific data, integrate them, interpret them, and store a selected sample.
The systems also draw on a specific memory residue to match with present experiences. (p. 22)

During periods of psychological distress, however, there is a "cognitive
shift" to a more "primitive" coding system that introduces a systematic bias
into inferences and interpretations of experiential data. These systematic
errors in cognitive processing are termed cognitive distortions and cate-
gorically include arbitrary inference, overgeneralization, selective abstraction, magnification or minimization, and dichotomous thinking.

Because cognitive distortions are presumed to be related functionally
to various forms of psychopathology, the primary aim of cognitive therapy
is to correct the patient's distorted inferences. Procedurally, this involves
therapist and patient participation in a process of collaborative empiricism
(Hollon & Beck, 1979; Beck & Weishaar, 1989), in which the patient's perceptions and beliefs are treated as hypotheses to be tested empirically. As
Beck and Weishaar (1989) point out

Collaborative empiricism engages the patient as a practical scientist who ordinarily interprets stimuli in a functional way but who has been temporarily
thwarted by the shift or bias in gathering and integrating information. The
therapist and patient work together in gathering evidence and testing hypotheses based on the patient's operating beliefs. (p. 30)

Similarly, Emery (in Beck & Emery, 1985) describes cognitive therapy as
relying on an inductive method in which

Patients are taught to consider beliefs as hypotheses, to pay attention to *all* available facts, and to revise hypotheses according to incoming data. They are also
taught to conduct experiments to test their hypotheses. The emphasis throughout therapy is on the patient's "getting the facts." (p. 188)

By challenging patients to code new information that is discrepant with ongoing beliefs about self and world, evaluative and discriminative functions
are expanded and a return to a "normal" coding system is established
(Beck & Weishar, 1989).

### Information-Processing Models

A dominant conceptual perspective in cognitive psychology is the information-processing paradigm (IPP). Ingram and Kendall (1986) state
that the IPP

. . . essentially conceptualizes the person as an information processing system
and focuses largely upon the structures and operations within the system and
how they function in the selection, transformation, encoding, storage, retrieval, and generation of information and behavior. (p. 5)

Although there are a number of cognitive approaches that operate under the umbrella of the IPP, most accounts employ a computer metaphor of human cognition and highlight the "inward" flow of information from the sense organs, its passage through a series of temporally defined stages of feature abstraction, and its subsequent storage in relatively static structures termed schemata (Lyddon, 1988). Schemata, in turn, are presumed to play a biasing role in the processing of new information (Tversky & Kahneman, 1974; Nisbett & Ross, 1980).

In recent years, clinical researchers have become interested in the prospect that schematic-processing biases may play an active role in the development and maintenance of various problems clients present in therapy (cf. Goldfried & Robbins, 1983; Hollon & Kriss, 1984; Meichenbaum & Gilmore, 1984; Turk & Salovey, 1985; Ingram, 1986; Kanfer & Hagerman, 1986; Winfrey & Goldfried, 1986). Schematic-processing biases hypothesized to account for inaccurate and distorted client perceptions include selective attention, confirmatory bias, egocentric bias, availability and representativeness heuristics, and illusory correlation (Turk & Salovey, 1985). Given the presumed moderating role of such biases, the primary task of the cognitive therapist from an information-processing perspective is to

> ... help clients recognize their faulty schematic processing and to make available evidence they can use to reinterpret these faulty views. The goal is to accumulate sufficient schema-inconsistent evidence to induce a new schema in which to embed the new self-referent information. (Winfrey & Golfried, 1986, p. 254)

Strategies designed to facilitate this outcome involve training clients in various "scientific-like" tasks, including systematic self-monitoring, multiple outcome (trials) observation, formal prediction generation and recording, the unobtrusive polling of other people, retrieval of past successes, and day-to-day monitoring of successful coping events (Hollon & Kriss, 1984; Winfrey & Goldfried, 1986).

Beckian cognitive therapy and information-processing approaches adhere to the assumption that emotional and behavioral problems are related to a lack of correspondence between persons' perceptions and external reality. In contrast to the rationalist cognitive emphasis on challenging the irrational, dogmatic, and absolute premises that people bring to bear on their interpretations of life events, empiricist approaches seek to correct the selective, misperceived, and overgeneralized inferences people make from experiential data. As a result, the strategic focus is to encourage clients to engage in a process of reality testing in which they pursue the empirical "evidence" for the validity of their beliefs. Therapeutic progress is a function of the degree to which clients beliefs correspond to "objective" reality. The etiological assumptions and methods of change identified with both

Beckian cognitive therapy and information-processing approaches indicate a dominant epistemic commitment to empiricism.

## Constructivist Approach

In contrast to rationalism and empiricism, which purport that reality is a singular, stable, and knowable category, constructivism assumes that realities are multiplistic dynamic human inventions and that all knowing comprises inherently imperfect conjectures about self and world. As a result, from a constructivist perspective, all knowledge is fallible, forever subject to revision or replacement, and may be evaluated best in terms of its present viability rather than in terms of any external criterion of validity (Mahoney, 1991). By explicitly endorsing a constructivist epistemology, constructivist approaches to psychotherapy similarly view psychological distress as indicative of construct systems that are no longer developmentally viable or adaptive. As Guidano (1988) states, psychotherapy based on this assumption

> . . . does not aim at persuading clients to adopt other standards for truth but rather at helping them to recognize, understand, and better conceptualize their own personal truth—this being their only possibility for making reality real for themselves. (p. 326)

From a constructivist perspective, personal realities and meanings are in need of change, not when they are irrational or invalid but when they reflect an outmoded solution to a salient developmental life challenge (cf. Carlsen, 1988; Guidano, 1988; Mahoney, 1991; Lyddon & Alford, in press).

### Constructivist Cognitive Therapies

Representing a convergence of both philosophical and psychological influences (Mahoney, 1988), the constructivist perspective in cognitive psychotherapy underscores the active, generative, and self-organizing aspects of human cognitive and emotional knowing (cf. Kegan, 1982; Ivey, 1986; Ford, 1987; Guidano, 1987, 1990; Neimeyer & Neimeyer, 1987; Carlsen, 1988; Mahoney, 1991). Constructivist metatheory reflects the confluence of several interrelated and overlapping theoretical frameworks, including (1) the formative influences of personal construct psychology (Kelly, 1955), developmental constructivist psychology (Piaget, 1954, 1970), and attachment theory (Bowlby, 1969,1979); (2) the contemporary theory of self-organization and the emerging view of humans as self-organizing and developing systems (see Ford, 1987; Mahoney, 1991, for comprehensive treatments of self-organization theory); (3) the study of evolving knowledge and knowing systems (Popper, 1972; Campbell, 1974; Radnitzky & Bartley, 1987); and (4) recent theoretical and empirical work on the role of experiential and emotionally focused interventions in psychotherapy (Clarke, 1989; Greenberg, Safran, & Rice, 1989). As Mahoney (1991) states, the constructivist cognitive perspective, instead of reflecting a singular theoretical influence, actually represents a family of theories of mind and cognition that

> . . . (1) emphasize the active and proactive nature of all perception, learning, and knowing; (2) acknowledge the structural and functional primacy of abstract (tacit) over concrete (explicit) processes in all sentient and sapient experience; and (3) view learning, knowing, and memory as phenomena that reflect the ongoing attempts of body and brain to organize (and endlessly reorganize) their own patterns of action and experience—patterns that are, of course, related to changing and highly mediated engagements with their momentary worlds. (p. 95)

From a constructivist perspective, psychological problems and their emotional expressions reflect discrepancies between current environmental and developmental challenges on one hand and a person's adaptive and self-organizing capacities on the other. As a result, constructivist conceptualizations of emotionality and the role of affective experience in the change process significantly differ from conceptualizations associated with rationalist and empiricist approaches. Constructivists tend to value emotions as another way of knowing, a way that is just as valuable to the human system as cognitive knowing. From a constructivist perspective, affective experiences are believed to exert a significant and functional role in the change process by providing opportunities for (1) the exploration of core beliefs about self and world and (2) the eventual construction of higher order patterns and cognitive structures (Mahoney & Lyddon, 1988; Clarke, 1989; Greenberg & Safran, 1989). Instead of viewing "negative" emotions (depression, anxiety) as problems to be eliminated by either more rational or more accurate thinking, constructivist theories tend to view various forms of emotional disequilibrium as significant signals of impending transition in a person's construct systems (Guidano, 1990; Lyddon, 1990; Mahoney, 1991). As Mahoney (1991) states

> . . . episodes of intense emotional "disorder" are often natural expressions of a human system's attempts to restructure itself in a viable manner. Systematic disorganization appears to be an important antecedent to reorganization. (pp. 208–209)

Following from these assumptions, the practice of constructivist cognitive therapy is conceptualized as more of a creative than a corrective endeavor (Neimeyer, 1990). In general, the goal of constructivist cognitive psychotherapy is to facilitate clients' self-construction of new cognitive organizations of experience and reality in the context of a safe, caring, and, at times, emotionally intense therapeutic relationship (Mahoney & Lyddon, 1988). In other words, rather than directly challenging the validity of a person's beliefs, constructivist therapists help clients invent new and perhaps more viable personal constructions and meanings. From a constructivist perspective, "all significant psychological change (in or out of therapy) involves change in the personal meaning that constitutes each individual's private reality" (Mahoney, 1990, p. 166). This fundamental therapeutic emphasis on clients' development and construction of more viable forms of knowing and personal reality underscores constructivist cognitive therapy's epistemic commitment to constructivism.

## Role of Epistemology in Psychotherapy

> . . . all theories of psychological change are fundamentally theories of learning, and all theories of learning ultimately entail a theory of knowing. (Mahoney, 1991, p. 26)

A central guiding assertion of this chapter is that the primary reason psychotherapists hold different positions on the theory and practice of psychotherapy is because they are committed to different epistemological frames of reference. From this premise, it is axiomatic that adherents to different models of cognitive therapy view psychopathology and change differently, because the very nature of knowing is conceived differently. Models of change based on a rationalist epistemology, for example, tend to view psychopathology as functionally related to the degree to which a person's beliefs correspond to warranted standards of rational thinking. Through rational appeal and disputation, clients are encouraged to challenge their irrational and dogmatic beliefs critically and to adopt more "rational" means of interpreting life events. Empiricist cognitive approaches, on the other hand, tend to view psychopathology as stemming from a person's inability to accurately make inferences about themselves and their experiences. In practice, these models emphasize empiricism and disconfirmation; clients are encouraged to adopt the role of personal scientists to systematically correct selective and distorted information processing.

In contrast, constructivist psychotherapies, through their explicit endorsement of constructivist epistemology, challenge rational and empirical assumptions about the nature of reality, psychopathology, and the process of change. Rather than view reality in terms of knowable categories of rational thought or objective inferences, constructivist approaches tend to favor a relativist position, a view of realities as both individual and collective constructions of order in experience. This view does not deny the existence of a world beyond our direct perceptual access, but suggests that any singular conception of "true" reality is not epistemologically justifiable. Constructivist conceptualizations of psychopathology similarly differ from rational and empirical views. Rather than view psychopathology and undesirable affect as a by-product of dysfunctional thinking, constructivist models tend to view various forms of psychological distress as natural expressions of the human system's attempt to reorganize itself in a viable manner. Intense emotions and disequilibria are conceptualized as powerful sources of personal knowledge, in and of themselves, that may function as important prerequisites to developmental change or cognitive reorganization. As a result, clients are encouraged to explore the unique *meaning* of their affective patterning against the backdrop of their developmental and relationship histories. Ultimately, the process involves working with rather than against various forms of emotional experience in order to facilitate the client's self-generation of new cognitive organizations of reality.

## Implications and Future Directions

The notion that different theories of cognitive psychotherapy presuppose different theories of knowledge and knowing leads to the conjecture that all cognitive therapies are means of conveying epistemologies and alternative views of reality. In other words, what a cognitive therapist chooses to do and how s/he chooses to do it may be seen as communicating to the client a deeper set of epistemic assumptions and values, the adoption of which becomes correlated with improvement. This view is consistent with Beutler and Guest's (1989) recent contention that psychotherapy, particularly cognitive therapy, can be understood best as a social persuasion process which, over the course of therapy, the attitudes and beliefs of the client begin to parallel those of the therapist. Such a view moves beyond the singular cognitive focus on the attitudes and beliefs of the client and suggests that a full rendering of the role of cognitive phenomena in psychotherapy must understand the belief system of the client in juxtaposition to that of the therapist. The point here is that, during the process of psychotherapy, the therapist's assumptive world interacts with that of the client and the unique confluence of the two determines the course and trajectory of the therapeutic process (cf. Highlen & Hill, 1984; Ivey, Ivey, & Simek-Downing, 1987).

The degree to which client–therapist similarity may influence psychotherapy process and outcome has been of long-standing interest to clinical researchers. (See Beutler, Crago, & Arizmendi, 1986, for a review.) The general findings associated with this line of inquiry suggest that client–therapist attitude and value similarities are potentially more significant than various client–therapist demographic variables in facilitating both relationship enhancement and favorable psychotherapeutic outcomes (Beutler & Bergan, 1991). These findings raise the intriguing possibility that similar facilitative effects may be found when a client adheres to a personal epistemology that is congruent with that being conveyed by his or her therapist during the course of psychotherapy. Although psychologists have begun to study individual differences in basic philosophical and epistemic assumptions (cf. Royce & Mos, 1980; Germer, Efran, & Overton, 1982; Johnson et al., 1988), the extension of this research to clinically relevant behaviors has been limited to the study of the relationship between epistemic commitment and such covariants as therapists' theoretical orientations and persons' preferences for different approaches to therapy (Schacht & Black, 1985; Lyddon, 1989b; Neimeyer et al., 1991). Lyddon (1989b), for example, recently examined the role of epistemic style in directing individuals' preferences for different therapy approaches. He found that persons significantly preferred therapy approaches that represented an "epistemic match" between their own personal epistemology and the epistemic orientation exemplified by each of the three approaches. Persons with dominant empirical, rational, and metaphorical epistemic styles (as measured via the Psycho-Epistemological Profile; Royce & Mos, 1980) respectively preferred behavioral, cognitive rationalist, and cognitive constructivist psychotherapy approaches. Although these and other data (Neimeyer et al., 1991) provide initial support for the possible facilitative role of epistemic compatibility between client and therapist, only research directed at assessing and defining the influence of such compatibility on psychotherapy process and outcome can substantiate its future significance. Future efforts, for example, may seek to address these questions.

1. How may the degree of client–therapist epistemic similarity influence a client's premature termination from therapy?
2. Does client–therapist epistemic similarity facilitate the development and quality of the "working alliance" in psychotherapy?
3. Do clients who continue in therapy adopt the epistemology of their therapist over the course of therapy?
4. Can the effectiveness of psychotherapy be improved by matching specific therapy approaches to a client's dominant epistemologies?

## Concluding Remarks

The evolving alliance between the fields of cognitive science and psychotherapy represents one of the most significant themes in late 20th-century psychology. Cognitive theories and therapies have come to occupy a prominent role amid the spectrum of contemporary psychotherapeutic efforts. In addition to these conceptual and practical developments, however, the convergence of cognitive and clinical science also has been accompanied by a growing appreciation for the way in which different approaches to psychotherapy are embodied by different assumptions about human knowing and change. As Mahoney (1991) reflects,

> . . . our professional aspirations in the realm of human helping and our efforts to facilitate development in those we serve are inseparable from our assumptions about human change processes. (pp. 16, 18)

This chapter is indebted to the wisdom of this assertion.

# Clinical Disorders

# 10

# Cognitive Science of Depression

**Rick E. Ingram**
*Department of Psychology*
*San Diego State University*
*San Diego, California*

**Christian Holle**
*Department of Psychology*
*State University of New York, Albany*
*Albany, New York*

Several theoretical approaches to depression have begun to emphasize information processing concepts as being at the core of depressive symptomatology. Beck's well-known model (1967), for instance, proposes that negative cognitive schemata distort the processing of information and serve to maintain depression. Although Beck's theory is the most widely known, compatible cognitive models by Kuiper (Kuiper, Derry, & MacDonald, 1982), Teasdale (1983,1986), and Ingram (1984b) also have assigned a central role to information processing in depression. Moreover, even the "behavioral" models proposed by Lewinsohn (Lewinsohn, Hoberman, Teri, & Hautzinger, 1985) and Rehm (1977) incorporate significant elements of information processing. Rehm (1977), for example, maintains that selective monitoring of negative information is an important component of depression whereas Lewinsohn's (Lewinsohn et al., 1985) revised model considers attentional processes to be at the root of a number of the cognitive and behavioral features associated with the disorder.

In parallel with this theoretical interest, empirical research on the information processing mechanisms of depression also has begun to accumulate. Although information processing may be defined operationally in a variety of ways (see Lachman & Lachman, 1986), several depression processing studies have examined specifically the encoding and retrieval of information. Encoding studies, for instance, are those that make information available to be processed by individuals with varying levels of depression, and then use some index (typically information recall) to generate inferences about how the material was encoded. In contrast, retrieval studies examine information that has been encoded and stored at some previous preexperimental time to determine the factors that affect its retrieval from long-term memory. Although they constitute only a subset of the cognitive factors addressed by extant depression research, encoding and retrieval processes are critical components of most information processing conceptualizations of depression and, as such, have important implications for understanding the processes that potentially mediate the multitude of cognitive deficits observed in depression. As these processes become better understood, it becomes increasingly possible to disentangle the ultimate contributions of cognitive mechanisms to depression and, hopefully, to develop accurate guidelines for generating optimally effective psychotherapeutic techniques. More broadly, an enhanced conceptualization of the information processing mechanisms operating in depression also portends an understanding of the relationship between affect and cognition in general. Thus, this chapter will review briefly and highlight the relevant outcomes of studies examining encoding and retrieval processes. Although this review will not be exhaustive, it will focus on research efforts that are representative of the empirical literature in depression. Then we will discuss the salient theoretical issues generated by encoding and retrieval empirical research (see also Blaney, 1986). Finally, we will discuss current research examining cognitive vulnerability, including some criticisms leveled against existing cognitive models.

## Encoding Studies

According to Tulving (1972), extant encoding studies can be conceptualized as focusing primarily on the processing of either semantic or episodic information.[1] *Semantic information* refers generally to knowledge and meaning; thus, it distinguishes studies that examine the processing of information relevant to an individual's self-knowledge or self-concept. *Episodic information,* on the other hand, is autobiographical in nature and therefore is concerned with memory for personal and behavioral events in the individual's experience (e.g., memory for task performance).

[1]It should be noted that the authors of these studies have not necessarily categorized the research in this manner. Nevertheless, such a distinction seems an accurate and reasonable way to organize the existing literature.

## Processing Semantic Information

Perhaps the first study to examine semantic information encoding in depression was reported by Davis (1979a), who employed a methodology from experimental cognitive psychology known as the depth-of-processing paradigm. Derived originally from memory research (Craik & Lockhart, 1972; Craik & Tulving, 1975) to determine the encoding of self-referent information (Rogers, Kuiper, & Kirker, 1977), the depth-of-processing paradigm presents individuals with stimulus adjectives and asks them to rate each adjective on a specified dimension. Theoretically, each dimension forces the individual to process the stimulus at a different cognitive level or depth to accurately perform the rating task. The deepest processing stage is thought to be the self-referent level, since the individual has the greatest store of information available at that level (i.e., information about the self or the self-schema). To assess the depth to which information is processed, an incidental recall task for the stimulus words is given immediately after the encoding phase of the paradigm. Craik and his colleagues have argued that information that is the most extensively (deeply) processed will leave a relatively stronger memory trace; thus, it is the most likely to be recalled in a free recall task.

According to current depressive information processing models, depressed people should have a greater store of negative information accessible at the self-referent level; thus, stimulus information that is depressive in nature should be processed efficiently by these individuals. Davis (1979a) thus presented depressed patients with a depth-of-processing task and examined recall rates for information encoded at various processing levels. For nondepressed control subjects, the expected recall superiority of self-referent processed information was found, indicating the presence of an organized schema to facilitate the encoding and subsequent recall of the information. For depressed subjects, this self-referent enhancement was not found; recall rates for self-referent information and information processed at a more general semantic level were roughly equivalent, a finding that caused Davis (1979a) to suggest the possibility that "the negative self-schema in depression does not exist" (p. 107). As has been pointed out several times, however, since Davis (1979a) examined only recall rates across the various processing tasks (i.e., how many stimulus adjectives were recalled) and not whether depressed subjects recalled more negative or depressive content adjectives, this particular use of the depth-of-processing paradigm was unable to test the conceptually appropriate question of negative information processing in depression (Derry & Kuiper, 1981; Kihlstrom & Nasby, 1981; Ingram, Smith, & Brehm, 1983). Two similar depressive information-processing studies (Davis, 1979b; Davis & Unruh, 1981) suffer the same inapplicability to the question at hand.

Building on Davis' examination of information processing in depression, Derry and Kuiper (1981) addressed the same issue with a more appropriate use of the depth-of-processing methodology. Employing the same paradigm, Derry and Kuiper (1981) developed an adjective list that contained both depressive (e.g., loser, inferior, hopeless) and nondepressive (e.g., amiable, sociable, capable) content. Consistent with the negative information processing hypothesis, Derry and Kuiper (1981) found that, by using these stimuli, clinically depressed subjects recalled significantly more depressive than nondepressive self-referent encoded content whereas both normal and nondepressed psychiatric control subjects showed a reversed pattern; they recalled more nondepressive than depressive self-referent information.

The same depth-of-processing paradigm also was used in two experiments reported by Kuiper and Derry (1982) with mildly depressed college students. In the first experiment, nondepressed subjects recalled more nondepressive than depressive self-referent information, whereas depressed subjects showed superior recall for both depressive and nondepressive self-referent content. In the second experiment, this pattern was repeated, although there was a nonsignificant trend for depressed subjects to recall more depressive than nondepressive self-referent adjectives. Based on a comparison of these results with their earlier research using clinically depressed subjects, Kuiper and Derry (1982) noted that "whereas mild depressives process both nondepressed and depressed content in terms of their self-schemas, more severe clinical depressives are only capable of effectively self-referencing pathologically oriented material" (p. 79). A closer inspection of the means reported in these studies, however, indicates that this conclusion may be somewhat premature. Although it is true that mildly depressed subjects processed positive and negative content with relatively equal facility, it is not true that clinically depressed subjects were completely devoid of any positive self-referent processing. In the Derry and Kuiper (1981) study, for example, clinically depressed subjects showed a self-referent positive information recall rate of 16%, precisely the same as that of the mildly depressed subjects in Experiment 2 and not substantially under the rate of the mildly depressed subjects in Experiment 1 of Kuiper and Derry's (1982) study. Thus, these studies suggest some equivalence between clinical and subclinical depression with respect to processing self-referent information.

Several other studies have examined incidental recall in depression. McDowall (1984), for instance, found that, in a free-recall situation, depressed patients recalled more previously presented unpleasant words (e.g., ridicule, misery) than pleasant words (e.g., beauty, kind). Employing a depth-of-processing paradigm, Hammen, Miklowitz, and Dyck (1986) found evidence that the strength of processing depressive information (i.e., stimulus adjectives with depressive content) is related not only to the severity of the depression but also to the duration of the depressive episode as well. Further, Hammen, Miklowitz & Dyck (1986) showed that when individuals were no longer depressed, they no longer evidenced enhanced processing of depressive information. Similarly, in a two-part study, Slife, Miura, Thompson, Shapiro, and Gallagher (1984) demonstrated that elderly depressed patients recalled more trigrams that they had previously said they disliked than trigrams that they had said they liked. Two control groups showed the opposite pattern. In the second part of the study, depressed patients who underwent psychotherapy reversed this trend over the course of therapy and showed enhanced recall of liked trigrams, a result consistent with Hammen and colleagues' (1986) finding that depressive information processing occurs only when the individual is actually depressed.

One study has examined the encoding of personal information in depression in the context of a social interaction. Gotlib (1983) had depressed and nondepressed inpatients and nondepressed controls interact with opposite-sex strangers. After this interaction, subjects were given a rating sheet that had purportedly been completed by a concealed observer of the interaction. Each sheet contained prearranged ratings on 13 bipolar adjectives that represented a number of evaluative dimensions (e.g., inadequate–adequate, unlikable–likable). After disclosing their reactions to these ratings, subjects were asked to reproduce from memory the ratings on a blank sheet. Results indicated that depressed subjects recalled these ratings to be significantly more negative than was actually the case, whereas neither of the nondepressed groups was inaccurate in recall. Gotlib (1983) suggested that these results clearly reflected a negative distortion by depressed individuals in the recall of social feedback.

Several studies also have examined the impact of situational manipulations on information encoding in depression. Ingram, Smith, and Brehm (1983), for instance, provided depressed and nondepressed college students with either a success or a failure experience immediately before administering a depth-of-processing task. Unlike Derry and Kuiper (1981) and Kuiper and Derry (1982), however, the stimulus adjectives in the processing task were not predetermined to be of depressive or nondepressive content. Instead, the stimulus words used by Rogers and colleagues (1977), that contain a range of content, were employed. After the depth-of-processing task, all subjects were asked to rate each word that had appeared on the task for favorability and self-descriptiveness. Based on these ratings, the mean personal favorability of the words recalled on the incidental recall portion of the task was examined. For nondepressed subjects, the self-referent favorability of recalled words encoded under the self-referent task was significantly higher in the success condition than in the failure condition. Nondepressed subjects also recalled significantly more favorable self-references in the success condition than did depressed subjects in the success condition. For depressed subjects, there were no differences in personal favorability recall between the success and failure conditions, a finding that led the authors to suggest that depressed subjects failed to make use of the success experience to activate the processing of positive self-referent information, as did the nondepressed subjects. Although the lack of a baseline comparison group that did not receive either a success or a failure experience makes these interpretations tentative, Ingram and associates (1983) suggested that depression might be characterized by a deficit in the ability to process positive information rather than an oversensitivity to negative information.

In another study addressing the impact of situational manipulations, Dyck (1983) found results that appeared to conflict with those of Ingram and co-workers (1983). In this study, depressed and nondepressed college students were instructed to recall a happy or a sad personal experience. After completing a manipulation check item that asked them to rate on a 7-point scale whether they felt happy or sad, the subjects participated in an incidental recall task in which depressive and nondepressive adjectives were rated on a self-referent scale and recall was assessed subsequently. Collapsed across the mood induction variable, results indicated that nondepressed subjects recalled significantly fewer negative words than did depressed subjects, whereas there was no difference between depressed and nondepressed subjects in the recall of positive words. When the mood induction variable was considered, findings showed that depressed subjects recalled significantly more theoretically defined schema-congruent words (i.e., negative words that were rated as descriptive and positive words that were rated as nondescriptive) in the sad condition than in the happy condition (29 as opposed to 16%). In contrast, nondepressed subjects did not show any differential recall as a function of the happy or sad mood manipulation (23% happy as opposed to 22% sad). Although Dyck (1983) concluded from these findings that information processing in depressed individuals might be more dependent on mood activation than it is in nondepressed individuals, interpretation of these results is problematic; the manipulation check employed appears to be highly susceptible to demand characteristics (e.g., subjects being asked to rate whether they felt happy or sad immediately after being told to think of something happy or sad). Thus, although significant effects certainly might be engendered by this kind of manipulation, particularly for already depressed subjects told to think of something sad in their own memory, it might be much less effective for subjects not currently experiencing any depression.

From a somewhat different vantage point than that of the studies previously described, several studies have examined whether ongoing information processing in depression might interfere with encoding of other information. Using a standard information-processing methodology, Krames and MacDonald (1985) presented depressed and nondepressed outpatients with a dual cognitive task in which they were required to learn a list of words (primary task) while being shown numbers of varying length and being asked to write them down (secondary task). This methodology assumes that an individual's cognitive processing capacity is limited; since two tasks vie for this capacity, performance on the primary task will deteriorate as the secondary task becomes more demanding. Under conditions of moderate and high secondary task interference (longer numbers), both depressed and nondepressed subjects showed equivalent interference effects on primary task performance. Interestingly, however, under low secondary task interference, depressed subjects continued to show poor performance relative to nondepressed subjects. These results were replicated subsequently in a study by Vredenberg and Krames (1983) using a conceptually similar experimental paradigm. Results of both studies suggested the possibility that, in conditions of low experimenter-controlled cognitive interference, current cognitive activity in depressed subjects is capable of interfering with external information processing significantly.

This conclusion receives additional support from a study by Gotlib and McCann (1984), who addressed the issue of cognitive interference in depression using a modified Stroop task. Depressed and nondepressed college students viewed rapidly presented words with depressed, neutral, and manic content; the subjects were asked to name the colors in which the words were printed. Gotlib and McCann (1984) reasoned that the presence of ongoing negative cognitive activity might interfere with the color-naming response latencies for depressive content words. Consistent with this hypothesis, they found slower response times to these words for depressed subjects but not for nondepressed individuals, who showed no differences across any of the word conditions. In a second experiment to test whether these results might be caused by transient mood effects, Gotlib and McCann (1984) repeated their procedure using Velten mood induction with nondepressed college students. Although results indicated significant group differences on a manipulation adjective checklist, no differences were found on the Stroop task among subjects given depression, elation, or neutral mood induction. Although this result was interpreted to indicate that mood itself is not a sufficient determinant of depressive interference effects, the possibility of demand characteristics on the manipulation item checklist must make this interpretation somewhat tentative.

## Episodic Processing Studies

In one of the first studies to investigate the processing of behavioral information in depression, Wener and Rehm (1975) presented a pseudotest of social intelligence to depressed and nondepressed subjects. Subjects ostensibly were reinforced for task performance accuracy, but actually were told that they were correct at a predetermined high (80%) or low (20%) rate and later were asked to recall the percentage of correct responses they received. In both the high- and low-reinforcement conditions, depressed subjects underestimated the percentage of correct feedback, a finding interpreted by the authors as indicating that depressed individuals were more sensitive to negative than to positive reinforcement.

Adding a punishment condition to this recall-of-reinforcement paradigm, Nelson and Craighead (1977) reinforced or punished college students for performance on an ambiguous task at a high (70%) or low (30%) rate. Depressed subjects recalled being reinforced significantly less accurately than did controls in the high-reinforcement condition, whereas in the low-reinforcement condition, estimates of reinforcement did not differ between the depressed and nondepressed groups. In the punishment conditions this pattern was largely reversed. There were no differences in recall of punishment at the high rate; both the depressed and nondepressed groups were fairly accurate. However, at the low-punishment rate, depressed subjects recalled receiving more punishment than did the nondepressed subjects, who significantly underestimated the negative feedback they had received. In other words, the depressed subjects were somewhat more accurate than the controls in the recall of punishment whereas the nondepressed subjects were generally more accurate in the recall of reinforcement.

Gotlib (1981) also addressed the recall of reinforcement in depression. Employing depressed inpatients, nondepressed inpatients, and nondepressed nonpatients, the recall of self-reinforcements and punishments administered on a verbal recognition task was examined. Gotlib (1981) found that depressed subjects recalled significantly more self-punishments than were actually made and significantly more than either of the control groups recalled. The biggest significant differences, however, were found for self-reinforcements. Here, depressed subjects recalled substantially fewer reinforcements than they actually made and fewer than either of the control groups recalled.

In another study, DeMonbreun and Craighead (1977) employed the same recall-of-reinforcement paradigm with clinically depressed and nondepressed control subjects. In addition to examining the recall of punishment and reinforcement, these investigators also sought to determine whether potential distortions in this recall occurred when individuals first perceived the reinforcing or punishing stimuli, or at some later information processing stage. To accomplish this end, an ambiguous task was employed, and performance feedback on each trial was conveyed to subjects by presentation of one of several slides, varying in shade from light gray to black. Subjects were instructed that the darkest slide indicated a 100% acceptable answer, the next darkest slide indicated a 75% acceptable answer, and the lightest and next lightest slides represented 100% and 75% unacceptable answers, respectively. A midrange gray or ambiguous slide that was not mentioned to subjects was included also. After performance feedback, subjects were to indicate which of the feedback slides they received. Additionally, the experiment was divided into two parts: in the first 40 trials, subjects received an equal number of all performance feedback slides, whereas in the last 40 trials, half the subjects received a high rate of "acceptable" responses while the other half received a low rate of acceptable responses.

Results indicated that all subjects responded to the undefined midrange slide as positive approximately half the time and as negative approximately half the time, thus providing no support for hypotheses of distortions in the initial perception of these stimuli. After the first half of the study, depressed subjects tended to recall receiving less positive feedback than they actually did, but the difference was not significant. After the subsequent 40 trials, depressed subjects in the high-reinforcement condition significantly underestimated the amount of positive feedback received and recalled significantly less of such feedback than did the control groups. In the low-reinforcement condition, no group differences were obtained. DeMonbreun and Craighead (1977) thus concluded that recall distortion in their depressed subjects occurs only when the rate of positive reinforcement is high.

Using a task similar to that employed by DeMonbreun and Craighead (1977), Craighead, Hickey, and DeMonbreun (1979) investigated recall as well as stimulus perception again, using ambiguous performance feedback (i.e., feedback from unidentified slides) with students who were selected to be depressed and anxious, nondepressed and anxious, or nondepressed and nonanxious, respectively. Inconsistent with previous depression theory and research, no significant differences were found among the groups on any measure. As noted by Sacco (1981), however, these negative findings were most likely the result of a lack of significant differences in depression or anxiety among any of the experimental groups, that is, inspection of depression and anxiety means, on measures made immediately before the experiment was conducted, indicated that the previously selected depressed and anxious subjects were no longer depressed or anxious. Hence, this experiment does not appear to have employed groups with any meaningful psychopathological differences.

Employing a similar experimental paradigm, Dykman and Volpicelli (1983) presented depressed and nondepressed college students with 40 trials of a dot estimation task. Subjects then received good, average, poor, or ambiguous (i.e., undefined) feedback that was conveyed by brightness of a red light bulb. Additionally, to examine whether the subjective importance of the experimental task affected information processing, half the subjects were told that the task reflected the possession of "special mental abilities," whereas for the remaining half, the evaluative significance of the task was downplayed.

Initial analyses indicated no significant differences in recall, in classification of initial stimuli (as good, average, or poor), or on a measure of latency to classify the stimuli. However, after inspection of the data, subsequent analyses indicated significant differences among groups in ambiguous stimulus classification during the last 20 experimental trials. Although Dykman and Volpicelli (1983) interpreted this result as an indication that depressed individuals "negatively bias" their stimulus perception of ambiguous feedback, inspection of the means showed only that depressed and nondepressed subjects significantly differed and suggested that nondepressed individuals may have been more likely to overinterpret this feedback as positive (instead of depressed subjects showing a negative bias). Dykman and Volpicelli (1983) also found significant differences in response latencies, that is, depressed subjects showed progressively longer times to classify the feedback as it became more positive whereas nondepressed subjects showed the opposite trend. In contrast, no differences were found in the recall of feedback nor were any differences on any measure found for the personal importance manipulation.

Johnson, Petzel, Hartney, and Morgan (1983) examined the effects of successful completion of tasks compared with failure to complete tasks in a recall-of-reinforcement paradigm. The tasks involved were 20 paper-and-pencil tests of analytic abilities, half of which the subjects were allowed to complete and half of which were interrupted prior to completion. Depressed college students recalled significantly more of the uncompleted tasks than the completed tasks, whereas nondepressed college students demonstrated the opposite trend by recalling significantly more of the completed tasks than the uncompleted tasks. Based on these recall differences, Johnson and colleagues (1983) argued that these findings were "consistent with Beck's (1967) assumption that the depressive minimizes those things s/he does well and maximizes those things s/he does poorly" (p. 55).

Employing a different approach to examining the encoding of behavioral information, Finkel, Glass, and Merluzzi (1982) provided depressed and nondepressed college students with a high proportion of positive self-referent statements, a low proportion of positive self-referent statements, or neutral non-self-referent statements, and asked them to rate each statement on a 7-point scale of how positively or negatively they perceived the statement. After these ratings were made, subjects were asked to recall how many of the statements they had "judged to be any degree positive." Recall results indicated that depressed subjects recalled judging significantly fewer statements positive than nondepressed subjects when the proportion of such statements was high, but not when the predetermined proportion was low or when the statements were neutral. It is not clear from the data presented, however, whether this decreased recall of positive statements for the depression group was a cognitive underestimate of the amount of statements they rated positively, or an accurate reflection of the fact that they rated fewer statements as positive than did nondepressed subjects (which other data in the study suggest that they did).

In a study employing depressed and nondepressed psychiatric patients, Roth and Rehm (1980) examined the processing of both semantic and episodic information. After rating a group of positive and negative adjectives on a personal accuracy scale, subjects were asked to choose the 10 positive and 10 negative words that were most self-descriptive. After a 10-minute filler task, the subjects were given a recall and recognition task for these words, neither of which later yielded significant group differences. Subjects also participated in a social interaction task in which they were videotaped in a role-playing procedure and later asked to rate their number of positive social responses (e.g., head nods) and negative social responses (e.g., hand rubbing). Comparison with objective videotape raters indicated that depressed subjects perceived an accurate number of negative responses and significantly fewer positive responses than were actually made. Nondepressed subjects perceived significantly fewer of both positive and negative responses than did the objective raters. Roth and Rehm appropriately pointed out that these results might be due to differences in selective information processing or to differences in the stringency of decision criteria employed. It seems clear, however, that depressed individuals in this study "underperceived" their socially appropriate responses.

### Studies of Retrieval of Personal Memory

As previously described, retrieval studies refer to those that examine the factors affecting the retrieval of preexperimentally stored information. Although retrieval studies can take several different methodological approaches, in this section we will limit our review to those studies in which depressed subjects retrieve previously stored personal memories.

Lloyd and Lishman (1975) reported probably the first study of this type. In this study, depressed patients were presented with a series of neutral stimulus words and asked to recall a pleasant or an unpleasant personal experience that was somehow associated with each word. Employing the latency to retrieve each of these experiences as the dependent measure, the investigators found that the more severe the depression, the less time it took to retrieve unpleasant memories and the greater time it took to report pleasant experiences.

Noting the strictly correlational basis of the Lloyd and Lishman (1975) findings, Teasdale and Fogarty (1979) followed up this study by manipulating mood in normal college students and examining the retrieval time of pleasant and unpleasant memories. Using the same strategy as Lloyd and Lishman (1975), college students were induced into either an elated or a depressed state with the Velten mood induction procedure (Velten, 1968) and were asked to recall a pleasant or an unpleasant experience in response to a neutral stimulus word. Results indicated that pleasant memories were recalled significantly more quickly when subjects were in an elated state than when in a depressed condition. No significant differences in response latencies for unpleasant memories were found between the elated and depressed states. Thus, only pleasant, not unpleasant, material appeared to be affected by the experimenter-induced mood.

In two similar experiments, Teasdale, Taylor, and Fogarty (1980) and Teasdale and Taylor (1981) examined the probability of memory retrieval in depression. Subjects again were induced into an elated or a depressed mood and were asked to recall a memory but were not given any instructions about the kind of memory to recall. On a different day and not under the effects of the mood manipulation, subjects were asked to rate the pleasantness of the previously recalled memories. Using these ratings to determine which memories were pleasant, results of both studies indicated that, in the depressed mood, subjects recalled significantly fewer pleasant memories than when in the elated condition. The opposite was true for unpleasant memories: fewer were recalled in the elated mood than in the depressed mood. Similar results were obtained by Teasdale and Russell (1983) and by Clark and Teasdale (1985), although the latter findings were limited to females, suggesting the possibility of potential sex differences in depressive information processing.

Next assessing clinical depression, Clark and Teasdale (1982) subsequently replicated the earlier results by examining diurnal variations in the mood of depressed inpatients. Using the same paradigm, with natural mood variations rather than mood inductions, it was found again that high levels of depression were related to significantly more unpleasant than pleasant memories recalled. During times of relatively low depression levels in these same patients, more pleasant than unpleasant memories were retrieved.

At least two other studies have examined personal memory retrieval processes in individuals with depressed mood. In one, Natale and Hantas (1982) found that college students who had been induced into an elated mood using the Velten procedure recalled a significantly greater number of happy memories than subjects induced into a depressed mood. Elated subjects also recalled significantly more happy than sad memories whereas induced-depression subjects recalled a fairly equal number of happy and sad memories. When compared with a baseline group not receiving any mood induction, the elation induction significantly increased the number of happy memories recalled whereas the depression induction significantly decreased the number of happy memories retrieved. For sad content, there was a decrease in memory only in the elation condition. For the induced depressed condition, no increase was seen in sad memories relative to the baseline group; both induced-depressed and normal-mood subjects recalled roughly the same number of these memories. These results are generally consistent with an experiment reported by Snyder and White (1982) that is relevant to the actual retrieval of information. In the first of three experiments, college students were induced into either an elated or a depressed mood and were asked to recall events that happened to them in the past week, good events that happened to them the past week, and, finally, bad events that happened to them in the past week. Results indicated that, when asked to recall these events, elated subjects recalled more happy events whereas depressed subjects recalled more unhappy events. The number of neutral events did not differ as a function of the mood manipulation. When subjects were specifically asked to recall either good or bad events, once again elated subjects recalled more positive events and depressed mood subjects recalled more negative events.

## General Findings

As always, diverse methodologies, different conceptual perspectives, and a variety of specific research questions make it difficult to draw conclusions about an area as a whole. Considering the methodological and theoretical issues that remain to be addressed, more than tentative conclusions concerning encoding and retrieval in depression are not possible. Nevertheless, based on the research available to date, we will attempt to delineate some general, and hopefully promising, trends in the data.

With respect to the encoding of semantic information, the bulk of available evidence suggests that depressed individuals, relative to nondepressives, do indeed experience an enhanced processing of negative or depressively oriented information. The efficient processing of positive or nondepressive information, on the other hand, seems to be more variable; some studies indicate decrements in positive processing (e.g., Ingram et al., 1983) and others suggest no such decrements (e.g., Kuiper & Derry, 1982). Such findings may identify positive information encoding as simply a variable process in depression; alternatively, extant research may have been variable in its ability to assess this process accurately. The most consistent conclusion emerging from the data so far, however, is that enhanced negative encoding may be the key factor in semantic information processing.

This idea somewhat contrasts with episodic information encoding studies. In these studies, depressed individuals seem to be impacted at the positive rather than at the negative information level, that is, the less accurate encoding (underestimation) of positive information seems to be the critical process for depressed individuals, not the distorted overestimation of negative information. It may thus be that, since depressed individuals are primed by extant and salient negative semantic structures, congruent episodic information is processed efficiently whereas incongruent (positive) information is distorted.

Although there are some exceptions, when retrieval studies are considered, the processing of positive and negative information in depression appears to be more symmetrical than for either semantic or episodic encoding processes, that is, although the retrieval of negative information seems to be enhanced consistently, the retrieval of positive information appears to be diminished more consistently as well. Of the several reasons for this result, one might be primarily methodological. Whereas encoding studies typically employ already depressed students or patients, retrieval studies usually rely on the manipulation of mood in normal student subjects. Although differences may be due to different subject populations per se, an intriguing possibility involves the mood assessed, particularly when subjects in retrieval studies are given elation manipulations. In encoding studies, control subjects, although not depressed, probably are not elated either (consider the attitude of many introductory psychology students sitting in a psychology experiment) and, thus, probably have a more "neutral" mood. More symmetrical retrieval findings, particularly with respect to positive processing therefore may be partially due to the added mood dimension that an elated condition brings to previously neutral mood subjects.

An additional possibility for different encoding and retrieval patterns may reflect the operation of somewhat different processes. Encoding, for example, is more restrained by factors external to the person, for example, the kind of information available in the environment. Variable positive or nondepressive processing hence may be a function of the information available to be processed. Even if the depressed individual's cognitive system more efficiently encodes negative information, positive information may be encoded accurately if, for example, a large amount of positive information "overwhelms" the system. Retrieval of information, on the other hand, would seem less constrained by these external factors and more dependent on solely internal factors. Without these constraints, affect may be more likely to be the prime determinant of the information that is retrieved, facilitating retrieval of consistent information and inhibiting retrieval of inconsistent information. Therefore, retrieval processes may be more related to "pure" mood than encoding is.

## Theoretical Issues

Several potentially important theoretical questions arise from this preceding review. One particularly relevant issue that has yet to be addressed explicitly concerns the parameters of the information to be processed and how it interacts with depressive characteristics. Information can vary in a number of dimensions. Gotlib (1983) and Dykman and Volpicelli (1983) have noted, for instance, that a number of studies of information processing in depression employed information that is highly impersonal (e.g., performance feedback on a letter recognition task). On a somewhat more abstract level, in this review we also have distinguished between semantic and episodic information. As evidenced by the data currently available, these different kinds of information indeed may be processed differently as a function of depression level and, more importantly, also may contribute to the maintenance or features of depression in different ways. Although by no means complete or mutually exclusive, several other potentially interesting categories of information also can be distinguished. Some examples include the target of the information (whether it is information specifically about the individual or social information concerning others), the general favorability of the information (e.g., positive/favorable or negative/unfavorable), the content of the information (e.g., neutral, depressive, anxious, manic, assertive, or aggressive), information congruence (does the information fit with the individual's own self-concept?), and, finally, as previously suggested by Gotlib (1983), the personal relevance of the information. All these categories would seem to be important and interactive dimensions that merit theoretical and empirical scrutiny. At the very least, however, future studies would be wise to refrain from drawing conclusions about how depressives process information without reference to the specific type of information under study.

Related to the issue of information categories in depressive processing is the issue of depressive categories. Although we have used the generic term depression to refer to a multifaceted symptom constellation with depressed mood as the defining characteristic, it is recognized widely that depression is not a unitary homogeneous disorder. It also is recognized widely that there is very little consensus concerning the classification, symptoms, and conceptual boundaries of various depressive disorders (Andreason, 1982; Depue & Monroe, 1978). Despite acknowledging the disagreement over depression classification, however, several broad categories in the most general sense do seem to be agreed on. We already have touched on the severity distinction in studies that have employed subjects ranging from normal subjects with induced depression to mildly depressed college students to clinically depressed inpatients. Although the extant research has shown some evidence generally supportive of the notion that information processing in these disorders is similar in at least a qualitative sense, research has yet to examine explicitly the specifics of potential information-processing differences in different severity levels.

One classification that also merits study is the unipolar–bipolar distinction. Previous research either has limited itself exclusively to unipolar depression or has not made a distinction between the two. Finding information-processing differences in unipolar and bipolar depression would not only be of great theoretical interest but, because much psychosocial-cognitive therapy is based on the premise that "correcting faulty information processing" is the basis for effective treatment (see Ingram & Hollon, 1986), such research also may have direct practical importance. An examination of other categories such as reactive–endogenous and neurotic–psychotic might prove interesting as well. More broadly, how information processing is affected by, and in turn affects, a variety of different moods (e.g., depression, mania) is of tremendous theoretical interest for understanding the relationship between affect and cognition (Hammen, 1983a). Finally, addressing information processing in individuals that are theoretically vulnerable to depression but not presently depressed and in children experiencing depressive affect, as Kuiper (Kuiper, Olinger, MacDonald, & Shaw, 1985) and Hammen (Hammen & Zupan, 1984; Hammen, 1985; Hammen, Marks, Mayol, & deMayo, 1985a; Hammen, Marks, deMayo, & Mayol, 1985b), respectively, have taken the lead in doing, also may provide important data on how information processing may ultimately contribute to depression.

One current controversy in the depression literature pertains to the relative accuracy or distortion of cognition in depression. Beck's (1967) traditional position that depressed people distort the processing of information in systematically negative ways has been challenged by several sources (e.g., Alloy & Abramson, 1979,1982; Lewinsohn, Mischel, Chaplin, & Barton, 1980; Sackeim, 1983). Ultimately, the challenge is that "a rapidly growing body of empirical work suggests that depressed peoples' perceptions and inferences are actually more realistic and accurate than those of nondepressed people" (Alloy, 1982, p. 2). Although the research discussed in this chapter was not designed specifically to address this issue, several studies do bear on it. Generally, these studies have shown mixed results, suggesting that sometimes depressed individuals "distort" information (e.g., Nelson & Craighead, 1977, reinforcement condition; Gotlib, 1983) and sometimes they do not (Nelson & Craighead, 1977, punishment condition). These mixed results therefore strongly suggest that the accuracy of information processing in depression is determined by a number of complex factors and that general conclusions about distortion or accuracy are probably premature. More fundamentally, although accuracy can be operationalized easily in laboratory situations, the notion of accuracy and distortion has not been defined adequately conceptually (Roth & Ingram, 1985). Beck's (1967) contention, for example, implies a "distortion by commission" definition in which depressed individuals somehow "change" positive or neutral information into negative information to fit their depressive schema. An equally likely but very different definition of distortion is a "distortion by omission" notion. In such a case, depressed individuals may process negative information very accurately but may cognitively ignore positive information (the converse may be just as likely for nondepressed individuals). The overall effect of this processing style thus would be distortion, because of the imbalance of information attended to relative to information available. Whether this or other conceptualizations of distortion are useful, it is important for future research to reach some degree of consensus about what constitutes distortion or accuracy before the phenomenon can be examined and conclusions be drawn.

## Cognitive Vulnerability

To date, the evidence for negative information processing in the depressed state is quite impressive. It must be noted, however, that cognitive depression models are ultimately causal models, that is, cognitive variables are postulated to play a contributory role in the onset of the depressive state. However, the existing empirical data pertaining to the cognitive features of the depressive state may not be relevant to this conceptualization of causality; several recent studies have provided evidence that appears to challenge cognitive causal models of depression. In a review of the evidence against cognitive theories, Persons and Miranda (in press) group the criticisms into three categories. First, longitudinal studies of depressed people throughout the duration of the disorder reveal that, when the depression reverts, it is difficult to continue to detect indications of negative cognition (e.g., Persons & Rao, 1985; Dobson & Shaw, 1987; Barnett & Gotlib, 1988). Second, comparisons of normal controls and recovered depressed individuals have shown no differences in dysfunctional attitudes or attributions (Dohr, Rush, & Bernstein, 1981; Hamilton & Abramson, 1983; Hollon, Kendall, & Iumry, 1986). Third, prospective longitudinal studies have not produced consistently supportive evidence showing that negative cognitive structures predispose individuals to later depressive episodes (Lewinsohn, Steinmetz, Larson, & Franklin, 1981; Hammen et al., 1985b).

As Garber and Hollon (1991) have noted, to infer onset, researchers must demonstrate temporal antecedence, that is, cognitive features must precede the onset of the disorder. Nevertheless, a lack of temporal antecedence does not diminish all the causal possibilities of the cognitive variables assessed in cross-sectional studies. We would argue, for instance, that causality is not synonymous with onset, although it tends to be treated as such by some investigators. For a disorder such as depression that, if untreated, usually persists for a minimum of 6 months, it is important to examine the factors that maintain the disordered state. Thus, factors involved in the perpetuation of depression have very real causal significance, not for the onset of the disorder, but for the maintenance of the disorder. It is legitimate to ask whether this aspect of causality is any less important than causal onset perspectives. The cognitive features assessed in the depressed state therefore may have a considerable degree of casual relevance if we look at causality from a broader perspective. This idea, of course, still must be demonstrated empirically, but it suggests that it is inappropriate simply to dismiss these variables as mere consequences or epiphenomena, as some investigators have done (e.g., Coyne & Gotlib, 1983).

Despite the possibility that cognitive variables studied to date may have causal relevance from a maintenance standpoint, it is still reasonable to inquire about their etiological importance. The answer to the onset question appears rooted in diathesis–stress conceptualizations of depression. Beck's theory (1967) proposes that dysfunctional beliefs remain latent until activated by stressful life events. Thus, a diathesis–stress model suggests that some individuals have negative self-representations available that interact with life events to bring about the disorder. More specifically, Segal and Shaw (1986) have argued that some individuals have a predisposition (or diathesis) in which certain "stressors precipitate a pattern of negatively biased, self-referent information processing that initiates the first cycle in the downward spin of depression . . . this predisposition consists of the operation of latent but reactive cognitive structures that are activated by events interpreted as personally significant" (p. 674).

In a study examining the cognitive diathesis–stress hypothesis, Miranda & Persons (in press) measured dysfunctional thinking after stressful life events, that were defined operationally as the number of life change events occurring in the last 6 months. Outpatients with and without a history of depression were assessed for dysfunctional thinking using the Cognitive Events Schedule (CES; Munoz, 1977) and also were asked to estimate the probability, from 0 to 100%, that statements from the Subjective Probability Questionnaire (SPQ; Munoz, 1977) applied to themselves. The SPQ measure includes negative views of the self, world, and future. Results indicated that after experiencing stressful life events, formerly depressed people reported significantly higher subjective probabilities of negative events than did never-depressed patients. In addition, the interaction of History of Depression by Stressful Life Events was significantly predictive of negative CES scores, reporting endorsement of global, rigid, and negative cognitions. Although the study was correlational in nature, and therefore unable to show dysfunctional cognitions as causal vulnerability factors for depression, it does give supporting evidence to the diathesis–stress approaches that predict increased negative cognitions for vulnerable individuals after stressful life events.

The hopelessness theory of depression represents another cognitive diathesis–stress model. In this cognitive subtype of depression, it is hypothesized that the tendency of an individual to make internal, stable, and global attributions to explain negative events increases the likelihood of developing depressive episodes (Alloy, Abramson, Metalsky, & Hartlage, 1988; Abramson, Metalsky, & Alloy, 1989). Thus, in the presence of stress, this depressogenic attributional style is considered neither a necessary nor a sufficient cause for depression, but only a contributory cause to depression activation. Current research strategies (e.g., Hamilton & Abramson, 1983; Fennel & Campbell, 1984; Dohr, Rush, & Bernstein, 1989) developed to test whether attributional style is a vulnerability factor for depression, however, have assumed that this style is a necessary cause of depression, that is, subject selection is determined by the presence or absence of depression, either in the past or future, and comparison is made based on the hypothesized vulnerability factor of attributional style. Thus, studies that fail to find differences in attributional style between currently depressed individuals and remissives are argued by some researchers (e.g., Barnett & Gotlib, 1988) to demonstrate a lack of empirical support for this attributional style to be a vulnerability factor for depression. Alloy and Lipman (in press), however, propose that subject selection to test the vulnerability hypothesis of the hopelessness theory instead should be based on the presence or the absence of the hypothesized depressogenic attributional style rather than the presence or absence of depression. Because subjects are selected on the basis of a behavioral characteristic, namely, attributional style, this research strategy has been termed a "behavioral high-risk paradigm" (Depue, Slater, Wolfstetter-Kausch, Klein, Goplerud, & Farr, 1981).

This high-risk paradigm has been employed by Alloy and Lipman (in press) in a retrospective study to test the attributional vulnerability hypothesis. In this study, nondepressed college students (BDI < 11) who scored in the highest quartile on the Attributional Style Questionnaire (ASQ; Seligman, Abramson, Semmel, & von Baeyer, 1979) for negative events were compared with similar students whose ASQ scores fell in the lowest quartile. Then, during a semistructured diagnostic interview, the occurrence, duration, and severity of major depressive episodes experienced by high-risk and low-risk subjects over the past 2 years were examined. Results indicated that attributionally vulnerable high-risk students experienced significantly higher rates, larger numbers, and greater severity of major depressive disorder episodes than did low-risk students. Although the duration of episodes was nonsignificant between the two groups, there was a trend for the high-risk group's depressive episodes to be of a longer duration. As in the Miranda study described previously, the retrospective design of this study limits determination of the causal direction between depressogenic attributional style and increased rates of past depression. Nevertheless, these findings give evidence to validate attributional style as a diathesis for depression.

Some investigators have argued (e.g., Ingram, 1991; Miranda & Persons, in press) that the key to understanding cognitive vulnerability from a diathesis–stress perspective is to study the activation processes of negative self-referent cognitive structures. Current research has begun to assess cognitive processing patterns in individuals who are not currently in a depressed state. The critical aspect of this research is to prime the resurgence of negative cognitive schemata by inducing a negative mood state. Miranda and Persons (in press), for example, have formulated a mood state hypothesis that proposes that dysfunctional attitudes and attributions are stable traits, but current mood state determines an individual's ability to report them. In addition, the probability of an individual's ability to report negative cognitions varies directly with the level of negative mood. Etiologically consistent with the cognitive theories, the mood state hypothesis asserts that unless priming occurs previously, underlying depressogenic cognitions are "not observable, measurable, or reportable even though they are present in a 'latent' or unconscious form" (Miranda & Persons, in press).

Miranda and Persons (in press) have used this mood state hypothesis to offer an explanation of the negative evidence against the cognitive theories. First, as a patient's mood state improves over time, underlying dysfunctional cognitions become inaccessible and, therefore, unobservable, leading to the conclusion that the beliefs also have "remitted." These attributions and cognitions, however, are believed to remain in a latent form. Second, these underlying beliefs also would be inaccessible to recovered depressed people because of an elevation in mood state. Thus, assessment of postmorbid depressives will fail to show previously high endorsements on dysfunctional cognition measures, despite their presence in a latent form. Third, asymptomatic patients vulnerable to depression should not show dysfunctional cognitions that could be employed in predicting subsequent depressive episodes unless a negative mood state was induced during assessment.

In concurrence with the mood state hypothesis, several studies have examined depression vulnerability using a mood priming procedure. In the Miranda and Persons (1988) study, a variation of the Velten (1968) technique was used to induce a positive or a negative mood. Reports of dysfunctional beliefs varied as a function of the mood state induced. However, higher endorsements occurring during a depressed mood occurred only for those women with a history of depression. Similarly, using nondepressed individuals with a history of a previous depressive episode, Miranda, Persons, & Byers (1990) reported elevated dysfunctional attitude scores only if the subjects were assessed in a negative mood state. In addition, the presence of a negative mood state in individuals with no history of depression did not result in elevation of dysfunctional attitude scores. Finally, using a depth-of-processing paradigm described previously, Teasdale and Dent (1987) assessed cognitive functioning in never-depressed and previously depressed women after a sad mood induction using music. Results indicated that 28% of remitted depressives recalled one or more negative self-rated adjectives as opposed to 5% of the never-depressed group. Although the stability of dysfunctional attributes is not demonstrated directly, these studies do support and are consistent with the mood state hypothesis.

Dysfunctional attitudes are among many other potentially important cognitive diatheses. For example, how attention is allocated is thought to be a schema-driven process that functions to structure information processed by the individual. Once the negative schema is activated, such attention allocation may prove to be a cognitive feature that helps maintain the depressed state. Several cognitive models (eg., Beck, 1967; Lewinsohn, 1985), for example, suggest that depressed people selectively attend to the least favorable information and, thus, build up a reservoir of negative self-references that perpetuates depressive affect (Ingram, 1991).

Using a modified dichotic listening paradigm developed in basic experimental cognitive psychology, Ingram (1991) examined the effect of negative mood on allocation of attention for subjects vulnerable to depression. In the dichotic listening task, subjects were presented with two messages, one in each ear. Subjects were instructed to attend to a story presented in one ear by repeating it word for word while a series of distractor words grouped into three blocks was presented in the other. Distractor blocks consisted of depressive personality descriptors, neutral words, and generally positive nondepressive personality adjectives, respectively. The number of tracking errors in each block was measured.

This task was administered to two groups of currently nondepressed subjects: a vulnerable group who had experienced a major depressive episode previously and a nonvulnerable control group with no history of significant depression. Each group was split into an experimental group that received a mood induction procedure to induce sad mood and an experimental group that received no mood manipulation. Results revealed that the mood induction was equally effective for vulnerable and nonvulnerable subjects, and that no differences were found, in any condition, between the vulnerable and nonvulnerable controls. For vulnerable subjects who received a sad mood induction, however, errors increased in both emotional stimulus blocks, whereas errors decreased for the nonvulnerable subjects when exposed to a sad mood.

The results of the study are consistent with past research on cognitive vulnerability, that is, no differences between vulnerable and nonvulnerable individuals in the control condition would be expected because depressive cognitive processes are difficult to detect after the depressive episode has remitted, although the negative self-schema are postulated to be present in a latent form. As evidenced by the increase in errors for vulnerable individuals who received a sad mood priming procedure, the occurrence of a negative mood thus does appear to activate a process in vulnerable people that has been suggested to be schema controlled: the allocation of attention.

This attentional allocation, however, appears to be fairly diffuse with respect to emotional stimuli, that is, not only depressive-content distractor blocks received enhanced attentional resources, but stimuli that had nondepressive affective connotations also were attended to. At the early preattentive processing stage that this task may assess, there does not seem to be much discrimination between positive and negative emotional stimuli; instead, the emotional nature of the stimulus appears to receive some attentional processing. This attentional allocation may be the equivalent of an "emotional early warning system" that alerts the individual of an impending threat to the self and processes anything with emotional connotations.

In fact, this perspective is consistent with a suggestion by Mathews (1989) in his studies of information processing in anxiety and depression. He has suggested that, although there are specific memory differences in depression and anxiety for respective depression and anxiety relevant information, at the early perceptual stages of information processing, there is enhanced attention to both depressive *and* anxiety stimuli, regardless of whether one is specifically depressed or anxious. Thus, information processing at early perceptual stages is nonspecific; the cognitive differences between the two states occur at a later processing stage. Likewise, the first sign of a dysfunctional schema being activated in vulnerable people may be the initiation of a perceptual process that focuses on the detection of any emotional information. At somewhat later processing stages, this information appears to be filtered so negative self-referent information receives enhanced elaborative processing whereas more positive or benign self-referent information is discarded in some way.

Data reported by Miranda and Persons (in press), Teasdale and Dent (1987), and Ingram (1991) empirically point to the availability of latent but reactive schemata in some individuals that may predispose them to depressive episodes when key activating events occur, presumably by providing access to an articulated network of negative self-referent information. These findings thus indicate that cognitive factors potentially are involved in the onset of depression. Once activated in vulnerable individuals, dysfunctional cognitive structures serve to direct the encoding, organization, and retrieval of information in a manner that provides access to a steady flow of negative self-referent information from both internal and external sources.

In closing, elucidating the role of cognitive variables in depression is an extremely complicated and demanding challenge. If, however, it is reasonable to assume that cognition contributes to depression in some nontrivial manner, then understanding the information-processing basis of this disorder ultimately can help researchers successfully meet this challenge. Depressive information-processing research has shown signs of steady growth in recent years. Through continued growth, both in uncovering the information-processing mechanisms of depression and in integrating knowledge of these mechanisms with other cognitive and noncognitive perspectives, it is our hope that this research can bring us closer to an understanding of the essential elements that underlie depression.

# 11

# Anxiety Disorders

**W. Jake Jacobs, Lynn Nadel, and Vanessa C. Hayden**

*Department of Psychology*
*University of Arizona*
*Tucson, Arizona*

## The Problems of Anxiety

### Prevalence and Risk

A person suffering one of the anxiety disorders usually feels intense and irrational fear, as if something dreadful is about to happen. The person is not out of contact with reality; the dreadful feeling does not render the person incapable of coping with daily life.[1] Instead, this feeling makes the person miserable. The feeling is common to the anxiety disorders and is what unites anxiety disorders as a class.

Nearly 29 million people (7.3% of the population) in the United States suffer from anxiety disorders. Approximately 1 in 5 will receive professional treatment. Primary care physicians will treat about 5 million; only about 1 million will receive care from a mental health professional. The

---

[1] In some cases, agoraphobia for example, the person may become seriously incapacitated.

remaining 23 million get help from family, friends, or the clergy, or do not get help (Regier et al., 1988; Pasnau & Bystritsky, 1990).

The lives of those afflicted with an anxiety disorder are at risk. A person suffering panic disorder, for example, is at risk for suicide. Indeed, a proportionally larger number of people diagnosed with panic disorder than of those suffering clinical depression will commit suicide (Lonnqvist & Kuoppasalmi, 1989; Weissman, Klerman, Markowitz, & Ouellette, 1989). Increased rates of death associated with hypertension, heart trouble, and stress-related disease also show up in this population (Wiessman, Markowitz, Ouellette, Greenwald, & Kahn, 1990). This is troublesome given that nearly 80% of those with an anxiety disorder will not receive any professional help. It is especially troublesome because powerful clinical tools, both biological and psychological, are available to help fight these afflictions.

This chapter begins with an overview of the problem of anxiety and a description of the bits and pieces from which anxiety seems to be constructed. We then offer a model (SIR) based in cognitive science that integrates cognitive, behavioral, and physiological perspectives on anxiety. Finally we use SIR to organize the major treatment procedures.

## Diagnostics

The anxiety disorders seem to be composed of four separable constellations of symptoms, interactions among which produce anxiety in its various manifestations.

### Constellations

**Affective Constellation (Emotion)**  Almost all the data we have about the affective constellation come from self-report, that is, from "I feel" statements. We should not trivialize these data. A sense of anxiety, impending personal catastrophe, apprehension, dread, and misery is what brings the sufferer to treatment. This sense is what the clinician seeks to control and what the researcher seeks to explain.

**Cognitive Constellation (Thought)**  The data we have about the cognitive constellation also come from self-report, although they have achieved a somewhat higher status in the scientific community than the data about the affective constellation. These data are the *content* of thought. The individual reports thoughts such as "I am going to die," "I cannot cope with this feeling any longer," or "If I do not perform (or withhold) this act, dire results will follow."

One may infer the existence of certain *processes* as the basis of such content statements. For example, a set of statements may show consistently a negative misinterpretation of life events, suggesting that a maladaptive cognitive *schema* is in operation. This schema forces a certain type of interpretation on the individual. Other statements may show that an individual diagnosed with an anxiety disorder is impaired on complex cognitive tasks, reflecting difficulty concentrating, making decisions, or remembering commitments. "Letters go unmailed; appointments are missed; it may take a half hour to scrutinize a menu" (Bootzin & Acocella, 1988, p. 174). Such self-reported data also suggest a pervasive disturbance in the processes that control attention, memory, and judgment.

**Behavioral Constellation (Action)** The data that we have for the behavioral constellation come from both self-report and direct observation. Behaviors from this constellation appear to be manifestations of primitive flight, fight, or freeze responses.[2] Components of this constellation may include impaired speech or motor functioning.

**Physiological Constellation** The data we have for the physiological constellation come from self-report, direct observation, and events recorded by instruments. The events of interest are usually peripheral, for example, increased respiration, blood pressure changes, changed heart rate, increased muscle tension, changes in galvanic skin response, dry mouth, nausea, diarrhea, or frequent urination. These events, which result from arousal of the sympathetic nervous system, may lead to muscle aches or twitches, headaches, difficulty breathing, racing pulse, tingling in the hands or feet, clammy hands, indigestion, and insomnia.

### Source of Anxiety Disorders

The causal interactions, if any, among elements of these constellations remain obscure. We do not know how components from each of these constellations combine to form particular anxiety disorders, which could be partial manifestations of a single underlying system (the universalist view), manifestations of independent processes (the modular view), or the product of partially interacting, partially independent processes.

A given anxiety disorder may be an unfortunate juxtaposition of components from four independent constellations that occasionally coalesce, or it may be a coherent system with affective, cognitive, behavioral, and physiological components.

We do know that events in the affective, cognitive, behavioral, and physiological constellations do not synchronize perfectly (Lang, 1970;

---

[2]There are other primitive response classes that are less well known. Rats, for example, will bury a source of danger (Pinel & Symans, 1989) or copulate if the appropriate environmental support is present (e.g., Barfield, & Sachs, 1968).

Rachman, 1978; Mavissakalian, 1987). An individual may, for example, show extensive physiological signs, yet not complain of emotional distress, or may show no behavioral or physiological signs while complaining vociferously of subjective terror.

The Diagnostic and Statistical Manual of the American Psychiatric Association DSM-III(R), the most commonly used diagnostic system in North America, identifies eight seemingly distinct anxiety disorders:

1. panic disorder with or without agoraphobia
2. agoraphobia without a history of panic disorder
3. obsessive–compulsive disorder
4. posttraumatic stress disorder
5. generalized anxiety disorder
6. anxiety disorder NOS
7. social phobia
8. simple phobia

The self-reported cognitive and behavioral contents certainly differ among the various anxiety disorders (but see Argyle, 1988; Kenardy, Evans, & Oei, 1989; Street, Craske, & Barlow, 1989; Warren, Zgourides, & Englert, 1990), but the physiological and affective components may not.

In summary, the anxiety disorders, as defined by DSM-III(R), include characteristics from four constellations of symptoms: affective, cognitive, behavioral, and physiological. Various combinations of symptoms yield a given disorder.[3]

## Current Perspectives

Most current perspectives on anxiety disorders take a linear view of causality, which has dominated science and scientific psychology for several centuries. The cognitive view suggests that thought causes anxiety; the behavioral view suggests that stimuli in the internal or external milieu[4] cause anxiety; the (neuro)biological view suggests that the activation of a given (neuro)biological system causes anxiety. In all cases, it is assumed that there is a specific cause—an event that will bring about a given state of anxiety or

---

[3]There is a small and active research literature pursuing the classification problem (e.g., Achte, 1989; Borden & Turner, 1989; Gabriel, 1989; Kenardy, Evans, & Oei, 1990; Hiller, Zaudig, von Bose, & Rummler, 1989; Kuoppasalmi, Lonnqvist, Pylkkanen, & Huttunen, 1989; Oei, Gross, & Evans, 1989; Pasnau & Bystritsky, 1990; Sanderson & Barlow, 1990).

[4]We use the term *milieu* in lieu of the term *context*. The latter term has a technical meaning within the Stress-Induced Recovery (SIR), which we use extensively in our theoretical work (e.g., Jacobs & Nadel, 1985; Nadel, & Willner, 1980, 1989; O'Keefe & Nadel, 1978; Tataryn, Nadel & Jacobs, 1989).

panic. The hope is that identification of sufficient or necessary causal conditions will provide therapeutic targets. Thus, cognitive therapists focus on changing either the content or the process of thought, behavioral therapists focus on changing reactions to given stimuli, and (neuro)biological therapists focus on changing specific (neuro)biological systems.

Our position is that linear models such as those just described neither offer a comprehensive picture of what the clinician faces, nor allow the practitioner to describe adequately, to predict, or to explain the material at hand.

We describe an integrative model, known as the Stress-Induced Recovery (SIR), that derives from a cognitive science perspective. Whereas classical models of anxiety argue that the properties of the parts (constellations) determine the nature of that disorder, SIR argues that this view is only partially true; SIR suggests instead that the properties of the disorder as a whole also regulate the properties of the parts. (See also Barlow, 1988, for another approach to this issue.) Thus, if cognition affects anxiety and anxiety affects the autonomic system and the autonomic system affects behavior, which in turn affects anxiety, which affects cognition, we have a disorder (anxiety) that cannot be accounted for neatly by linear models.[5]

## An Integrative Model

Jacobs and Nadel (1985; in preparation) proposed the SIR model of simple phobias, which argues that simple phobias (and perhaps other anxiety disorders) result from a confluence of several factors, all necessary for the development of a clinically significant problem. Briefly, we argued that learning experiences occurring before the full development of the brain, particularly before hippocampal formation (12–24 months of age in humans), are critical to the later development of some anxiety disorders. In proper temporal order, these factors are (1) aversive learning episodes that occur early in life, well before the anatomical and physiological maturation of the hippocampal formation (e.g., Squire, Cohen & Nadel, 1984);

---

[5]This approach, of course, is not new. Behavioral therapy, for example, makes use of such a multilevel approach by relying on a *functional analysis* before behavioral interventions occur. A functional analysis, by definition, looks at the person in a larger environmental context that may include reinforcers, discriminative stimuli, social interaction, and much more. Behavioral therapy, moreover, often makes use of the larger context to effect change. Behavioral therapists who, for example, teach parents to use token economies to bring their children's behavior under control are affecting change in the child by first *affecting change in the parent*. The whole point of therapy is to get the parent to behave differently toward the child (usually through instruction, thus violating one of their own basic principles)—and the whole therapy relies upon changes in the supporting context to bring about change in the target system, the misbehaving child.

(2) anatomical and physiological maturation of the hippocampal formation (Bayer & Altman, 1991); (3) the occurrence of severe physiological stress some time after this maturation; (4) the resultant "disabling" of the hippocampal formation and uncovering of the learning that occurred in early maturing learning/memory (taxon) systems (e.g., Micco, McEwen & Shein (1979); (5) the simultaneous exposure to stimuli resembling (in a feature-based sense) those stimuli to which infantile learning had occurred; and (6) a reinstatement of primitive event memories that activate latent neural circuits (e.g., Campbell & Jaynes, 1966; Riccio & Haroutunian, 1979). If all the elements come together in proper temporal and spatial order, an anxiety disorder will appear (see also Tataryn, Nadel, & Jacobs, 1989). Jacobs and Blackburn (in press) have provided an algebraic model that captures many of the events critical to the original account.

Jacobs and Nadel (in preparation) have shown that SIR may be elaborated to explain the etiology of an initial panic attack that may later be elaborated into panic disorder and further elaborated into agoraphobia. The first panic or phobic attack results from a learning experience that occurs before hippocampal maturation. To be manifested in adulthood, both disorders require stress and a concurrent re-exposure to the stimulus features encoded during the critical infant experience. The difference between the disorders is the developmental time-window during which the original learning experience occurs, leading to a difference in the content of that learning experience.

According to SIR, learning that occurs in infancy never truly disappears. Instead, it appears that taxon learning and memory is buried by the maturation of the fast-acting, highly cognitive, hippocampally based locale learning and memory system. The later maturing locale system is, however, biased by the retention of early experience held in taxon learning and memory systems. The locale system makes reference to taxon contents and uses these contents to bias what is learned and the speed at which any previously established learning extinguishes. Thus, many of the constraints observed during adult learning are, in truth, savings effects.

SIR proposes that, during a simple extinction procedure, the content of the taxon systems remains unchanged. Extinction, in this case, results from a new set of principles acquired by the fast-acting locale system, namely, a cognitive rule that ". . . in this place, the cue no longer has biological meaning" (Jacobs & Nadel, 1985, p. 523). We shall call this phenomenon pseudoextinction. In contrast, extinction that takes place in the absence of the locale system appears to be true extinction; the contents of the taxon systems are changed. There should be no remnants of the former conditioning experience in either the locale or the taxon system after true extinction. The implications of properties of taxon and locale systems will be made clear in subsequent text.

## Issues of Integration

We now turn to ideas that are fundamental to traditional approaches to the treatment of anxiety. We shall treat three seemingly disparate ideas; our purpose is to illustrate how SIR integrates them and makes them coherent.

### Cognitive Therapy

The idea that unites cognitive-behavioral therapy is intuitive and straightforward. When one changes distorted views about the self, the future, and the world, one changes affect and behavior. It is difficult, however, to determine exactly what the cognitive therapist means by this statement (Arkowitz & Hanna, 1989). For some, the statement means that when we change thought *content* we bring about emotional or behavioral change in a person. For others, changing thought itself does not matter; instead the target of therapy must be the *process* producing thought. Changing processes underlying thought will bring about emotional or behavioral change in a person. In the following discussion we address some of the implications of these positions.

**Content Position** Those who hold the content position argue that thoughts[6] mediate or cause emotional behavior (see Mahoney, 1974,1977; Meichenbaum, 1979,1985; Clark, 1986; Salkovskis & Clark, 1990). First, one experiences physiological change associated with anxiety. Then one becomes aware of the physiological change. This awareness produces specific thoughts, for example, "I am about to die." The content of a specific thought produces anxiety or even terror. An awareness of threat or terror produces more frightening thoughts, which escalates anxiety.[7]

Cognitive content therapists define cognition as "... a specific thought, such as an interpretation, a self-command, or a self-criticism." They also apply the term to wishes (such as suicidal desires) that have verbal content (Beck, 1963, p. 326). Content therapists assert that a change in thought content, for example, "My heart is pounding because I am excited," will accomplish therapeutic change (see Argyle, 1988; Laraia, Stuart, & Best, 1989; Alford, Freeman, Beck & Wright, 1990). Cognitive content therapies are, thus, "... a set of treatment techniques that aim to relieve symptoms of psychological distress through the direct modification

[6]The use of the term 'thought' is fraught with difficulty. The term 'cognition' or the phrase 'cognitive content' suffers the same confusion. We use 'thought' in its intuitive sense, acknowledging the extreme difficulty of this term.

[7]Many models describe this causal chain, which begins with perceived threat. This may, for example, lead to apprehension which leads to overbreathing. Overbreathing leads to a decrease in $pCO_2$ and increases in blood ph. These physical changes lead to unpleasant body sensations which lead to more apprehension (see Clark, Salkovskis, & Chalkley, 1985).

of the dysfunctional ideation that accompanies them" (Bedrosian & Beck, 1980, p. 128). Therapies of this type are, therefore, designed to restructure the content of thought.

The content position has generated much of the data in the recent literature (e.g., Chambless & Gracely, 1989; Himle, Himle, & Thyer, 1989; Holt & Andrews, 1989; Kenardy et al., 1989; Warren, Zgourides, & Jons, 1989; Borkovec & Inz, 1990; Warren, et al., 1990), some of which does not satisfy predictions generated by the content theorists. (For examples, see Klein & Klein, 1989; Street et al., 1989; Zucker et al., 1989; Gurnani & Wang, 1990; Hampl, Scott, Carmin, & Fleming, 1990; Kenardy, Evans, & Oei, 1990).

**Process Position** Those who hold the process position argue that thought content is but one manifestation of deeper-lying processes that regulate emotion, perception, learning, and other psychological states (see Ellis, 1987; Beck, 1988). This position proposes, for example, that panic attacks critically involve the catastrophic misinterpretation of some body or psychological experiences. This habitual misreading (a process), combined with the unwitting obstruction of access to corrective information (a second process) and a decline in the ability to reason (a third process), escalates the person's symptoms of panic.

The process therapist defines cognition as a set of processes that produces specific thoughts, interpretations, self-commands, or self-criticisms. The term also is applied to processes such as schemata. Cognitive process therapies rest on the assumption that producing change in process leads to changes in thought content, behavior, and emotion. The strategy is less direct in its assertions about the causal relationship between thought, emotion, and behavior. The most conservative of these strategies might argue that changes in thought content result from process change. Manipulations of thought content, from this point of view, serve both as a way of changing processes responsible for thought and emotion and as an outcome measure. Changes in dysfunctional processing lead to changes in both the emotion and the behavior caused by the thought. (See Velmans, 1991, for a thoughtful discussion of these issues as they relate to cognitive science in general.)

### Behavior Therapy

A major idea of behavior therapy[8] is that when one changes relationships among conditional and unconditional stimuli, one changes affect, behavior, cognition, and physiology. The goal, then, is to identify the stimuli controlling each outbreak of anxiety and to apply well-known principles of extinction to eliminate the response they trigger. It is difficult, however, to

---

[8]There are two different varieties of behavior therapy: Those based in classical conditioning and those based in operant conditioning. We concentrate on the former. The therapies arising from the operant perspective require a different treatment.

identify the critical conditional and unconditional stimuli (McNally, 1990). To make the problem tractable, two assumptions have been common.

First, it is assumed that all stimuli are represented in the central nervous system and that associations are realized through neural connections among the sets of neurons representing the stimuli. Second, it is assumed that there is a fixed 1:1 correspondence between environmental events, as "psychologists/observers" might define them, and their neural representations. These assumptions have proven convenient, enabling those interested in learning and cognition to show that higher organisms take various features of the available environmental information and form associations among them in selective and complicated ways. (See, for example, Kamin, 1969; Wagner, 1971; Rescorla & Wagner, 1972; Wagner & Rescorla, 1972; Mackintosh, 1974,1975,1983; Pearce & Hall, 1980; Daly & Daly, 1982; Damianopoulos, 1987; Jacobs, 1987; Pearce, 1987; Jacobs & Blackburn, in press; for reviews.) These assumptions, however, leave the problem of specifying the relationships among observed events, represented events, and subjective experience primarily to those concerned with sensation, perception, and psychophysics.

**Clinical Neuroscience**

The idea that unites (neuro)biologically based therapy is that there are organic determinants of anxiety. When one changes biological systems, one changes cognition, affect, and behavior. It is assumed that we apply psychological treatments for a psychogenic disorder; we apply biological treatments for a somatogenic disorder. There is no need to expand on this position since it will form the basis of much of what follows.

**Resolution: Cognitive Science**

The ideas underlying the cognitive, behavioral, and neurobiological perspectives just outlined are not irreconcilable. The SIR model emphasizes the interdependence of these perspectives and the phenomena on which they are based. Anxiety disorders incorporate contributions from affective, cognitive, behavioral, and biological systems, as well as from the relationships among them.

SIR assumes that anxiety derives from a variety of sources, each of which is manifested in a specific way. At the cognitive level, one might see maladaptive thoughts; at the behavioral level, it could be stereotypy and behavioral inflexibility; at the neurobiological level, it might be tachycardia. These manifestations are not separate, but interrelated. Thus, cognitive processes produce more than cognitive effects; they also may contribute to the production of behavioral or neurobiological effects. These effects may, in turn, feed back to the cognitive process, enhancing or diminishing its intensity. People may be frightened by thoughts as well as by physical pain, the pounding of their heart, or the trembling of their hands.

There are similarities between the cognitive science perspective, as exemplified by SIR, and the behavioral approach, but there is a critical difference between them that lies at the core of SIR. The behavioral approach assumes that people are frightened not by particular thoughts, but by environmental stimuli that are initially neutral and are associated with aversive stimuli. SIR agrees with the assumption that anxiety derives from learning, and also accepts the view that this learning involves the formation of associations instantiated in the central nervous system. The critical distinction between SIR and traditional behavioral approaches lies in SIR's assertion that there is not a fixed, immutable correspondence between environmental stimuli and their neural representations. How a person's brain represents stimuli, or indeed what stimuli it represents, depends critically on the kinds of experiences to which the person is exposed early in life. These early formative experiences shape not only the person, but also the person's neural machinery, determining how it will deal with later events. Behavioral approaches are silent on this level, failing to take into account the extraordinary plasticity of the nervous system, especially in developmental terms.

Thus, SIR contends that, although the environment may contain a triggering stimulus, the trigger itself resides in the specific neural circuitry of the anxiety-ridden individual. In this way, it accounts for how stimuli that trigger anxiety for one person can have no impact on another. From this perspective, a conditioned (environmental) stimulus that triggers anxiety is equivalent to a thought, a pain, a pounding heart, or trembling hands, all of which reflect activity of the system as an integrated whole.

The characteristic feature of this approach, and of cognitive science in general, is that it insists on the integration of cognitive, behavioral, and neurobiological perspectives, none of which is allowed to exist on its own, isolated from the impact of the others. Anxiety, and the anxiety disorders, involves thoughts and behaviors that are linked, on the one hand, to experiences and events in the environment and, on the other, to the way in which these are represented in the afflicted person's nervous system. SIR asserts that we will neither understand, nor successfully treat, anxiety disorders unless we take this complex situation into account.

## Treatment[9]

It don't have to be true to be useful.
(Overheard in a bar in Tucson, Arizona)

Although what should change seems obvious when we talk about an anxiety disorder, the problem becomes more complicated when one con-

[9]See Barlow & Cerny (1988), Beck & Emory (1985), Freeman & Simon (1989), Fried (1990), Kennerley (1990), Marks, (1987), Munoz (1986), Pasnau (1984), Thyer (1987), and Turner, (1984) for more complete descriptions of these and other procedures.

siders the question at a practical level. Some therapists claim we must change affect, others claim we must change cognition, others claim we must change behavior, and still others claim that physiological change is sufficient to accomplish our therapeutic goals. If we concentrate on the afflicted individual, then we want to know more specifically what aspect of affect, cognition, behavior, or physiology must change.

We need theory to guide our choices here. Theory allows us to postulate causes of the disordered affect, cognition, behavior, or physiology at the root of an anxiety disorder, to make predictions about the results of manipulating those causes, and to develop the principles leading to effective treatment aimed at ameliorating the disorder.

SIR asserts that the properties of anxiety arise from interactions among various components. These properties also may affect the parts themselves (the interior milieu) and the context within which they exist (the exterior milieu). As is evident from our summary of SIR's treatment of conditional and unconditional stimuli, we concentrate primarily on the interior milieu. Change, however, often originates in the exterior milieu.

According to SIR, anxiety serves a purpose in reflecting poor adaptation to the external milieu.[10] Poor adaptation leads to stress. Stress induces changes in cognition (a narrowing of attention), behavior (stereotypy), and biochemistry (a shut-down of the hippocampal formation). This cascade exposes early formed, fundamental taxon structures that are then changed in response to internal and external environmental pressures. If these changes produce satisfactory adaptation, then stress lifts. The lifting of stress induces changes in cognition (an enriching of attention and other processes), behavior (increased behavioral flexibility), and biochemistry (returning hippocampal formation to its normal spatial, cognitive, and behavioral functions), and anxiety lifts. Thus, the stress produced by poor adaptation increases the chance of continued satisfactory adaptation of the individual to the external milieu. Anxiety serves as a critical component in setting the stage for corrective action.

Corrective action may come in the form of cognition, behavior, or physiology. Interventions may range in intensity from simple reframing to serious physiological and behavioral challenge. Therapy is designed to increase satisfactory adaptation to circumstances of which the victim may have no control, or to change those circumstances that may be corrected.

The therapeutic consequences of entering the system through each of these routes may be quite different. It is most convenient, then, to classify

[10]Poor adaptation might enter the system through cognitive (recognizing a maladaptive situation), behavioral (an inability to accomplish fundamental behavioral goals), or physiological (sickness or chronic starvation) means. Satisfactory adaptation might enter the system through the same means: Cognitive (recognizing or interpreting a situation as satisfactory), behavioral (accomplishing fundamental behavioral goals), or physiological (a well balanced diet).

these interventions in terms of what they do, rather than in terms of the route by which they enter the system. We suggest that interventions encourage the person to comply, to cope, to circumvent, to cure, or to conserve treatment gains. We shall use this as a theme to unify our discussion of the common treatment modes for anxiety disorders. The classification rests fundamentally on the way in which SIR regards treatment modes.

We will present this classification subsequently (see "Developing a Treatment Strategy"). Before doing so, we return to the ideas of symptom constellations and the content–process distinction to organize our discussion of data collection and diagnosis.

## Data Collection

Many well-understood and highly treatable physiological conditions include components of the affective, cognitive, behavioral, or physiological constellations that make up an anxiety disorder. These components can mask as an anxiety disorder. Among them, hyperthyroidism, inner ear infection, congestive heart failure, chronic pulmonary disease, acute pulmonary infection, asthma, orthostatic hypotension, anemia, paroxysmal atrial tachycardia, mitral valve prolapse, endocrinophaty, temporal lobe epilepsy, hyperventilation syndrome, and low grade infections are the most common. Knowing the medical condition of the individual enables clinicians to be sensitive to the possibility of organic disease and to the psychological side effects of any disease the person may have. Clinicians should remain sensitive to the possibility of organic disease and be willing to work closely with a physician during diagnosis and treatment.[11]

One also should consider the possibility of drug-induced anxiety or panic. The side effects of many of the drugs prescribed for organic disease present as mental disturbances. Unfortunately, such drugs may be prescribed without forewarning about these side effects. Nonprescription drugs (including vitamins, amino acids, and the like) may also precipitate anxiety or panic or mask as such. The withdrawal of drugs, including alcohol, nicotine, caffeine, cocaine, amphetamines, and others, also can precipitate panic attacks or severe anxiety.

## Diagnosis

When all medical factors have been eliminated as possible contributors to the symptoms, one can diagnose more precisely. The Anxiety Dis-

[11]The converse is also true. Ballenger (1987) estimates that 6–10% of the patients in a primary care setting and 10–14% of the patients in a cardiology unit suffer from misdiagnosed panic disorder. This phenomenon is well documented among researchers but many primary care physicians seem unaware of it (Watkins, Lidren & Champion, 1991).

orders Inventory Schedule-Revised (ADIS-R) [12] can be a useful supplement to DSM-III(R) and is fully compatible with it.

Having made the diagnosis, the therapist and the patient gather data. They work together to determine what affective, cognitive, behavioral, and physiological content needs to be changed. They identify automatic thoughts that occur during an episode of anxiety, any environmentally or physiologically based stimuli that might trigger an attack, and the physiological manifestations of anxiety as well as its time course, severity, and intensity. Their task during this phase is to describe the problem well enough to be able to tailor an efficacious treatment regime to the individual and his or her needs. This development requires both science and art.

**Thought Content**

Accurately identifying thought content is critical. The therapist eventually will direct the entire cognitive component of therapy at changing the content. Most therapists try to measure cognitive content by recognition, recall, prompted recall, or expressive methods (Glass & Merluzzi, 1981) by using, among others, the Social Interaction Self-Statement Test, the Assertiveness Self-Statement Test, and the Cognitive Interference Questionnaire. (See Merluzzi & Boltwood, 1989, for more complete descriptions of these tests.)

It is preferable to record cognitive content during a period of anxiety or shortly thereafter when the data have a greater chance of being accurate. The different methods available attempt to do this through a variety of means. Recall methods rely primarily on having the person list thoughts that he or she may have during an attack of anxiety. Prompted recall methods include videotaped or enacted scenes during which the individual supplies thought dialogue. This allows the therapist to record the thoughts as they unfold, revealing temporal characteristics as well as content. Diaries, which the person keeps for several weeks, are quite useful for collecting data on-line. Expressive methods, which are perhaps the best of the lot, ask the person to think aloud while experiencing an attack. This is easily done, for example, with simple or social phobias, agoraphobia, and obsessive–compulsive disorders, and can be used for panic disorder by inducing panic under controlled conditions. [13] These methods also may be used to collect affective, behavioral, and physiological data.

---

[12]Available from Graywind Publications, c/o Center for Stress and Anxiety Disorders, 1535 Western Avenue, Albany, New York, USA. 12203. The cost is between $3.50 and $4.00 (US) apiece, depending on how many you order. A specimen set is available with one instruction manual and a bound ADIS-R. If you want to use the ADIS-R as a research tool, contact Dr. Peter DiNardo at the Center for Stress and Anxiety Disorders. They will make video tapes and training sessions available to you. Additional training in the use of the ADIS-R is available from Barlow's Center for Stress and Anxiety Disorders at Albany, New York.

[13]Barlow & Cerny (1988) have provided a systematic program for gathering such data. It could be easily adapted to most of the anxiety disorders.

### Thought Process

It is important to understand the schemata and the attributional styles the person uses in thought process, typically by interpreting the content data collected in the previous phase. Interpretation of these data involves methods ranging from intuitive analysis through content analysis and extends to factor analysis or structural analysis. Litz and Keane (1989) have reviewed the selective information processing exhibited by people suffering from anxiety disorders. Further development along these lines holds a promise of providing a powerful diagnostic tool to identify thought processes that might be targeted for change (see also Lang, 1985).[14]

### Behavior

The clinician also wants to know about the behaviors the patient is exhibiting and the stimuli that might be triggering them. Acquiring this information is harder than it might seem, partly because the person is, generally, the primary observer. The therapist trains the individual in basic observational methodology by constructing questionnaires, creating diaries, and checking reliability, making sure the person records all behaviors associated with the anxiety. It is critical that the person's training include basic formal observational methods, including reliability checks. Acquiring reliable data on behavior is essential, because these observations will be primary material for designing behavioral interventions (see Barlow & Cerny, 1988).

### Functional Analysis

It is a good idea not only to explore the symptoms the individual exhibits, but also the functions those symptoms may have. To do so, one must examine both the individual and the broader context within which the individual functions. In some cases a symptom may serve purposes other than those that are obvious at first glance. This systemic approach, which is compatible with a behavioral approach, seeks to explore interactions among important individuals, including the person and other people in the social group (usually members of the family). Changing the cognition or behavior of an individual is fruitless if he or she receives pressure not to change from the social or physical environment. Treatment in cases such as this should include the person *and* the individuals who are intimately involved in the system (Shoham-Salomon & Bootzin, 1990).

---

[14]The goal of therapy itself may be a function of whether one focuses on content or process. A Content therapist might argue, ". . . the goal of C[ognitive] T[herapy] is not to cure, but rather more effective coping . . ." Freeman & Simon (1989, p. 360), but the Process therapist might profoundly disagree, asserting that the goal would be to change the process and thereby affect a cure.

Having gathered information about thought content and process, about behaviors and their possible patterns, and clinician and the client define the goals of therapy. The practitioner and patient together prioritize the list of goals and arrive at some decision about reasonable achievements. Then, a treatment strategy incorporating the data and the priority list must be developed.

### Developing a Treatment Strategy

The question most critical for the therapist, no matter what the persuasion, is where to enter the system to effect change. SIR asserts that answering this question correctly relies on understanding that the causes of behavior, both normal and abnormal, arise at many levels of the complex system that we call a person.

Some therapies aim only at one level, leaving the other levels untouched. This approach, from the perspective of SIR, appears naive at best. Other therapies aim at more than one level, although some practitioners might deny this. Therapeutic procedures are typically classified by the level at which they direct treatment. We feel that it is more direct to classify therapeutic procedures by what they accomplish rather than by their level of entry. This approach, however, requires theoretical guidance. We now offer a functional taxonomy guided by SIR. We concentrate on the major functions of each class.

The first job of the therapist is to insure compliance. The therapist then teaches procedures that allow a person to cope with anxiety, to circumvent anxiety, to cure the maladaptive anxiety, and to conserve treatment gains.

#### Compliance

No therapeutic intervention can succeed without the patient's cooperation. Treatment may fail because of a failure to comply with treatment recommendations (Meichenbaum & Turk, 1987). The procedures in this section, from the perspective of SIR, serve mainly to facilitate compliance. They do not seem to facilitate true extinction, in which associative bonds are broken. These procedures may bring about some change in locale (cognitive) systems, and thereby affect a variation of pseudoextinction, but taxon systems remain unchanged. Nonetheless, their main affect is to encourage the client to engage in other more therapeutically efficacious procedures.

**Psychoeducation** First, through the use of a treatment rationale, the therapist convinces the patient that the procedures will work by convincing the person that the diagnostic model of the disorder is correct. The next task is to convince the person that feelings of anxiety or panic are normal.[15] Finally, a person learns, when frightened, to recognize the signs of fear (or panic).

Explaining these ideas not only provides reassurance, but also allows the patient to reattribute anxiety to the effects of agents that can be controlled and to predict the occurrence of such anxiety. The notion that the procedures they are about to learn will work helps insure that the person will follow the treatment plan.

Although we realize that the goal of the treatment rationale (to convince the person of the truth of something) defies the very basis of scientific training (to doubt, maintain skepticism, and disconfirm), this step is essential before trying other interventions. [See Barlow and Cerny's (1988) instructional manual for specific suggestions regarding the treatment rationale for many cognitive interventions.] The person's belief in the model and its efficacy seems critical to successful treatment (see, for example Lick & Bootzin, 1975; Southworth & Kirsch, 1988).

**Paradoxical Interventions** Paradoxical interventions operate to the benefit of the most resistant persons (Shoham-Salomon, Avner, & Neeman, 1989). They rely on the assumption that a major problem in an anxiety disorder is that the afflicted individual struggles against both anxiety and its ensuing symptoms. The therapist encourages the person to try to increase symptoms such as palpitations and to allow the dreadful event to happen when an anxiety attack occurs. One intention of this procedure is to allow habituation to the symptoms by demonstrating that the feared consequences, for example, dying or losing control, will not occur (Frankl, 1960; Gerz, 1966; Goldstein, 1978).

The primary intention is to use noncompliance as a tool. The therapist may, for example, encourage the person to have anxiety attacks. If nothing changes and anxiety attacks continue, the person has followed the therapeutic prescription. They have had a demonstration that the feared consequences will not occur and have had habituation experience with the attacks. This can be used as a starting point for other therapeutic interventions. If, on the other hand, the anxiety attacks stop (and this can happen in highly reactant persons), then the person already has accomplished a main therapeutic goal—cessation of the anxiety attacks. (See Shoham-Salomon & Rosenthal, 1987, for a quantitative review of this literature.)

---

[15]Many call such a strategy *reframing*, which means that the therapist (or another) provides a different, usually positive, perspective from which the individual might view an emotion or situation. Usually reframing involves changing a negative connotation, "I am anxious all the time and it is abnormal" to a positive, "I am in touch with my feelings, my feelings are normal, and all of this gives me an opportunity to learn."

## Coping

A person also needs to be able to abort either panic or anxiety. Coping procedures are skills that may be applied to prevent an attack from developing. To do so, the person applies the procedures in the presence of prodromal symptoms. Coping procedures may come to serve as safety signals (inhibitors of fear) that act much like the rituals, talismans, sunglasses, or safe persons of the agoraphobic (see e.g., Mathews, Gelder, & Johnston, 1981).

Let us explain how this might work. Each time an efficacious procedure is used (e.g., Xanax®), a pairing of the procedure (presence of or swallowing the capsule) with relief of anxiety is achieved. This approach may lead to a superstitious dependence on the presence of the procedure (having the capsule within reach). The procedure, of course, parallels those used to produce conditioned inhibition. The presence of a conditioned inhibitor of fear, known in other parts of the literature as a safety signal, may serve as a powerful reinforcer (LoLordo, 1969). Once an association has been made between Xanax® and the relief of anxiety, for example, Xanax® becomes a reinforcer for the panic-ridden individual and s/he carries it at all times.

The superstitious relief a person receives from the presence of Xanax® finds its basis in locale (cognitive) systems (see Jacobs & Nadel, 1985). The argument applies mainly to the coping procedures, but also to other effective treatment procedures.

**Drugs**  The benzodiazapines are the most common pharmacological coping tool. Some, Xanax® for example, are used to abort a panic attack. Librium® or Valium® may be used to help control low-grade anxiety. Many people learn to recognize prodromal symptoms of anxiety and use one or another of the high-potency benzodiazepines as a coping tool. Although useful as coping tools, these drugs seem ineffective as circumvention tools (see Altesman & Cole, 1984; Ballenger, 1984; Goldberg, 1984; Lydiard & Roy-Byrne, 1988; subsequent discussion).

**Controlled Respiration Training**  Controlled respiration training relies on the notion that hyperventilation plays a crucial role in anxiety (see Huey & Sechrest, 1983; Gorman et al., 1986; Fried, 1987; Ley, 1988a,b; 1989; Fried & Golden, 1989). The individual learns slow abdominal breathing, usually while lying down, practicing on a daily basis until it is mastered. The therapist then encourages the person to use controlled breathing to overcome sensations of anxiety and panic (see Fried, 1990). Some use this procedure with imagery and biofeedback (see Fried, 1987b).

**Imagery**  In imagery procedures, patients receive instructions in imagining pleasant scenes or situations. They then receive instructions to use these well-practiced images when experiencing the prodromal or actual symptoms of a panic attack.

**Coping Self-Statements**   In the development of coping self-statements, the therapist begins with psychoeducation, convincing the person that thoughts exacerbate panic and interfere with coping self-statements. The person and therapist then identify negative self-statements (thoughts), images, and feelings that occur before (during prodromal symptoms), during, and after an attack. The person and therapist then generate specific self-statements to cope with negative thoughts. Statements about competence and control, for example, focusing on the present, taking things as they come, and ignoring possible future consequences, seem most efficacious. The person then receives instructions and practice designed to ingrain these thought patterns and instructions on how to use these strategies during various stages of an attack.

**Applied Relaxation**   The applied relaxation method uses a variety of procedures to encourage a person's self-directed in vivo exposure to fear-producing situations. The person first learns progressive muscle relaxation (see "Circumvention") and then applies the skill in therapist-guided situations. For example, the therapist and patient role-play, learning to relax in the presence of the therapist as well as in therapist-assisted exposure situations. The purpose of the training is to teach the person to recognize early signals of muscular tension and to respond to those signals adaptively (see Öst, 1987).

**Modeling**   A model initially exhibits fearful behaviors, remarking on both the fear and the symptoms, such as sweating, heart palpitations, and difficulty breathing. The model then demonstrates coping behaviors, such as instructions to relax, to breath deeply, to overcome the fear, and statements such as "I will get through this." This demonstration may be done by another individual or by videotape. The person then is encouraged to model or imitate the behavior seen during the demonstration.

#### Circumvention

An afflicted person needs a way to circumvent unwanted or uncontrolled anxiety. The circumvention procedures are skills that, when applied properly, prevent the occurrence of attacks of panic and anxiety.

The circumvention procedures seem uniformly designed to relieve current levels of stress. Like the compliance and coping procedures we have described, circumvention procedures produce changes in the locale system but not in the taxon system. The relief of stress appears to decrease the sensitivity of the taxon system, both in terms of the ease with which anxiety is triggered and in terms of the taxon system's ability to change.

**Drugs**  The four major classes of drugs used in dealing with anxiety disorders are benzodiazapines, tricyclic antidepressants, monoamine oxidase (MAO) inhibitors, and beta blockers. The drugs that are effective in circumventing panic or anxiety tend to be the slow onset type (tricyclics or MAO inhibitors), requiring that the person take medication daily to circumvent, rather than abort, an attack (Lydiard & Ballenger, 1987). Tricyclics and MAO inhibitors are used to circumvent panic attacks and may help with low-grade anxiety (Pohl & Rainey, 1983; Goldberg, 1984; Sheehan, 1984; Liebowitz & Fyer, 1988; Beiderman, 1990). The beta blockers seem efficacious in circumventing performance anxiety or social phobias (Fonte & Stevenson, 1985; Lydiard & Roy-Byrne, 1988; Roy-Byrne & Katon, 1987).

**Biofeedback**  Biofeedback procedures are useful in controlling specific physiological symptoms (Orne, 1980), an advantage that might be worth the special equipment. One might use the procedure to teach a person to relax particularly difficult areas (the face and jaw are often problem areas) or to control responses that normally are outside voluntary control (heart rate or frontalis muscle, for example).

**Progressive Muscle Relaxation**  Progressive muscle relaxation finds its basis in the work of Jacobson (1938). The training provides the person with procedures that allow peripheral relaxation on demand. It begins with progressively tensing and relaxing groups of muscles throughout the body. After practice, an individual can relax muscles on command (bring relaxation under stimulus or instructional control) (see Bernstein & Borkovec, 1973). If practiced enough, this procedure also relaxes the person, making anxiety more difficult to trigger.

**Systematic Desensitization**  Systematic desensitization springs from Wolpe's (1958) integration of Jacobson's work on induced relaxation and Watson and Raynor's (1920) empirical extension of Pavlov's (1927,1928) work on classical conditioning. The therapy proceeds in three steps. The therapist first teaches the person progressive muscle relaxation. The person and therapist then construct a fear hierarchy that contains panic-evoking sensations and situations, ranging from the least to the most feared. The therapist next presents imaginary scenes from the hierarchy, in order of increasing difficulty, while the person relaxes. The goal is for the person to be able to relax while exposed to each item. When the person accomplishes the goal, the next more difficult item in the hierarchy is presented. This continues until the person can tolerate the imagined presence of the most feared items.

**Programmed or Reinforced Practice**  In programmed or reinforced practice, the therapist encourages a person to approach a feared situation or stimulus gradually. The therapist instructs the person to turn back whenever the level of anxiety becomes too extreme. The person receives praise from the therapist for improvement and for continued practice, generally on a continuous reinforcement schedule.

The therapist usually assigns specific homework to the person. The therapist also directs the person to keep diaries recording examples of exposure, the level of anxiety felt during exposure, and so on. The therapist and person then review the data and make adjustments to encourage further exposure and comfort in the presence of the feared items.

**Cognitive Restructuring** The cognitive restructuring procedure tries to make an individual aware of the role that cognition plays in potentiating and maintaining anxiety. The therapist first elicits the individual's thoughts, feelings, and interpretations about anxiety attacks. The therapist then points out the way in which the individual thinks about anxiety, for example, catastrophizing, overgeneralizing, absolute thinking, selective focus, or jumping to conclusions. The individual, in collaboration with the therapist, then gathers evidence for or against such interpretations, challenges such interpretations, and arranges for personal experiments (usually involving exposure) to test the validity of the predictions.[16] The goal is to change a cognitive style from one based on belief (indisputable fact) to one based on possibilities (testable hypotheses).

**In Vivo Desensitization** The person undergoing in vivo desensitization meets with a therapist to construct a hierarchy of feared stimuli, situations, or activities. The person then experiences these feared stimuli, beginning with the least feared and progressing to the most feared in real life. Exposure is accordingly gradual; increased duration and intensity of exposure is the eventual goal (see Marks, 1987). This procedure may use relaxation, cognitive coping strategies, or no additional strategy to cope with the later occurrence of fear.

**Bibliotherapy** The bibliotherapy method involves giving the person readings or instructional manuals designed to change behavior and cognition programmatically. These manuals may range from booklets (instructions on relaxation techniques, for example) to full cognitive-behavioral programs. Although many researchers are uncomfortable with bibliotherapy, at least one clear demonstration of its usefulness in dealing with an anxiety disorder is available. Clum and his colleagues (Gould, Clum, & Shapiro, 1991) have reported that bibliotherapy using the Clum (1990) text is as effective in controlling panic disorder as an individual

---

[16]Pure cognitive interventions are rare. Most cognitive procedures demand the use of behavioral strategies in order to accomplish cognitive change.

therapy using the same procedures. Such methods are cost effective and easier on both therapist and patient. Bibliotherapeutic methods, of course, include compliance, coping, and circumvention procedures.

## Cure

SIR takes the position that a cure requires a change in the content of taxon systems. This change will lead to concomitant changes in the content of affect, cognition, behavior, and physiology as reported by the individual. We have argued that few of the procedures now available accomplish this goal (Jacobs & Nadel, 1985; Tataryn et al., 1989). This chapter is not the appropriate place to outline the argument; let us say, however, that ruthless exposure therapies, those evoking high levels of stress, may be the only procedures now available that accomplish true change in the way in which individuals approach the world.

**Flooding** Flooding involves continuously exposing the person in vivo to high-intensity anxiety-producing stimuli until the anxiety disappears. The idea is that exposure to a feared stimulus will abolish the fear that has been, in the past, associated with it.[17]

**Implosive Therapy** In contrast to flooding, the implosive procedure exposes the person to imagery of feared stimuli (see Stampfl & Levis, 1967). This is done by first identifying the phobic stimuli for each person, then practicing neutral imagery to test the person's ability to use imagery, and finally creating scenes and describing them in enough detail to elicit fear. Thus, one exposes the person indirectly to fear-producing situations through imagination or symbols. The person is encouraged to face the imagery and to avoid escaping the sensations associated with it during the implosive therapy session and during homework assignments (see Boudewyns & Shipley, 1983; Laraia et al., 1989). The therapeutic task is to block avoidance behavior and thereby permit exposure to the full range of triggering stimuli (see Levis, 1987).[18] The procedure includes a method

---

[17]There has been some question if it is ethically correct, or even humane, to use flooding techniques in the clinic. Obviously, it is beyond the scope of this paper to fully explore the problem, so we shall leave it with the following: There are theoretical reasons to believe that flooding may be the most effective of the exposure therapies, others leaving the client with traces of the former psychopathology, traces which, if left untreated may, under the right circumstances, burst back into emotional life (e.g., Jacobs & Nadel, 1985; Lang, 1977; Foa & Kozak, 1986).

[18]Levis asserts that flooding and implosive therapy do not differ in kind "The term 'flooding' is frequently used interchangeably with Implosive Therapy" p. 451, and "In the interest of efficiency and to reduce resistance, symptom-correlated cues are presented first. These are presented *in vivo* when possible or, if *in vivo* exposure is difficult, an imagery method of presentation is used." Pp. 452–453. We shall ignore the claim for the purposes of this paper.

resembling paradoxical intervention (see previous text) to accomplish this goal (Levis, 1987).

### Conserving Treatment Gains

The treatment procedures that we have reviewed have a number of troubling implications. According to SIR, these procedures help with compliance, coping, and circumvention, but they do not cure. Even worse, they may prevent cure. We have argued that stress serves an adaptive function. It exposes taxon systems for modification. Relief of stress seems to decrease the degree of control exhibited by taxon systems, thus decreasing its sensitivity and proclivity to change.

Any procedure that reduces stress before change occurs in taxon systems prevents that change and thus leaves the basis of the disorder untouched. The use of such procedures theoretically demands the use of additional procedures that will help prevent the recurrence of taxon-based anxiety or panic. We now turn to these procedures.

**Stress Management**   The fact that early learning, once acquired, may never be eliminated suggests that when we use the procedures described earlier to eliminate symptoms, the original basis of the disorder lies untouched in the form of neural circuits prepared by early experience. Even when the presenting problems of a person suffering from an anxiety disorder are brought under control, the therapist's job is not finished. The therapist is obliged to provide additional training for the client. Most effective would be procedures designed to reduce stress (daily practice of deep muscle relaxation, for example) and to cope with stress. The person may apply coping procedures to the broader class of stressful situations or may use one of the many stress management packages that are now available.

**Extensive Exposure**   SIR, at its present stage of development, implies that continued long-term controlled exposure to thoughts and stimuli that trigger aspects of an anxiety disorder will lead a person away from mere coping and toward a cure. We suspect, on empirical grounds, that taxon systems are not entirely invulnerable to current experience. Cognitive systems (locale) appear to protect these deeply buried circuits from change only partially (see Jacobs & Nadel, in preparation). If, as we suggest, practice will bring about long-term change, then continued presentation of the former trigger stimuli may serve to decrease the likelihood of reacquisition of the disorder.

Of course, the therapist must convince the client that continued practice is necessary, which may require using compliance procedures and continuing to monitor the client long after the symptomatology has been brought under control.

**Exposure to Many Settings**   SIR also suggests that it is necessary to provide controlled exposure to thoughts and environmentally based stimuli in many different settings to achieve the generality that is needed in effective psychotherapy. Barlow and Cerny (1988) and Clum (1990) stress the need for generality and describe generalization methods that might be used to accomplish this goal.

## Prevention

At present, little or no work is directed at the prevention of anxiety disorders. However, a number of implications from SIR, from Lang's (1985) model, and from Foa & Kozak's (1986) extension of that model are appropriate to consider briefly.

According to SIR, learning experiences occurring before the full development of the hippocampal formation (12–24 months of age in humans) are critical to the later development of at least some anxiety disorders and to the way in which cognitive systems process information. Early experience, held in the form of prepared taxon circuits, influences the information that enters the cognitive (locale) systems and influences the sense that these systems make of such information (see Jacobs & Nadel, 1985).

Lang (1985) proposed that stimuli relevant to fear are encoded and held in memory as propositions. These semantic fear networks contain information about (1) stimulus cues that elicit fear; (2) potential psychophysiological, behavioral, and cognitive responses; and (3) the meaning of these responses. These stimuli are encoded in a way that facilitates appropriate responding to them (Litz & Keane, 1989).

Melding these two models suggests a way in which predispositions to anxiety disorders might be detected early. If early experience influences later developing cognitive systems to encode and hold these stimulus types as propositions, then we can detect predispositions toward an anxiety disorder of one type or another. This extension of SIR suggests that attentional biases toward potentially threatening cues (see, e.g., Foa & McNally, 1986; MacLeod, Mathews, & Tata, 1986; Watts, McKenna, Sharrock, & Trezise, 1986) might be found before the development of an anxiety disorder. In addition, one may be able to detect weak memory biases in these individuals if tested under the correct circumstances (e.g., Norton, Schaefer, Cox, Dorward, & Wozney, 1988; McNally, Foa, & Donnell, 1989).[19] With early detection of such predispositions, one might design programs to prevent their occurrence. An application of this idea awaits both theoretical refinement and improvements in methodology. We note here that early detection programs and preventative measures may save more human misery than all the treatment procedures devised thus far.

---

[19]Indeed, the presence of 'latent' processing biases may explain some of the variability found in this type of study. This raises the possibility that the control groups in these studies are contaminated by latently-held processing biases.

# 12

# Cognitive Science and Obsessive–Compulsive Disorder

**Dan J. Stein and Eric Hollander**

*Department of Psychiatry*
*College of Physicians and Surgeons*
*Columbia University*
*and*
*New York State Psychiatric Institute*
*New York, New York*

Neurobiology
Psychoanalysis
Behaviorism
Cognitive Science
Integration
Implications

Perhaps the most striking aspect of the recent literature on obsessive–compulsive disorder (OCD) is the dramatic growth in our understanding of the neurobiology of this illness (Hollander, DeCaria, & Liebowitz, 1989). OCD once was considered typical of the functional disorders in psychiatry; many now think of it as a neuropsychiatric disorder. Insofar as the growth of knowledge in neuroscience has important implications for integrative cognitive science models of the mind and its disorders, OCD is therefore a useful exemplar. We will attempt to focus our discussion of OCD, then, on the biological underpinnings of the symbolic or representational level. We begin by reviewing advances in the biology of OCD and by considering previous psychological models of OCD.

## Neurobiology

The initial impetus to neurobiological research of OCD was the finding that patients, for whom there were few treatment options, experienced considerable improvement with clomipramine, a predominantly serotonergic antidepressant, but not with desipramine, a predominantly noradrenergic antidepressant. This finding was unusual, because psychiatric disorders such as depression and panic disorder respond to both kinds of medication. The development of specific serotonin reuptake blockers confirmed that medications that act on the serotonin neurotransmitter system are most effective for the treatment of OCD (Zohar and Insel, 1987).

Further advances in biological psychiatry have substantiated the involvement of the serotonin system in this disorder. Measurement of cerebrospinal fluid serotonin before and after effective pharmacotherapy indicated that at least in some patients, serotonin is high prior to treatment and decreases with treatment; this decrease may correlate with clinical improvement (Thoren et al., 1980). Some agents that activate serotonin receptors (agonists) have been found to exacerbate the obsessions and compulsions of OCD (Zohar, Mueller, Insel, Zohar-Kadouch, & Murphy, 1987; Hollander, Fay, Cohen, Campeas, Gorman, & Liebowitz, 1992). Agents that block serotonin receptors (antagonists) prevent the effects of these activating agents. Treatment with serotonin reuptake blockers appears to change serotonin neurotransmission. Thus, after a course of medication, the exacerbating effect of such serotonin agonists on obsessions and compulsions is reduced (Zohar, Insel, Zohar-Kadouch, Hill, & Murphy, 1988; Hollander et al., 1991a).

Some evidence exists for the involvement of neurochemical systems other than the serotonergic system in OCD. Dopamine involvement, for example, is suggested by the response of some OCD patients and of patients with obsessive–compulsive related disorders, such as Tourette's syndrome, to dopamine blockers. Also, certain medications and substances that activate the dopamine system can exacerbate symptoms in patients with OCD and related disorders or lead to repetitive motor symptoms in normal subjects (Goodman, McDougle, Price, Riddle, Pauls, & Leckman, 1990).

In addition, our understanding of the neuroanatomical locus of the neurochemical changes in OCD has advanced. For example, much evidence indicates the involvement of the basal ganglia and frontal cortex in OCD. Patients with neurological disorders affecting these structures may develop OCD (Kettle & Marks, 1986), and surgical interruption of pathways between these structures has alleviated OCD (Martuza, Chiocca, Jenike, Giriunas, & Ballantine, 1990). Also, patients with OCD have been found to have subtle neurological abnormalities (Hollander et al., 1990). Computed tomography (CT) of the basal ganglia in patients with OCD has indicated the appearance of damage to these structures (Luxenberg, Swedo, Flament, Friedland, Rapoport, & Rapoport, 1988). Most recently, positron emission tomography (PET) has demonstrated abnormalities in cerebral metabolism of the orbitofrontal cortex and the basal ganglia in OCD (Baxter, Phelps, Mazziotta, Guze, Schwartz, & Selin, 1987).

In light of these considerable advances, it may be argued that OCD is best thought of as a neuropsychiatric rather than a psychological disorder. Along this line of thinking, further advances in our understanding of OCD will follow more precise investigation of the neuroanatomical and neuro-chemical bases of the disorder, and an understanding of OCD may not require a model of the mind.

However, neurobiology does not seem to answer a number of questions about OCD that appear to require some model of the mind. The symptoms of OCD are both specific, that is, the same kinds of concerns and rituals are seen in different patients, and diverse, that is, the range of these concerns and rituals is broad. What is the relationship between the neurobiological research findings and the particular symptomatology of OCD? Further, psychological events may be important in the etiology of the disorder, and psychological interventions may be efficacious in its treatment. Thus, the phenomenology of OCD and its causal mechanisms require a psychological level of understanding.

Psychoanalysts have been concerned longest with understanding OCD using a model of the mind; we will turn next to their work.

## Psychoanalysis

In October, 1907, Freud began his treatment of Paul Lorenz, the "Rat Man." The analysis lasted for almost a year and proved highly successful. Long-term follow-up was, however, impossible, since the patient was killed in World War I. Freud's classic case report of Lorenz (1909) provides a detailed account of the symptoms seen in obsessional neurosis or OCD, as well as a complex formulation of their development and change.

Central to this model is a concept of psychic energy. Early on, Freud (1894) defined psychic energy as "a quota of affect or sum of excitation" that can be discharged, displaced, or repressed. In his case report, Freud argued that in OCD "this energy makes itself felt now in commands and now in prohibitions, according as the affectionate impulse or the hostile one snatches control of the pathway leading to discharge" (1909, pp. 244). He concluded that

> a thought-process is obsessive or compulsive when, in consequence of an inhibition (due to a conflict of opposing impulses) at the motor end of the psychical system, it is undertaken with an expenditure of energy which (as regards both quality and quantity) is normally reserved for actions alone. (1909, pp. 244)

In *The Disposition to Obsessional Neurosis* (1913), Freud expanded his argument that in OCD representation of the genital instincts is taken over by a pregenital organization, dominated by hatred and anal erotism. He suggested that this shift was determined by constitutional rather than environmental factors. Later, in *Inhibitions, Symptoms and Anxiety* (1926), Freud also referred to the rigid and implacable character of the superego in OCD. He again emphasized that, although obsessional ideas are conscious, they are disguised and distorted substitutes for repressed unconscious impulses.

Freud's model of OCD is valuable. It offers an account of a number of the phenomena of the disorder, including the patient's ambivalence, the need for control, the struggle against what are experienced as forbidden wishes, and the severe prohibitions. The model includes a valuable focus on the developmental antecedents of the disorder and on the psychological aspects of treatment, such as transference. Finally, the model allows theoretical space for an integration with neurobiological advances.

On the other hand, Freud's view of psychic energy, central to his metapsychology (Gill, 1977), may be criticized (Swanson, 1977). Modern biology does not view the nervous system as operating according to the laws of 19th century physics, and modern psychoanalysis predominantly has concluded that it is useful to replace a focus on energy-based models with an emphasis on the relational aspects of the mind when accounting for psychological phenomena (Mitchell, 1988).

For Freud, obsessional neurosis was "the most interesting and repaying subject of psychoanalytic research" (1926, pp. 113). In recent years, however, apart from the occasional attempt to replace classical models with a more relational or interpersonal model (Salzman, 1985), there has been a dearth of psychoanalytic writing on OCD (Esman, 1989). This retreat may be considered somewhat surprising in view of our argument that Freud's observations on OCD are detailed and precise, that his model is complex and fertile, and that it addresses the possibility of biological advances. The retreat of analysts is not surprising, however, since contemporary neuroscience contradicts various aspects of Freud's metapsychology, psychoanalysis is relatively unable to theorize about recent neurobiological advances, and psychoanalytic treatment apparently fails with OCD (Esman, 1989).

One alternative at this point is to attempt to retain Freud's clinical theory, but discard his metapsychology. After all, although Freud acknowledged that his constructs might one day be demonstrated to have biological foundations, he also declared that they had their own intrinsic value in accounting for psychopathological phenomena (1940). Many contemporary analysts have argued for this strategy (Gill, 1977).

Our own view, however, is that contemporary cognitive science allows for the replacement of the psychic energy model with more sophisticated concepts. Cognitive science, in other words, provides a metapsychology for psychopathology. Just as Freud began with a biological model and moved to psychological structures, so our cognitive science strategy will be to focus on how neuroscientific findings underpin the representational level. Our aim, therefore, is neither to disregard nor to retreat from classical analytic theory, but to reframe such theory in terms of contemporary models and discoveries.

## Behaviorism

Another psychological model of OCD is that of the behaviorists. This model argues that OCD develops in two stages. Initial OCD symptoms, such as obsessions, are classically conditioned anxiety stimuli. Subsequent OCD symptoms, such as neutralizing thoughts or compulsive rituals, avoid or terminate exposure to the stimuli and reduce anxiety or anticipated anxiety. There is little evidence for the first stage, since traumatic events rarely lead directly to OCD, but there is some evidence for the second stage. For example, experimentation confirms that contamination leads to increased anxiety in washers and cleaning leads to a decrease in anxiety (Hodgson & Rachman, 1972). The behavioral model leads to various techniques, such as exposure and response prevention, for extinguishing OCD symptoms (Rachman & Hodgson, 1980; Marks, 1981).

The behavioral model of OCD can be criticized for not explaining a number of cognitive aspects of the disorder (Salkovskis, 1990). A more cognitive model is that of McFall and Wollersheim (1979), who suggest that a cognitive "primary appraisal" process of threat is central in OCD. This process is likely to be influenced by a number of irrational beliefs, such as the ideas that one should be perfect to avoid disapproval and that one is powerful enough to prevent disaster via ritualizing. In therapy, these beliefs can be challenged.

Similarly, Salkovskis and Warwick (1988) suggest that individuals with OCD have been socialized to be particularly sensitive about the degree of responsibility they have when experiencing intrusive thoughts, and therefore will exaggerate the harm associated with those thoughts. Neutralizing is associated with a perceived reduction in the risk of being responsible for harm. In therapy, underlying assumptions about responsibility for harm and evaluations of intrusive thoughts can be challenged.

Once again, the behaviorist and cognitive models are useful for the clinician. They postulate various environmental antecedents to OCD and provide a heuristic account of how to approach treatment and of how treatment works.

However, the metapsychology of this view, that is, its assumptions about the mind and its disorders, is open to criticism. Early behaviorists, after all, specifically argued that models of the mind should be replaced by models of behavior. Further, cognitively oriented theorists have avoided the biological basis of cognitive processes. Thus McFall and Wollersheim (1979) and Salkovskis and Warwick (1988) do not account for the biological underpinnings of the appraisal of threat or harm. This neglect of the biological may be responsible for the failure of cognitive-behavioral models to account for the specific forms that OCD symptoms take.

Although OCD can be helped by cognitive-behavioral interventions, cognitive-behaviorists have not employed a sufficiently complex model of mind and of treatment. We must, then, theorize that cognitive-behavioral interventions are efficacious within a more comprehensive theory.

## Cognitive Science

We propose that a cognitive science model of OCD can incorporate important biological, analytic, and behavioral findings, while avoiding certain limitations of each individual approach. The concepts of mental goals and feedback loops have been employed by several cognitive scientists; we employ these cybernetic constructs in our model of OCD. However, we focus in particular on the biological basis of the goals and feedbacks involved in OCD.

One of the key progenitors of cognitive science was Norbert Wiener, who published the landmark volume *Cybernetics* in 1948. During the war, Wiener, a young mathematician, was asked to develop more accurate anti-aircraft machinery. As a result of his work on the feedback mechanisms that kept artillery on course, he became interested in self-regulation devices. Wiener noted that there were important analogies between feedback devices in engineering systems and homeostatic mechanisms in nervous systems. As he wrote:

> The central nervous system no longer appears as a self-contained organ, receiving inputs from the senses and discharging into the muscles. On the contrary, some of its most characteristic activities are explicable only as circular processes, emerging from the nervous system into the muscles, and reentering the nervous system through the sense organs, whether they be proprioceptors or organs of the special senses. (Weiner, 1961, p. 8)

Such feedback and homeostatic mechanisms allow both organisms and machines to be purposeful. The word cybernetics emphasizes the need for a science devoted to issues of control and communication, whether in machines or in minds.

The cybernetic framework permeates the work of later cognitive scientists. One idea, for example, has been that both minds and machines have current states and goal states. When a difference is perceived between these states, behavior is altered to bring the current state closer to the goal state. If current state and goal state are not perceived as different, then behavior is maintained or a new goal is set (Miller, Gallanter, & Pribram, 1960). The cybernetic framework also has been expanded to account for various mental phenomena. Hierarchies of goals have been proposed, for example, many of which are ordinarily out of awareness. However, when there is a disruption of goals, conscious control becomes important (Bruner, 1957) and often emotion is generated (Mandler, 1975).

Certain cognitivists, such as Wiener's contemporaries McCullough and Pitts (1943) and Von Neumann (1958), have focused explicitly on the parallels between brain and machine. Similarly, Piaget (1971) placed the cybernetically related notion of equilibriation at the heart of his biologically based cognitive theory. Nevertheless, one aspect of Wiener's work develops Shannon's (1938) seminal work and argues that information can be conceptualized independent of its particular medium. A subsequent functionalist movement in cognitive science has argued that mental states can be defined and investigated independent of their physical instantiation. Indeed, the biological basis of mental goals and feedback loops is emphasized only rarely by cognitive scientists.

The notion of a biologically based system for determining and controlling goal discrepancy may, however, be useful in addressing the psychopathology of OCD. Indeed, recent work indicates that the particular neuroanatomical and neurochemical systems that were noted to be involved in OCD may have a cybernetic role. Early authors saw the basal ganglia as a route from cortical association areas to the motor cortex, thereby participating in the initiation and control of movement. More contemporary research suggests that an array of parallel basal ganglia-thalamocortical circuits may have perceptual, cognitive, and motor functions (Alexander, DeLong, & Strick, 1986). Basal ganglia circuitry may have a role both as a store of innate motor programs and in the processing of sensory information (Schneider, 1984).

We can hypothesize that some OCD patients have a disrupted goal-feedback mechanism that results in the persistence of particular sequences. Several authors have discussed OCD in precisely these terms. Gray (1982), for example, has reviewed evidence that the septohippocampal system and associated limbic areas function to detect and correct mismatch, and has suggested that OCD patients suffer dysfunction in brain match–mismatch mechanisms. Pitman (1987) has employed a cybernetic model of OCD, proposing that, in OCD, high error signals (produced by the limbic system) cannot be reduced through behavioral output (produced by the basal ganglia). Rapoport and Wise (1988) have suggested that in OCD there is activation of an "internal motivation detector" in the absence of sensory input (for example, of dirtiness), resulting in repetitive behaviors (such as compulsive handwashing).

What about the role of serotonin? Gray (1982) has hypothesized that the role of ascending serotonin projections to the septohippocampal system is to add information about punishment and, therefore, to lead to an inhibition of motor behavior. Depue and Spoont (1986) have advanced a similar model of serotonergic pathways exerting an inhibitory influence. Conversely, a great deal of evidence suggests that decreased serotonergic function is associated with increased impulsivity (Coccaro et al., 1989). Although the complexity of the serotonin system should not be underestimated, current results provide some indication that decreased serotonergic function may involve the underestimation of possible harm.

It may be hypothesized that, in some OCD patients, serotonergic dysfunction results in the overestimation of possible harm (Liebowitz & Hollander, 1991). Concurrent with this concept is Carr's (1974) finding that there is an abnormally high subjective estimate of the probability of unfavorable outcome in OCD patients. Similarly, premorbid personality may be characterized by shyness and cautiousness.

Disturbances in the biological basis for the determination and assessment of goal discrepancy may be observed in animals other than humans. Indeed, Goldberger and Rapoport (1991) have suggested that excessive grooming in canines, or acral lick dermatitis, is a neuroethological analog of OCD. Grooming behaviors constitute animal motor programs or fixed action patterns that may be mediated by basal ganglia circuitry. Like OCD, acral lick dermatitis appears to respond selectively to serotonergic medications (Goldberger & Rapoport, 1991; Stein, *et al.*, 1992).

A neurobiologically based model does not rule out developmental antecedents to or environmental precipitants of OCD. For example, it has been suggested that early learning about danger may be a factor in the pathogenesis of OCD (Salkovskis, 1990). Environmental frustrations (Martin & Tesser, 1989) or losses (Tait & Silver, 1989), on the other hand, may lead to goal discrepancy and subsequent ruminations. In animals, perserverative motor programs or fixed action patterns are triggered similarly by frustration (Stein et al., 1992).

A cognitive science model of biologically based determination and assessment of goal discrepancy in OCD can be studied empirically. In our work with OCD patients, we have employed a number of biological and neuropsychological measures, including neurological soft signs, neuroendocrine and behavioral responses to serotonergic challenges, and reflection-impulsivity on cognitive processing tasks such the Matching Familiar Figures Test ( MFFT ) (Hollander, Liebowitz, & Rosen, 1991).

The MFFT is a tin.ed test that requires selecting one matching figure from a choice. The target figure is very detailed and the mismatches differ in a single detail. OCD patients tended to be fast and inaccurate or slow and accurate on the MFFT. These patterns contrasted with the control group's intermediate latency and low error rate. One hypothesis, then, is that patients with a short latency and high error rate have visual discrimination difficulties whereas patients with a long latency and low error rate have a low tolerance for risk taking.

Indeed, patients who were fast and inaccurate on the MFFT had a high number of soft signs and a poor response to treatment. These characteristics suggest a more diffuse neurological impairment, perhaps accompanied by discriminatory failures. The findings in this subgroup of patients may be consistent with abnormal goal-feedback mechanisms, which lead to rapid perseverative behaviors. On the other hand, patients who were slow and accurate on the MFFT showed exacerbations with methyl-chlorophenylpiperazine (MCPP), a partial serotonin agonist, and responded to fluoxetine, a specific serotonin reuptake blocker. This suggests the presence of serotonin dysfunction. The findings in this subgroup of patients may be consistent with overestimation of harm, which leads to slow perseverative behaviors.

A second way to test this cognitive science model of OCD is to employ it to consider the various phenomena seen in OCD. Consider first the affects of OCD, which traditionally include anger (from the id) and guilt (from the superego). In cognitive science terms, these affects may be an intrinsic aspect, such as harm overestimation, of cybernetic discrepancy or its assessment in OCD. The link between serotonergic dysfunction and impulsive aggression provides some support for this view. On the other hand, these affects may reflect psychological reactions, for example, to the perpetual overestimation of harm or to the perpetual disruption of goals. In the terms of the DSM-III(R), obsessive–compulsive personality (OCP) disorder may develop as a result of OCD, that is, inflexible attitudes may follow overvaluation of harm. The person with OCD may be more or less aware of these affects.

Similar analyses may apply to various defense mechanisms or mental processes that classically are seen in OCD. Ambivalence, for example, may be a result of an intrinsic inability to prevent certain thoughts from taking place again and again, or it may reflect attempts to compensate for the perpetual overestimation of harm. Similarly, intellectualization may represent an intrinsic aspect of the disorder or may be a reaction to harm estimations that are out of control. If OCD involves the dopamine system, one possibility is that this system underpins such processes as magical thinking and overvalued ideation. Again, the person with OCD may be more or less aware of these mental processes.

In cognitive science terms, then, it may be suggested that OCD involves a biologically based deficit in determining goal discrepancy or in assessing the degree of harm associated with such discrepancy. Environmental factors such as learning about danger or increases in stress may exacerbate or precipitate this deficit. These processes take place automatically, and the person with OCD may be intellectually aware of the senselessness of symptoms.

However, the emergence of conscious control processes does not necessarily resolve the mismatch problems. Rather, secondary problems such as ambivalence and indecision, perfectionism, and the need for control, may arise. Treatment involves biological manipulation, learning to stop a sequence of behaviors, or learning to downplay possible harm.

## Integration

We stated earlier that our model includes many of the best aspects of previous models, and excludes their weaknesses. In this section, we argue this claim more fully by comparing the cognitive science model of OCD with the biological, analytic, and learning models.

Consider first the cognitive science and the biological models. The cognitive science model outlined here clearly is based on important advances in contemporary neurobiological research, and is therefore close to the biological model. However, insofar as our model incorporates such concepts as mental goals and feedback loops, it is also a model of mind, and therefore differs from a purely biological approach.

Indeed, it may be suggested that the cognitive emphasis of our model is helpful in explaining some of the biological heterogeneity of the disorder. Thus, some OCD patients seem to have abnormal serotonergic responsiveness whereas others are characterized by more neurological impairment. A model of cybernetic discrepancy provides a way for both these abnormalities to lead to OCD symptoms.

Consider next the relationship between the cognitive science model and the psychoanalytic approach. The cognitive approach follows the classical analytic approach insofar as it begins with a biologically based view of the mind, and postulates how changes in underlying mechanisms lead to pathological symptoms. However, instead of being grounded in outdated ideas about psychic energy, the cognitive science model is grounded in current neurobiology. Indeed, the model follows modern analytic thought insofar as it conceives of mental structures as cognitive rather than energy-based constructs. However, the model, instead of avoiding metapsychology, is based on the computational framework of cognitive science. Thus, the model attempts to tackle psychopathology with the same scrutiny and rigor as analytic theory, but also has the advantage of a solid metatheoretical foundation.

The similarities and differences between the cognitive and the analytic approaches to OCD are exemplified in the way that each tackles the important unconscious aspects of the disorder. Both the cognitive and the analytic approaches postulate mental processes of which the patients is unaware to explain OCD symptoms and phenomenology. Freud argued, for example, that patients are unconscious of the meaning of their OCD symptoms. Thus, "the patients themselves do not know the wording of their own obsessional ideas" (1909, pp. 79). The cognitive science perspective is one of automatic mental processes in OCD, and of patients who, although perhaps aware of the senselessness of resulting psychic events (such as a particular obsession), may be more or less aware of how processes (such as the overestimation of harm) lead to this event in a meaningful way. Whereas the psychoanalytic model conceives of the unconscious as a locus of sexual and aggressive energies and postulates that these energies are defended against when they become excessive, the cognitive model contends that various mental processes, such as harm estimation and anger arousal, may be automatic in nature and psychological strategies for dealing with these processes when they are impaired may be available. Although both models provide explanations for a series of complex phenomena, the cognitive science models avoids the metapsychology of the analytic perspective. Other constructs and parameters that are central to analytic theory also may be reformulated in cognitive science terms.

Finally, consider the relationship between the cognitive science model and learning theory. Both models allow a role for psychological processes in the pathogenesis and treatment of OCD. In particular, both models emphasize harm overestimation in the pathogenesis and treatment of OCD. However, the cognitive model differs from learning models because it focuses on a biological basis for such mental processes rather than conceiving of the pathogenesis and treatment of OCD in purely psychological terms. The model is, therefore, able to incorporate cognitive psychology research without having to restrict its observations, explanations, and interventions.

## Implications

The cognitive science model of OCD has a number of clinical and research implications. The model emphasizes, for example, the neurobiological underpinning of mental processes involved in the production of OCD symptoms. An immediate clinical implication is the importance of psychopharmacological intervention in the treatment of OCD. In particular, serotonergic medications may play a role in altering the way in which cybernetic discrepancy is judged by the individual. Dopaminergic medication also may play a role in patients who also display magical thinking or overvalued ideation.

On the other hand, our model also indicates that not all patients will be responsive to medication. Thus, patients in whom there is a neuroanatomical basis for increased cybernetic discrepancy rather than a serotonergic dysfunction with accompanying harm overestimation may not be as responsive to serotonergic medication.

However, the cognitive model also suggests that, in both medication responsive and medication nonresponsive patients, psychotherapeutic interventions may be helpful. For patients who exhibit harm overestimation, cognitive interventions may be directed toward changing this estimation (Salkovskis, 1990). Such interventions may include disputation of irrational beliefs (Emmelkamp, Visser, & Hoekstra, 1988) or learning to better manage affects (Emmelkamp & Van der Heyden, 1980). For patients who display repetitive rituals, behavioral interventions may be directed toward decreasing these. Such interventions may include exposure and response prevention (Emmelkamp, 1987).

A cognitive science approach to OCD encourages future research on OCD that combines assessments of cognitive processing with constructs and parameters highlighted by the neurobiological, analytic, and learning models. Initial work correlating measures of reflection-impulsivity with neurochemical and neuroanatomical measures, for example, requires further development. The inclusion of measures of environmental precipitants or transference processes in OCD also may be helpful.

Cybernetic discrepancy may affect processing in a variety of spheres including the area of language. Cognitive processing research therefore should not be restricted to the exploration of obviously symptomatic processes. Conversely, cognitive scientists interested in cybernetic mechanisms may benefit from extending their studies of normal subjects to include patients with obsessive–compulsive and related disorders.

## Acknowledgments

This chapter was supported in part by a NARSAD Young Investigator Award to Dan J. Stein and a Research Scientist Development Award (MH-00750) to Eric Hollander from the National Institutes of Mental Health, Bethesda, Maryland.

# 13

# Dissociative and Conversion Disorders

**John F. Kihlstrom**

*Amnesia and Cognition Unit*
*Department of Psychology*
*University of Arizona*
*Tucson, Arizona*

The Vicissitudes of Diagnosis
Conversion and Somatization
Contradictions in Conversion and Dissociation
Implicit Memory and Implicit Perception
The Rise and Revival of Dissociation Theory
Consciousness, Dissociation, and the Self
A Return to Diagnosis and a Call for Research

Keep it well in mind, and this should not require great effort, that the word "hysteria" means nothing, and little by little you will acquire the habit of speaking of hysteria in man without thinking in any way of the uterus.

Charcot (1877, p. 37)

The word "hysteria" should be preserved, although its primitive meaning has much changed. It would be very difficult to modify it nowadays, and truly it has so great and beautiful a history that it would be painful to give it up.

Janet (1901, p. 527)

The dissociative and conversion disorders constitute a disorder that once was referred to as "hysteria:" symptoms and syndromes suggestive of neurological disease that occur in the absence of diagnosable insult, injury, or disease in the brain.[1] Hysterical symptoms and syndromes were studied and catalogued by Janet and Freud, who both first encountered them in Charcot's clinic at the Salpetriere (Chertok, 1970; Macmillan, 1986); later, their observations formed the bases for the first (rival) psychogenic theories of mental illness. These theories continue to fascinate us, even today.

In current usage, the dissociative disorders include amnesia, a loss of autobiographical memory (either general, covering an entire period in the person's life, or selective, covering only certain classes of events); fugue, a general amnesia coupled with loss of identity and, perhaps, relocation; multiple personality, in which a single individual seems to display two or more distinct personalities; depersonalization, in which the person perceives him- or herself as somehow changed or unreal; and derealization, in which the person perceives the surrounding world as changed or unreal instead. What unites these syndromes is a functional disorder of memory, broadly construed (Kihlstrom & Evans, 1979; Schacter & Kihlstrom, 1989; Kihlstrom, Tataryn, & Hoyt, 1990; Tasman, 1991); in some sense the patients forget what they did, who they are, or both.

The conversion disorders include psychogenic deafness, blindness, and other impairments of sensory-perceptual function, either general (i.e., affecting the entire modality) or selective (i.e., affecting the perception of only certain categories of objects and events), as well as paralysis, aphonia, and other impairments of voluntary motor function (these, too, may be general or specific). Again, these are functional disorders of perception and action (Kihlstrom, Barnhardt, & Tataryn, 1991), mimicking neurological disease but occurring in the absence of organic damage.

## The Vicissitudes of Diagnosis

The categories "dissociative disorder" and "conversion disorder" are unique in the psychiatric nosology, because they are the only syndromes

---

[1]This is not to deny that the symptoms of the dissociative and conversion disorders have a biological base. All mental states, including functional amnesia and similar disorders, are accompanied by correlated changes in brain state, but these brain states do not cause the disorders in the same way that damage to perihippocampal structures causes organic amnesia or lesions in the striate area cause cortical blindness. Moreover, it must be recognized that some dissociative and conversion disorders arise in association with physical injury, even if they cannot be attributed to lasting organic problems. Also, some apparently "functional" disorders may reflect the early stages of organic illness, the true nature of which becomes clear only after the disease has progressed. The fact that organic factors are implicated in some dissociative and conversion disorders should not be taken to imply that they are not analyzed most appropriately in psychological (or, according to some authors, sociocultural), rather than neurobiological, terms.

whose labels carry etiological significance. Schizophrenia may be caused by defective genes or double binds; depression may be caused by neurotransmitter abnormalities or a life history of helplessness and hopelessness; anxiety may reflect hormonal imbalances or an environment characterized by unpredictable aversive events. On the other hand, the dissociative disorders are caused by dissociation, ostensibly, and the conversion disorders by conversion. In this way, both sets of syndromes continue the line established by the ancient diagnosis of hysteria, the name of which derives from the attribution of symptoms to a wandering uterus.

In the earliest attempts to develop a standard nomenclature for psychopathology, introduced during and after World War I, the dissociative and conversion disorders were, in fact, linked under the general label of "conversion hysteria," a label that obviously reflects the heavy influence of psychoanalytic thought on psychiatry at the time. Even within that framework, however, the label was somewhat of a misnomer. Conversion might be invoked to explain disorders of the sensory and motor systems, when the anxiety associated with unacceptable impulses is converted into physical symptoms that symbolically represent the repressed content, but it cannot explain disorders of memory and personality.

After World War II, the conceptualization of dissociation and conversion changed as psychiatry and psychopathology attempted to find a firmer scientific footing for the diagnostic system. The first edition of the *Diagnostic and Statistical Manual* (DSM-I; American Psychiatric Association, 1952) abandoned explicit reference to hysteria, yet the classical psychoanalytic conception of these disorders continued to dominate psychopathological thought. Conversion and dissociation were categorized as psychoneurotic disorders in which anxiety was "unconsciously and automatically controlled by various defense mechanisms"—specifically, dissociation and conversion—rather than "directly felt and expressed" (p. 31). The dissociative syndromes included, among others, depersonalization, multiple personality, fugue, (psychogenic) amnesia, and somnambulism (a second listing of somnambulism was defined as sleepwalking, proper). The conversion syndromes included anesthesia (in various sensory modalities), paralysis, and dyskinesia.

The second edition of DSM (DSM-II; American Psychiatric Association, 1968) reverted to the pre-DSM practice of explicitly classifying dissociation and conversion disorders as subtypes of hysteria, again defined in classical psychoanalytic terms as involving the unconscious and automatic control of anxiety. Hysterical Neurosis, Dissociative Type, was conceptualized as involving alterations in consciousness and identity, whereas Hysterical Neurosis, Conversion Type, involved disruptions in the special senses or the voluntary motor system.

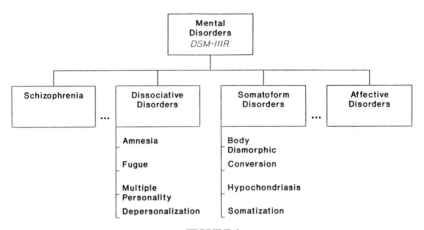

**FIGURE 1**

The classification of dissociative and conversion disorders by DSM-III(R), showing dissociative disorders and conversion disorders on separate branches.

The next editions, DSM-III and DSM-III(R) (American Psychiatric Association, 1980,1987), dispensed with both neurosis and hysteria as technical terms; for the first time, the dissociative and conversion disorders were defined descriptively in theory-neutral language (Kluft, Steinberg, & Spitzer, 1988). Moreover, for the dissociative disorders at least, a structured interview—the SCID-D—was developed that made diagnosis more reliable (Steinberg, Rounsaville, & Cicchetti, 1990; Steinberg, 1991; for an alternative instrument, see Ross, Heber, Norton, & Anderson, 1989). Finally, for the first time, dissociation and conversion were no longer linked in the hierarchical arrangement of the nosology (although, admittedly, they are described in adjacent chapters). As shown in Fig. 1, the dissociative disorders constitute their own category in DSM-III(R) on the same level as schizophrenia, mood disorders, anxiety disorders, and the like. In contrast, the conversion disorders are located under a different major branch, as a subtype of the somatoform disorders, along with body dysmorphic disorder, hypochondriasis, and somatization disorder. Moreover, conversion disorder continues to be characterized in psychoanalytic terms, including the notions of primary and secondary gain and the idea that the patient's symptoms are expressions of conflict.

In the forthcoming DSM-IV, the diagnosis of the dissociative disorders has been refined greatly (Spiegel & Cardeña, 1991). For example, the criteria for psychogenic fugue include the loss of personal identity as well as the assumption of a new one. Most important, interpersonality amnesia is returned to a central place in criteria for multiple personality disorder. DSM-IV also adds a new subcategory of culture-specific disorders with dissociative overtones, for example, amok, berserk, and koro. At the same time, DSM-IV persists in segregating the dissociative disorders from their conversion counterparts, which continue to be listed under the somatoform disorders. The diagnosis of the somatoform disorders, apparently, is largely unchanged.

A major thrust of this chapter is to argue that this classification separation between the dissociative and conversion disorders is, literally, a category mistake (Ryle, 1949), and that the conversion disorders are named misleadingly. Viewed from a cognitive perspective, the dissociative and conversion disorders have much in common, whereas the conversion disorders bear little or no resemblance to other somatoform illnesses.

## Conversion and Somatization

The classification of conversion disorders as somatoform in nature appears to have resulted from the fact that their presentation focuses on physical symptoms that have no demonstrable organic basis. Conversion patients complain of blindness, deafness, tactile anesthesia, and paralysis of the skeletal musculature. In body dysmorphic disorder (previously known as dysmorphophobia), patients with normal appearance complain of defects in their appearance, such as wrinkled or spotted skin, enlarged or shrinking hands or feet, excessive facial hair, or misshapen facial features. In hypochondriasis, the patient shows a preoccupation with a particular disease and misinterprets bodily signs or sensations accordingly, despite competent professional reassurance to the contrary. In somatization disorder, formerly called Briquet's syndrome (or, alternatively, hysteria), the patient presents with repeated, multiple somatic complaints, against a long and complicated medical history of unsuccessful hospitalizations, uninformative tests, and unnecessary treatments.

Linking all these syndromes under a heading of "baseless physical complaints" ignores important differences among them. For example, the symptoms of hypochondriasis are fear of and concern for disease, not actual complaints of illness or loss of function; in this way, it can be distinguished from both conversion disorder and somatization disorder. More relevant to the present argument, however, are the many differences between conversion disorder and somatization disorder (Maxmen, 1986; Goodwin & Guze, 1989). Conversion disorder generally involves neurological symptoms (although admittedly psychogenic vomiting and pseudocyesis also have been classified as instances of conversion), whereas somatization disorder typically involves symptoms of the gastrointestinal, genitourinary, and cardiopulmonary systems. Conversion disorders usually present in one system, whereas somatization disorders usually involve multiple complaints. Patients with conversion disorder may be rather casual about their symptoms (*la belle indifference*), whereas their counterparts with somatization disorders are more dramatic, bordering on histrionic. Conversion disorders erupt suddenly, whereas somatization disorders appear gradually. Conversion symptoms often respond, at least temporarily, to hypnotic suggestion or barbiturate infusion; somatization symptoms do not. Conversion disorders often remit spontaneously, whereas somatization disorders persist despite active and prolonged treatment. If they reappear, conversion symptoms usually involve the system originally involved; the complaints in recurrent somatization disorder more commonly affect a different system.

These differences have been recognized for a long time (Chodoff, 1954,1974; Chodoff & Lyons, 1958), but apparently this knowledge has not affected diagnostic practice. Despite the views of Charcot (1877) and Janet (1901) quoted at the outset of the chapter, we can be glad to see the disappearance of the term "hysteria" with its ancient sexist connotations (Veith, 1965) and long service in modern health care as a vehicle for patient abuse. However, there is a sense in which the baby has been thrown out with the bathwater; the field has failed to recognize the features that originally led classifiers to link the dissociative and conversion disorders under a single rubric. To understand these common characteristics and their theoretical significance, we turn to the classic literature in descriptive psychopathology, as well as to a small body of experimental literature concerned with these syndromes. (For fuller descriptions, see Schacter & Kihlstrom, 1989; Kihlstrom et al., 1990,1991).

## Contradictions in Conversion and Dissociation

The classic description of the conversion disorders is found in Janet's treatises, *The Mental State of Hystericals* (1901) and *The Major Symptoms of Hysteria* (1907). Here, Janet noted the apparent contradictions between patients' complaints of losses of sensory, perceptual, and motor functioning, and their behavior, which was often inconsistent with these claims. (For more detail, see Kihlstrom et al., 1991.) In hysterical anesthesia, for example, Janet observed that reflexes could be elicited by stimulation in the anesthetized area, and that the patients' limbs and digits did not show the scars and blisters characteristic of those whose insensitivities were caused by neurological damage. Janet contrived a clever test (for a review of research on a modern version, see McConkey, Bryant, Bibb, Kihlstrom, & Tataryn, 1990) in which one anesthetic patient was given the paradoxical instruction to say "yes" when she felt a touch and "no" when she did not; when stimulated randomly on sensitive and anesthetized portions of her body, she invariably said "yes" to the former and "no" to the latter, clearly making a discriminative response that belied her claims of insensitivity.

In other cases, Janet noted that the functionally deaf could still hear a ticking watch or vibrating tuning fork applied to their teeth or skull. In unilateral blindness, he showed that pressure to one eye produced a doubling of the image, and that patients could read both red and blue letters through eyeglasses, one of whose lenses passed only blue light, the other only red. In functional tunnel blindness, patients moved in response to events in the periphery; in functional hemianopsia, they responded to events in their scotoma. All such demonstrations indicate that vision in both eyes is intact.

Janet's patients said that they could not see, hear, or feel yet, at the same time, their behavior was obviously responsive to visual, auditory, or tactile events. Similar observations were made by others, including William James (1890; see Taylor, 1983), and passed quickly into established clinical lore: the way to distinguish a functional disorder from malingering is that the malingerer attempts to construct an internally consistent self-presentation; the genuine hysteric displays indisputable contradictions, and makes no attempt to hide or reconcile them. A similar notion underlies Orne's (1959) notion of trance logic in hypnosis. It should be noted that, although this kind of test may once have been valid, the diffusion of cultural knowledge about these contradictions may have rendered current reliance on it unsound (see McConkey et al., 1990).

Since the appearance of Janet's treatises, numerous formal experiments have confirmed his essential observations. (For a more complete review, see Kihlstrom et al., 1991.) For example, Hilgard and Marquis (1940) showed that a patient with functional anesthesia and paralysis was able to acquire a conditioned finger-withdrawal response; Malmo, Davis, and Barza (1952,1953) found that a functionally deaf patient showed electromyographic responses to an auditory conditioned stimulus for shock. Brady and Lind (1961) and others (Grosz & Zimmerman, 1965,1970; Theodor & Mandelcorn, 1973; Bryant & McConkey, 1989) found that patients who complained of total blindness were able to make visual discrimination. Barraclough (1966) made a similar observation in a case of functional deafness. Levy and his colleagues obtained event-related potentials (ERPs) in response to somatosensory stimulation in cases of functional hemianesthesia (Levy & Behrman, 1970) and anesthesia (Levy & Mushin, 1973), whereas Moldofsky and England (1975) showed enhanced ERPs in a group of patients with hemianesthesia and weakness. Knutsson and Martensson (1985) found a normal pattern of torque and electromyographic activity in the muscles of patients with functional paresis.

Interestingly, similar sorts of contradictions have been observed in patients with the dissociative disorders of psychogenic amnesia, fugue, and multiple personality. (For reviews, see Schacter & Kihlstrom, 1989; Kihlstrom et al., 1990.) Thus, Janet's report on Madame D., a case of hysterical somnambulism and functional retrograde amnesia: the woman had been victimized by a cruel joke, and had no conscious recollection of the prank; nevertheless, her nocturnal dreams and somnambulistic episodes recapitulated the episode, and she froze whenever she passed the location where the event occurred. Ansel Bourne, a case of fugue studied by William James (1890), had no memory for his life as a lay minister, yet during his fugue he attended church regularly and related episodes that ultimately were traced back to his premorbid life.

These observations have been repeated in the 20th century. An amnesic patient studied by Gudjonsson (1979; Gudjonsson & Haward, 1982), who had been suicidal before her illness began, showed a predominance of death themes on the Rorschach and electrodermal responses to items of personal relevance. Schacter, Wang, Tulving, and Freedman (1982) studied a patient who showed complete loss of autobiographical memory and personal identity, but was able to identify people and events from the time covered by his amnesia. Lyon (1985) asked a fugue patient to dial a telephone number at random; her mother answered. Kaszniak, Nussbaum, Berren, and Santiago (1988), treating a patient who was amnesic for a homosexual rape, observed that he became upset when presented with a TAT card showing one person possibly attacking another from behind. Christianson and Nilsson (1984) observed that an amnesic rape victim became upset when she returned to the scene of the crime. All these patients claimed amnesia for the events in question, yet in some sense memory for the events continued to influence them.

As in the case of the conversion disorders, these clinical observations are supported by formal experimental studies. (For reviews, see Schacter & Kihlstrom, 1989; Kihlstrom et al., 1990.) In the first of these studies to appear in the history of modern experimental psychopathology (for early examples, see Sidis, 1902; Sidis & Goodhart, 1904; Prince, 1939), Ludwig and his colleagues (Ludwig, Brandsma, Wilbur, Bendfeldt, & Jameson, 1972) administered a variety of tests of learning and memory to a patient who showed a complex pattern of amnesia among four alter egos. Although the primary personality could not recall paired associates learned by the others, it did show considerable time savings in relearning the list. Analogous findings were obtained on other tests involving fear conditioning and interpersonality transfer of knowledge.

Later experimental studies have produced the same kinds of results. For example, Silberman and his colleagues (Silberman, Putnam, Weingartner, Braun, & Post, 1985) conducted a study of verbal learning in nine multiple personality disorder (MPD) patients. Interestingly, proactive and retroactive interference were not reduced when lists were studied by two different alter egos of the same subject. Nevertheless, each alter ego claimed an amnesia for events experienced by the other, and list discrimination between alter egos was very poor. Similarly, Dick-Barnes and her colleagues (Dick-Barnes, Nelson, & Aine, 1987) administered a test of paired-associate learning and pursuit-rotor learning to a single case of MPD. The paired-associate learning task showed an interpersonality amnesia, whereas the pursuit-rotor task showed interpersonality transfer.

In the most thorough study of memory in MPD performed to date, Nissen and her colleagues (Nissen, Ross, Willingham, Mackenzie, & Schacter, 1988) compared performance on a number of different memory tests in a single MPD patient with 22 alter egos, at least 8 of which were separated from the others by an amnesic barrier. On tests of cued recall and yes–no recognition, each ego state was unable to remember items presented to the others. However, on several other tasks, including four-alternative forced-choice recognition, repetition priming in perceptual identification and word-fragment completion, and sequence learning in serial reaction time, one personality appeared to capitalize on the experiences of the other.

## Implicit Memory and Implicit Perception

To summarize, despite the patients' claims that they cannot remember or cannot perceive, careful testing in both the conversion disorders and the dissociative disorders reveals that the unremembered or unperceived events continue to influence ongoing experience, thought, and action. One way to make sense of these contradictions is to dismiss the complaints of the patients and conclude that the hysterically blind and deaf actually see and hear perfectly well, but are enacting a socially prescribed "sick role" in compliance with situational demands and constraints, or to gain strategic advantage in interpersonal affairs. This idea is fundamental to certain social–psychological approaches to hysteria and, indeed, mental illness in general (Szasz, 1961,1970; Sarbin, 1964,1968; Braginsky, Bräginsky, & Ring, 1969; Sarbin & Coe, 1979; Sarbin & Mancuso, 1980).

However, Janet (1907) himself rejected the "crude explanation" (p. 171) of deception and fraud, and offered a different perspective. Hysterical patients are unaware of the events in question and, although the patients are affected by these events nonetheless, these effects occur outside of awareness. From a theoretical point of view that rejects the notion of unconscious mental processes, such an argument might appear to be *ad hoc*. More recently, however, the argument has gained force from similar observations that have been made in cases in which the facts rule out interpretations in terms of a sick role and strategic self-presentation.

Consider, for example, cases of the amnesic syndrome observed in patients suffering bilateral lesions in the hippocampus and related brain structures (Squire & Zola-Morgan, 1991). This memory disorder involves a gross anterograde amnesia, so patients cannot recall or recognize things that they have done or experienced since the time that the brain damage occurred. If tested in other ways, however, they clearly show the aftereffects of these events. For example, if they have forgotten a list of words, and subsequently are presented with a word stem or fragment and asked to complete it with the first word that comes to mind, they are more likely to produce items from the list than if they had never seen the list, a phenomenon known as a priming effect. Similarly, these patients show savings in relearning items from a forgotten word list. Finally, they are able to acquire and display new cognitive and motor skills, although they do not consciously remember how they acquired them and they do not realize that they possess them.

These contradictions resemble those that are observed in the functional amnesias of the dissociative disorders. Interestingly, they are known as dissociations, a technical term that has found considerable use in recent cognitive psychology and cognitive neuropsychology (Dunn & Kirsner, 1988). In cognitive psychology, the term *functional dissociation* refers generally to a situation in which some state, condition, or manipulation has an effect on one dependent variable but not on another. Several dissociations have been documented in the domain of memory. For example, the amnesic syndrome affects recall and recognition but not priming, savings in relearning, or performance of a cognitive skill. Similarly, elaborative activity at the time of encoding has an effect on recall but not on priming; on the other hand, a shift in the modality of presentation between study and test has an effect on priming but not on recall. However, dissociations are not limited to memory. In perception, damage to the striate cortex impairs object identification but not object location. In neuropsychological studies of language processing, it has been found that global dyslexics perform poorly when reading nonsense and irregular words, whereas normal individuals perform well on both tasks. Surface dyslexics can read nonsense words but not irregular words, whereas phonological dyslexics can read irregular but not nonsense words.

The general pattern of functional dissociations is illustrated in Fig. 2. In the case of single dissociation (Fig. 2A), some variable selectively affects performance on one task but not on another. In the case of double dissociation, there are two variables as well as two tasks: Variable A affects performance on Task X but not Task Y, whereas Variable B affects performance on Task Y but not on Task X. Double dissociations come in two forms: uncrossed, reflecting the co-occurrence of two single dissociations

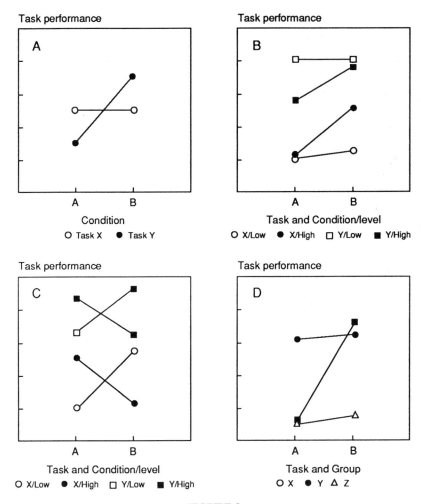

**FIGURE 2**

Varieties of dissociations, after Dunn & Kirsner (1988). (A) Single dissociation. The difference between Condition A and Condition B has no effect on Task X (O) but a large effect on Task Y (●). (B) Double dissociation, uncrossed. High (●) and low (O) levels of Condition X have no effect on Task A, but a large effect on Task B; similarly, high (■) and low (□) levels of Condition Y have a large effect on Task A, but no effect on Task B. (C) Double dissociation, crossed. High (●) and low (O) levels of Condition X increase performance on Task A, but decrease performance on Task B; similarly, high (■) and low (□) levels of Condition Y decrease performance on Task A, but increase performance on Task B. (D) Reversed association. Group X (O) shows low levels of performance under both Condition A and Condition B, whereas Group Y (●) shows high levels of performance under both conditions, but Group Z (□) shows low levels of performance under Condition A, but high levels of performance under Condition B.

in opposite directions (Fig. 2B), and crossed, similar to the crossover interaction familiar in the analysis of variance (Fig. 2C). Single dissociations support the inference that two different processes underlie performance on the two tasks, an inference that is strengthened by the finding of double dissociations, especially crossed double dissociations. Even so, as Dunn and Kirsner (1988) have noted, the existence of two separate processes is by no means guaranteed. For that reason, they proposed a further criterion of reversed association (Fig. 2D), in which there is a positive correlation between two tasks under one pair of experimental conditions and a negative correlation in another pair of conditions.

In the domain of memory, these kinds of dissociations have been considered probative evidence for two different forms of memory, commonly known as explicit and implicit memory (Schacter, 1987), memory with and without awareness (Jacoby & Dallas, 1981; Eich, 1984), or direct and indirect memory (Johnson & Hasher, 1987; Richardson-Klavehn & Bjork, 1988).[2] Explicit memory refers to the person's conscious recollection of some previous event, the ability to say "This event happened to me" or "I did this thing at such-and-such a time and in such-and-such a place." Explicit memory is exemplified by tasks that ask subjects deliberately to remember a particular episode: free recall, cued recall, and recognition. Implicit memory, in contrast, is revealed by any change in experience, thought, or action that is attributable to some past episode. Priming, savings, and skilled activity are examples of such changes; note that they do not refer to specific prior episodes in the person's life, nor do they require that such episodes be remembered consciously. Explicit and implicit memory are dissociable in two broad senses. First, implicit memory can be spared when explicit memory is impaired and, second, variables can affect explicit memory but not implicit memory and vice-versa. Some theorists (e.g., Tulving & Schacter, 1990; Schacter, 1991) construe such dissociations as evidence that explicit and implicit memory correspond to different underlying memory systems; others disagree (e.g., Roediger, 1990). For our purposes it suffices to recognize them merely as different expressions of episodic memory.

Similar dissociations appear in neurological disorders of perception. The most dramatic of these is the report of "blindsight" in the patient D. B. (Weiskrantz, 1986) and others with damage in the primary visual projection area. This patient suffered a left hemianopia following surgical destruction of the right striate cortex. Although he has virtually no vision in his left visual field, he is able to judge accurately the presence or absence

---

[2]There are important differences between these sets of terms, but for our purposes they are treated as equivalent. The explicit–implicit distinction is preferred for reasons outlined elsewhere (Roediger, 1990; Schacter, 1990).

of visual stimuli, and reach accurately for objects presented in his scotoma; moreover, he is able to discriminate among horizontal, vertical, and diagonal lines and discriminate among such stimuli as Xs, Os, Ts, and 4s. He claims to be unable to see the objects to which he is responding. Although under some circumstances D. B. reports that he *knows* that something is in his field, he does not describe his experience as seeing; his test performance, although accurate, has the phenomenal quality of intuition.

Based on reports such as these, Kihlstrom et al. (1991) have proposed a distinction between explicit and implicit perception. Paralleling the case of memory, explicit perception may be defined as the person's conscious perception of some object or event in the current stimulus environment, manifested in tasks that require the subject to detect, describe, and identify the stimulus. By the same token, implicit perception is reflected in any change in experience, thought, and action that is attributable to some event in the current stimulus field. Explicit and implicit perception, so defined, apparently are dissociable; it is possible to respond discriminatively to a stimulus without having the experience of perceiving it.

It should be understood that the explicit–implicit distinction is not confined to the neurological syndromes. Dissociations of explicit and implicit memory are observed in posthypnotic amnesia, surgical anesthesia, young children, and aging memory; they also are observed in college students participating in conventional laboratory experiments, for example, elaborative activity at the time of encoding affects explicit but not implicit memory (Kihlstrom et al., 1990). Similarly, dissociations of explicit and implicit perception are observed in so-called "subliminal" perception, perceptual defense, hypnotic analgesia, and other negative hallucinations induced by hypnosis (Kihlstrom et al., 1991). Apparently, dissociations of explicit and implicit memory are observed in the dissociative disorders as well, just as dissociations of explicit and implicit perception are observed in the conversion disorders. These dissociations are what Janet had in mind when he argued that the syndromes of hysteria were united by an unconscious influence and behavior without awareness.

## The Rise and Revival of Dissociation Theory

As Ellenberger (1970) notes, the hysterias played a seminal role in the development of psychogenic theories of psychopathology. The first such theory was articulated around the turn of the century by Janet (1889,1907; for fuller descriptions, see Ellenberger, 1970; Perry & Laurence, 1984; for an autobiographical account, see Janet, 1930). According to Janet, mental life can be analyzed into a large number of psychological automatisms or elementary structures (today we might think of them as schemata or

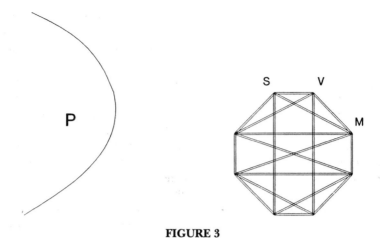

**FIGURE 3**

Janet's (1907) depiction of dissociation in the case of Irene. Ideas S, V, and M, all related to the death of her mother, are isolated from the ideas constituting the conscious personality, P (after Hilgard, 1977).

modules) that control experience, thought, and action in various domains. These automatisms, which combine both perception and action, are finely tuned to environmental circumstances. They are not restricted to whole faculties and modalities, such as cognition or emotion, perception or language, or vision or hearing. Rather, they involve content: memories of self, perception of a certain portion of space, or execution of certain actions.

According to Janet, each person possesses a vast repertoire of such automatisms, bound together into a single unified stream of consciousness. As such, the inputs to these automatisms are accessible to phenomenal awareness and the outputs are amenable to voluntary control. However, under circumstances of stress or exhaustion, the unity of consciousness can be broken when one or more of these separates from the rest. These dissociated automatisms continue to operate, but they are detached from the executive functions of phenomenal awareness and voluntary control. In Janet's view, this occurs in hysteria; the unity of consciousness is broken, and some subset of automatisms becomes split off from the rest, resulting in a state of désaggrégation (in French) or dissociation (in English). If the automatisms control vision, the result is hysterical blindness; if they control hearing, hysterical deafness; if voluntary motor function, paralysis; if autobiographical memory, amnesia. Moreover, the fact that automatisms are content-bound, rather than content-free, offers the possibility of selective dissociations: tunnel blindness, an ability to hear some voices but not others, the loss of memory for one time, place, or person but not another. Figure 3 presents a graphical representation of Janet's system.

In Janet's view, this state of disaggregation accounts for some of the peculiar features that distinguish the dissociative and conversion disorders from their organic analogs. For example, one of the hallmarks of the functional disorders is the remarkable set of paradoxes and contradictions apparent in the patients' behavior. These observations reflect the continued processing of information by the dissociated automatisms—the fact that they still receive inputs, and generate outputs, outside of executive awareness and control. These autonomous activities permit a high level of adaptive behavior on the part of the patient; Janet's case of the patient with functional tubular blindness who nevertheless was able to play ball games comes to mind. Because their symptom has a limited impact on adaptive behavior, it is not surprising that functional patients, but not organic patients, exhibit a rather blase attitude about their symptoms and their consequences.

Janet was mistaken about one point. The occurrence of paradoxes and contradictions does not necessarily distinguish the functional disorders from their organic counterparts. Dissociations of explicit and implicit memory occur in the amnesic syndrome and dissociations of explicit and implicit perception occur in blindsight. In fact, dissociations are ubiquitous.[3] Fortunately, such rules are no longer needed; modern neurology offers a wide variety of brain-imaging techniques, including positron emission tomography and magnetic resonance imaging that can be used to determine the presence, location, and extent of brain damage. However, Janet was right to draw attention to the existence of dissociations, and to try to understand them in psychological terms.

Although dissociation was soon overshadowed by Freud's concept of repression and his psychosexual theory of neurosis, Janet's ideas eventually experienced a revival in the form of Hilgard's (1977) neodissociation theory of divided consciousness. (For an appreciation of Hilgard's theory, see Kihlstrom, 1991.) Like Janet, Hilgard (1977) characterizes the mind as a set of separate components, called cognitive control structures, that monitor and control mental functioning in different domains. These various components are organized in a tangled hierarchy so each is in communication with the others and all are in communication with an executive ego. This central control structure serves as the ultimate endpoint for all inputs and the ultimate starting point for all outputs, and provides the basis for the phenomenal experience of awareness and intention. When inputs received by a subordinate control structure are processed through to the

---

[3]Actually, Janet may have anticipated this situation. In his autobiographical essay, he writes, "From the medical viewpoint, I still believe that one will eventually be compelled to return to interpretations of neuropathic disorders similar to those which I have proposed in regard to hysteria" (1930, p. 127). In this light, we may conclude that Janet would have looked kindly on the appropriation of his concept by psychology, neuropsychology, and cognitive science.

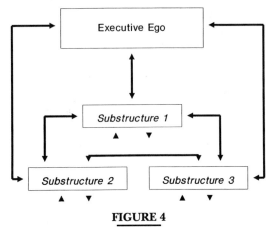

**FIGURE 4**

Hilgard's system of multiple controls (after Hilgard, 1977). In this depiction of a unified cognitive system, each of the substructures is able to communicate with the others and with the executive ego.

executive ego, then the person is aware of them (or, more precisely, of their mental representation). When outputs are generated by a subordinate structure in response to commands initiated by the executive ego, then the person has the experience of intentional action. Finally, the interconnections among subordinate cognitive controls allow them to pass information to and otherwise influence each other. Hilgard's system of controls is portrayed in Fig. 4.

Hilgard makes clear that the situation just portrayed is an ideal, and that the unity of consciousness is actually illusory. Some subordinate cognitive structures may have no direct connection to the executive ego, meaning that they process inputs and generate outputs outside of awareness and independent of voluntary control. Similarly, the function of some substructures can become habitual, or routinized, by constant repetition or practice. This idea is closely related to the notion that some mental processes are innately automatic (Hasher & Zacks, 1979) or may become automatized through a process of routinization (Anderson, 1982; Shiffrin & Schneider, 1984).

Other circumstances also can disrupt the normal relationships among cognitive structures. Certain environmental conditions, such as those involved in "subliminal" stimulation, can make it difficult for information processed by a substructure to reach the executive ego. Alternatively, certain organic conditions, such as brain damage, physiological conditions induced by sleep, anesthetics, or other drugs, or mental states such as daydreaming, absorption, and hypnosis may temporarily or permanently alter the connections between individual structures. For example, if the communication routes between a subordinate structure and the executive ego are cut, the subordinate structure may engage in certain forms of information processing outside of phenomenal awareness and without the subjective experience of intention. Such a state is defined by Hilgard as dissociation.

Hilgard's system was devised with the dissociations of hypnosis in mind, but also provides a way of conceptualizing the dissociations observed in the dissociative and conversion disorders. (For applications of Hilgard's scheme to other areas of cognitive psychology and cognitive neuropsychology, see Kihlstrom, 1991.)

1. Imagine a circumstance in which the subsystem responsible for visual perception is cut off from the executive ego, but remains able to communicate laterally with other subordinate systems. A person in this situation will be denied the experience of seeing yet, because the visual subsystem continues to process inputs, execute outputs, and pass information to (and receive information from) other subsystems, the person may still be able to respond adaptively to visual events, a common observation in cases of functional blindness.

2. In another case, the subsystems responsible for sensory and motor activity in the arm and hand are cut off from the executive ego. Under these circumstances, the person will be denied awareness of tactile and kinesthetic events, and deliberate attempts to move the limb will be without effect. However, at the same time, the subsystems in question may operate autonomously to develop conditioned escape and avoidance responses to mild shock applied to the affected limb, the sort of outcome obtained by Hilgard and Marquis (1940) in their pioneering exercise in behavior therapy.

3. Disruptions of links between the executive ego and substructures representing autobiographical memory will produce the symptoms of psychogenic amnesia and psychogenic fugue, respectively. However, this amnesic barrier will not prevent the person from gaining access to procedural and semantic memories that are not part of the episodic memory system. Multiple personality disorder represents a special case in which there appear to exist two or more executive ego structures; some substructures are shared between them, others are not. Activation of one executive ego gives it the ability to monitor and control the substructures to which it is connected; it is denied awareness of and control over the substructures that are unique to its counterparts. Under these circumstances, it would be possible to develop coexisting sets of identities, autobiographical memories, and mental functions, only one of which would be obvious at any one time. At the same time, each alter ego can influence the others implicitly, outside of awareness, by passing information between shared subsystems.

Hilgard's idea of dissociation reflecting a disruption in the normal relationships among mental subsystems is especially interesting at a time when cognitive science, especially cognitive neuropsychology, is attracted to the idea of modules, each geared to performing some information-processing task, with built-in constraints on cognitive penetrability and the possibilities of disconnections between them (e.g., Geschwind, 1965; Fodor, 1983). Contemporary neuropsychology provides evidence for brain structures mediating the encoding and decoding of speech, of language, of visual and auditory stimulation, of nouns and verbs, and even of vowels and consonants, each of which can be spared selectively (Shallice, 1988; McCarthy & Warrington, 1990). However, there are two important differences between Hilgard's notions and the dominant view of modules. First, Fodor's modules are tied at least implicitly to particular brain structures (Wernicke's and Broca's areas, for example, or the striate cortex), whereas Hilgard's subsystems are functional in nature, not isomorphic to any biological formations. Also, Fodor's modules are content-free mental faculties, such as language, speech, and vision; in contrast, Hilgard's subsystems can be associated with content as well as with function.

Whether in Janet's original form or Hilgard's updated form, dissociation theory provides a perspective of nonconscious mental functioning that is rather different from that proposed by classical psychoanalytic theory. Classical psychoanalysis restricts the unconscious to primitive sexual and aggressive ideas and impulses, and contends that unconscious mental processes are irrational and imagistic. In contrast, dissociation theory asserts that nonconscious mental structures and processes do not differ qualitatively from their conscious counterparts, except for the fact that they are not accessible to conscious awareness. Moreover, classical psychoanalysis argues that the restriction of awareness is motivated by purposes of defense. Thus, repression reflects an attempt to cope with anxiety aroused by conflicting ideas and impulses; rendering some mental content unconscious has the effect of reducing anxiety. In contrast, dissociation theory does not impart a defensive function to dissociation. Dissociations can occur as a by-product of stress and conflict without being regarded as coping mechanisms; dissociations also can occur under circumstances that are free from intrapsychic conflict, for example, hypnosis. When repressed contents intrude on consciousness and behavior, they do so in highly disguised symbolic form; dissociated contents express themselves more directly.

Dissociation and repression theory do agree, however, on one fundamental point: the percepts, memories, and thoughts denied to conscious awareness nevertheless may intrude on the person's ongoing experience, thought, and action. For Freud, the "return of the repressed" is reflected in neurotic symptoms, dreams, and slips of the tongue and other reflections of the psychopathology of everyday life. For Janet, the impact of dissociated "fixed ideas" is seen in the contradictions of hysteria, but also in the phenomena of hypnosis, for example, posthypnotic suggestion. From the perspective of present-day cognitive theory, both kinds of influences may be construed as instances of implicit perception and implicit memory, that is, as reflections of the processing of current or past events outside of phenomenal awareness.

## Consciousness, Dissociation, and the Self

An alternative information-processing account of dissociation (Kihlstrom, 1987,1990; Kihlstrom et al., 1990,1991) begins with James' (1890) proposal that the self is the key to conscious awareness.

> The personal self rather than the thought might be treated as the immediate datum in psychology . . . It seems as if the elementary psychic fact were not *thought* or *this thought* but *my thought*, every thought being *owned* . . . The universal conscious fact is not "feelings and thoughts exist" but "*I* think" and "*I* feel." (p. 221; emphasis original)

A similar idea was expressed by Janet.

> The complete consciousness which is expressed by the words, "I see, I feel a movement," is not completely represented by this little elementary phenomenon [i.e., of a sensation of vision or of motion]. It contains a new term, the word "I," which designates something very complicated. The question here is of the idea of personality, of my whole person . . . There are then in the "I feel," two things in presence of each other: a small, new, psychological fact, a little flame lighting up—"feel"—and an enormous mass of thoughts already constituted into a system—"I." These two things mingle, combine; and to say "I feel" is to say that the already enormous personality has seized upon and absorbed that little, new sensation which has just been produced. (pp. 304–305)

On the other hand, Claparede (1911) remarked on the absence of self-reference in the mental activity of certain brain-damaged patients.

> If one examines the behavior of such a patient, one finds that everything happens as though the various events of life, however well associated with each other in the mind, were incapable of integration with the *me* itself. (p. 71)

The problem is how to represent the self within the framework of contemporary cognitive theory. One option is provided by associative-network models of memory such as the ACT* theory of Anderson (1976,1983). Anderson argues that memory stores two types of knowledge, declarative and procedural. Declarative memory consists of factual knowledge about objects and events; procedural memory includes the person's repertoire of cognitive and motor skills. In ACT*, declarative knowledge is represented

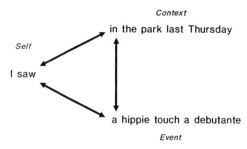

**FIGURE 5**

Schematic memory network representation of an episode. The event node represents the episode itself; the context node the time and place that the event took place; and the self node represents the person as the agent or experiencer of the event (after Anderson, 1976).

by semantic (actually propositional) networks, in which nodes represent concepts and features and associative links represent the relationships between them. Procedural knowledge is represented by productions (or systems of productions), *IF–THEN* rules in which the nodes stand for processing goals, conditions, and actions. Whereas declarative knowledge is available to introspection, procedural knowledge is unconscious in principle. A special segment of declarative memory, know as working memory, contains representations of the organism, its environment, and its currently active processing goals, as well as nodes representing knowledge activated by perception, memory, and thought.

According to this view, the self is a declarative memory structure representing the person's knowledge of him or herself: the physical and psychosocial attributes that most characterize the person and serve to distinguish him or her from others (Kihlstrom & Cantor, 1984; Kihlstrom, Cantor, Albright, Chew, Klein, & Niedenthal, 1988; Kihlstrom, 1992). This knowledge structure resides in working memory, where it can make contact with other knowledge represented in the course of perception, memory, thought, and action. The proposal is that contact with the mental representation of self is a necessary condition for representation in phenomenal awareness.

Consider the following schematic representation of an event in which the person perceives (or remembers) an occasion on which a hippie touches a debutante (Fig. 5; for a full propositional representation, see Anderson, 1976).

<blockquote>
I saw<br>
a hippie touch a debutante<br>
in the park last Thursday.
</blockquote>

In such a representation, there are three central important links

1. between the event node (representing a hippie touching a debutante) and the context node (representing the fact that the touching took place in a particular park on a particular Thursday);
2. between the self node (representing the self as the observer of the event) and the event node; and
3. between the self node and the context node (representing the location of self at a particular time and place).

When the self node is connected to the event node, the person is aware of the event in question. In this way, just as James and Janet proposed, the personal self has become part of the mental representation of the event, as the agent or experiencer of whatever occurred. Of course, there are other ways in which the self could be represented in the event. The self could be the hippie who touched the debutante or the debutante who was touched by the hippie. In any case, the link to the self provides the mental basis for the phenomenal experience of consciousness, the moment when we inject ourselves into our thoughts, feelings, and desires; when we take possession of them; when we experience and acknowledge them as our own rather than someone else's.

When the link between event and self is disrupted, the person is not aware of the event in question. Even so, however, there is nothing to prevent the activated mental representation of the event from influencing the person's ongoing experience, thought, and action, outside of awareness, and generating the classic phenomena associated with implicit memory. Thus, the event node can serve as a source of activation that can spread to other conceptually related nodes. Suppose the experience of viewing a hippie touch a debutante was so shocking that the person lapsed into an episode of psychogenic amnesia or fugue, reflecting the dissociation of the mental representation of self from the mental representation of the event. Such a person will not be able to remember the event in question. Nevertheless, activation of the mental representation of a hippie touching a debutante would facilitate the perceptual identification of hippies and debutantes in a scene, and the retrieval of factual information about these social types (i.e., that hippies have long hair and wear beads or that debutantes have long hair and wear white dresses); it might lead hippies and debutantes to appear in the person's thoughts and images, including dreams and daydreams. Moreover, if the event (or any of its constituents) appears as a condition in a production system, the person may engage in certain behaviors. Thus, if the person is offended by the mingling of different socioeconomic classes, he or she might experience feelings of anger or disgust. Note, however, that the individual will be unaware of why he has these thoughts, images, and feelings. The source of the spreading activation, in his own personal experience, will remain unknown to him.

A variant of the model can be used to represent the conversion disorders. Assume, for example, that our hypothetical patient has been struck blind (rather than rendered amnesic) by the sight of a hippie touching a debutante. This blindness represents the disconnection of the mental representation of the self from coexisting mental representations of visual input. Because these representations remain activated in working memory, however, they continue to play a role in the person's ongoing experience, thought, and action. For example, if the patient is unknowingly placed in the same room with a hippie, he or she might feel uneasy and ask to be relocated, might spend more (or less) time oriented in the direction of the hippie than would be expected by chance, or might attempt to catch a ball thrown by the hippie.

Obviously, the details of such a view must be worked out. In the present context, the primary value of the model is to show that it is possible, in principle, to represent dissociations of the sort that interested Janet and Hilgard within the confines of a widely accepted model of the human information-processing system. Moreover, it is of interest to note that variants of this model can account for other dissociations, occurring outside the domain of the dissociative and conversion disorders (Kihlstrom, 1991; Kihlstrom et al., 1991). Thus, for example, in hypnosis the links to the self that are so critical to consciousness might be set aside temporarily, resulting in such phenomena as posthypnotic amnesia and hypnotic blindness. It may turn out that the hippocampus, destruction of which results in the amnesic syndrome, plays a critical role in linking the mental representation of self to the mental representation of ongoing experience. In cases of so-called subliminal influence, it might be that degraded stimuli, either because they are too weak or presented too briefly, do not get processed into working memory and, thus, do not have the opportunity to make contact with the self node. Many possibilities along similar lines exist.

## A Return to Diagnosis and a Call for Research

It seems clear, at this point, that the dissociative and conversion disorders should be returned to their historical status as closely related diagnostic entities. Both types of syndrome share in addition to their pseudoneurological nature, the disruption of consciousness (Nemiah, 1990), of the normal integration of percepts, memories, and actions with the self. Percepts and memories that ordinarily would be linked with the self, and thus be consciously accessible, are not, yet they continue to influence experience, thought, and action outside of awareness in the form of implicit percepts and implicit memories. Goal-directed actions consciously willed by the self do not connect with their corresponding pro-

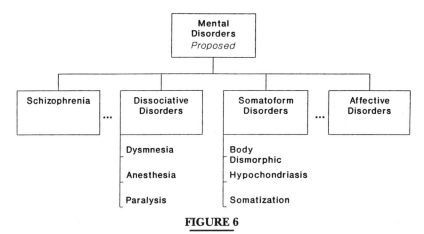

**FIGURE 6**

Proposed classification of dissociative disorders, with varieties of functional abnormalities of memory, perception, and action listed as subtypes.

duction systems, and thus remain unexecuted, yet these same systems can be activated, outside of awareness, by other appropriate conditions. The dissociative disorders are not simply disorders in which dissociations occur; rather, the term should be reserved for those cases in which the primary feature is a disruption of the monitoring and controlling functions of consciousness.

Looking forward to the future DSM-V, the foregoing considerations suggest a reclassification of the dissociative and conversion disorders as suggested in Fig. 6. First, the dissociative disorders should be retained as a broad category of psychopathology, listed in the same level of the nosology as schizophrenia, affective disorder, anxiety disorder, somatization disorder, psychophysiological disorder, and other major categories of mental illness. This label should be reserved for functional disorders of the monitoring and controlling functions of consciousness, that is, failures of conscious perception, memory, or motor control attributable to instigating events or processes that do not result in brain insult, injury, or disease, but produce more difficulties than normally would occur in the absence of those events and processes (Schacter & Kihlstrom, 1989). The pathognomic feature of the dissociative disorders is disruptions in phenomenal awareness and the voluntary control of action, coupled with evidence of information processing outside of awareness. Thus, the "dissociation" in the dissociative disorders refers to the links between the self on one hand, and perception, memory, and action on the other. Somatization disorders, which do not involve disruptions in the monitoring and controlling functions of consciousness, are classified separately.

The dissociative disorders are further divided into three subcategories, depending on the mental functions lost to consciousness. (1) Dissociative dysmnesia would include all the failures of identity and personal memory, presently classified as dissociative disorders: psychogenic amnesia, fugue, multiple personality disorder, and depersonalization and derealization; (2) dissociative anesthesia would include all the sensory-perceptual syndromes presently listed under the conversion disorders, including all the sensory modalities and pain: psychogenic blindness, deafness, tactile anesthesia, analgesia, and so forth; and (3) dissociative paralysis would include the losses of voluntary motor control listed under the conversion disorders, including paralysis of the extremities, aphonia, astasia-abasia, and weakness.

Issues of diagnosis aside, a cognitive approach to the dissociative and conversion disorders begins with an appreciation of their pseudoneurological nature. To a first approximation, the symptoms of dissociation and conversion are those of brain-damaged individuals. Concussed individuals show retrograde amnesias; certain brain tumors can induce massive personality changes; feelings of depersonalization and derealization often accompany epileptic seizures; anesthesia and paralysis are common consequences of strokes; striate damage can produce blindness. These disorders, however, are cognitive disorders, and can be studied with the experimental procedures developed by cognitive neuropsychologists (Kihlstrom & McGlynn, 1991). It is a pity that, for all the attention devoted to the dissociative disorders (and, for that matter, to the somatization disorders of which the conversion disorders are currently a part), there has been so little experimental work done on them.

## Acknowledgments

Preparation of this chapter, and the research contributing to the point of view represented herein, was supported in part by Grant MH-35856 from the National Institute of Mental Health. I thank Terrence Barnhardt, Lawrence Couture, Martha Glisky, Lori Marchese, Susan McGovern, Robin Pennington, Sheila Mulvaney, Victor Shames, Douglas Tataryn, and Irene Tobis for their comments.

# 14

# Schema Approach
# to Personality Disorders

**Dan J. Stein**
*Department of Psychiatry*
*College of Physicians and Surgeons*
*Columbia University*
*and*
*New York State Psychiatric Institute*
*New York, New York*

**Jeffrey E. Young**
*Department of Psychiatry*
*College of Physicians and Surgeons*
*Columbia University*
*and*
*Cognitive Therapy Center of New York*
*New York, New York*

Each of the major schools of psychology has contributed to the theory of personality and its disorders. The conceptual divergence of this body of ideas is reflected in the existence of a variety of conflicting therapeutic approaches to the personality disorders. It has been argued elsewhere in this volume that the cognitive revolution in psychology and its applied sciences may provide a unifying paradigm and facilitate interdisciplinary cohesion. Unfortunately, cognitive science has paid relatively little attention to either individual differences or to the more complex phenomena that constitute personality, personality disorder, and personality treatment. The contrast between a wealth of divergent theories and therapies of personality, and an increasingly consolidated theory of mind that has neglected to focus on this area, makes the intersection of personality and cognitive science particularly interesting. The nature of such an intersection is the subject of this chapter. The cognitive science concept of schemas will be focused on and argued to be theoretically valuable in understanding personality and clinically valuable in treating personality disorder. The chapter will begin with a brief overview of existent approaches to personality and its disorders to highlight continuities and contrasts with a cognitive science approach.

## Biological Views

Since the time of Hippocrates, it has been hypothesized that personality and its disorders have constitutional roots. In post-Darwinian thinking, this hypothesis has been supported by the argument that various traits can be seen as having emerged in the context of evolution. The precise nature of the constitutional hypothesis has changed with time. Hippocrates focused on four temperaments that resulted from the bodily presence of black bile, blood, yellow bile, and phlegm. With increasing interest in and knowledge of anatomy, personality traits were correlated with protuberances of the skull. The development of histology saw the division of people into endomorphic, ectomorphic, and mesomorphic types, each group resulting from a predominance of one or another layer of the egg. The rise of physiology led to a concern with overreactive or underreactive autonomic nervous systems as the basis for extroversion and introversion. Finally, the impact of neurochemistry led to Cloninger's (1987) hypothesis that the three major neurotransmitters—dopamine, serotonin, and noradrenaline—underlie the various dimensions of personality and personality disorder.

Various findings have solidified such views. Family and twin studies indicate a strong heritability of certain personality traits (Zuckerman, 1990) and disorders (Robins, 1966). Developmental studies have indicated the consistency of individual temperament, which is observable from an early age (Thomas & Chess, 1984; Kagan, 1989). Biological correlates of personality increasingly have been established (Siever, Klar, & Coccaro, 1985). Finally, psychopharmacological intervention has proved valuable in particular disorders (Cowdry & Gardner, 1988).

Although biological correlates may underlie personality, biology itself does not provide an account of the psychological phenomena with which it correlates. Biology provides important models of various neurochemical and neuroanatomical systems and of their role in particular behaviors, but does not provide a sufficiently complex model of the emergent phenomena, such as personality and the personality disorders, that are composed of such behaviors.

On the other hand, models of these emergent psychological phenomena need to consider biological realities. We would argue that because neuroscience is a central discipline of cognitive science, models that are constructed by cognitive scientists can include biological substrates as well as emergent phenomena. In formulating a cognitive science model of personality, we will need to retain this biologically informed aspect of personality theory.

## Analytical Views

The importance and limitations of biology were noted by Freud (1937), who wrote, "Each ego is endowed from the first with individual dispositions and trends, though it is true that we cannot specify their nature or what determines them." Freud abandoned his early studies in biology and constructed a psychodynamic model of mind and of personality. His psychological theory of personality focuses on what analysts term "character." This focus is first articulated in his account of anal character in *Character and Anal Erotism* (Freud, 1908), and is extended in a number of later papers.

Several key points about this theory should be noted. First, it is an energy-based model. Freud accounts for observable character traits on the basis of underlying psychic structures. The interplay between these underlying structures of character is, however, conceived of in terms of an economics of energy: instincts dam up and are transformed or discharged. Second, it is a wide-ranging model. The psychic structures that account for character traits also account for a variety of other phenomena, ranging from normal to pathological, including dreams, fantasy, and acting out; defenses and symptoms; sexual identity and sexual relations; self concept; and object relations. Third, Freud's model focuses on change. The theory accounts both for the development of character traits, and for their change in the course of an analysis. Character traits and their underlying structures emerge from the interaction of constitutional factors and environmental ones, and thereafter remain in place, manifesting in ideas, feelings, and behaviors at different stages of life. Although character traits may have adaptive features at the time of their emergence, at a later point they may prove maladaptive. In therapy, character traits may lead to resistance and may emerge in the transference. With interpretation and working through, however, progress may occur. Finally, the model emphasizes the unconscious. The nature of the patient's character traits, and their underlying structures, is more or less unknown to the patient.

Freud's model of character clearly undergoes continual revision. Whereas character is formulated initially as a derivative of libidinal drives, a later emphasis is on character as the formation of identifications by means of structured ego representations (Liebert, 1984). Later analysts may be seen to focus even less on the energetic aspects of this model than on character as it develops in relationship to others. Although the energy model is good for phenomena such as movement and momentum, it fails to provide an adequate account of the subtle differentiations that constitute personality. The cumbersome nature of this model has been shown consistently to result in a variety of theoretical impasses (Swanson, 1977). Thus, the focus of post-Freudian theorists is on the self, the other, and the space between them (Mitchell, 1988). Kohut and the self-psychologists highlight a failure in empathy of the nurturing environment, arguing that this loss leads to arrest in the maturation of self. Interpersonal analysts such as Erikson and Sullivan emphasize the consequences of the dynamic interplay between caretakers and children for character formation. Kernberg and other object-relations theorists highlight character as comprising structured object relations.

A strength of contemporary cognitive science lies in its convergence with post-Freudian analytic theory in replacing a focus on psychic energetics with an emphasis on the mind as concerned with representation and symbol manipulation. In contrast, cognitive science may be viewed as weak in the other key areas of analytic thought. Thus, cognitive scientists have focused primarily on cognition in the laboratory, and have paid relatively less attention to the broad array of mental phenomena not included under the rubric of cognition, to the development and change of cognitive structures, and to the unconscious aspects of mind. Again, in formulating a cognitive science model of personality, we will need to consider these analytically informed areas of personality theory.

## Behavioral Views

Whether behaviorists have accepted the notion of personality and personality disorder is debatable. Skinner (1974), for example, argued that to posit an internal construct, such as personality, that directed behavior was to approach the level of primitive animism. On the other hand, behaviorism has influenced several important works on personality (Dollard, Doob, Miller, Mowrer, & Sears, 1939; Mowrer, 1950). A focus on the observable also has influenced the factor-analytic approach, which has dominated empirical personality research (Mischel, 1968).

Further, in recent years behaviorists have contributed to the literature on the therapy of personality disorder (Linehan, 1989). Two different behavioral strategies are discernable (Turner & Turkat, 1988). The first is to treat each symptom of the personality disorder patient as a separate behavior that requires change. The second is to develop a formulation of an underlying behavioral problem that accounts for the various symptoms of the patient.

Behaviorist theory fails to provide an adequate description of the internal workings of the mind. On the other hand, it may be argued that the behavioral model was instrumental in bringing to the psychological sciences a concern with empirical measurement and operational definition. Cognitive science clearly has been influenced by this concern. Once more, in constructing a cognitive science model of personality, this behaviorally informed aspect of model building will require attention.

## Cognitive Science

A number of personality theorists have attempted to develop a cognitively oriented approach to personality. Kelly's (1955) personal construct theory of personality has been particularly influential in cognitive psychology. More recently, Forgus and Sulman (1979) have described a cognitive theory of personality that emphasizes core rubrics that cover self-perception, world view, and instructions for action. An early work by Tomkins and Messick attempted to employ artificial intelligence methodologies to develop models of personality. In social psychology, Bandura (1973, 1986) and others have developed a social-cognitive theory of personality (Nasby & Kihlstrom, 1986; Cantor & Zirkel, 1991; Higgins, 1991).

An interest in cognitive constructs has been apparent also among clinicians working with personality disorder patients. The increasingly cognitive orientation of post-Freudian psychoanalysis has been mentioned already. In cognitive therapy, whereas early work focused on depression, current work shows increasing interest in personality disorder (Beck et al., 1990; Young, 1990).

In addition, a dialogue between cognitivists and clinicians interested in personality has been initiated. Thus, for example, there has been empirical work on disorders of personality styles (Weinberger, Schwartz, & Davidson, 1979), object relations (Blatt, Brenneis, & Schimek, 1976), and their development (Emde, 1983; Stern, 1985). Perhaps the most widely used construct in this dialogue, however, is that of schemas (Stein, 1992). In the following section, we will focus on the schema construct as one that is central to the various disciplines that constitute cognitive science. We then explore the use of this term by two theorists, one a cognitive-behavioral therapist and the other a psychodynamically oriented analyst, who have written extensively about schemas and the psychopathology and psychotherapy of personality disorders. The cognitive science and clinical conceptions of schemas are then compared. Finally, we assess whether the employment of schema theory can integrate usefully the behavioral, analytic, and learning views of personality that we have discussed already.

## Schemas in Cognitive Science

The concept of the schema may be seen to have roots in each of the central disciplines of cognitive science (Stein, 1992). In philosophy, Kant used the concept to describe the interdigitation of properties of the mind (a priori categories) and raw sensory data (of a posteriori experience). "This representation of a universal procedure of the imagination in providing an image for a concept, I entitle the schema of the concept" (quoted in Gardner, 1985). It may be argued that Kant employed concepts of representation to move beyond the impasse between the empiricists, who argued that knowledge has its origins in the external world, and the rationalists, who argued that knowledge is a product of the mind. Thus, he may have helped develop a conceptual science that accounts for the possibility of scientific knowledge.

Indeed, the schema concept was developed by subsequent natural scientists. The neurologists Head and Holmes (1911), for example, studied the spatial perceptions patients have of their bodies, referring to the basis of these perceptions as the postural schema. The postural schema integrated sensations that were triggered by postural change. In lesions of the parietal lobe, the schema may be destroyed, with the possible outcome that patients ignore part of their body, treating it as if it were not their own. Conversely, an amputee may have an intact brain schema, and therefore perceive movements in the missing limb. Today the term body schema is used more widely (Frederiks, 1969).

Kant was not optimistic about the possibilities of psychological science. Nevertheless, a short while later, Piaget again employed the concept of the schema, formulating a wonderfully complex and sustained argument in developmental psychology. Piaget originally had philosophical interests, but soon came to the conclusion that the time was ripe for knowledge to be studied from a scientific viewpoint (Piaget, 1972). According to Piaget, the initial schemas of the child comprise biological sensorimotor reflexes that coordinate the child's interactions with the environment. Gradually, these biological schemas allow adaptation to the environment by two complementary processes, assimilation and accommodation. Piaget provides a detailed description of the gradual transformation of sensorimotor schemas to operations of formal thought (Piaget, 1952).

The concept of schemas was introduced to cognitive psychology by Bartlett (1932), a former student of Head, who was interested in memory. Bartlett felt that memory was a social phenomenon and that the context of an experience had crucial effects on what was retained and recalled. Although Ebbinghaus had pioneered the experimental study of memory using nonsense syllables, this methodology did not seem suitable to

Bartlett's concerns. A conversation with Wiener, the founder of cybernetics, was instrumental in helping Bartlett find an experimental methodology for developing his ideas. Wiener suggested that Bartlett explore the Russian Scandal parlor game, in which a story is passed around the room, and the original and final version are compared. Bartlett found that subjects showed consistent patterns of error in the recall of narratives. Thus, for example, an American Indian narrative would be revised regularly by subjects until it resembled a Western tale. Bartlett developed the construct of the schema to explain this, describing a schema as a component of memory that is formed from encounters with the environment, and that organizes information in specific ways. Such schemas aid the recall of a typical (Western) narrative, but systematically distort the recall of an unusual (American Indian) narrative.

Finally, cognitive scientists have developed the concept of schemas of self (Markus, 1977; Greenwald, 1980; Rogers, 1981) and others (Cantor & Mischel, 1977; Fiske, 1981; Taylor & Crocker, 1981; Uleman & Bargh, 1989). These constructs allow cognitive science to incorporate theories and methods from social psychology and sociology.

The fertility of the concept of schemas is apparent in the extent to which it has infiltrated the literature of contemporary cognitive science. Schema theory has been employed in theories of memory (Schacter, 1989), concept representation (Smith, 1989), problem solving (VanLehn, 1989), movement (Jordan & Rosenbaum, 1989), and language (Arbib, Conklin & Itill, 1987). A variety of empirical data about schemas has emerged. Schemas have been found to facilitate recognition and recall, to influence speed of information processing and problem solving, to allow for the chunking of information into more meaningful units to enable inference about missing data, and to provide a basis for prediction and decision making. Schemas are thought to engender bias by relying on confirming evidence at the expense of disconfirming evidence, but this characteristic maintains schemas (Meichenbaum & Gilmore, 1984; Winfrey & Goldfried, 1986; Williams, Watts, MacLeod, & Matthews, 1988).

It may be argued, however, that the elasticity of the concept of schemas indicates a lack of theoretical rigor. The number of different definitions of schemas by various authors is consistent with this argument. Nevertheless, some degree of consensus has emerged. Thorndyke and Hayes-Roth (1979), for example, describe three universal assumptions made by different authors: a schema is an organization of conceptually related elements representing a prototypical abstraction of a complex concept, a schema gradually develops from past experience, and a schema guides the organization of new information. Further, a metatheory of schemas gradually has been constructed. Thus, it generally is recognized that a schema comprises an architectural element (its structure) and a propositional element (its content) that may be verbal or nonverbal. Schemas are involved in operations (e.g., encoding, retrieval) in which events (e.g., thoughts, images) are produced and processed (Ingram & Kendall, 1986). Schemas are thought to be highly interdependent and hierarchically organized, and to vary in the extent to which they are open to awareness (Craik & Lockhart, 1972; Thorndyke & Hayes-Roth, 1979). The extent to which different theorists who employ the concept of schemas have both divergent and convergent ideas is seen also in the following discussion of the use of schema theory by clinicians.

### Schemas in Clinical Science

The schema concept has been employed by several clinical theorists in both the cognitive-behavioral (Arnkoff, 1980; Goldfried & Robbins, 1983; Turk & Speer, 1983; Greenberg & Safran, 1984; Young, 1990) and the psychoanalytic (Wachtel, 1982; Slap & Saykin, 1983; Eagle, 1986) traditions. Perhaps the most extensive contributions, however, are by Beck (1964, 1967), a founder of cognitive therapy, and Horowitz (1988,1991), a psychoanalyst with a strong interest in cognitive science.

Beck (1964) introduced the concept of schema in the context of his work on a diathesis–stress model of depression. He defined a schema as "a [cognitive] construct for screening, coding, and evaluating the stimuli that impinge on the organism" (Beck, 1967). The formation of schemas was also characterized.

> The theory proposes that early experiences provide the basis for forming negative concepts about the self . . . These . . . may be latent but can be activated by specific circumstances which are analogous to experiences initially responsible for embedding the negative attitude. (Beck, Rush, Shaw, & Emery, 1979)

The content of schemas was discussed in detail. Kovacs and Beck (1978) wrote

> Schemata that predispose to and become overly active in a depressive episode . . . organize those aspects of the person's experience that concern self-evaluation and relationships with other people . . . Depressogenic schemata code and organize information about life situations or events that the individual perceives as real or potential subtractions from his personal domain.

More recently Beck and his colleagues have elaborated the notion of schemas further in discussing their relevance to the cognitive therapy of personality disorders (Beck et al., 1990). They classify schemas into different categories, for example, personal, familial, cultural, religious, gender, and occupational. Different types of schemas have different functions. Cognitive schemas are concerned with abstraction, interpretation, and recall; affective schemas are responsible for the generation of feelings; motivational schemas deal with wishes and desires; instrumental schemas prepare for action; and control schemas are involved with self-monitoring and self-regulation, as well as with controlling relationships with the external environment. In turn, schemas form subsystems, so cognitive schemas include schemas concerned with self-evaluation and evaluation of others, schemas concerned with memory and recall, and schemas concerned with expectancies and predictions. Beck and associates argue that schemas can be viewed as operating in a logical linear progression. Thus a dangerous stimulus activates a "danger schema," which in turn activates affective, motivational, action, and control schemas. The person then interprets the situation as dangerous (cognitive schema), feels anxiety (affective schema), wants to get away (motivational schema), and becomes mobilized to flee (instrumental schema). If the person determines that running away is unhelpful, he or she may inhibit that impulse (control schema).

Beck and his colleagues (Beck et al., 1990) use this framework to account for the production of various psychopathological phenomena. Dysfunctional thoughts, feelings, and behaviors, for example, are due to schemas that produce consistently biased judgments. The schemas of personality disorder resemble those of the symptom disorders, but are involved in the everyday processing of information and are therefore operative on a more continuous basis. When compared with the schemas of normal people, schemas in personality disorder can be seen to be evoked across many or most situations, to have a compulsive quality, and to be difficult to control or modify. Thus, they are more overgeneralized, imperative, inflexible, and resistant to change. In personality disorder, certain patterns of thinking, feeling, and behaving therefore will be overdeveloped, whereas others will be underdeveloped. There also will be a vulnerability to certain life experiences that interfere with these patterns. Schemas may be more or less active; at these vulnerable times there may be increased activation of maladaptive schemas and decreased processing of more appropriate schemas, resulting in further dysfunction and the appearance of a symptom disorder.

Beck and co-workers (1990) also use the schema framework to discuss development and change. Schema development is influenced by both constitutional and environmental factors. A particular schema may develop in response to developmental experiences or as a result of identification with family members. Certain patterns of thinking, feeling, and behaving may be derived from or may compensate for such schemas. Therapists use cognitive, affective, and behavioral strategies to change cognitive, affective, and behavioral schemas. Changing a schema is difficult and causes anxiety. On the other hand, emotionally charged topics arouse dysfunctional schemas, and change depends on a certain kind of affective experience. Schemas regarding change, self, and others can impede therapy. Schemas regarding the therapist may be labeled transference cognitions. Change comprises a continuum from restructuring of schemas to more subtle modifications. Such changes require time for the reworking that takes places in therapy.

Finally, to what extent are such schemas known to the patient? According to Beck and colleagues (1990), although such structures are not conscious, we can identify their content. Recognition and evaluation of such schemas in therapy allows their change.

Horowitz (1988a,b) categorizes schemas somewhat differently, and also emphasizes different features of schemas. Horowitz notes that schemas summarize past experience into holistic composite forms that allow incoming information to be compared with preexisting patterns. This comparison allows rapid processing, but also leads to certain biases. Schemas readily process input that fits the schematic view, and impede processing of input that does not. There are schemas of both self and other.

Subordinate schemas, including one for complex body movement, are brought together in a self-schema. Self-schemas include ways to gain pleasure or avoid displeasure (motivational schema), positioning in relation to the world (role schema), and ways to help decide which of two motives to choose (value schema). Superordinate schemas that articulate self and other schemas in ways that organize a script of wishes, fears, and likely reactions are called role-relationship models. Every individual has a repertoire of multiple schemas of self and others. Schemas operate simultaneously along multiple parallel channels. Schematic transorderings of information may allow mind–body links. The organization and repertoire of self-schemas changes slowly, enabling self-identity. However, different patterns of schema activation exist in the same person, and these are accompanied by shifts in state of mind and in the pattern of experience and behaviors. Horowitz postulates the existence of control processes that prevent the emergence of certain states of mind. Personality comprises the schemas, the states of mind, and the habitually used controls of an individual.

Horowitz has used this framework to account for maladaptive interpersonal patterns, and for maladaptive reactions to stress. In some people, schemas and patterns of control of schemas are insistent and inappropriate. These patterns constitute personality problems. Changes in the environment may lead to a poor fit between external reality and preexisting role-relationship models. Emotional response to stress is due, in part, to the discord between the new situation and enduring schemas.

Horowitz also uses his schema framework to give an account of development and change. Self-schemas develop from a basis of genetic and environmental interaction. Role-relationship models develop in the context of interpersonal behavioral patterns. Common issues are those of love and care, power and control, and sexuality and status. In therapy, the schemas of the patient become manifest in the role-relationship models of clinician and patient. The therapeutic alliance allows the patient to develop insight into such schemas and, during a process of working through, gradually to replace or modify them.

Horowitz notes that schemas and control processes persist unconsciously, but also emphasizes that they can be named, thus allowing recursive conscious representation.

## Integration

The question of the extent to which cognitive and clinical views of schemas are consistent is raised immediately. We would argue that, although different cognitive scientists and different clinicians clearly have somewhat different perspectives, there is considerable overlap. We have discussed the philosophical, biological, developmental, psychological, and sociological aspects of the cognitive science concept of the schema. It may be argued that both Beck and Horowitz view schemas as representational constructs that account for psychic processes, acknowledge that schemas are biologically based and formed during a developmental process, see schemas as psychological constructs open to empirical study, and think of schemas as manifesting in the interpersonal world. Further, the cognitive science metatheory of schemas is duplicated in their work. Both theorists describe schemas as representing a prototypical abstraction of a complex concept, as gradually developing from past experience, and as guiding the organization of new information. They attend to the structure and content of schemas, postulate how schema operation results in psychic events, and give some indication of how schemas are organized hierarchically and whether they operate consciously or unconsciously. Further, a good deal of empirical work on patient schemas is consistent with the findings of experimental cognitive science. In his review, Segal (1988) concludes that there is good evidence in the clinic that schemas engender bias by relying on confirmatory evidence at the expense of disconfirming evidence. Such work, however, has been done mostly with depressed patients, and there is a relative lack of empirical studies of schemas in personality disorder.

This overlap between conceptual and clinical approaches results in many convergences in the conceptual approach that Beck and Horowitz take toward personality and its disorders. Both emphasize personality as involved with the representations of self of other, and of self–other the relationships. Both note the biological basis of personality, and describe the gradual development and change of personality over time. Both view the psychology of personality as open to empirical study, and think of personality as manifesting in the social world. They view the schemas of personality as representing abstract prototypes, as emerging out of past experience, and as guiding mental processing. They note the structure and content of personality schemas, postulate how such schemas result in different psychic events, describe the hierarchies of such schemas in personality, and describe their unconscious aspects. Empirical work on the overlap between the views of Beck and Horowitz on personality has not, however, been undertaken.

The views of Beck and Horowitz may be seen to supplement the biological, analytic, and behavioral views of personality described earlier. In acknowledging the biological underpinnings of schemas, they suggest that biological findings can be incorporated into their models without reducing the models to biological ones. Both, therefore, allow for a biology of personality as part of the cognitive science of personality. Beck and Horowitz concur with the analytic emphasis on the range of phenomena accounted for by psychic structures, on their development and change, and on their unconscious operation, yet also are able to go beyond an energy-based account of such structures. Both theorists use cognitive theory to construct a complex view of the relationship between personality and other psychic phenomena (including psychiatric symptoms), of the development and change of personality, and of the unconscious aspects of personality. Finally, Beck and Horowitz emphasize the necessity for empirical work with schemas, so falling under the methodological influence of behaviorism without falling prey to its elision of the mind. Thus, both stress an empirical and experimental approach to personality.

### Assessment

Research on personality disorders has been given an important stimulus in recent years by the publication of the DSM-III and the DSM-III (R). These manuals not only placed the personality disorders on a separate axis, but also provided them with operational diagnostic criteria. Nevertheless, categorical diagnosis is only one aspect of clinical assessment. The clinician needs to assess underlying patterns of thinking, feeling, and behaving to determine the precise nature of the psychological dysfunctions present in the patient.

The biological, analytic, and behaviorist perspectives have been only partly helpful in measuring such underlying constructs. Biological measures in personality disorder remain a research tool. Analysts have measured such constructs as ego functioning and defense mechanisms. Unfortunately, not only are such constructs difficult to operationalize, but quantitative measures have not been widely accepted in analytic circles. Although a behaviorist approach has been adopted by a number of psychometricians interested in the measurement of individual differences, these measures have not found wide use in the clinical setting.

Information processing and other cognitivist approaches may be able to contribute to personality assessment (Nasby & Kihlstrom, 1986). Once again, we will focus on the concept of the schema. Broad strategies for measuring schemas in the clinic include self-rated questionnaires and clinician-rated structured interviews or projective tests. Further, within a particular theoretical conceptualization of schemas, it appears that reliable assessment of schemas in taped psychotherapy sessions can be achieved (Horowitz, 1991).

Young (1990) has described a self-rated Schema Questionnaire for the assessment of schemas of self in relation to the environment. Young (1990) focuses on "early maladaptive schemas" (EMSs), schemas that are dysfunctional in some significant and recurring manner, and are the result of early problematic interpersonal experiences. Each schema comprises cognitive, behavioral, affective, and interpersonal components. He has identified 16 EMSs that reflect the most common thematic contents in personality disorder. EMSs are grouped into six broader domains corresponding to six hypothesized developmental paths. (1) instability and disconnection, (2) impaired autonomy, (3) undesirability, (4) restricted self-expression, (5) restricted gratification, and (6) impaired limits.

Although the self-rating of schemas may be questioned insofar as schemas operate out of awareness, we have found this to be a useful first step in the assessment of personality. During psychotherapy, schemas are triggered in a variety of ways (Young, 1990), including discussions of the meaning of current events that cause distress or strong feelings, including events within the therapeutic relationship; imagery techniques such as allowing spontaneous images to come to the patient's mind or describing specific situations that are likely to trigger schemas; exploration of dreams; and homework assignments such as keeping thought records, topics related to schemas, or reading relevant books. A subjugation schema including the emotion of anger, for example, is likely to be triggered outside the therapy by events such as having to follow parental directives and within the therapy by having to conform with the therapist's instructions. Images, dreams, and thoughts of submitting to the control of others can be used to explore the beliefs and affects associated with this schema; for example, the idea that failure to submit will lead to negative consequences and the feeling of anger about having to submit.

Determination of the operation of a schema in psychotherapy may be difficult because a wide variety of cognitions and affects may reflect a single schema or a single schema may be responsible for a variety of different cognitions and affects. Young (1990), for example, has described the phenomena of schema maintenance, avoidance, and compensation. Schema *maintenance* is the continuous cognitive-affective confirmation and behavioral enactment of a schema. Schema *avoidance* comprises the

# TABLE 1

## Early Maladaptive Schema

| Schema | Description | Specific characteristics |
|---|---|---|
| Instability and disconnection | Expectation that one's needs for security, safety, stability, nurturance, and empathy will not be met in a predictable manner within the context of intimate or family relationships; typical family origin is detached, explosive, unpredictable, or abusive | **Abandonment/instability (AB)**<br>The perceived *instability* or *unreliability* of those available for support and connection; involves the sense that significant others will not be able to continue providing emotional support, connection, strength, or practical protection because they are emotionally unstable, unpredictable, unreliable, or erratically present; because they will die imminently; or because they will abandon the patient in favor of someone better<br>**Abuse/mistrust (MA)**<br>The expectation that others will hurt, abuse, humiliate, cheat, lie, manipulate, take advantage, or explode with violence or anger. Usually involves the perception that the harm is intentional or the result of unjustified and extreme negligence. May include the sense that one always ends up being cheated relative to others or "getting the short end of the stick."<br>**Emotional deprivation (ED)**<br>Expectation that one's desire for a normal degree of emotional support will not be adequately met by others.<br>Deprivation of nurturance: Absence of attention, affection, warmth, or compansionship<br>Deprivation of protection: Absence of strength, direction, or guidance from others<br>Deprivation of empathy: Absence of understanding, listening, self-disclosure, or mutual sharing of feelings from others |
| Impaired autonomy | Expectations about oneself and the environment that interfere with one's perceived ability to separate, survive, and function independently; typical family origin is enmeshed, undermining of child's judgment, or overprotection | **Functional dependence/incompetence (DI)**<br>Belief that one is unable to handle one's everyday responsibilities in a competent manner, without considerable help from others (e.g., take care of oneself, solve daily problems, exercise good judgment, tackle new tasks, make good decisions); often presents as a pervasive passivity<br>**Vulnerability to harm and illness (VH)**<br>Exaggerated fear that disaster is about to strike at any time (natural, criminal, medical, or financial), and that one is unable to protect oneself; may include unrealistic fears that one will have a heart attack, get AIDS, go crazy, go broke, be mugged, crash, and so on<br>**Enmeshment/undeveloped self (EM)**<br>Excessive emotional involvement and closeness with one or more significant others (often parents), at the expense of full individuation or normal social development; often involves the belief that at least one of the enmeshed individuals cannot survive or be happy without the constant support of the other; may also include feelings of being smothered by, or fused with, others; *or* insufficient individual identity or inner direction; often experienced as a feeling of emptiness or of floundering |
| Undesirability | Expectation that one will not be desirable to—or is different from—other people, in terms of any of the following: physical attractiveness, social skills, inner worth, moral integrity, interesting personality, career accomplishment, values, interests, masculinity/femininity; socioeconomic background; typical origin is criticalness or rejection from family or peer group | **Defectiveness/shame (DS)**<br>The feeling that one is *inwardly* defective, flawed, or invalid; that one would be fundamentally unlovable to significant others if exposed; or a sense of shame regarding one's perceived internal inadequacies; often involves excessive self-criticism, self-punishment, comparisons with others, and exaggerated expectations of rejection and blame in *intimate* relationships<br>**Social undesirability/alienation (SU/SI)**<br>The belief that one is *outwardly* undesirable to others (e.g., ugly, sexually undesirable, low in status, poor in conversational skills, dull) *or the* feeling that one is isolated from the rest of the world, different from other people, and/or not part of any group or community; often involves self-consciousness, alienation, comparisons with others, and insecurity in *social* situations<br>**Failure to achieve (FA)**<br>The belief that one will inevitably fail, or is fundamentally inadequate relative to one's peers, in areas of achievement (school, career, sports); often involves the belief that one is stupid, inept, untalented, ignorant, and so on |

| Restricted self-expression | Inordinate restriction, suppression, or ignoring of one's emotions or daily preferences; typical family origin is suppression of feelings and domination by adults | Subjugation (SB)<br>Excessive surrendering of control over one's own decisions and preferences, usually to avoid anger, retaliation, or abandonment; involves the perception that one's own desires are not valid or important to others; often leads to anger at the subjugator; frequently presents as excessive compliance and eagerness to please.<br>Emotional inhibition (EI)<br>Excessive difficulty expressing or discussing feelings (anger, hurt, sadness, joy), because one expects their expression to result in loss of esteem, harm to others, embarrassment, retaliation, or abandonment |
| Restricted gratification | Excessive emphasis on work, status, duty, standards, responsibility to others, or the negative aspects of life, at the expense of happiness, pleasure, natural inclinations, pleasure, health, optimism, or creativity; typical family origin is grim: pain, performance, sacrifice, self-control, and negativity predominate over pleasure, playfulness, and optimism | Self-sacrifice/overresponsibility (SS)<br>Excessive focus on meeting the needs of others, at the expense of one's own gratification; most common reasons are to prevent causing pain to others, to avoid guilt, to gain in esteem, to maintain the connection with others perceived as needy; often results from an acute sensitivity to the pain of others; often involves an exaggerated sense of duty and responsibility to others, usually leads to a sense that one's own needs are not being adequately met and sometimes to resentment of those who are taken care of<br>Unrelenting/unbalanced standards (US)<br>Relentless striving to meet high or unbalanced expectations of oneself or others, at the expense of happiness, pleasure, relaxation, spontaneity, playfulness, health, sense of accomplishment, or satisfying relationships; usually involves undue emphasis on any of six broad areas: (1) achievement or competition; (2) money, physical appearance, or social status; (3) self-control or discipline; (4) perfectionism, order, or attention to detail; (5) control and mastery of the environment; (6) moral, ethical, or religious precepts (other than self-sacrifice)<br>Negativity/pessimism (NP)<br>Pervasive lifelong focus on the negative aspects of life (pain, death, loss, disappointment, conflict, guilt, resentment, unsolved problems, potential mistakes, betrayal, things that could go wrong) while minimizing or neglecting the positive or optimistic aspects; may include feelings of help-lessness or uncontrollability, based on the expectation that one cannot prevent negative outcomes in life |
| Impaired limits | Deficiency in internal limits, leading to difficulty respecting the rights of others or meeting one's own personal goals; typical family origin is permissiveness and indulgence | Entitlement/self-centeredness (ET)<br>Insistence that one should be able to have whatever one wants, regardless of what others consider reasonable or the cost to others; often involves excessive control over others, demandingness, and lack of empathy for others' needs<br>Insufficient self-control/self-discipline (IS)<br>Pervasive difficulty exercising sufficient self-control and frustration tolerance to achieve one's personal goals, or to restrain the excessive expression of one's emotions and impulses |

cognitive-affective and behavioral processes performed by a patient to avoid a schema and its accompanying unpleasant affect. Schema compensation occurs when a patient manifests thoughts, feelings, or behaviors that represent exaggerated attempts to resolve schema issues, and constitutes a different form of schema avoidance. Patients with a subjugation schema, for example, maintain their belief that one must submit to the control of others to avoid negative consequences by always pleasing others and not considering themselves. Such patients may avoid their subjugation schema by procrastinating or may compensate by rebelling and not doing anything for anyone. The demonstration of schema maintenance, avoidance, and compensation during psychotherapy further enhances schema identification.

Although the reliable identification of schemas within a particular theoretical conceptualization is possible, the validity of any particular set of ratings remains problematic. Within the EMS classification, for example, the empirical correlation of schema categories with environmental antecedents may help establish validity. Further theoretical and empirical work is necessary to establish which schema classifications have the most explanatory value in the clinical setting.

## Treatment

The treatment of personality disorder is one of the most difficult therapeutic tasks facing the clinician. Biologists, analysts, and behaviorists all have struggled with the personality disorder patient, and achieved only limited success. In this section, we will, once again, use the concept of the schema to help consider a therapeutic approach to the personality disorder patient.

We can begin by recalling that the schemas that are responsible for personality disorder develop during a gradual process, concern basic life themes such as intimacy and autonomy, are associated with a great deal of affect, are pervasive, and are part of the core self and cognitive organization. Changing schemas is, therefore, a slow and anxiety-provoking process. Change processes may involve changing existing schemas or learning new schemas. Change also can take place on a variety of different levels; schemas may be tackled at various places in the hierarchy. Schemas may, however, interfere with therapeutic change. Schemas about self and others, or about change, may undermine the patient, the therapist, or the therapeutic process. Patients with a subjugation schema, for example, may maintain the schema by constantly deferring to the therapist. Finally, longstanding schemas may be reverted to in times of stress, even after completion of therapy. Although patients with a subjugation schema, for example, may succeed through therapy in establishing romantic relationships in which there is a balance between their needs and those of others, having to work for a controlling employer at some later time may trigger the subjugation schema again.

A central goal of treatment is to provide a relationship within which schemas can be identified, labeled, and laid open to change. Schemas of self and other that themselves affect the therapeutic process can then be pointed out. Since schemas are developed and maintained through interpersonal experience, they can be modified best by working with the patient's interpersonal relationships, including the therapeutic relationship. The therapeutic relationship itself counteracts the formation of early maladaptive schemas. To return to the example of subjugation schemas, a therapeutic relationship in which the patient is able to express his or her needs and does not have to submit to the control of the therapist will be helpful.

Techniques for changing schemas include experiential (affective), cognitive, behavioral, and interpersonal interventions (Young, 1990). Affect allows schemas to be mobilized, which may be necessary for their change. Emotive techniques include creating imaginary dialogues and emotional catharsis. Insight into the operation of schemas is also a valuable part of therapy. Cognitive techniques include reviewing evidence in support of schemas, examining the support critically, reviewing evidence contradicting the schema, illustrating how the patient discounts contradictory evidence, contradicting and challenging the schema, and developing flashcards to strengthen the new perspective. Behavioral techniques include practicing new behaviors or changing the environment. For patients with subjugation schemas, then, it is helpful to focus on their associated feelings of anger, to explore their negative thoughts related to expressing their needs, and to establish a relationship in which there is a balance between their needs and those of the other person.

A schema-based view of personality therapy may be a useful supplement to the biological, behavioral, and analytic theories of therapy. We can use it to reformulate classical concepts of change or of aspects of therapy such as transference. For example, there is a formidable analytic literature on the nature of change. The classical analytic model asserts that change involves dynamic catharsis; more modern analytic models emphasize the importance of empathic reparenting. According to behavioral models, on the other hand, change involves reinforcement or relearning. The approach presented here includes these various aspects of change. In a similar vein, the classical analytic model contends that transference is a distorted neurotic repetition, whereas the modern analytic view emphasizes the genuine holding environment that the therapist provides. The view here highlights the empathic entry into the patterns of the patient, and the gradual reshaping of those patterns. A cognitive science view of the therapy of personality also leads to a rationale for the use of eclectic techniques; schema changes can be brought about by cognitive, affective, behavioral, or interpersonal methods.

## Conclusion

In considering the intersection between personality theory and cognitive science, we have focused on one cognitive science construct, that of the schema. This concept has been used not only by a variety of cognitive scientists, but also by clinicians of divergent schools. Despite the predictable diversity engendered by these various uses of the concept, there is surprising unanimity about certain theoretical ideas and empirical findings. The concept supplements aspects of the biological, analytic, and behaviorist approaches to personality, and suggests new ways of conceptualizing personality, of assessing personality, and of treating personality disorders. Further work on the intersection between cognitive science and personality theory appears warranted.

## Acknowledgment

Parts of this chapter were adapted from the paper by D. J. Stein, (1992). "Schemas in the cognitive and clinical sciences: an integrative construct," *Journal of Psychotherapy Integration*, **2**, 45–63.

# 15

# Cognitive Studies
# of Alzheimer's Disease

**Marcus Richards and Yaakov Stern**

*Department of Neurology*
*and*
*Gertrude H. Sergievsky Center*
*College of Physicians and Surgeons*
*Columbia University*
*New York, New York*

Primary degenerative dementias are among the most frequent neurological disorders that occur in old age. In a population-based survey, Alzheimer's disease (AD) alone accounted for one-half to two-thirds of all incident cases of dementia over a period of 15 years (Kokmen, Chandra, & Schoenberg, 1988). AD remains an incurable disease, is currently the fourth leading cause of death among the elderly in the United States, and is increasing in prevalence in most countries. The adequate management of AD, based on a detailed understanding of the neurological, neuropathological, cognitive, and behavioral changes that constitute the disease process, is thus a large and serious concern for the international public health community. In this chapter, the impact of cognitive science in advancing our understanding of some of these changes in AD will be discussed and directions for continuing investigation will be highlighted.

## Diagnosis of Alzheimer's Disease

AD is a progressive dementing disorder, usually with an insidious onset, ranging in severity from mild forgetfulness and disorganization to total intellectual and functional incapacity requiring continual supervision. The presence of AD is confirmed by histopathological evidence obtained from biopsy or autopsy. However, in the absence of such evidence, a presumptive diagnosis of Alzheimer's disease (probable AD or pAD) is based on a number of formal clinical criteria. Initially, the presence of dementia must be established, based on standardized criteria, such as those set forth in the revised *Diagnostic and Statistical Manual of Mental Disorders DSM-III(R)*.

Additional criteria for pAD have been recommended by the NINCDS-ADRDA workgroup (McKhann, Drachman, Folstein, Katzman, Price, & Stadlan, 1984) and have been adopted widely. These additional criteria require a disease onset between ages 40 and 90 and evidence of progressive worsening of memory and other cognitive functions. In addition, the diagnosis of pAD is supported by evidence of a family history of similar disorders and evidence of progressive cerebral atrophy on computerized tomography studies, along with a normal lumbar puncture and a normal pattern or nonspecific changes in electroencephalogram (EEG). Impairments should be observed in the absence of clouded consciousness and systemic disorders or other brain diseases that could account for them. Although changes in activities of daily living are identified by careful history-taking, cognitive changes usually are documented by neuropsychological examination.

Neuropsychological tests have many advantages: they are typically flexible and capable of use within a wide range of ability, from normal individuals who are highly functioning to patients with severe dementia. Moreover, most neuropsychological tests are standardized and normalized and have been assessed for reliability. However, diagnostic neuropsychological assessment typically is intended to document cognitive changes at a level sufficient for diagnosis and does not explore mechanisms of deficit. For example, in order to demonstrate memory impairment in AD, it is usually sufficient to demonstrate defective short-term verbal and visual memory or a rapid decline in the retention of these memory traces over time. However, as Brown and Marsden (1988) point out, there are many potential causes of such memory impairment, including lack of adequate registration of information through an attention deficit, difficulties in organizing and encoding the material to be learned, problems in the learning process itself, rapid decay of the memory store once learned, increased vulnerability to interference from competing information, and difficulties with retrieval strategies. Similarly, language impairment is widely observed in AD and is usually sufficient for evaluative neuropsychological assessment to document deficits in simple language function, such as confrontational naming and word fluency. However, there is evidence that language in AD is impaired in additional ways, for example, in semantic versus syntactic content, in semantic priming during verbal learning, and in the development of narrative. To untangle these complex problems, controlled experimental strategies must be employed. How has cognitive science advanced our understanding of AD? For convenience, studies will be reviewed in the categories of memory, language, reasoning, attention, and visuospatial function.

## Cognitive Studies

### Memory

#### Memory Complaints

Evidence of acquired memory impairment is required for the diagnosis of dementia. AD patients almost universally present with symptoms of memory loss in daily life; these symptoms are among the most striking aspects of the disease. During the early stages of impairment, AD patients typically complain of difficulty in recalling new information, such as recent events and conversations, and in learning new material or procedures, along with an apparent preservation of old stores of information. There is also increased difficulty in remembering short lists, such as those required for shopping or for planning the day's agenda. During the more advanced stages of the disease, these impairments become so severe that even simple routines are disrupted and new memory impairments are observed, for example, inability to recognize faces. Consistent with this clinical presentation, neuropsychological examination tends to reveal deficits in both short- and long-term memory in AD patients (cf. Brown & Marsden, 1988). Can deficits that underlie these changes be elucidated by cognitive investigations?

Memory can be classified according to its temporal aspects (e.g., immediate, short-term, long-term, remote), the kind of information processed (e.g., verbal, visual), or the nature of the processing (e.g., priming, encoding, recall, recognition). There is evidence that most, if not all, of these aspects of memory are impaired in AD (Morris & Kopelman, 1986; Brown & Marsden, 1988). An obvious issue, therefore, is whether AD patients have a global memory deficit, that is, whether multiple memory processes are disrupted by multiple causes, or whether the disease affects a single process or a limited number of processes common to all these aspects of memory, for example, registration or retrieval. To address this issue, a detailed review of memory function in AD is necessary.

## Short-Term or Primary Memory

Short-term or primary memory refers to the retention of material over brief intervals, typically 1 minute or less. Perhaps the most simple measure of primary memory, one that is used widely in the clinical setting, is that of memory span, in which item strings of increasing length are presented until recall of the whole string in correct sequence fails. Numerous studies have documented impaired memory span in AD, using a variety of stimuli, such as digits (Kaszniak, Garron, & Fox, 1979; Kopelman, 1985), letters (Morris, 1984), words (Miller, 1973; Corkin, 1982; Morris, 1984), and blocks (Cantone, Orsini, Grossi, & De Michelle, 1978; Corkin, 1982). There is also evidence that degree of impairment increases with disease severity (Corkin, 1982; Berg et al., 1984). In contrast, AD patients show only a modest impairment in the recency effect, that is, the recall of the last few items in a series during free recall (Miller, 1971; Wilson, Bacon, Fox, & Kaszniak, 1983). What factors are responsible for this selective impairment?

An heuristic framework for interpreting these findings is provided by the working memory model proposed by Baddeley and Hitch (1974) and elaborated by Baddeley (1986). According to this model, working memory consists of a controlling Central Executive System (CES) with limited processing capacity and a number of slave systems that the CES coordinates and allocates resources to. These systems include the articulatory loop system, which allows storage of verbal information in primary memory and permits the recycling of this information while it is being processed, and a visuospatial scratchpad, which permits storage and manipulation of visuospatial imagery. The articulatory loop is thought to be intact in AD (Morris, 1984). The CES is a planning and coordinating system that allows an interface between incoming environmental information and information in long-term memory. Baddeley (1986) has equated this system with the Supervisory Attentional System of Norman and Shallice (1980). Evidence suggests that CES functioning is impaired in AD (Baddeley, Logie, Bressi, Della Sala, & Spinnler, 1986). Baddeley and colleagues (1986) suggest that performance on span tasks depends at least in part on CES function, because these tasks require the holding of item sequences in short-term memory. This is not the case, on the other hand, with the recency effect, since the latter is based on passive storage in the absence of concurrent load.

One important role of the CES is to schedule two or more concurrent tasks, a facility that enables, for example, the storing of information while processing a heavy cognitive load. This phenomenon has been investigated using the Brown–Peterson task (Peterson & Peterson, 1959). During this task, subjects are presented with three verbal items, such as CVC (consonant–vowel–consonant) trigrams, are given a distracting subsidiary task, such as serial subtraction, and then are required to recall the three items in correct order. Under these circumstances, all individuals, whether normal or cognitively impaired, show rapid forgetting of the items, with total forgetting in less than 1 minute. However, AD patients show significantly more forgetting than normals (Corkin, 1982; Morris, 1986; Sullivan, Corkin, & Growdon, 1986) and the magnitude of this deficit is related to disease severity (Corkin, 1982). As Crowder (1982) notes, this phenomenon is an analog of everyday experience: "momentary distraction and the subsequent loss of very recent information." However, reasons for this rapid forgetting have been a matter for extensive investigation.

The most simple explanation—that the memory trace decays as a function of time taken up by the distractor task—has been discredited; a more widely held view is that material presented during the distractor task displaces or interferes with the to-be-remembered material and prevents its rehearsal. It has been suggested that maintenance rehearsal, involving the recycling of untransformed material in a short-term loop, rather than elaborative rehearsal, where to-be-retained material is encoded by more complex means such as chunking, imaging, or the formation of associations, is required for retention during the Brown–Peterson task (Vallar & Baddeley, 1982). Importantly, maintenance rehearsal is thought to place significant demands on central processing resources (Vallar & Baddeley, 1982). In addition, several studies have shown substantial forgetting with distractor tasks that exert minimal interference on the to-be-remembered items (such as tone-shadowing during the learning of verbal items), but place heavy demands on central processing resources (e.g., Watkins, Watkins, Craik, & Mazuryk, 1973). It is argued that such a distractor task prevents rehearsal by diverting limited central processing resources. Further, Morris (1986) has shown that very simple distractor tasks (such as tapping or articulating the word "the"), which cause little or no forgetting in normal controls, are sufficient to disrupt short-term retention of verbal material in AD patients. This suggests that central processing resources themselves are attenuated in AD. The significance of this result will be considered again in subsequent sections.

### Long-Term or Secondary Memory

Not only is the registration of material in short-term memory inadequate in AD, but long-term storage of information also is impaired (cf. Morris & Kopelman, 1986; Brown & Marsden, 1988). Indeed, much weight is attached to poor performance on neuropsychological memory tests during diagnostic evaluation of AD. These tests include Logical Memory (recall of thematic material), Visual Reproductions (drawing geometric figures from memory), and Associate Learning (associating pairs of words) subtests of the Wechsler Memory Scale (Weschsler, 1945), the Selective Reminding Test (a test of verbal list learning; Buschke & Fuld, 1974), or the Benton Visual Retention Test (requiring the ability to reproduce or recognize geometric figures; Benton, 1955). Not only is performance usually impaired during immediate testing, but a rapid decay of memory traces over time (15–30 minutes) typically is observed with Ad patients. Inadequate registration of to-be-learned material in short-term memory clearly will result in insufficient representation of this material in long-term store. An important question, however, is whether the short-term rehearsal deficit provides a sufficient explanation of these difficulties, or whether there are independent deficits in additional processes, such as encoding, storage, decay, or retrieval, that must be considered. Most of the following discussion concerns episodic memory, that is, memory for consciously experienced facts and events. Implicit memory and semantic memory (the representation of abstract knowledge and meaning) will be dealt with more fully in the next section.

An operational distinction has been drawn between the processes of acquisition, retention, and retrieval in the recall or recognition of episodic memories. Although the validity of these distinctions has been questioned (Tulving, 1979; Schacter and Tulving, 1982), they remain useful nodal points for identifying the source(s) of memory deficits in AD. A valuable experimental strategy is to hold one or more of these processes constant while manipulating the target process. At the acquisition level, the process of encoding has been investigated most frequently.

Encoding refers to the manner in which material is organized in memory. Particular encoding strategies, such as organizing words according to membership of a semantic category, can enable recall of larger quantities of information than can be held in short-term span. However, evidence suggests that AD patients are poor at such strategies. For example, when AD patients are presented with words that are either unrelated to each other or drawn from two semantic categories, they do not appear to benefit from this organization during a free-recall task, and do not impose an efficient organization of their own onto the words; normal controls tend to cluster words across trials whereas AD patients show no such strategy (Weingartner, Kaye, Smallberg, Ebert, Gillin, & Sitram, 1981).

Some investigations in this area have been influenced by the "levels of processing" approach to memory hypothesized by Craik and Tulving (1975). These authors hypothesized that memory traces strengthen as they become more "deeply" processed; the deepest level of processing operates at the level of stimulus meaning. Corkin (1982) manipulated the level of processing by directing the attention of AD patients to either sensory aspects of a spoken word ("was the word said in a man's or woman's voice?"), phonemic aspects ("does it rhyme with?"), or semantic aspects ("is it a type of?"). The patients then were given a word recognition task. As expected from the model, normal individuals recognized words that had been followed by semantic questions more frequently than those that had been followed by phonemic or sensory questions. However, AD patients had equally poor memory for all words. Similarly, Rosenbaum, Soule, and Drexler (1988) gave patients and controls a paired-associate recall task in which the associates either rhymed or were semantically related. Whereas controls recalled more target words from the latter condition than the former, AD patients performed equally poorly in both cases.

In contrast, however, Martin, Brouwers, Cox, and Fedio (1985) found no difference between AD patients and normal controls when encoding was self-generated. These authors presented subjects with lists of objects with either no instructions about how to encode or instructions to generate a rhyme for each object (phonemic), identify where it could be located (semantic), or act out how it could be used (semantic-praxic). Although patients recalled fewer words overall, both groups recalled more words from the semantic categories than from the phonemic category. However, in a separate experiment, these authors also demonstrated that patients made recognition errors by choosing distractors that were related to the targets semantically, suggesting that semantic processing was not sufficiently deep to allow adequate discrimination between target and distractor.

One distinctive feature of the experiment by Martin and colleagues (1985) is that subjects were required to use self-generated stimuli. However, other studies have cast doubt on the ability of AD patients to benefit from such active processing. Mitchell, Hunt, and Schmitt (1986) used sentences in which the object either was given or was omitted and had to be self-generated. Subjects were later required to recall the object when given the subject of each sentence. Whereas normal controls recalled more self-generated objects, AD patients showed no difference in the recall of given and self-generated objects. In addition, Dick, Kean, and Sands (1989a,b) found that, unlike normal controls, AD patients did not benefit from either acting out or self-generating words to be remembered.

The consensus of these studies is that AD patients show an encoding deficit in secondary memory and are unable to organize material in a manner that can be recalled efficiently. What about the fate of material retained over time? Intuitively, it seems reasonable to expect that rapid forgetting by AD patients would be easy to demonstrate. However, experimental investigations of forgetting curves have yielded controversial results. A number of authors have used the recognition memory paradigm developed by Huppert and Piercy (1979). Here, pictoral stimuli are presented and subsequently tested for recognition over three delay intervals, 10 min, 24 hr, and 1 wk. The use of a recognition paradigm is thought to eliminate the role of retrieval. In addition, exposure time during acquisition is adjusted to match subjects for recognition performance at the 10-min delay interval. Under these circumstances, Corkin, Growdon, Nissen, Huff, Freed, and Sagar (1984), Freed (1984), and Kopelman (1985) found similar rates of forgetting in AD patients and normal controls when tested at the 24-hr and 1 wk intervals. Becker, Boller, Saxton, and McGonigle-Gibson (1987) administered the Story Retell and Rey Figure memory tests to AD patients and controls and found that, although performance on immediate recall was significantly poorer on both tests for AD patients, both groups showed parallel rates of forgetting over a 30-min delay interval. Only one study departs from this consensus. Hart, Kwentus, Taylor, and Harkins (1987) exposed mild AD patients and matched controls to line drawings of common objects and varied exposure time until all subjects reached criterion performance during a 90-sec delay recognition test. They were retested subsequently over intervals of 10 min, 2 hr, and 48 hr. Although all subjects showed forgetting between the 2-hr and 48-hr intervals, only the AD patients showed forgetting by the 10-min interval. Thus, although AD patients may show similar overall rates of forgetting over extended intervals, the latter study suggests that retention loss may occur more rapidly in AD patients over very short delays and that controls "catch up" over a longer period, thus accounting for the negative conclusions of the other authors. Interestingly, Hart and co-workers (1987) used a yes/no recognition procedure, so that total forgetting would have been represented by chance responding at the 50% level. However, although forgetting in AD patients reached asymptote more rapidly than normals, this asymptote always remained above the chance level. These authors suggest that mild AD patients retain some portion of the stimuli at the expense of forgetting the remaining information at a very rapid rate.

These studies demonstrated that the organization of secondary memory is impaired at the acquisition level and that there is also evidence of a retention deficit superimposed on this problem. A further component of memory is retrieval of material from storage. A widely used technique for investigating the retrieval process is that of recognition memory, in which the subject is required to identify a previously presented target from an array of distractors. Several studies have demonstrated that recognition memory is impaired in AD (cf. Brown & Marsden, 1988), with the degree of impairment increasing with disease severity (Vitaliano, Breen, Albert, Russo, & Prinz, 1984; Flicker, Ferris, Crook, & Bartus, 1987a). An obvious question, however, is whether the retrieval deficit stands alone or whether it results primarily from poor acquisition and retention.

One method that has been used to help tease apart these problems is that of cued recall. Miller (1975) showed that patients with presenile dementia were able to recall words if the first letter of the word was given. However, Morris, Wheatley, and Britton (1983) found that cued recall yielded superior performance to forced-choice recognition. In both studies, cueing yielded recall performance that was similar to that of controls; the authors interpret these findings as demonstrating an independent retrieval deficit. However, Davis and Mumford (1984) compared the effects of free recall, recall with a letter cue, and recall with a semantic cue. They showed that, although AD patients performed more poorly than controls under all conditions, letter cueing yielded similar degrees of improvement in both groups. However, semantic cues were only found to be beneficial to controls. Davis and Mumford suggest that the lack of effectiveness of semantic cueing in patients indicates that the information was not processed adequately according to its semantic properties and that, as a consequence, these results suggest an encoding deficit rather than a retrieval deficit in AD. These authors fail to explain, however, why letter cueing was effective at all in patients, so the role of retrieval failure remains a likely one in AD. The question of retrieval will be considered further in the section on remote memory.

### Remote Memory

The memory tasks discussed thus far involve the presentation of new material. What is the fate of memory for information from the patient's premorbid past? As noted earlier, the clinical profile of early AD tends to emphasize deficits in the learning and retention of new material, with the relative preservation of memory for remote events and autobiographical information. Is this apparent preservation corroborated by experimental investigation? In fact, a number of studies have shown that remote memory is impaired in AD with respect to controls (Wilson, Kaszniak, & Fox, 1981; Corkin et al., 1984; Beatty, Salmon, Butters, Heindel, & Granholm, 1988; Sagar, Cohen, Sullivan, Corkin, & Growdon, 1988; Dall'Ora, Della Sala, & Spinnler, 1989; Kopelman, 1989). These studies employed tests of memory for public events and faces, personal facts, and autobiographical incidents. However, with the exception of the study by Corkin and associates (1984), all demonstrated a significant temporal gradient (or a nonsignificant trend toward one), in which distant memories were preserved relative to recent ones. Why should remote memory be preserved selectively in this manner? One clue comes from the study by Sagar and coworkers (1988). These authors found that the gradient was abolished when recognition tasks were introduced, as a result of improvement in recent memories. They suggest that different memory processes are involved along the temporal gradient and that the facilitating effect of cueing on the more recent portion of the gradient indicates a retrieval deficit that affects recent memories more than remote memories. Concurrent with this distinction, Cermak (1984) has suggested that new memories are mainly episodic in nature and only become transferred to more abstract (semantic) storage systems much later in time. According to Beatty and colleagues (1988), this semantic system is more resistant to neurological insult than is memory for consciously experienced facts and events, at least during the early stages of AD. It is clear, however, that semantic memory itself is impaired in AD (see subsequent text). This may explain why remote memory in AD patients, although more preserved than recent memory, is still defective relative to that of normals.

Further clues are provided by Dall'Ora and associates (1989), who analyzed the qualitative characteristics of autobiographical memories in AD patients and noted an inability to sustain searching activity to "find their way about" their own biographies. These authors suggest that failure of remote autobiographic memory in AD results from defective organization of search rather than defective storage of old memories. Corroborative evidence for this suggestion comes from Kopelman (1989) and Finley, Sharp, and Agramont (1990), who noted significant improvements in the expression of remote memory from a recall baseline when responses were facilitated by recognition procedures.

### Summary and Conclusions

The previous sections indicate widespread memory deficits in AD, no matter how memory is partitioned for experimental investigation. Concerning memory for new information, there is clear-cut evidence that AD patients are impaired in immediate registration, in the maintenance of information in working memory, and in the encoding and organization of material for long-term storage. There is a suggestion that forgetting is more rapid and retrieval is more impaired in patients. However, until further evidence for the independence of storage and retrieval deficits from acquisition and encoding deficits is obtained, the most parsimonious explanation for recall and recognition failure in primary and secondary memory in AD is that of impaired acquisition and encoding.

In contrast, several studies indicate a relative preservation of memories acquired during the premorbid stage, although it is clear that remote memory in AD is impaired relative to normals. Available evidence suggests that this problem arises from failure of efficient access to remote memories rather than from decay of the material itself during storage.

### Language, Reasoning, and Semantic Memory

#### Nature of Semantic Memory

At first, the aggregation of language and abstract reasoning may seem too sweeping a maneuver to make. However, many of the difficulties that AD patients have in both areas can be discussed within a common framework of semantic memory, so this section naturally follows.

According to Cohen (1977), semantic memory concerns the structure, organization, and storage of knowledge and the representation of meaning. It contains an internal dictionary in which lexical terms are stored and defined, but is much more than this. The elements of semantic memory are concepts, some of which are nonverbal. Concepts represent propositions, link them in particular relationships, and combine them to form common areas of knowledge. A distinction has been drawn by Tulving (1983) between semantic and episodic memory. As noted earlier, episodic memory refers to memory for consciously experienced events, such as the contents of a recent conversation, the location of a misplaced item, or the kinds of food eaten for breakfast on a particular day. Semantic memory, on the other hand, concerns permanent abstract knowledge, such as knowledge that a ball is round, that an orange and a banana are both fruit, and that $100 - 7 = 93$. As Cohen (1977) notes, semantic memory is a "working system, in which new facts are constantly being incorporated, stored knowledge is being updated and reclassified, and particular items of information are being sought, located, assembled and retrieved." This definition should immediately alert us to potential sources of difficulty in AD, since the sections on memory have shown that AD patients are impaired especially in learning and organizing new information. However, the definition also introduces a new cognitive function, that of combining and recombining objects and attributes of objects in new ways, for example, in learning not only that an orange and a banana are members of the class of objects known as "fruit," but that fruit are members of class "means of reproduction." It also should be noted that the observations presented earlier provide a perspective for interpreting Verbal IQ, as determined by the Information, Vocabulary, Arithmetic, Comprehension, and Similarities sub scales of the revised Wechsler Adult Intelligence Scale (WAIS-R; Wechsler, 1981). A decline in Verbal IQ is found routinely during diagnostic evaluation of AD.

The several theoretical models of semantic memory include dictionary models (Katz & Fodor, 1963), network models (Collins & Quillian, 1969; Collins & Loftus, 1975), set-theoretic models (Meyer, 1970; Schaeffer & Wallace, 1970), and the marker-search model (Glass & Holyoak, 1975). However, with the exception of the network approach, these models rarely have provided either the starting point or a post-hoc interpretive framework for research into semantic memory in AD. Instead, a more empirical approach has been favored, guided by clinical findings of impairment in word-finding, comprehension, and conceptual ability. These problems shall be considered in turn.

### Word Finding

AD patients typically present with impaired word-finding abilities and associated circumlocution. These difficulties include impaired verbal fluency, poor verbal expression (e.g., increased paraphasic errors), and anomia (Rosen, 1983a). As the disease progresses, echolalia and palilalia also may be observed (Ajuriaguerra & Tissot, 1975). Although clinical assessment of these features is undertaken routinely during evaluation for dementia (Rosen, 1983a), a series of controlled studies has been carried out to elucidate the nature of word-finding difficulties in AD. Many of these are reviewed by Nebes (1989).

Everyday speech in AD has been studied by Bayles (1982), Hier, Hagenlocker, and Shindler (1985), Nicholas, Obler, Albert, and Helm-Estabrooks (1985), and Kempler, Curtiss, and Jackson (1987). These studies have shown that grammatical structure and complexity are more or less preserved in AD, but that content and information are reduced, with increased dependency on empty words (e.g. "thing" or "stuff") and phrases. Semantic accuracy is also impaired, with increased frequency of semantically related but incorrect words (e.g., calling a stool a chair) and increased circumlocution. Three basic components of language function—vocabulary, fluency, and naming—are assessed routinely by neuropsychological examination. Although there are some dissenting studies, there is a consensus that vocabulary is relatively resistant to deterioration in AD (Brown & Marsden, 1988). However, this is not true for verbal fluency. This cognitive domain usually is assessed by asking the patient to generate as many words as possible, within a time constraint, beginning with a particular letter, as in the Controlled Oral Word Association Test (Benton & Hamsher, 1978), or within a particular semantic category, for example, animals (Boston Diagnostic Aphasia Examination; Goodglass & Kaplan, 1983). Numerous studies have found AD patients to be impaired on these tests, although there is some controversy over whether the impairment is greater for letter category task or for semantic category (cf. Brown & Marsden, 1988; Nebes, 1989).

A detailed examination of verbal fluency in AD has been undertaken by Ober, Dronkers, Koss, Delis, and Friedland (1986). These authors found impaired fluency even in mild AD patients. Patients not only generated fewer words overall, but their rate of production tended to tail off more rapidly than that of normal controls and they produced more errors and perseverations However, Ober and colleagues found no difference between patients and controls in mean category dominance (i.e., the typicality of a word within each respective category) or the extent to which dominance decreased over time. These results are interpreted to suggest that low-frequency words are no less accessible in patients than in normals.

Naming ability usually is assessed clinically by requiring patients to name line drawings or pictures of decreasing familiarity, as in the Boston Naming Test (Kaplan, Goodglass, & Weintraub, 1983). Numerous studies have demonstrated some degree of anomia in AD, with impairment increasing as a function of disease severity (cf. Brown & Marsden, 1988). However, the cause of this anomia has been controversial. One putative deficit that can underlie difficulty in naming is the inability of AD patients to perceive the stimulus correctly. However, although there are some studies that support the perceptual basis of anomia in AD, a more widely held view is that the impairment is semantic in origin. For example, Bayles and Tomoeda (1983) and Martin and Fedio (1983) have shown that the errors that AD patients make in naming tasks tend to be semantic (e.g., calling a sofa a chair) rather than perceptual (calling an object by the name of something visually similar but semantically unrelated). In addition, Huff, Corkin, and Growdon (1986) demonstrated that naming performance in AD correlates with the number of words generated in the same categories as the naming stimuli, but not with a perceptual discrimination task. One inference from these studies is that AD patients suffer a loss of or shrinkage in the network of semantic attributes that underlies the conceptual basis of that which is denoted by a naming stimulus. However, an alternative account is that patients are unable to access the lexical handle of the stimulus. For example, Huff, Mack, Mahlmann, and Greenberg (1988) gave AD patients a sentence completion task (e.g., "A tool used to pound nails is called a _____."). These authors found that patients consistently failed to name one item or another across repeated testing. However, when patients were given a forced-choice recognition version of this task (e.g. "Is a tool used to pound nails called a hammer?"), performance improved, suggesting a lexical retrieval deficit. In accord with this suggestion, Harrold (1988) showed that AD patients were able to pantomime objects successfully (i.e., could access information about their semantic attributes) that they were unable to name. As Nebes (1989) points out, however, there is no reason to assume that these different accounts of anomia are mutually incompatible.

**Conceptual Structure**

Concepts and concept meaning appear to lose their richness in AD. However, several studies show that superordinate conceptual structure is preserved, whereas the network of specific semantic attributes that distinguish one concept from another is vulnerable. For example, Martin and Fedio (1983) found that AD patients could sort objects into categories and answer questions related to these categories. However, they had difficulty with particular features or functions of the objects. They were able to state, for example, that a saw is a tool, but had difficulty identifying the material it is made from or specifying its use. It may be, however, that these features, rather than being lost, are difficult to access by AD patients. Flicker, Ferris, Crook, and Bartus (1987b) showed that patients were able to choose items that had a common use from a multiple-choice array, although they could not describe the use of a particular object when presented.

The vulnerability of links between concepts in AD is demonstrated in a different way by Gerwith, Shinder, and Hier (1984). These authors required patients to generate associations to given words and recorded the frequency of syntagmatic associations (i.e., words from a different class that could follow sequentially from the target word in a sentence, such as shoes–wear) and paradigmatic associations (i.e., words from the same class that are related in meaning to the target word, such as shoes–feet). Gerwith and associates found that frequency of the former was preserved across levels of disease severity and suggested that this indicates preserved syntactic structure, whereas frequency of the latter declined with disease severity, suggesting a diminished semantic network.

Whatever the cause of this impairment, it is tempting to consider the network model of semantic memory proposed by Collins and Quillian (1969), in which information is organized in a hierarchical structure from superordinate class (e.g., animal), through subordinate classes (e.g., bird), to more specific exemplars (e.g., canary). It is tempting, also, to suppose that processing at these lower levels is differentially impaired in AD. This approach ignores, however, the importance of flexibility at higher levels where, for example, exemplars or intermediary categories are recombined into new higher-order ones. This skill is measured by the Similarities subtest of the WAIS-R. Here, subjects are asked to state how two objects or entities are alike and are awarded greater credit for higher levels of superordinate abstraction to link the entities. For example, more credit would be gained by stating that a coat and a suit are both garments than for merely stating that they are both made of cloth. Use of intermediate or lower levels of abstraction commonly is observed in AD patients during this test.

Another perspective from which to view this problem is that AD patients may have difficulty in identifying the defining features or "essence" of an entity or concept, that is, features that fundamentally distinguish one entity from another. Concurrent with this suggestion, Grober, Buschke, Kawas, and Fuld (1985) presented AD patients with a target word and three attributes (e.g., the word "table" and the attributes "furniture," "wood," and "department store") and asked them to rank the importance of these attributes to the target word. Patients were likely to rank nonessential attributes as highly as essential attributes. Along with the failure to link concepts by a superordinate structure during the Similarities subtest of the WAIS-R, this impairment is referred to clinically as concrete thinking and is a highly characteristic feature of cognitive functioning in AD.

### Semantic Context

Results of these studies imply that conceptual structures and the network of connections linking different concepts (Collins & Quillian, 1969) are impaired or attenuated in AD. One further way to investigate the nature of this impairment is to examine how the context in which information is presented can activate associations with and connections to that information. The most widely used technique to investigate this question is that of priming. In normals, prior exposure to a stimulus decreases the time to process a related stimulus. It is assumed that the prime activates connections to the target stimulus. If the network of connections is reduced in AD, then the effects of priming should not be as striking as they are in normals (Nebes, 1989). Not surprisingly, this issue has proved to be a complex one to resolve. Nebes, Martin, and Horn (1984) showed that prior exposure to a word decreased the time required by both AD patients and controls to name a semantically related word, and that naming latency in both groups was facilitated equally by the prime. However, the effect of priming appears to depend critically on the nature of the paradigm used. For example, AD patients appear to benefit from repetition priming (in which subjects process a word during a lexical-decision task faster if that word is repeated in the series) to the same extent as controls. On the other hand, when word-retrieval is required, AD patients show little benefit from priming. For example, Salmon, Shimamura, Butters, and Smith (1988) presented subjects with a series of words, followed subsequently by word-stems (the first few letters of a word). Whereas normal controls were likely to complete the stem correctly if the relevant word had been presented previously, AD patients did not show this benefit. Of interest is the fact that stem-completion has been likened to cued recall (Nelson, Canas, Bajo, & Keelean, 1987). This raises the possibility that the lexical search process, rather than the semantic network itself, is impaired in AD. The extent to which lexical search is impaired, however, may depend on context ambiguity. Nebes, Boller, and Holland (1986) showed that AD patients were slightly slower than normals in generating a word to complete a sentence if only few words would fit the sentence (e.g., "Cats see well at ____."). However, patients were markedly slower on this task if the sentence was more ambiguous (e.g., "In the distance, they heard a ____."), thus increasing the demand for self-guided search.

### Summary and Conclusions

There is little question that performance in verbal tasks that depend on semantic memory, such as word-generation and naming, are impaired in AD. This impairment may provide the basis for many of the language deficits with which AD patients present clinically. There is also evidence that the richness of conceptual structure and the complexity of links between concepts is impoverished in AD. However, whether these findings represent actual loss of semantic information or whether they reflect processing deficits, for example, impairment in organization, search, and retrieval, remains controversial. There is some suggestion that the core of semantic information is at least grossly intact in AD, but that patients have trouble with tasks that require self-generated search strategies. There are also indications that the dynamic nature of semantic memory—a property that enables stored knowledge to be updated, information to be assembled, and concepts to be combined and recombined—is attenuated in AD. Finally, the extent to which impairment in semantic memory is responsible for difficulties with episodic memory, and vice versa (Nebes, 1989), should be considered. An important question is whether a common deficit, such as one of encoding or retrieval, causes impaired performance in these two cognitive territories or whether separate independent deficits must be highlighted.

## Attention

It is important to assess attention in AD patients, partly because impaired attention can be an important (though not defining) clinical feature of the disease, but also because impaired attention can have a large and serious impact on performance on other cognitive tests, particularly memory tests (e.g., Ober, Koss, Friedland, & Delis, 1985).

Several pencil-and-paper neuropsycholgical tests contain an attentional component, including the Digit-Span and Digit-Symbol subtests of the WAIS-R, and the Cancellation Test, in which subjects are required to check off targets embedded in an array of distractors on a page as quickly and as accurately as possible (Sano, Rosen, & Mayeux, 1984). Performance on these tests tends to be poorer in AD patients than in age-matched controls. However, such findings reveal little about the extent and nature of impaired attention in AD.

### Controlled and Automatic Processing

One attempt to provide a coherent framework for interpreting attentional impairments in AD has been made by Jorm (1986), based on the distinction between controlled and automatic processing drawn by Schneider and Shiffrin (1977) and Shiffrin and Schneider (1977). Jorm proposed that controlled processing, which demands great attentional capacity, is affected differentially in early AD, whereas automatic processing, which requires less attentional capacity, is not affected until the disease is advanced. Accordingly, patients with early AD show particular difficulties with tasks containing a learning component (e.g., paired-associate learning, serial word-lists, and supraspan digit strings), those in which unfamiliar material is presented (e.g., naming rare objects or learning the definition of unfamiliar words), or those in which active retrieval from long-term memory is required. On the other hand, tasks that depend more on automatic processing, such as vocabulary, reading familiar words, and naming familiar objects, are relatively preserved in mild AD. However comprehensive this framework may be, it is couched at the descriptive level only and is vulnerable to circular reasoning. In order to understand fully the nature of attentional impairments in AD, it is necessary to move to a hypothetico-deductive approach.

### Global and Selective Attention

An important distinction is drawn by Posner and Bois (1971), and elaborated by Posner (1986), between nonspecific attentional processes and selective attention. Global attention refers to the process by which an event is prepared for following a warning, and typically is assessed in the laboratory using reaction-time (RT) tasks in which subjects are required to respond to a target as quickly as possible (Sano, 1988). Selective attention refers to the ability to allocate processing capacity among multiple inputs and to select which of these will be processed further (Nebes & Brady, 1989). Choice RT, in which RT and error rate are used as dependent measures, is employed widely to study selective attention, although other paradigms have been and will be described also. To examine differential impairment in these processes in AD, Sano (1988) gave patients a choice RT task in which patients were required to identify matches and mismatches between pairs of shapes. Global attention was investigated by preceding the pairs with a warning stimulus; selective attention was manipulated by arranging for one shape to briefly precede the other, so it cued the correct response. Performance in patients was similar to that in controls when either task was administered alone. However, when the two tasks were combined, by allowing the initial letter to act as both a warning and an encoding cue for the second letter, patients made more errors than controls did. Although combining the tasks in this way increased overall task difficulty, the increased error rate is suggestive of impaired selective attention.

A distinction within selective attention has been drawn by Nebes and Brady (1989) between divided and focused attention. The former refers to the simultaneous processing of multiple sources of independent information and the latter refers to the tuning out of irrelevant information to concentrate on one chosen source of information. To investigate whether one or both of these processes is impaired in AD, Nebes and Brady (1989) gave patients and matched controls a RT task in which subjects were required to search for a target letter among an array of letters that varied in number from two to six. The relationship between set size and search time thus provided a measure of divided attention. Focused attention was assessed by a similar task, except that the set size was held constant and, for half the trials, four of the letters were red and two were black ("cued" condition) whereas, for the remaining half, all letters were black ("noncued"). Subjects were informed that the target, when present, would always be black. A measure of focused attention therefore was provided by the magnitude of the decrease in RT from noncued to cued conditions. AD patients and normals were equally able to use the color cue to selectively search the target, that is, patients did not show differentially impaired focused attention. However, the search time for patients increased at a steeper rate than did that of normals as the letter set size increased, suggesting that divided attention is impaired in AD.

**Active and Passive Control**

A further distinction has been drawn by Norman and Bobrow (1975a,b) between selective attention governed by passive input, that is, by "external" events (data driven), and selective attention governed by active control, that is, driven by information stored in memory ("internal" cues). A good deal of evidence suggests that, whereas data driven selective processes are intact in normal old age, there are significant age decrements in memory driven processes. These impairments are thought to arise from poor central control over the optimal use of internally represented information for guiding attentional selectivity from moment to moment (Rabbitt, 1979). To investigate these processes in AD, Cossa, Della Sala, and Spinnler (1989) gave AD patients and age- and education-matched controls a letter-search task in which letters appeared one at a time in a circular array. Subjects were required to respond as quickly and accurately as possible whenever the letter T appeared. This letter appeared in a random position, in a selected position for 70% of the trials (memory driven condition), or in pairs of trials in which the target appeared in the same place in both trials of the pair and RT to each second trial was measured (data driven condition). Since degree of accuracy remained constant during all tasks for both groups, changes in RT provided the primary measure of interest. On this basis, Cossa and colleagues found that, although both data and memory driven conditions yielded improved RT in controls (with a superior improvement in the data driven condition), AD patients showed no significant benefit from either condition, suggesting overall impoverishment in selective attentional resources in AD, rather than a specific worsening of active control processes.

**Dichotic Listening**

A different paradigm to investigate selective attention is that of dichotic listening (Broadbent, 1954,1956). In this technique, subjects are presented with simultaneous, but conflicting, material to the left and right ears through headphones, and are required to attend selectively to one side, the other, or both sides simultaneously. One version of this test used with AD patients is the Staggered Spondaic Word test (SSW; Katz, 1962). Here, the first syllable of a spondaic word (a two-syllable word in which each syllable is stressed, e.g., upstairs) is presented monotically, then the first syllable of a second spondaic word (e.g., downtown) is presented to the other ear so it overlaps with the second syllable of the first word, that is, these two syllables are presented dichotically. Finally, the second syllable of the second word is presented monotically to the same ear as the first syllable of the second word. The task is to name all the words heard correctly. Using this technique, Grimes, Grady, Foster, Sunderland, and Patronas (1985) found that AD patients were able to repeat significantly fewer words than matched controls. In order to eliminate the possibility that this result was merely an artifact of an inability to perceive degraded auditory stimuli, Grady, Grimes, Patronas, Sunderland, Foster and Rapoport (1989) repeated the experiment, but also presented monotic word lists, either time compressed by 60% (TCS) or delivered through a low pass filter (filtered speech or FS). Whereas AD patients were impaired significantly on all conditions with respect to age-matched controls, the number of words they were able to repeat correctly was lower during the SSW test than during either the TCS or FS condition, suggesting that SSW performance reflects impaired ability to divide attention in AD patients. These results corroborate those of Nebes and Brady (1989) by highlighting the role of divided attention. It should be noted, however that an analogous test of focused attention, in which subjects would be required to "shadow" (i.e., selectively attend to) stimuli presented to one ear while distracting material is presented to the other ear, has not been attempted with AD patients. Finally, Mohr, Cox, Williams, Chase, and Fedio (1990) presented pairs of words dichotically and required subjects to recall the words under three conditions: free recall, left-ear first (i.e., "recall all the words you heard with the left ear, then all the words with the right ear"), and right-ear first. Whereas controls were able to preferentially allocate attention to the ear specified by the experimenter, AD patients were less able to shift in this way. It should be noted that inability to shift attention has been regarded as evidence of impaired executive function, arising from frontal involvement. Corroborative evidence for impaired executive function in AD has been obtained by LaFleche and Albert (1991).

### Summary and Conclusions

Consistent with both clinical observation and neuropsychological evidence, experimental cognitive investigations reveal impaired attentional processes in AD. However, the impairment may be confined to selective attention; the more global arousal mechanisms that enable an impending event to be prepared for appear to be relatively intact. Moreover, investigations employing target searching and dichotic listening techniques indicate that divided attention, enabling subjects to monitor multiple sources of information, is particularly vulnerable in AD. It is fair to state, however, that the ability to focus attention during distracting stimulation has not been investigated adequately in AD patients.

One construct that may provide a link between the selective attention deficit in AD and other cognitive processes, such as memory, is the Supervisory Attentional System of Norman and Shallice (1980), which has been linked to the Central Executive System (CES) of Baddeley and Hatch's (1974) model of working memory. As was described earlier, one function of these systems is to act as an interface between external stimuli and internally represented information and to direct attention consciously where it is needed. Since there is evidence to suggest that CES functioning is impaired in AD, it may be that a common breakdown underlies disruptions in both selective attention to the environment and processes of short-term memory. This issue clearly warrants further investigation.

## Visuospatial Function

Longitudinal neuropsychological studies have indicated that most aspects of visuospatial function remain relatively preserved until the more advanced stages of AD (Grady et al., 1988; Rebok, Brandt, Folstein, 1990). The extent to which deficits in visuospatial ability underlie clinical features such as spatial disorientation and impaired recognition memory has provided one focus for investigation in this area of AD. Unfortunately, few studies have employed detailed experimental techniques to identify causes of visuospatial difficulties; researchers have tended to rely on standard clinical instruments that document impairment at the descriptive level (Brown & Marsden, 1988). It is useful, however, to consider a range of visuospatial function and to identify the most basic level of impairment in this area in AD.

### Matching to Sample and Line Orientation

At the simple neuropsychological level, Eslinger, Damasio, Benton, and Van Allen (1985) and Ska, Poissant, and Joanette (1990) have shown that AD patients are impaired on the Benton Line Orientation Test (Benton, Hamsher, Varney, & Spreen, 1983), in which subjects are required to identify two lines from an array that have the same orientation as two target lines. Ska and co-workers found not only a greater overall impairment in patients than in controls, but also that patients made unusual errors, such as failure to identify true vertical or true horizontal. Huff and associates (1986) gave AD patients and age- and education-matched normal controls the Form Discrimination Test (LaBerge & Lawrence, 1957), in which subjects are presented with pairs of irregular 12-sided polygons of graded similarity and asked to determine whether the polygons in each pair are the same or not. These authors found that patients made significantly more errors on this test than did the controls. Using a different matching task, Brouwers, Cox, Martin, Chase, and Fedio (1984) found that AD patients were significantly more impaired than controls on the Mosaic Comparisons Test. During this test, subjects are presented with two complex random designs, partitioned by three rows and columns, and are required to identify a single block in which a difference between the pairs occurred. It should be noted, however, that a time limit was imposed on this task. Not all studies employing a matching to sample procedure have found impaired performance in AD, however. In particular, Sahakian, and co-workers (1988) found no difference between patients and controls when complex abstract patterns were used as stimuli.

### Drawing and Construction

The neuropsychological tests described so far require the ability to discriminate or match to sample. Mention should be made, however, of visuospatial tests that require drawing and construction, since AD patients also show visuomotor impairment that cannot be attributed to loss of fine motor control. Rosen (1983b) required normal controls, patients with mild AD, and patients with moderate to severe AD to copy the Visual Reproductions figures from the Wechsler Memory Scale (Wechsler, 1945) and found a significant decline in performance as a function of severity of dementia. Sunderland and colleagues (1989) required AD patients to draw the face of a clock reading the time of 2:45, a widely used bedside assessment measure. Drawings of patients were rated as significantly poorer than controls and these ratings showed significant negative correlations with AD severity. AD patients also have been shown to be both slower and less accurate than controls in copying the Rey–Osterrieth Complex Figure (Brouwers et al., 1984).

These studies indicate that AD patients are impaired on a wide range of clinical and neuropsychological tests of visuospatial and visuomotor function and that, by and large, degree of impairment shows a positive relationship with disease severity. An alternative idea is that AD patients with marked visuospatial deficits form a clinically distinct subgroup. de Leon, Potegal, and Gurland (1984) gave a range of parietal tests to AD patients residing in a nursing home. The battery included tests of matchstick construction, right–left orientation, graphesthesia, and clock-reading, along with measures of tactile sensory function. A subgroup of patients, who were classed as wanderers (i.e., patients who got lost within the facility, who required help or instruction to get from one location to another, or who were not responsive to street and traffic signs) was found to have significantly lower mean parietal scores than the other patients, in the absence of any overall difference in mental status between these two groups. Whether these wanderers form a distinct subgroup or whether wandering represents a milestone in the progression of the disease, this study highlights the functional and clinical significance of psychometrically determined visuospatial and visuomotor dysfunction.

### Right–Left Orientation and Mental Rotation

A further direction in the investigation of visuospatial ability in AD concerns the use of complex visuospatial tasks, in particular, those that challenge right–left orientation and mental rotation ability. Age decrements in these abilities have been demonstrated (cf. Flicker, Ferris, Crook, Reisberg, & Bartus, 1988). Surprisingly, however, there appears to be no further significant deterioration in AD, at least during the mild stages of the disease. Two studies have employed Money's Standardized Road Map Test of Direction Sense (Money, Alexander, & Walker, 1965). During this test, subjects are presented with a simulated street map of a town, on which a route with 32 turns is drawn. Subjects are then asked to imagine following the route (or watch the experimenter trace the route) and to indicate at each corner whether a left or right turn is required. Of the turns, 15 involve movement away from the subject, 15 are made while returning in the direction of the subject (and thus require mental rotation), and 2 turns are "hairpin" turns, moving in both directions. Dependent measures for this test consist of time to completion and number of correct responses (in both directions). Using this test, Brouwers and colleagues (1984) found no significant difference between the performance of AD patients and that of controls. Flicker and associates (1988) found a general decrement in performance across young controls, elderly controls, mild AD patients, and advanced AD patients. These authors found that mental rotation, but not right–left orientation, was affected by age. However, whereas mild AD patients made more errors than controls in either direction, suggesting a right–left orientation deficit in AD, the magnitude of the rotation effect was the same in elderly controls and in mild AD patients. A floor effect obscured the investigation of rotation in the advanced AD group. Flicker and co-workers conclude that mental rotation is not differentially impaired in AD. In a separate task, these authors found that, whereas the same mild patients made more errors than elderly controls in naming objects from the Boston Naming Test, patients were at no extra disadvantage to controls when these objects were rotated 180°.

### Summary and Conclusions

Results of visuospatial experiments in AD are unusual because deficits have been demonstrated at a simple level, for example, with tasks that require judgment of line orientation, matching to sample, and copying of geometric designs, whereas performance in the more complex task of mental rotation appears to be no worse than that of normal elderly individuals. It is fair to argue, however, that the issue has not yet been investigated fully. Although it is tempting to suggest that these visuospatial deficits play an important role in the etiology of spatial disorientation in AD, the experiments with mental rotation place limits on the utility of this suggestion. It is likely that investigations of visuospatial memory will be more revealing in this area. On the other hand, an association between impairment in visuospatial tasks used to assess parietal function and wandering in AD patients has been demonstrated. Further investigations of this kind will provide an important contribution to research in this area.

## Concluding Remarks

A large and diverse series of experiments, carried out largely over the past decade, has yielded major contributions to our understanding of the cognitive changes that occur during Alzheimer's disease. When considering the results of these experiments, several central themes emerge. For example, experiments with episodic and semantic memory suggest that mechanisms responsible for short-term registration, organization, and manipulation of material are highly vulnerable during even the early stages of the disease. By the same token, experiments investigating selective attention suggest that ability to allocate attentional resources to multiple inputs is compromised in AD also. These studies suggest that the concept of working memory and other dynamic information-processing systems are fruitful directions to pursue in AD research. A crucial role for cognitive science, therefore, is to develop and test hypotheses that can elucidate these processes further and relate them to other findings in the investigation of AD, for example, studies of neurochemical changes and of neuroimaging abnormalities, as well as to clinical and behavioral observations of AD patients.

Indeed, the gap between the detailed constructs and hypotheses of the experimental cognitive approach and the behavior of the AD patient at the level of the clinical syndrome is still discernible. For example, the process of temporal disorientation still is understood poorly. In addition, links between experimental cognitive tests and functional capacity, the impairment of which constitutes part of the clinical definition of dementia, often are inferred rather than investigated. An important challenge for cognitive science, therefore, is to strengthen these ties and to harness the momentum gathered to facilitate the progress of multidisciplinary models of AD. By furnishing both theory and data concerning mental changes at the level of the conceptual nervous system (Hebb), cognitive science offers a unique contribution to the study of AD but, like Janus, simultaneously faces the real nervous system and the clinical behavior to which it gives rise.

## Acknowledgments

Preparation of this chapter was supported by Federal Grants AG07370 and AG08702, the Parkinson's Disease Foundation, and the Charles S. Robertson Memorial Gift for Alzheimer's Disease.

# 16

# Information Processing, Experience, and Reading Disability

**Louise C. Spear**

*Department of Special Education*
*Southern Connecticut State University*
*New Haven, Connecticut*

**Robert J. Sternberg**

*Department of Psychology*
*Yale University*
*New Haven, Connecticut*

Most children learn to read with relative ease. Nevertheless, even a cursory examination of elementary school classrooms will reveal some youngsters with severe reading difficulties. Serious reading problems can be found among children with normal, even well above average, intelligence. This population, frequently labeled "learning disabled," "reading disabled," or "dyslexic," has intrigued practitioners and researchers for decades, and is the subject of this chapter.

Unfortunately, in the past, approaches to reading disability (RD) often have not been well motivated theoretically or based on solid empirical evidence. However, the relatively new multidisciplinary field of cognitive science seems to offer a better understanding of RD, as well as more effective long-term solutions to the problems faced by disabled readers. In this chapter, we will explore what our own research, as well as that of other cognitive scientists, suggests regarding a number of issues surrounding RD. Specifically, what kinds of cognitive deficits characterize RD? To what extent do disabled readers have intrinsic deficits, and to what extent are their problems the result of extrinsic factors, such as ineffective schooling? What kinds of educational interventions are needed for disabled readers?

We will focus on disabled readers, rather than on learning disabilities (LD) in general, for two reasons. First, disabled readers form the most frequently identified and most thoroughly researched group of learning disabled children. In addition, a consideration of other disabilities, such as those in mathematics, would seem to be beyond the scope of a single chapter. However, some of the issues we will raise here, such as the issue of extrinsic factors in RD, may be applicable to disabilities in other academic areas as well.

We will begin by discussing definitions of reading disability, and addressing some definitional issues. This background is essential for understanding the rest of the chapter. Next, we will discuss some traditional views of RD. This discussion will be followed by a more extensive discussion of research findings in reading disability, and models of RD from cognitive psychology, a branch of cognitive science. At this point, we also will present our own model (Spear & Sternberg, 1987) of RD. Next, we will address theories of causation, especially the extent to which RD involves causes intrinsic or extrinsic to the individual. Finally, we will conclude with some practical implications for assessment and remediation.

## Definitions and Defining Issues

Definitions of learning disabilities, including RD, tend to be framed in educational terms. The current federal law, P.L. 94–142, defines a learning disability as

> a disorder in one or more of the basic psychological processes involved in understanding or in using language, spoken or written, which may manifest itself in an imperfect ability to listen, think, speak, read, write, spell, or do mathematical calculations. The term includes such conditions as perceptual handicaps, brain injury, minimal brain dysfunction, dyslexia, and developmental aphasia. The term does not include children who have learning problems which are primarily the result of visual, hearing, or motor handicaps, of mental retardation, of emotional disturbance, or of environmental, cultural, or economic disadvantage. (*Federal Register*, Dec. 29, 1977, p. 65083)

Federal law further stipulates that LD children must show a severe discrepancy between ability (typically measured with an IQ test) and achievement in at least one of seven specified areas: basic reading (i.e., word identification skills), reading comprehension, written expression, math calculation, math reasoning, listening comprehension, and oral expression.

Other definitions of learning disabilities, including the various state definitions and the current DSMIII(R) definitions (American Psychiatric Association, 1987) of specific developmental disorders, are similar in spirit if not in actual wording to the P.L. 94–142 definition. All these definitions of learning disabilities in general, and of RD in particular, tend to share the following three components: the child must have a severe discrepancy between ability and actual achievement; that discrepancy cannot be attributable primarily to some other handicapping condition, such as sensory impairment or economic disadvantage; and the disability is assumed to be intrinsic to the individual, for example, caused by central nervous system dysfunction rather than by an extrinsic factor such as poor instruction or lack of stimulation in the home. A fourth component of many state definitions and of the federal definition, but not of the DSM-III(R) definition, is that the disability is associated with a psychological processing disorder.

These definitions of RD intertwine with numerous problems faced by practitioners and researchers in the field. One problem involves the fact that regression effects, the tendency for very high and very low scores to regress toward the mean on remeasurement, rarely are considered when children are identified as reading disabled. A second problem involves the lack of consistency across school systems and states in determining what constitutes a "severe" discrepancy; a child who is identified as RD in one school system might not be identified as RD in a neighboring town. Third, there is little consensus in the field about how to measure a psychological processing disorder, and many of the processing measures that have been used in the past have dubious validity or reliability (Hammill, 1972; Vellutino, 1979).

Studying school-labeled LD children has been said to reveal more about sociology and politics than about learning disabilities (Senf, 1986). Certainly, numerous social factors are important in determining who is labeled LD or RD and who is not. Many authorities (e.g., Smith, 1991) have suggested that the relative palatability of the LD label, compared with other labels such as "mentally retarded" or "emotionally disturbed," has resulted in the tendency to overidentify children as LD. Smith (1991) also notes that LD placements have been affected by changes in guidelines for identifying mentally retarded (MR) individuals that were enacted in the mid-1970s. Children with IQs in the 70s, who formerly might have been classified as retarded, no longer met MR guidelines. These children were sometimes funnelled into LD classes, whether or not they met LD guidelines, because they had difficulty succeeding in a regular classroom setting without extra help. Many other socially relevant factors, including a child's behavior, gender, and socioeconomic status, may influence whether or not that child is identified as LD. Thus, it is crucial for researchers to verify independently the existence of a discrepancy between ability and achievement, rather than merely using school-labeled LD or RD children.

## Traditional Views of Reading Disability

At least three broad views of RD may be identified. One view, historically the oldest, emphasizes the role of brain injury or dysfunction in RD and is represented by writers such as Orton (1937). These authorities searched for evidence of neurological problems during assessment (evidence that is not necessarily convincing from a contemporary viewpoint), but focused on direct remediation of academic skills when initial assessment was complete. A second view, which was especially popular in the 1960s and early 1970s, contended that RD was caused by perceptual problems, particularly visual perceptual problems. These authorities (e.g., Frostig, 1967) generally advocated the use of perceptual testing and training, practices that were found later to be ineffective (see Vellutino, 1979, for an extensive review). The third and most current view attributes RD to a variety of verbal deficits and is represented by Vellutino (1979), the Haskins Laboratories group of investigators (e.g., Brady, Shankweiler, & Mann, 1983; A. Liberman, 1989; I. Y. Liberman, 1989), and our group, among others. Predictably, those who hold the verbal-deficit view emphasize language skills in assessment and remediation of RD.

At least two important points should be made about the three different views of RD. First, there is some overlap among the views. For example, although writers such as Orton (1937) emphasized the causality of brain disorders in RD, they also thought that disabled readers demonstrated perceptual problems as symptoms of brain disorders. Other authorities (e.g., Boder, 1973) have suggested the possibility of different subtypes of RD, in which at least one subtype involves a perceptual deficit and another subtype involves a verbal deficit. Also, although each view has been most prevalent at different periods in time, currently each view still has advocates. For instance, in spite of overwhelmingly negative research evidence, many laypersons, as well as some practitioners, continue to adhere to the perceptual deficit view of RD.

## Models of Reading Disability from Cognitive Psychology

Most cognitive psychology models of RD implicate verbal processes and, thus, can be seen as part of the verbal-deficit view. In this section, we will begin by reviewing the most well-documented verbal deficits of disabled readers, including several different models of RD. Most of these models propose specific lower-level deficits as the source of RD. Next, we will discuss some alternative, but less well-documented, models of RD that propose broader cognitive deficits among disabled readers. Finally, we will review our own (Spear & Sternberg, 1987) framework for understanding RD.

## Well-Documented Verbal Deficits of Disabled Readers

### Word Recognition, Automatization of Word Recognition, and Reading Comprehension

Poor reading is strongly associated with word recognition problems involving accuracy, speed, or both (Barron, 1978; Perfetti, Finger, & Hogaboam, 1978; McCormick & Samuels, 1979). In fact, Perfetti (1986) comments that the task that he has consistently found the most discriminating for reading skill at all grade levels "is the vocalization or naming task, in which the subject reads a single word or nonword presented on a screen and names the word as quickly as possible" (p. 17). The differences between normal and poor readers are especially large for long words, for pseudowords or "nonwords," and for low-frequency words.

Some investigators (Ehri, 1991; Gough & Juel, 1991) distinguish different stages in the acquisition of word recognition skills. They propose that the earliest stage is characterized by paired-associate learning involving the selection of visual cues, such as the overall shape of the word, whereas a later stage is characterized by knowledge of letter-sound correspondences or decoding. Children must acquire this decoding knowledge to become proficient readers. Gough and Juel (1991) further suggest that early acquisition of decoding is critical.

> What seems essential is to insure that children learn to decode in first grade. If decoding skill does not arrive then, it may be very hard to change the direction that reading achievement takes: Poor decoding skill leads to little reading and little opportunity to increase one's basic vocabulary and knowledge, leaving a shaky foundation for later reading comprehension. (p. 55)

Not surprisingly, experience, particularly in the form of school instruction, appears to play an important role in the acquisition of decoding skills. For instance, Vellutino and Scanlon (1991) found that different instructional procedures fostered different reading strategies among second and sixth grade readers. Subjects tended to read in a more global (focusing on whole words) or a more analytic (using decoding knowledge) manner, depending on the type of instruction they had received. Byrne (1991) presents evidence that young children find it difficult to infer decoding knowledge from whole-word instructional approaches; rather, they need to be taught this knowledge directly.

Other writers (Smith, 1973; Goodman, 1976) have claimed that proficient reading is driven by comprehension processes, not by relatively low-level processes such as word recognition. According to this view, proficient readers generate hypotheses about the text as they read, focusing on the recognition of individual words only when the hypothesis fails to be confirmed. The centrality of fast, accurate word recognition to proficient reading certainly would appear to undermine hypothesis-testing models of reading. In addition, evidence that poor readers actually make more use of context to facilitate word recognition than do good readers (Perfetti, 1982; Stanovick, 1986a) also tends to disconfirm these models, since use of context is a comprehension-based process. Because proficient reading is characterized by accurate and rapid word recognition, good readers have no need to rely on context to recognize words; their word recognition processes operate more rapidly than do the comprehension-based processes involved in using context. Poor readers, on the other hand, may sometimes rely on comprehension-based processes to supplement their slow or inaccurate word recognition skills. However, this use of context by poor readers may come at a cost: it leaves fewer mental resources free for higher-level comprehension.

A number of authors (LaBerge & Samuels, 1974; Perfetti & Lesgold, 1977; Sternberg & Wagner, 1982) have emphasized the importance of automatization of word recognition to proficient reading. According to the automatization failure hypothesis, poor readers might continue to demonstrate reading comprehension problems even after they have mastered basic recognition skills because their recognition continues to require conscious effort, thus consuming mental resources that would be free for comprehension in the normal reader.

### Phonological Awareness

Phonological awareness, or awareness of the sound structure of spoken language, typically has been measured by the use of tasks such as counting phonemes in a spoken word (e.g., "fish" has three phonemes); phoneme blending (blending separate sounds to form a word); and phoneme deletion, or deletion of a sound from a spoken word (e.g., the child is asked to "say 'snow' without the /s/"). All these tasks appear to be measuring a single underlying skill, rather than multiple unrelated skills (Lundberg, Olofsson, & Wall, 1980; Wagner & Torgesen, 1987). Phonological awareness has been well established as a predictor of early reading ability, independent of IQ (Lundberg et al., 1980; Mann & Liberman, 1984; Vellutino & Scanlon, 1987). In addition, there is some evidence that phonological awareness can be trained and that training has a beneficial effect on reading skill (Bradley & Bryant, 1983; Vellutino & Scanlon, 1987).

The typical theoretical explanation for these findings is that, in an alphabetic orthography such as English, the beginning reader must be able to map visual symbols, the letters, onto the sounds in the spoken language. If the child lacks awareness of the sounds in the speech stream, this mapping process will be difficult. Moreover, since phonemes in spoken language are processed automatically, below the level of consciousness, there is ordinarily little reason for children to have become aware of phonology simply by hearing spoken language (A. Liberman, 1989; I. Y. Liberman, 1989). However, it is possible that some specific types of spoken language activities may enhance phonological awareness. For instance, MacLean, Bryant, and Bradley (1987) found that preschoolers' knowledge of nursery rhymes was predictive of phonological awareness and of later reading skill.

Is phonological awareness a natural cognitive achievement, that is, an ability that simply develops with maturation, or is it dependent on receiving instruction in reading? Phonological awareness does appear to be influenced by instruction in reading, particularly by instruction in an alphabetic orthography (Read, Ahang, Nie, & Ding, 1984; Byrne & Ledez, 1986). Phonological awareness is almost certainly a skill involving reciprocal causation (Stanovich, 1986a), that is, a certain degree of phonological awareness appears to facilitate or even enable beginning reading, but reading acquisition itself contributes to phonological awareness. This increased level of phonological awareness in turn appears to result in further growth in reading, so that phonological awareness and early reading skill may be viewed as developing in tandem (Perfetti, Beck, Bell, & Hughes, 1987).

### Memory for Verbal Information and Phonological Coding in Short-Term Memory

There is ample evidence that poor readers differ from normal readers on short-term memory tasks involving verbal material, and that this difference is associated with difficulty in using a phonological code. For instance, poor readers typically have not differed from normal readers in their ability to recall items that do not lend themselves to verbal or phonological coding, for example, pictures of unfamiliar faces or nonsense doodles; however, on memory for items that can be coded phonologically, for example, words, letters, numbers, and pictures, consistent differences between normal and poor readers have emerged (Katz, Shankweiler, & Liberman, 1981; Vellutino & Scanlon, 1987). Further, the differences between normal and poor readers in phonological coding are independent of IQ (Wagner & Torgesen, 1987). Phonological coding usually is inferred experimentally by comparing recall for lists of phonologically confusable (e.g., b, c, g, t, z) and nonconfusable (e.g., f, h, j, q, r) letters or words. Poorer performance on the confusable than on the nonconfusable lists is assumed to be evidence that subjects are making use of phonological coding.

Phonological coding in short-term memory is thought to be important for permitting both listeners and readers to hold and integrate larger units of discourse, such as clauses and sentences (Perfetti & Lesgold, 1977). A phonological code appears to be a particularly efficient means of retaining ordered linguistic information. Perhaps the most persuasive evidence of the importance of phonological coding to reading involves the finding (Hanson, 1989) that, even among profoundly deaf individuals, skill at phonological coding predicts reading skill. This finding also demonstrates that both phonological awareness and phonological coding involve abstract linguistic units rather than "sounds," as we would ordinarily think of them. Hanson's subjects developed phonological coding skill even in the complete absence of the ability to hear spoken language; she hypothesizes that this skill may have been acquired through lipreading, speech training, or experience with English orthography in reading.

Although there is some controversy about whether phonological coding is always necessary in reading, especially among proficient readers (e.g., Crowder, 1982), many researchers would agree that phonological coding is important during acquisition of reading skill. Wagner and Torgesen (1987) have suggested that efficiency of phonological coding might be related strongly to the success of initial attempts at using word recognition skills, since recognizing words would require the ability to use phonological codes to store letter sounds when blending sounds to form words. These authors further suggest that performance on phonological awareness tasks may be a function of phonological coding skill.

Poor phonological coding ability sometimes has been hypothesized to cause poor reading ability. However, in general, the nature of the relationship between phonological coding and reading ability has been studied less intensively than has the relationship between phonological awareness and reading ability. Although Mann and Liberman (1984) found efficiency of phonological coding in kindergartners to be predictive of reading ability at the end of first grade, it seems likely that the relationship between these two skills is at least bidirectional, that is, involves reciprocal causation. Developmental studies of normal readers have found dramatic increases in the use of phonological coding in the early elementary school years (Conrad, 1971; Rapala & Brady, 1990), just when most children are learning to read. A few writers (Morrison, 1991; Tunmer, 1991) have suggested that learning to read develops phonological coding ability, not the other way around.

Finally, some investigators suggest that phonological coding problems may play a role in poor readers' difficulties with spoken, as well as written, language. These difficulties will be discussed more fully in the next section.

**Spoken Language Difficulties**

Both in clinical observations and in controlled research, poor readers have been found to demonstrate difficulties with spoken language comprehension (Vellutino, 1979; Smith, Macaruso, Shankweiler, & Crain, 1989) and production (Brady et al., 1983; Brady, Poggie, & Rapala, 1989). It should be emphasized that these spoken language problems are generally subtle ones, particularly in comparison with the reading deficit. In the research investigating this topic, syntactically complex sentences are required for the differences between poor and normal readers in spoken language comprehension to emerge; multisyllabic words or pseudowords typically are required for the differences in speech repetition skills to emerge.

Shankweiler and Crain (1986) argue for a "unitary hypothesis" to explain the wide-ranging problems of poor readers. According to the perspective of these researchers, and their colleagues at Haskins Laboratories, difficulties at the phonological level are the common thread underlying poor readers' problems with word recognition, reading comprehension, and speech comprehension and production. These investigators also argue that reading is more taxing of short-term memory resources than is speech, at least in beginning or poor readers. These readers have inaccurate or slow word recognition abilities, which constitute a drain on memory resources that is not present in spoken language. This discrepancy would explain the finding that the spoken language deficits of poor readers are typically much more subtle than are their reading problems.

Whereas the Haskins Laboratories group views disabled readers as having a problem primarily in phonological processing, other investigators (Vellutino, 1979; Vellutino & Scanlon, 1991) suggest that there may be different subgroups of disabled readers displaying a variety of verbal deficits. These deficits might be phonological, semantic, or syntactic in nature. Of course, any of these deficits could be expected to affect spoken language ability as well as reading ability.

## Alternative Models of Reading Disability

The models of RD that we have just discussed have all implicated specific verbal deficits as the source of RD. However, a number of researchers have proposed that RD involves broader cognitive deficits. Here we will review briefly some of these alternative models.

Wolford and Fowler (1983) suggest that disabled readers have difficulty making use of partial information. These authors obtained the typical finding of less efficient use of phonological coding in poor readers than in good readers, but also found that poor readers made more visual confusions on a visual whole-report task. Thus, the problems of poor readers appear to go beyond phonological coding.

Tunmer (1991) suggests that phonological awareness may be more related to nonverbal problem-solving ability than to overall verbal ability. He proposes that phonological awareness is linked to the Piagetian process of decentration, since phonological awareness requires the child to shift attention (i.e., decenter) from the content, or meaning, of language to the form of language. In Tunmer's view, both phonological awareness deficits and poor reading may be associated with a lag in nonverbal cognitive development.

Disabled readers typically have deficient knowledge about the orthographic structure of words, that is, deficient knowledge about sound–symbol relationships and phonic rules (Morrison & Manis, 1982; Gough & Juel, 1991). Morrison and Manis (1982) and Morrison (1991) contend that this deficient orthographic knowledge may be symptomatic of a broader difficulty in learning complex or irregular rule systems. These authors view mathematics as involving a more regular system of rules, which would explain the fact that disabled readers are sometimes high achievers in math.

A number of investigators have studied the strategic problems of poor readers. For example, some writers (Torgesen & Goldman, 1977; Bauer, 1982) have attributed the short-term memory problems of disabled readers to the failure to use memory strategies such as verbal rehearsal. Other writers (e.g., Wong, 1982) have studied the difficulties of disabled readers in using various reading strategies. Ceci (1983) found that disabled readers were deficient in the use of purposive semantic processing, which requires conscious planning and intent.

If the models of RD described in this section are correct, it would be difficult to defend the firm distinction made by most practitioners, as well as most researchers, between RD and mental retardation. Instead, disabled readers might be viewed as "slow learners" at the low end of normal cognitive functioning. However, in general, the research evidence supporting these models is scantier, and the evidence that exists is less convincing than the evidence in favor of the verbal-deficit models discussed in the previous section. Some of these studies are flawed methodologically or employ subjects that may not be typical of disabled readers. For instance, Ceci (1983) calls his subjects "language/learning disabled" and appears to use youngsters with relatively broad impairments in both spoken language and reading.

Another issue in interpreting these findings, and one which we view as critical, concerns experiential differences between disabled and normal readers, particularly experiential differences created by poor reading itself. For example, reading strategies may be acquired during the process of learning to read, through practice, particularly at more advanced reading levels. If disabled readers never attain an advanced reading level, they may never generate certain reading strategies. However, in this case, deficient reading strategies would be related more to the experience of being a poor reader than to a cognitive difficulty in generating or using strategies. Indeed, when Taylor and Williams (1983) matched disabled and normal readers on reading level, the disabled group was not deficient in awareness of text organization, which is one aspect of strategy acquisition.

A similar argument might be advanced for many of the other higher-level cognitive areas discussed in this section. In fact, one investigator (Stanovich, 1986b) suggests that long-standing reading problems actually might create higher-level cognitive impairments, since some higher-level cognitive skills, such as vocabulary, may be acquired primarily through reading. Our own (Spear & Sternberg, 1987) framework for understanding RD emphasizes the importance of experiential factors in RD, particularly in older disabled readers. In developing this framework, our thinking was guided by a number of influences, including our own research and practice, our triarchic view of intelligence (Sternberg, 1985), and the work of many other investigators, particularly LaBerge and Samuels (1974), Perfetti and his colleagues (e.g., Perfetti et al., 1978,1987), Stanovich (1986a,b), and the Haskins Laboratories group (e.g., Mann & Liberman, 1984; Shankweiler & Crain, 1986).

### Framework for Understanding Reading Disability

Central to our framework is the idea that some of the underlying deficits associated with RD change over time. Therefore, very young poor readers will show somewhat different patterns of deficits than will older poor readers. Moreover, very young poor readers (early elementary level) will tend to show lower-level cognitive deficits whereas older poor readers (middle elementary and older) will tend to show higher-level cognitive deficits. However, these higher-level deficits are not attributable to a true higher-level processing deficit, as explained here.

Four types of deficits characteristic of young (first or second grade) poor readers are word recognition deficits, deficits in verbal short-term memory and phonological coding, subtle spoken language deficits, and difficulties with phonological awareness. All these difficulties appear to share a problem at the phonological level. Thus, reading failure is certainly a language-based, and most probably a phonology-based, disorder.

The early difficulties of poor readers rapidly impinge on other areas. For instance, relatively lengthy text is encountered as early as the end of first grade; here the poor reader is already multiply handicapped: word recognition problems tax a verbal short-term memory system that is already impaired, so the poor reader often begins to experience reading comprehension as well as word recognition problems. In the middle to upper elementary grades, academic areas that are affected directly by the reading impairment also become problem areas, for example, content subjects such as social studies and science, spelling, and written expression. On the other hand, by the later grades, difficulties in areas that are affected by the acquisition of some reading ability, such as phonological awareness, many have abated. However, poor readers' word recognition deficits tend to persist throughout the elementary grades and beyond because, even when poor readers can recognize some words, they have difficulty automatizing the recognition process.

As suggested earlier, we propose three main sources for the higher-level problems of disabled readers, none of which involves a true higher-level cognitive deficit. One source involves the original constellation of lower-level deficits in areas such as word recognition and verbal short-term memory, which creates numerous secondary problems in higher-level areas such as reading comprehension. A second source involves the difficulty disabled readers have in automatizing decoding, a difficulty that handicaps them increasingly in later grades as reading demands increase.

The third source of the higher-level problems involves experiential factors. In particular, the experience of being a poor reader would deprive the RD youngster of the opportunity to learn a wide variety of reading-related skills, such as reading strategies (which normal readers appear to induce as they acquire increasing reading skill), knowledge about the orthographic structure of words (which normal readers appear to acquire as they pass beyond the earliest stage of reading ability), vocabulary, and knowledge in a wide range of content areas. These secondary deficits will, in turn, impinge on other areas, including reading, in a cascade of academic failure. Of course, the experience of being a poor reader is also likely to create a range of attitudes and emotions about reading, and perhaps about schooling in general, that, like the secondary academic and cognitive deficits, will exacerbate the child's problems.

Although we have discussed some possible sources for the higher-level deficits of disabled readers, we have said little about possible sources for the lower-level deficits, that is, deficient word recognition skills, lack of phonological awareness, deficient phonological coding, and subtle spoken language problems. We will consider this issue in the next section. First, however, we will need to review evidence regarding possible intrinsic and extrinsic causes of RD.

## Theories of Causation

Most investigators and practitioners in the field of RD assume the locus of RD to be intrinsic to the individual, the result of subtle neurological damage or dysfunction. However, considering the widespread and longstanding nature of this assumption, actual evidence in favor of an intrinsic disorder is surprisingly weak. Although early authorities such as Orton (1937) and Strauss and Lehtinen (1947) did include youngsters with obvious brain damage in their subject populations, they also worked with many youngsters for whom no evidence of brain injury could be found. In these cases, the early authorities assumed that brain damage or dysfunction was present, based on cognitive similarities between RD children and brain-injured adults. This assumption is being made still in some contemporary research. For example, Kelly, Best, and Kirk (1989) studied the performance of disabled and nondisabled readers on a variety of cognitive tasks, such as verbal fluency, facial recognition, and card sorting. Based on the disabled readers' performance on the cognitive tasks, and on similar performance by brain-injured adults in previous research, Kelly and associates advance a "prefrontal cortical hypothesis" to explain RD.

Perhaps the most direct contemporary evidence of brain impairment in RD individuals involves the autopsy studies of Galaburda and his colleagues (Galaburda, Sherman, Rosen, Aboitiz, & Geschwind, 1985; Galaburda, 1986). These researchers have found cellular abnormalities in dissected brains of RD children and adults. However, a number of questions can be raised about this research and the extent to which it can be generalized to RD youngsters as a whole, or even to a subgroup of RD youngsters. First, and not surprisingly, the number of subjects autopsied has been extremely small. As Coles (1987) points out, this kind of research is difficult to replicate, since many researchers lack the facilities, not to mention the brain donations, required for autopsy studies of RD brains. Coles also raises questions about the nature of the subjects autopsied and the basis for classifying them as RD.

Cognitive psychologists have focused on psychological description rather than causation. Many cognitive psychologists do not even address the issue of causation, although there are some exceptions to this statement. For instance, the Haskins Laboratories researchers suggest that the unitary phonological deficit that they propose in RD readers may be due to "a more general deficiency in the biological specialization that processes phonological structure in speech" (I. Y. Liberman, 1989, p. 209) or that RD youngsters may constitute the low end of a continuum of normal phonological processing (Rapala & Brady, 1990). Vellutino and Scanlon (1991) suggest that, although cases of RD characterized by a phonological processing deficit may have an intrinsic basis, many cases of poor reading stem from instructional factors.

### Evidence Regarding Extrinsic Factors in Reading Achievement

Evidence for the importance of extrinsic factors in reading achievement, for example, schooling and home environment, is abundant, but is not typically the focus of RD research, since RD definitions theoretically exclude children whose problems are primarily the result of these factors. Researchers in RD usually assume that if a youngster has come from a middle-class background and has attended school regularly, then schooling and home environment cannot be causes of poor achievement. However, there is evidence (see Coles, 1987, for an extensive review) that a middle-class environment does not necessarily guarantee optimal preparation for learning, that is, there are specific, and in some cases rather subtle, home and school characteristics that relate significantly to reading achievement, and may vary considerably even within a middle-class environment.

For example, with respect to variables in the home, Wells (1981) found that the style and content of language that parents used with preschool children predicted later reading achievement. Specifically, children whose parents engaged them in extended conversations that encouraged the children to reflect on past experiences appeared to have an advantage in learning to read. In addition, children whose parents expose them to a wide array of knowledge about the world, particularly the kind of knowledge that is important in school achievement, will have an advantage over those who are not exposed to this knowledge, since reading comprehension depends heavily on background knowledge (Anderson, Hiebert, Scott, & Wilkinson, 1985).

Anderson and associates (1985) further suggest that reading aloud to children is especially crucial in preparing them for reading instruction. Moreover, how children are read to is also important. Parents who actively engage children in the story, who ask thought-provoking questions, and who talk about word meanings and letter names, provide the greatest benefit to their children.

There is also considerable evidence regarding the importance of certain instructional and programming variables to gains in reading achievement. Some of these variables include the amount of classroom time allocated to reading instruction (Rosenshine & Stevens, 1984), which can vary considerably from teacher to teacher; the amount of independent silent reading done in school (Allington, 1984); the pace of instruction, which also can vary considerably depending on the teacher, even among groups in the same grade and at similar ability levels (Gambrell, 1984); and the manner in which the teacher responds to oral reading errors (Hoffman, O'Neal, Kastler, Clements, Segel, & Nash, 1984). On the other hand, although studies indicate that time spent on worksheet and workbook activities is not related to gains in reading achievement (Rosenshine & Stevens, 1984), these activities consume a large portion of the reading period in many classrooms.

The dominant reading approach in most classrooms continues to be the basal approach (Anderson et al., 1985), which involves complete programs for teaching reading, including curricula, teachers' manuals, readers, and workbooks, organized by grade level. However, the basal approach has been criticized on many counts. Flesch (1955) and Chall (1967), among others, criticized the approach for its lack of emphasis on decoding skills. Basal publishers responded to these criticisms by including more phonics in the basal programs, but phonics as taught in the basals often is oriented toward analysis of words children can read already, not on using phonics to decode unfamiliar words. This approach may not be the most effective one, especially for poor readers, for whom most words are likely to be unfamiliar. In addition, three other criticisms of the basal approach (Anderson et al., 1985) are the tendency of the early books to include a large number of words that have not yet been covered in the phonics component of the program; the lack of a coherent narrative structure in many first grade basal selections; and the lack of nonfiction selections in the early books, which may make the transition to content area texts in the later grades more difficult.

A current major rival to the basal approach is the "whole language" approach to teaching reading (Goodman, 1986). This approach emphasizes, among other things, integration of reading with writing, and having children read children's literature and trade books rather than basal readers. (However, it should be noted that many basal programs are beginning to include selections of children's literature in the basal readers, so that, at least with respect to reading material, the distinction between the two approaches is becoming less sharp). There are aspects of "whole language" that might be incorporated very profitably into a total reading program, as we will discuss in the next section. However, one problem with the "whole language" approach is that decoding skills frequently are not taught at all, a practice that has been criticized justifiably as disastrous for poor readers (e.g., Liberman & Liberman, 1990).

Two important points should be made about the home and school variables just discussed. The first point is that a parent need not be a "bad" parent or a teacher a "bad" teacher to have provided unwittingly a mediocre, or at least less than optimal, learning environment for a child. For instance, one might be an excellent parent but not be particularly skilled at engaging a child during reading or at asking the right kinds of questions. A conscientious teacher might be constrained by a required curriculum and reading program, or by lack of appropriate training. The second point is that a child need not come from a generally deprived or disadvantaged background to lack important preparation for reading instruction. In other words, children who appear to meet exclusionary criteria and are characterized as RD might actually have problems that stem from extrinsic factors.

One question that might be raised at this juncture concerns the fact that all children are not affected in the same way by these characteristics.

For example, many children whose parents never read to them in the preschool years have no difficulty learning to read in school, and many children learn to read well with the basal approach. Does this suggest that the children who do have difficulty must have some kind of intrinsic disorder?

We would argue that this is not necessarily the case. Reading achievement is determined by a variety of factors, including the child's own abilities and temperament, home environment, and schooling. In one case, a less than optimal home environment might be offset by exceptional schooling or strong motivation to succeed; in another case, less than optimal schooling might be offset by high ability or an excellent home environment for learning. Coles (1987) proposes an interactivity theory to explain LD, including RD. According to interactivity theory, myriad factors, including those just mentioned, actively interact to determine whether or not a given child develops reading problems. Coles contends that RD children do not have an intrinsic biological disorder, although they may in some cases have an intrinsic difference (e.g., in learning style) that predisposes them to difficulty in school. Sternberg (1988b) has described different cognitive styles that, depending on the teacher and classroom environment, may produce varying educational outcomes.

## Causation and the Reading Disability Framework

We now return to the question raised at the end of the last section of this chapter. What is the source of the lower-level deficits of disabled readers? Recall that these deficits include word recognition, phonological awareness, phonological coding, and subtle spoken language problems, and that the deficits are particularly prominent in young disabled readers.

It is difficult to argue with the claim that at least some disabled readers have problems stemming from intrinsic causes. For instance, some RD youngsters may indeed come to school with a biologically based disorder in phonological processing, as suggested by I. Y. Liberman (1989). In addition, there is considerable evidence that prenatal exposure to a variety of harmful substances, such as alcohol, lead, and cocaine, is associated with later cognitive difficulties (Smith, 1991), including poor reading. Cognitive science frameworks of RD that are integrative in nature, such as our own, can include intrinsic or biological factors without being limited to them.

However, for several reasons, we would urge caution in assuming an intrinsic basis for most cases of RD. First, the actual evidence in favor of an intrinsic cause, particularly for the vast majority of RD children, is weak. Second, we know that a number of extrinsic factors are very important in reading achievement; most critically, we know, from the plethora of commissions and reports (e.g., Anderson et al., 1985), if not from personal experience, that many schools are not teaching reading particularly well. Third, the very notion of a biologically based disorder, not to mention terms like "brain damage" and "brain dysfunction," has negative connotations. Given the nature of the research evidence, and the potentially damaging consequences of unwarranted assumptions about intrinsic disorders, it seems that we should exercise caution when assuming an intrinsic basis for RD.

Further, even in cases involving intrinsic dysfunction, extrinsic factors would be extremely important, since they could exacerbate and compound, or alternatively, greatly ameliorate a child's problems. For example, suppose there is a subgroup of RD children who do have a biologically based disorder in phonological processing. For those youngsters, an instructional approach that failed to teach decoding skills would be utterly disastrous. On the other hand, an excellent instructional program, and a home environment highly conducive to school achievement, certainly would lessen the effects of the child's phonological processing disorder; in some cases, the child's "disorder" might never even be recognized.

How might purely extrinsic factors account for deficits in word recognition, phonological awareness, spoken language, and phonological coding? Let us consider each area in turn.

It is perhaps easiest to see how extrinsic factors, particularly poor instruction, might affect the acquisition of word recognition skills. The research that we have reviewed here suggests the importance to beginning readers of grasping the alphabetic principle, that is, mastering decoding skills. Certainly there is more than one way to approach the teaching of decoding. However, two of the most commonly used approaches to teaching reading, the basal approach and the whole-language approach, frequently have a faulty or a nonexistent decoding component.

What about disabled readers' difficulties with automatization of word recognition skills? Experience also can affect the development of automatization (Sternberg, 1988a). For instance, Sternberg (1986) suggests two factors that are particularly important to the development of automatization; practice, particularly practice without mistakes, and motivation. As early as first grade, poor readers begin to get significantly less practice reading, even in school, than do good readers (Stanovich, 1986b). No one will quarrel with the assertion that poor readers are generally less motivated to read than are good readers. Thus, automatization failure may begin.

We know that direct efforts at training phonological awareness appear to be effective (e.g., Bradley & Bryant, 1983). It is likely that some children are exposed naturally, in the home or elsewhere, to language activities that tend to promote phonological awareness, such as rhyming games, poetry, songs, and the like. Indeed, at least one study (MacLean et al., 1987), mentioned earlier, has found that 3-year-olds' knowledge of nursery rhymes predicted phonological awareness, as well as later reading achievement. In addition, some of the easier phonological awareness tasks, such as rhyming and alliteration, are traditional "reading readiness" skills typically covered in kindergarten programs. However, programs would vary in the amount of coverage given to these skills and in the types of activities used to teach the skills. Some kindergarten programs undoubtedly would be better than others in promoting phonological awareness.

With respect to the subtle spoken language problems of disabled readers, most of the studies reviewed here have used school-aged children. Thus, it is entirely possible that difficulties in comprehension of syntactically complex sentences and in speech repetition tasks are the product of, rather than causally related to, poor reading. Even assuming that the spoken language problems precede school entrance, it is certainly possible that an aspect of the home environment, such as the type of language parents use with children or the extent and type of parent–child conversations, causes these problems.

Phonological coding deficits also might be caused by extrinsic rather than intrinsic factors. First, if learning to read develops phonological coding, as we and others (e.g., Tunmer, 1991) have suggested, then phonological coding deficits might be largely a product of poor reading. On the other hand, if phonological coding deficits precede poor reading, as some researchers (e.g., Mann & Liberman, 1984) suggest, one might still envision extrinsic causes for these deficits. For example, some investigators, such as Wagner and Torgesen (1987), suggest a link between phonological awareness and phonological coding skills; perhaps early exposure to rhyming games, songs, poetry, and so on develops skill in phonological coding as well as in phonological awareness. Alternatively, early experience with verbal memory tasks in general might promote verbal short-term memory and phonological coding skill. Even if all four lower-level deficits discussed here reflect a single processing deficit, as claimed by the Haskins Laboratories group, there is no particular reason to assume that this deficit has an intrinsic cause, since extrinsic factors, such as socialization or instructional approach, can affect cognitive processing (Sternberg, 1988a; Vellutino & Scanlon, 1991).

As we have discussed, all these lower-level deficits tend to appear among younger poor readers (e.g., first and second grade), and perhaps also among older children who are still functioning at a very low reading level. Although some youngsters undoubtedly are able to overcome a poor start in reading, one should not underestimate the importance of the first few years in school, particularly of the child's experience in first grade. A number of writers (Stanovich, 1986b; Gough & Juel, 1991) have suggested that poor initial achievement in reading may set a youngster back irretrievably, because it may set in motion a host of other problems such as decreased motivation, lowered expectations, and so on. The common school practice of ability grouping worsens the outlook for first-grade low achievers. Research indicates that, whereas ability grouping may benefit youngsters designated as high-ability, it tends to place low-ability groups at a disadvantage (Anderson et al., 1985); in fact, it has been argued (Allington, 1983) that the future reading achievement of a young child may be determined more by the initial reading group placement than by the child's actual ability. In other words, even if the child is capable of learning to read, being designated as a low achiever may be a self-fulfilling prophecy.

As we discussed when presenting our framework for understanding RD, higher-level deficits in areas such as reading comprehension and the use of reading and memory strategies tend to appear in older poor readers, those at a third or fourth grade level and beyond. We proposed three main sources for these higher-level deficits: the earlier lower-level deficits, failure to automatize word recognition, and experiential factors (Spear & Sternberg, 1987). It should be evident from the preceding discussion that all three of these sources may involve exclusively extrinsic, not intrinsic, causes. We recognize that the possibility of an intrinsic dysfunction in at least some disabled readers certainly cannot be ruled out, and we also recognize that part of our presentation here is purely speculative. However, with respect to causation, our proposal is no more speculative than the unsubstantiated belief in an intrinsic brain dysfunction that has characterized much of the RD field in the past. As Coles (1987) contends, perhaps there is a message in the repeated failure to find solid evidence of brain dysfunction in disabled readers, despite dogged efforts to do so over many years. Perhaps it is time to investigate more fully other possible causes of RD, specifically extrinsic ones. Moreover, extrinsic causes are more likely than an intrinsic brain disorder to be amenable to change.

Extrinsic factors could affect reading acquisition and cause a reading disability in many ways. For instance, we already have discussed some problems with the way that most regular classrooms approach the teaching of reading, especially the teaching of decoding skills in the early grades. In particular, decoding skills may not be taught directly, children may not be taught how to apply decoding skills to unfamiliar words, or there may be a poor mapping between what is covered in the phonics component of the reading lesson and the kinds of words that children are expected to read in books. Even perfectly normal youngsters can find the alphabetic principle quite difficult to grasp, and can have difficulty inferring phonic generalizations on their own, as the research of Byrne (1991), among others, suggests. Children who enter first grade with a genuine weakness in phonological skills, a weakness that may be constitutional or experientially acquired, are likely to have particular difficulty grasping the alphabetic principle. In other words, without appropriate instruction, some children are likely to fail in their initial attempts at reading. In turn, failure to acquire beginning decoding skills might result in lessened motivation and assignment to a low reading group, triggering a variety of other factors such as lowered expectations and less practice reading. Decreased motivation and limited practice would tend to interfere with automatization of any decoding skills that were eventually acquired, and inaccurate or effortful decoding would impair comprehension, resulting in RD. Although many poor readers eventually receive remedial services, sometimes including excellent instruction in decoding, it may prove very difficult to undo the harmful effects of a poor start in reading, especially if several years pass before extra help is provided.

Extrinsic factors could cause RD in many other scenarios, including ones in which the quality of reading instruction is not a culprit. Moreover, because children begin school with a variety of experiences, abilities, temperaments, and motivational levels, a given instructional program might be adequate for some children, but inadequate for others, who might still learn to read well with an instructional approach suited to their needs. The important point is that, once a child has failed to acquire decoding skills, whatever the reason for the initial failure, the same chain of negative effects is triggered, and may result in RD.

The characteristics that distinguish our view of RD from the views of other investigators include its relatively broad scope, its emphasis on extrinsic factors in RD, its emphasis on the changing and expanding nature of the deficits seen in RD, and its inclusion of automatization failure (Sternberg & Wagner, 1982). Our view of RD is most different from one that associates RD with broad cognitive deficits, such as Wolford's or Tunmer's. Except for our emphasis on extrinsic factors, our view of RD in beginning readers is compatible with the views of the Haskins Laboratories group. On the other hand, our emphasis on extrinsic factors is similar to the view of Coles. However, unlike Coles, we have tried to articulate how the specific processing deficits seen in RD might be caused and might develop.

One might wonder, if RD is caused by extrinsic variables, what the purpose is of knowing about the processing deficits seen in RD. In emphasizing possible extrinsic causes of RD, we certainly do not mean to suggest that psychological description is unimportant. Knowledge about the specific processing deficits seen in disabled readers, for example, poor word recognition skills and lack of phonological awareness, has provided crucial insights about reading acquisition in general, and about the kinds of instructional techniques most needed for poor readers. Knowledge about these processing deficits has aided also in developing assessment tools that may be used to identify young children at risk for reading problems. However, although understanding the cognitive processes used in reading is crucial, it is also important to surpass psychological description to understand RD completely. Ultimately, prevention and remediation are linked to an understanding of causation.

## Practical Implications

In this final section of the chapter, we would like to present some of the practical implications of our view of RD. First, we will discuss implications for assessment of RD, then implications for instruction.

### Implications for Assessment

One of the most crucial implications of our framework and, indeed, of the research of many other investigators concerns the importance of early identification of reading problems. Delay in identification and remediation tends to result in a rapidly expanding constellation of academic, motivational, and sometimes emotional problems, thereby making remediation progressively more difficult and complex.

A number of measures can identify children at risk for reading failure, even at a kindergarten level and certainly by the middle of first grade. These measures include tests of verbal short-term memory, such as the Digit Span subtest of the Wechsler Intelligence Scale for Children—Revised (Wechsler, 1974), and tests of phonological awareness (e.g., Rosner, 1975). Mann, Tobin, and Wilson (1987) have shown that phonological awareness also may be measured by analyzing the invented spellings of kindergarten youngsters, an approach that may be more practical for the classroom teacher than for individual testing. In addition, measures of oral language functioning, such as tests of syntactic comprehension, may be a useful adjunct to some of the other tests suggested here.

Most important, once formal reading instruction has begun, teachers should be especially alert to those youngsters who lag behind other children in acquiring decoding skills. At very early reading levels, some children are able to compensate for lack of decoding knowledge by using context to guess at unfamiliar words or by memorizing whole words by sight. However, limited decoding knowledge is likely to result in reading problems at later grade levels, when the demands on reading comprehension escalate. At present, many published tests are available for assessing the decoding skills of young children, for example, the Word Attack subtest of the Woodcock Reading Mastery Tests (Woodcock, 1973). An oral reading inventory is an excellent way to evaluate reading skill in a number of important areas, including decoding, fluency, and comprehension.

With older children, particularly those functioning at a third or fourth grade level and beyond, measures of reading comprehension and automatization of decoding probably will be more helpful than measures of decoding accuracy or phonological awareness. In educational settings it is difficult to assess automatization skills formally, since experimental measures of automatization frequently have relied on computerized procedures not feasible for educational use. However, one might use two informal methods to assess the extent to which a child has automatized decoding. One of these involves timed speed drills on lists of words the child can decode. (See Gallistel, Fischer, & Blackburn, 1977, for one description of this technique). Another method simply involves informal observations of fluency during oral reading.

IQ tests are used frequently with disabled readers of all ages to determine whether or not there is a significant discrepancy between ability and achievement. It is important to note that some IQ tests, particularly those administered to groups, require reading. Obviously an IQ test that involves reading will underestimate a poor reader's true ability and should not be used.

A final point that we would like to make about assessment concerns the issue of labeling. If RD is the result of extrinsic causes, as we have argued it may be, at least in some cases, then the use of terms such as "disability" may be unjustified as well as potentially harmful in creating low expectations, decreased motivation, and so on. Although we have used the term "reading disability" here because it is the accepted terminology, it is probably best in practice to avoid terms that imply an intrinsic brain dysfunction. Instead, a descriptive term such as "poor reader" might be used. Avoidance of unduly negative labels is particularly preferable for very young children, for whom testing is least reliable and the long-term dangers of labeling greatest.

## Implications for Instruction

A major implication of our framework for instruction involves the need to emphasize decoding knowledge in teaching children to read, particularly in the early grades. Although some children appear to acquire this knowledge by induction, without ever being taught directly, other children have difficulty in inducing decoding knowledge (Byrne, 1991). Further, it would seem sensible, certainly, to make information so crucial to reading acquisition an explicit part of an instructional program. Some examples of programs that teach decoding directly include the Orton–Gillingham approach (Orton, 1937; Gillingham & Stillman, 1966) and the Slingerland program (Slingerland, 1976).

For young children, particularly kindergartners and first graders, phonological awareness training would be an important part of instruction in decoding. Some examples of phonological awareness activities may be found in Engelmann (1969) and Blachman (1987). Treiman (1991) suggests that intrasyllabic units, which are units intermediate in size between syllables and phonemes, may be easier units than phonemes for children to become aware of and, thus, may be a good starting point for instruction.

Decoding must become automatic for children to become proficient readers. A number of techniques may be useful in developing automatization, for example, speed drills on familiar words (Gallistel, et al., 1977) and practice reading and rereading familiar selections. Anderson and associates (1985) point out that, although musicians would never be expected to perform a piece well without a chance to practice repeatedly, elementary school children are expected to do just that during oral reading. Finally, since motivation appears to be especially important in the development of automatization, techniques that improve a poor reader's motivation to read may help improve automatization. Encouraging children to read appropriate library books, newspapers, or magazines about topics of interest to them as part of daily reading instruction is one way to enhance motivation to read.

Although we think that the direct teaching of decoding skills and the development of automatization of decoding are crucial aspects of any reading program, decoding need not and should not be taught to the exclusion of everything else. Listening comprehension and reading comprehension are two other areas that are especially important. In this respect, some aspects of the "whole language" approach (Goodman, 1986) may be quite helpful to disabled readers. Although we strongly disagree with the tendency of many "whole language" advocates to ignore the importance of decoding knowledge in reading acquisition, we also think that some aspects of "whole language," such as the emphasis on having children read good trade books and children's literature and on reading aloud to children, might be combined very profitably with a decoding approach. For instance, older disabled readers who have some decoding knowledge could read a variety of children's literature and might find this more motivating than the usual school fare. Books can be chosen based on the child's interests and reading skills, so greater individualization is possible. Differences in reading ability among children also are highlighted less obviously in this approach.

Younger disabled readers would find many children's trade books too difficult, because of their limited decoding skills, but they still might be able to read some very easy books, such as books with predictable text (e.g., Carle, 1984). These children might be given a controlled phonetic reader to develop decoding skills in context and easy trade books to develop comprehension and enhance motivation. Further, the use of listening comprehension activities, such as having children listen to and discuss a story read by the teacher, would be particularly beneficial for young disabled readers. These types of activities, if done well, build motivation for reading and also develop comprehension skills that should serve disabled readers well when they are able to decode more difficult text.

A reading program emphasizing explicit and early instruction in decoding, combined with activities that enhance motivation to read and encourage spoken language development, is likely to be most beneficial for disabled readers. Indeed, for many children, such a program might be preventive rather than remedial. However, for older disabled readers, prevention obviously is not a possibility, and remediation is likely to be a more difficult enterprise. Although the general techniques suggested here should prove helpful with older as well as younger children, with older disabled readers it will also be necessary to remediate a number of secondary deficit areas. Thus, for example, reading strategies and content knowledge in areas such as social studies and science probably will need to be taught directly. Nevertheless, even for older children, considerable improvement is possible with a good instructional program, and the eventual goal for most disabled readers should be grade-appropriate reading performance.

# Bibliography

Abelson, R. P. (1981). Psychological status of the script concept. *American Psychologist*, **36**, 715–729.

Abramczyk, R. R., Jordan, D. E., & Hegel, M. (1983). "Reverse" Stroop effect in the performance of schizophrenics. *Perceptual and Motor Skills*, **56**, 99–106.

Abramson, L. Y., Alloy, L. B., & Metalsky, G. I. (1988). The cognitive diathesis-stress theories of depression: Toward an adequate evaluation of the theories' validities. In L. B. Alloy (Ed.), *Cognitive processes in depression.* (pp. 3–30). New York: Guilford.

Achte, K. (1989). Treatment of anxiety disorders. Proceedings of the World Psychiatric Association on the Psychopathology of Panic Disorders: Many faces of panic disorder (1988, Espoo, Finland). *Psychiatria Fennica, Supplement*, 102–111.

Ader, R., Felten, D. L., & Cohen, N. (1991). *Psychoneuroimmunology* (2nd ed.). San Diego: Academic Press.

Alexander, G. A., DeLong, M. R., & Strick, P. L. (1986). Parallel organization of functionally segregated circuits linking basal ganglia and cortex. *Annual Review of Neuroscience*, **9**, 357–381.

Alford, B. A., Freeman, A., Beck, A. T., & Wright, F. D. (1990). Brief focused cognitive therapy of panic disorder. *Psychotherapy*, **27**, 230–234.

Allington, R. L. (1983). The reading instruction provided readers of differing ability. *Elementary School Journal*, **83**, 255–265.

Allington, R. L. (1984). Oral reading. In P. D. Pearson (Ed.), *Handbook of reading research.* (pp. 829–864). New York: Longman.

Alloy, L. B. (1982). Depression, nondepression, and cognitive illusions. In N. S. Jacobson (Ed.), *Cognitive theories of depression: A critical reappraisal.* Symposium presented at the meeting of the Association for the Advancement of Behavior Therapy, Los Angeles, California.

Alloy, L. B., & Abramson, L. Y. (1979). Judgment of contingency in depressed and nondepressed students: Sadder but wiser? *Journal of Experimental Psychology: General*, **108**, 441–485.

Alloy, L. B., & Abramson, L. Y. (1982). Learned helplessness, depression and the illusion of control. *Journal of Personality and Social Psychology*, **42**, 1114–1126.

Alloy, L. B., Abramson, L. Y., Metalsky, G. I., & Hartlage, S. (1988). The hopelessness theory of depression: Attributional aspects. *British Journal of Clinical Psychology*, **27**, 5–21.

Alloy, L. B., & Lipman, A. J. (in press). Attributional style as a vulnerability factor for depression: Validation by past history of mood disorders. *Cognitive Therapy and Research.*

Allport, A. (1989). Visual attention. In M. I. Posner (Ed.), *Foundations of cognitive science.* Cambridge: MIT Press.

Altesman, R. I., & Cole, J. O. (1984). Psychopharmacologic treatment of anxiety. *Journal of Clinical Psychiatry*, **44**, 12–18.

American Psychiatric Association (1952). *Diagnostic and statistical manual: Mental disorders.* Washington D.C.: American Psychiatric Association.

American Psychiatric Association (1968). *Diagnostic and statistical manual: Mental disorders* (2nd ed.). Washington D.C.: American Psychiatric Association.

American Psychiatric Association (1980). *Diagnostic and statistical manual: Mental disorders* (3rd ed.). Washington D.C.: American Psychiatric Association.

American Psychiatric Association (1987). *Diagnostic and statistical manual: Mental disorders* (3rd ed., rev.). Washington D.C.: American Psychiatric Association.

Anderson, J. R. (1976). *Language, memory, and thought.* Hillsdale, New Jersey: Erlbaum.

Anderson, J. R. (1982). Acquisition of cognitive skill. *Psychological Review*, **89**, 369–406.

Anderson, J. R. (1983). *The architecture of cognition.* Cambridge: Harvard University Press.

Anderson, J. R. (1990). *Cognitive psychology and its implications* (3rd ed.). New York: W. H. Freeman.

Anderson, R. C., & Pichert, J. W. (1978). Recall of previously unrecallable information following a shift in perspective. *Journal of Verbal Learning and Verbal Behavior*, **17**, 1–12.

Anderson, R. C., Hiebert, E. H., Scott, J. A., & Wilkinson, I. A. G. (1985). *Becoming a nation of readers: The report of the commission on reading.* Champaign, Illinois: Center for the Study of Reading.

Anderson, W. T. (1990). *Reality: It isn't what it used to be.* San Francisco: Harper & Row.

Andreason, N. C. (1982). Concepts, diagnosis, and classification. In E. S. Paykel (Ed.), *Handbook of affective disorders.* New York: Guilford Press.

Anlezark, G. M., Crow, T. J., & Greenway, A. P. (1973). Impaired learning and decreased cortical norepinephrine after bilateral locus coeruleus lesions. *Science*, **181**, 682–684.

Arbib, M. A., Conklin, E. J., & Hill, J. C. (1987). *From schema theory to language.* Oxford: Oxford University Press.

Argyle, N. (1988). The nature of cognitions in panic disorder. *Behaviour Research and Therapy*, **26**, 261–264.

Aristotle. *Complete works.* Revised Oxford translation in 2 Volumes. J. Barnes (Ed.), 1984. Princeton, New Jersey: Princeton University Press.

Arkowitz, H., & Hanna, M. T. (1989). Cognitive, behavioral, and psychodynamic therapies: Converging or diverging pathways to change? In A. Freeman, K. M. Simon, L. E. Beutler, & H. Arkowitz (Eds.), *Comprehensive handbook of cognitive therapy* (pp. 143–167). New York: Plenum.

Arnkoff, A. (1980). Psychotherapy from the perspective of cognitive theory. In M. J. Mahoney (Ed.), *Psychotherapy process: Current issues and future directions* (pp. 339–361). New York: Plenum Press.

Arnkoff, D. B., & Glass, C. R. (1982). Clinical cognitive constructs: Examination, evaluation, and elaboration. In P. C. Kendall (Ed.), *Advances in cognitive-behavioral research and therapy* (Vol. 1, pp. 1–34). New York: Academic Press.

Aslin, R. N. (1981). Development of smooth pursuit in human infants. In D. F. Fisher, R. A. Monty, & J. W. Senders (Eds.), *Eye movements: Cognition and visual perception* (pp. 31–51). Hillsdale, New Jersey: Erlbaum.

Baars, B. J. (1986). *The cognitive revolution in psychology.* New York: Guilford Press.

Bachrach, A. J. (1970). Diving behavior. In *Human performance and scuba diving.* Chicago: Athletic Institute.

Bacon, S. J. (1974). Arousal and the range of cue utilization. *Journal of Experimental Psychology*, **102**, 81–87.

Baddeley, A. (1986). *Working memory.* Oxford: Oxford University Press.

Baddeley, A. (1990). *Human memory: Theory and practice.* Boston: Allyn and Bacon.

Baddeley, A., & Hitch, G. (1974). Working memory. In G. H. Bower (Ed.), *The psychology of learning and motivation* (Vol. 8). New York: Academic Press.

Baddeley, A., Logie, R., Bressi, S., Della Sala, S., & Spinnler, H. (1986). Dementia and working memory. *Quarterly Journal of Experimental Psychology,* **38A**, 603–618.

Baillargeon, R. (1986). Representing the existence and the location of hidden objects: Object permanence in 6 and 8 month old infants. *Cognition,* **23**, 21–41.

Ballenger, J. C. (1984). Psychopharmacology of the anxiety disorders. *Psychiatric Clinics of North America,* **7**, 757–771.

Ballenger, J. C. (1987). Unrecognized prevalence of panic disorder in primary care, internal medicine and cardiology. *American Journal of Cardiology,* **60**, 39–47.

Bandura, A. (1978). The self-system in reciprocal determinism. *American Psychologist,* **33**, 344–358.

Bandura, A. (1986). *Social foundations of thought and action: A social cognitive theory.* Englewood Cliffs, New Jersey: Prentice-Hall.

Barfield, R., & Sachs, B. (1968). Sexual behavior: Stimulation by painful electric shock to skin in male rats. *Science,* **161**, 392–395.

Bargh, J. A., & Pietromonaco, P. (1982). Automatic information processing and social perception: The influence of trait information presented outside of conscious awareness on impression formation. *Journal of Personality and Social Psychology,* **43**, 437–449.

Barlow, D. H., & Cerny, J. A. (1988). *Psychological treatment of panic.* New York: Guilford.

Barlow, D. H., & Maser, J. D. (1984). Psychopathology in anxiety disorders. *Journal of Behavioral Assessment,* **6**, 331–348.

Barnett, P. A., & Gotlib, I. H. (1988). Psychosocial functioning and depression: Distinguishing among antecedents, concomitants, and consequences. *Psychological Bulletin,* **104**, 97–126.

Baron-Cohen, S. (1987). Autism and symbolic play. *British Journal of Developmental Psychology,* **5**, 139–148.

Baron-Cohen, S., Leslie, A. M., & Frith, U. (1985). Does the autistic child have a theory of mind? *Cognition,* **21**, 37–46.

Baron-Cohen, S., Leslie, A. M., & Frith, U. (1986). Mechanical, behavioural and intentional understanding of picture stories in autistic children. *British Journal of Developmental Psychology,* **4**, 113–125.

Barraclough, M. (1966). A method of testing hearing based on operant conditioning. *Behavior Research and Therapy,* **4**, 237–238.

Barrios, B. A. (1989). On the changing nature of behavioral assessment. In A. S. Bellack & M. Hersen (Eds.), *Behavioral assessment: A practical handbook* (3rd ed, pp. 3–41). New York: Pergamon.

Barron, R. W. (1978). Access to the meanings of printed words: Some implications for reading and learning to read. In F. Murray (Ed.), *The recognition of words: IRA series on the development of the reading process.* Newark, Delaware: International Reading Association.

Bartlett, F. C. (1932). *Remembering: A study in experimental and social psychology.* Cambridge: Cambridge University Press.

Bauer, R. H. (1982). Information processing as a way of diagnosing and understanding learning disabilities. *Topics In Learning and Learning Disabilities,* **2**, 33–45.

Baxter, L., Phelps, M., Mazziotta, J., Guze, B., Schwartz, J., & Selin, C. (1987a). Local cerebral glucose metabolic rates in obsessive–compulsive disorder: A comparison of rates in unipolar depression and in normal controls. *Archives of General Psychiatry,* **44**, 211–218.

Baxter, L., Thompson, J., Schwartz, J., Guze, B., Phelps, M., Mazziotta, J., Selin, C., & Moss, L. (1987b). Trazodone treatment response in obsessive-compulsive disorder correlated with shifts in glucose metabolism in the caudate nuclei. *Psychopathology,* **20**, 114–122.

Bayles, K. A. (1982). Language function in senile dementia. *Brain and Language,* **16**, 265–280.

Bayles, K. A., & Tomoeda, C. K. (1983). Confrontation naming in dementia. *Brain and Language,* **19**, 98–114.

Beatty, W. W., Salmon, D. P., Butters, N., Heindel, W. C., & Granholm, E. L. (1988). Retrograde amnesia in patients with Alzheimer's disease or Huntington's disease. *Neurobiology of Aging,* **9**, 181–186.

Bebbington, P. E., Hurry, J., Tennant, C., Sturt, E., & Wing, J. K. (1981). Epidemiology of mental disorders in Camberwell. *Psychological Medicine,* **11**, 561–579.

Beck, A. T. (1963). Thinking and depression. *Archives of General Psychiatry,* **9**, 324–333.

Beck, A. T. (1964). Thinking and depression. II. Theory and Therapy. *Archives of General Psychiatry,* **10**, 561–571.

Beck, A. T. (1967). *Depression: Clinical, experimental and theoretical aspects.* New York: Harper and Row.

Beck, A. T. (1976). *Cognitive therapy and the emotional disorders.* New York: International Universities Press.

Beck, A. T. (1988). Cognitive approaches to panic disorder. In S. Rachman & M. D. Maser (Eds.), *Panic: Psychological perspectives.* Hillsdale, New Jersey: Erlbaum.

Beck, A. T., & Emery, G. (1985). *Anxiety disorders and phobias: A cognitive perspective.* New York: Basic Books.

Beck, A. T., Freeman, A., and Associates (1990). *Cognitive therapy of personality disorders.* New York: Guilford.

Beck, A. T., Rush, A. J., Shaw, B. F., & Emery, G. (1979). *Cognitive therapy of depression.* New York: Guilford Press.

Beck, A. T., & Weishaar, M. E. (1989). Cognitive therapy. In R. J. Corsini & D. Wedding (Eds.), *Current psychotherapies* (4th ed., pp. 285–320). Itasca, Illinois: Peacock.

Becker, J. T., Boller, F., Saxton, J., & McGonigle-Gibson, K. L. (1987). Normal rates of forgetting of verbal and non-verbal material in Alzheimer's disease. *Cortex,* **23**, 59–72.

Bedrosian, R. C., & Beck, A. T. (1980). Principles of cognitive therapy. In M. J. Mahoney (Ed.), *Psychotherapy process* (pp. 127–152). New York: Plenum Press.

Benjamin, T. B., & Watt, N. F. (1969). Psychopathology and semantic interpretation of ambiguous words. *Journal of Abnormal Psychology,* **74(6)**, 706–714.

Benton, A. (1955). *The visual retention test.* New York: Psychological Corporation.

Benton, A., & Hamsher, K. (1978). *Multilingual aphasia examination.* Iowa City: University of Iowa Hospitals.

Benton, A., Hamsher, K., Varney, N., & Spreen, O. (1983). *Contributions to neuropsychological assessment.* New York: Oxford University Press.

Berg, L., Danzinger, W. L., Storandt, M., Cohen, L. A., Gado, M., Hughes, C. P., Knesevich, J. W., & Botwinick, J. (1984). Predictive features of mild senile dementia of the Alzheimer type. *Neurology,* **34**, 563–569.

Berman, K. F., Illowsky, B. P., & Weinberger, D. R. (1988). Physiological dysfunction of dorsolateral prefrontal cortex in schizophrenia: Further evidence for regional and behavioral specificity. *Archives of General Psychiatry,* **45**, 616–622.

Bernstein, D. A., & Borkovec, T. D. (1973). *Progressive relaxation training.* Champaign, Illinois: Research Press.

Beutler, L. E., & Bergan, J. (1991). Value change in counseling and psychotherapy: A search for scientific credibility. *Journal of Counseling Psychology,* **18**, 16–24.

Beutler, L. E., & Guest, P. D. (1984). The role of cognitive change in psychotherapy. In A. Freeman, K. Simon, L. E. Beutler & H. Arkowitz (Eds.), *Comprehensive handbook of cognitive therapy* (pp. 123–142). New York: Plenum.

Beutler, L. E., Crago, M., & Arizmendi, T. G. (1986). Therapist variables in psychotherapy process and outcome. In S. L. Garfield & A. E. Bergin (Eds.), *Handbook of psychotherapy and behavior change* (3rd ed., pp. 257–310). New York: Wiley.

Biederman, J. (1990). The diagnosis and treatment of adolescent anxiety disorders. *Journal of Clinical Psychiatry*, **51**, 20–26.

Bjork, R. A. (1989). Retrieval inhibition as an adaptive mechanism in human memory. In H. R. Roediger, III, & F. I. M. Craik (Eds.), *Varieties of memory and consciousness: Essays in honor of Endel Tulving*. (pp. 195–210). Hillsdale, New Jersey: Erlbaum.

Bjork, R. A., & Woodwary, A. E., Jr. (1973). Directed forgetting of individual words in free recall. *Journal of Experimental Psychology*, **99**, 22–27.

Blachman, B. A. (1987). An alternative classroom reading program for learning disabled and other low-achieving children. In W. Ellis (Ed.), *Intimacy with language: A forgotten basic in teacher education*. Baltimore: The Orton Dyslexia Society.

Blaney, P. H. (1974). Two studies on the language behavior of schizophrenics. *Journal of Abnormal Psychology*, **83**(1), 23–31.

Blaney, P. H. (1986). Affect and memory: A review. *Psychological Bulletin*, **99**, 229–246.

Blatt, S. J., Brenneis, C. B., & Schimek, J. G. (1976). Normal development and psychopathological impairment of the concept of the object on the Rorschach. *Journal of Abnormal Psychology*, **85**, 364–373.

Bleuler, E. (1911/1950). *Dementia praecox: or The group of schizophrenias*. New York: International Universities Press.

Bloom, F. E., Schulman, J. A., & Koob, G. F. (1989). Catecholamines and behavior. In U. Trendelenburg & N. Wiener (Eds.), *Handbook of experimental pharmacology* (pp. 27–88). Berlin: Springer Verlag.

Bobrow, D. G., & Winograd, T. (1977). An overview of KRL, a knowledge representation language. *Cognitive Science*, **1**, 3–46.

Boder, E. (1973). Developmental dyslexia: A diagnostic approach based on three atypical reading-spelling patterns. *Developmental Medicine and Child Neurology*, **15**, 663–687.

Bootzin, R. R., & Acocella, J. R. (1988). *Abnormal psychology: Current perspectives*. New York: Random House.

Borden, J. W., & Turner, S. M. (1989). Is panic a unique emotional experience? *Behaviour Research and Therapy*, **27**, 263–268.

Borkovec, T. D., & Inz, J. (1990). The nature of worry in generalized anxiety disorder: A predominance of thought activity. *Behaviour Research and Therapy*, **28**, 153–158.

Boudewyns, P. A., & Shipley, R. H. (1983). *Flooding and implosive therapy*. New York: Plenum.

Bourne, H. R., Lichtenstein, L. M., Melmon, R. L., Henney, C. S., Weinstein, Y., & Shearer, G. M. (1974). Modulation of inflammation and immunity by cyclic AMP. *Science*, **184**, 129–148.

Bower, G. H. (1981). Mood and memory. *American Psychologist*, **36**, 129–148.

Bower, G. H. (1983). Affect and cognition. *Philosophical Transactions of the Royal Society, London, Series B*, **302**, 287–402.

Bower, G. H., & Morrow, D. G. (1990). Mental models and narrative comprehension. *Science*, **247**, 44–48.

Bower, G. H., Black, J. B., & Turner, T. J. (1979). Scripts in memory for text. *Cognitive Psychology*, **11**, 177–220.

Bower, G. H., Gilligan, S. G., & Monteiro, K. P. (1981). Selectivity of learning caused by affective states. *Journal of Experimental Psychology*, **110**, 451–473.

Bowers, K. S. (1984). On being unconsciously influenced and informed. In K. S. Bowers & C. Meichenbaum (Eds.), *The unconscious reconsidered*. (pp. 227–272). New York: Wiley.

Bowers, K. S. (1987). Intuition and discovery. In R. Stern (Ed.), *Theories of the unconscious and theories of the self* (pp. 91–108). Hillsdale, New Jersey: Erlbaum.

Bowers, K. S., & Meichenbaum, D. (Eds.). (1984). *The unconscious reconsidered*. New York: Wiley.

Bowlby, J. (1969). *Attachment and loss* (Vol. 1, *Attachment*). New York: Basic Books.

Bowlby, J. (1973). *Attachment and Loss* (Vol. 2, *Separation*). London: Hogarth Press and Institute of Psychoanalysis.

Bowlby, J. (1979a). The making and breaking of affectional bonds. II. Some principles of psychotherapy. *British Journal of Psychiatry*, **130**, 421–431.

Bowlby, J. (1979b). Reasonable fear and natural fear. *International Journal of Psychiatry*, **9**, 79–88.

Bradley, B., & Mathews, A. (date). Memory bias in recovered clinical depressives. (Submitted).

Bradley, L., & Bryant, P. E. (1983). Categorizing sounds and learning to read—A causal connection. *Nature*, **301**, 419–421.

Brady, J. P., & Lind, D. L. (1961). Experimental analysis of hysterical blindness. *Archives of General Psychiatry*, **4**, 331–339.

Brady, S., Poggie, E., & Rapala, M. M. (1989). Speech repetition abilities in children who differ in reading skill. *Language and Speech*, **32**, 109–122.

Brady, S., Shankweiler, D., & Mann, V. (1983). Speech perception and memory coding in relation to reading ability. *Journal of Experimental Child Psychology*, **35**, 345–367.

Braginsky, B. M., Braginsky, D. D., & Ring, K. (1969). *Methods of madness: The mental hospital as a last resort*. New York: Holt, Rinehart, and Winston.

Bray Garretson, H., Fein, D., & Waterhouse, L. (1990). Sustained attention in children with autism. *Journal of Autism and Developmental Disorders*, **20**, 101–114.

Brazelton, T. B., Krslowski, B., & Main, M. (1974). The origins of reciprocity. In M. Lewis & L. Rosenblum (Eds.), *The effect of the infant on its caregiver*. New York: Wiley.

Breger, L. (Ed.) (1969). *Cognitive-clinical psychology: Models and integrations*. Englewood Cliffs, New Jersey: Prentice-Hall.

Brenner, C. (1976). *Psychoanalytic technique and psychic conflict*. New York: International Universities Press.

Breuer, J., & Freud, S. (1893/1955). The psychical mechanism of hysterical phenomena: Preliminary communication. In J. Strachey (Ed.), *The standard edition of the complete psychological works of Sigmund Freud* (Vol. 2, pp. 1–18). London: Hogarth Press.

Brewin, C. R. (1989). Cognitive change processes in psychotherapy. *Psychological Review*, **96**, 379–394.

Bridgeman, B. (1988). *The biology of behaviour and mind*. New York: John Wiley & Sons.

Broadbent, D. E. (1954). The role of auditory localization in attention and memory span. *Journal of Experimental Psychology*, **47**, 191–196.

Broadbent, D. E. (1956). Successive responses to simultaneous stimuli. *Quarterly Journal of Experimental Psychology*, **8**, 145–152.

Bronson, G. W. (1974). The postnatal growth of visual capacity. *Child Development*, **45**, 873–890.

Brouwers, P., Cox, Martin, A., Chase, T., & Fedio, P. (1984). Differential perceptual-spatial impairment in Huntingdon's and Alzheimer's dementias. *Archives of Neurology*, **41**, 1073–1076.

Brown, G. D. A. (1990). Cognitive science and its relation to psychology. *The Psychologist*, **3**, 339–343.

Brown, G. W., & Harris, T. O. (1978). *The social origins of depression*. London: Tavistock.

Brown, G. W., Davidson, S., Harris, T., Maclean, U. Pollock, S., & Prudo, R. (1977). Psychiatric disorder in London and North Uist. *Social Science and Medicine*, **11**, 367–377.

Brown, R. G., & Marsden, C. D. (1988). "Subcortical dementia": The neuropsychological evidence. *Brain*, **2**, 363–387.

Brozoski, T. J., Brown, R. M., Rosvold, H. E., & Goldman, P. S. (1979). Cognitive deficit caused by regional depletion of dopamine in prefrontal cortex of Rhesus monkey. *Science*, **205**, 929–931.

Bruner, J. S. (1957). On perceptual readiness. *Psychological Review,* **64**, 123–152.

Bruner, J. S. (1983). *In search of mind.* New York: Harper & Row.

Bruner, J. (1986). *Actual minds, possible worlds.* Cambridge: Harvard University Press.

Bryant, R. A., & McConkey, K. M. (1989). Visual conversion disorder: A case analysis of the influence of visual information. *Journal of Abnormal Psychology,* **98**, 326–329.

Buchsbaum, M. S., Ingvar, D. H., Kessler, R., Waters, R. N., Cappelletti, J., van Kammen, D. P., King, C. A., Johnson, J. L., Manning, R. G., Flynn, R. W., Mann, L. S., Bunny, W. E., & Sokoloff, L. (1982). Cerebral glucography with positron tomography. *Archives of General Psychiatry,* **39**, 251–259.

Burgess, I. S., Jones, L. N., Robertson, S. A., Radcliffe, W. N., Emerson, E., Lawler, P., & Crow, T. J. (1981). The degree of control exerted by phobic and non-phobic verbal stimuli over the recognition behaviour of phobic and non-phobic subjects. *Behaviour Research Therapy,* **19**, 223–234.

Burnod, Y., & Korn, H. (1989). Consequences of stochastic release of neurotransmitters for network computation in the central nervous system. *Proceedings of the National Academy of Science (U.S.A),* **86**, 352–356.

Buschke, H., & Fuld, P. A. (1974). Evaluating storage, retention and retrieval in disordered memory and learning. *Neurology,* **24**, 1019–1025.

Byrne, B. (1991). Experimental analysis of the child's discovery of the alphabetic principle. In L. Rieben and C. A. Perfetti (Eds.), *Learning to read: Basic research and its implications.* (pp. 75–84). Hillsdale, New Jersey: Erlbaum.

Byrne, B., & Ledez, J. (1986). Phonological awareness in reading-disabled adults. *Australian Journal of Psychology,* **35**, 185–197.

Callaway, E., III., & Dembo, D. (1958). Narrowed attention: A psychological phenomenon that accompanies a certain physiological change. *AMA Archives of Neurology and Psychiatry,* **79**, 74–90.

Campbell, D. T. (1974). Evolutionary epistemology. In P. A. Schilpp (Ed.), *The philosophy of Karl Popper* (Vol. 14., I and II, pp. 416–463). LaSalle, Illinois: Open Court.

Cannon, W. B. (1930). The Linacre lecture on the autonomic nervous system: An interpretation. *Lancet,* **218**, 1109–1115.

Cantone, G., Orsini, A., Grossi, D., & De Michelle, G. (1978). Verbal and spatial memory span in dementia (an experimental study of 185 subjects). *Acta Neuropsychologia (Naples),* **33**, 175–185.

Cantor, N., & Kihlstrom, J. F. (Eds.) (1981). *Personality, cognition, and social interaction.* Hillsdale, New Jersey: Erlbaum.

Cantor, N., & Mischel, W. (1977). Traits as prototypes: Effects on recognition memory. *Journal of Personality and Social Psychology,* **35**, 38–48.

Cantor, N., & Zirkel, S. (1990). Personality, cognition, and purposive behavior. In L. A. Pervin (Ed.), *Handbook of personality theory and research* (pp. 135–164). New York: Guilford.

Capra, F. (1983). *The turning point.* New York: Bantam.

Carle, E. (1984). *The very busy spider.* New York: Philomel Books.

Carlsen, M. B. (1988). *Meaning-making: Therapeutic processes in adult development.* New York: Norton.

Carnap, R. (1947). *Meaning and necessity.* Chicago: University of Chicago Press.

Carr, A. T. (1974). Compulsive neurosis: A review of the literature. *Psychological Bulletin,* **81**, 311–318.

Carroll, D. (1972). Repression–sensitization and duration of visual attention and relationship patterns—Three samples inspected. *Perceptual and Motor Skills,* **34**, 949–950.

Caspar, F., Rothenfluh, T., & Segal, Z. (1991). *The appeal of connectionism for clinical psychology.* Unpublished manuscript.

Ceci, S. J. (1983). An investigation of the semantic processing characteristics of normal and language/learning disabled children. *Developmental Psychology,* **19**, 427–439.

Cermak, L. S. (1984). The episodic-semantic distinction in amnesia. In L. R. Squire & N. Butters (Eds.), *Neuropsychology of memory*. New York: Guilford Press.

Chadwick, J., & Mann, W. N. (trans.) (1978). *Hippocratic writings*. G. E. R. Lloyd (Ed.). Harmondsworth: Penguin.

Chall, J. (1967). *Learning to read: The great debate*. New York: McGraw-Hill.

Chambless, D. L., & Gracely, E. J. (1989). Fear of fear and the anxiety disorders. *Cognitive Therapy and Research*, **13**, 9–20.

Chapman, L. J., & Chapman, J. P. (1978). The measurement of differential deficit. *Journal of Psychiatric Research*, **14**, 303–311.

Chapman, L. J., Chapman, J. P., & Miller, G. A. (1964). A theory of verbal behavior in schizophrenia. In B. A. Maher (Ed.), *Progress in experimental personality research* (Vol. 1, pp. 135–167). New York: Academic Press.

Charcot, J.-M. (1877). *Lectures on the diseases of the nervous system*. London: New Sydenham Society.

Cheesman, J., & Merikle, P. M. (1986). Word recognition and consciousness. In D. Besner, T. G. Waller, & G. E. Mackinnon (Eds.), *Reading research: Advances in theory and practice* (Vol. 5, pp. 311–352). New York: Academic Press.

Cherry, E. C. (1953). Some experiments on the recognition of speech, with one and with two ears. *Journal of the Acoustical Society of America*, **25**, 975–979.

Chertok, L. (1970). Freud in Paris: A crucial stage. *International Journal of Psycho-Analysis*, **51**, 511–520.

Chiodo, L. A., & Berger, T. W. (1986). Interactions between dopamine and amino acid-induced excitation and inhibition in the striatum. *Brain Research*, **375**, 198–203.

Chodoff, P. (1954). A re-examination of some aspects of conversion hysteria. *Psychiatry*, **17**, 75–80.

Chodoff, P. (1974). The diagnosis of hysteria: An overview. *American Journal of Psychiatry*, **131**, 1073–1078.

Chodoff, P., & Lyons, H. (1958). Hysteria, the hysterical personality, and "hysterical" conversion. *American Journal of Psychiatry*, **114**, 734–740.

Chomsky, N. (1959). A review of B. F. Skinner's *Verbal Behavior*. *Language*, **35**, 26–58.

Christianson, S.-A., & Loftus, E. S. (1991). Remembering emotional events: The fate of detailed information. *Emotion and Cognition*, **5**, 81–108.

Christianson, S.-A., & Nilsson, L.-G. (1984). Functional amnesia as induced by psychological trauma. *Memory and Cognition*, **12**, 142–155.

Christianson, S.-A., Loftus, E. F., Hoffman, H., & Loftus, G. R. (1991). Eye fixations and memory for emotional events. *Journal of Experimental Psychology: Learning, Memory, and Cognition*, **17**, 693–701.

Christianson, S.-A., & Nilsson, L.-G. (1989). Hysterical amnesia: A case of aversively motivated isolation of memory. In T. Archer & L.-G. Nilsson (Eds.), *Aversion, avoidance and anxiety: Perspectives on aversively motivated behavior* (pp. 289–310). Hillsdale, New Jersey: Erlbaum.

Claparede, E. (1951). Recognition and 'me-ness.' In D. Rapaport (Ed.), *Organization and pathology of thought* (pp. 58–75). New York: Columbia University Press. [Reprinted from *Archives de Psychologie* (1911) **11**, 79–90.]

Clark, A. (1989). *Microcognition*. Cambridge: MIT Press.

Clark, D. M. (1986). A cognitive approach to panic. *Behaviour Research and Therapy*, **24**, 461–470.

Clark, D. M., Salkovskis, P. M., & Chalkley, A. J. (1985). Respiratory control as a treatment for panic attacks. *Journal of Behavior Therapy and Experimental Psychiatry*, **16**, 23–30.

Clark, D. M., & Teasdale, J. D. (1982). Diurnal variations in clinical depression and accessibility of memories of positive and negative experiences. *Journal of Abnormal Psychology*, **91**, 87–95.

Clark, D. M., & Teasdale, J. D. (1985). Constraints of the effects of mood on memory. *Journal of Personality and Social Psychology*, **48**, 1598–1608.

Clarke, K. M. (1989). Creation of meaning: An emotional processing task in psychotherapy. *Psychotherapy*, **26**, 139–148.

Cleeremans, A., Servan-Schreiber, D., & McClelland, J. L. (1989). Finite state automata and simple recurrent networks. *Neural Computation*, **1**, 372–381.

Clippinger, J. (1977). *Meaning and discourse: A computer model of psychoanalytic speech and cognition*. Baltimore: Johns Hopkins University Press.

Cloitre, M., & Liebowitz, M. R. (1991). Memory bias in panic disorder: An investigation of the cognitive avoidance hypothesis. *Cognitive Therapy and Research*, **15**, 371–386.

Cloninger, R. (1987). A systematic method for clinical description and classification of personality variants: A proposal. *Archives of General Psychiatry*, **44**, 573–588.

Clum, G. A. (1990). *Coping with panic: A drug-free approach*. Pacific Grove, California: Brooks-Cole.

Coccaro, E. F., Siever, L. J., Klar, H. M., Maurer, G., Cochrane, K., Cooper, T. B., Mohs, R. C., & Davis, K. L. (1989). Serotonergic studies in patients with affective and personality disorders: Correlates with suicidal and impulsive-aggressive behavior. *Archives of General Psychiatry*, **46**, 587–599.

Cohen, G. (1977). *The psychology of cognition*. New York: Academic Press.

Cohen, J. D., Dunbar, K., & McClelland, J. L. (1990). On the control of automatic processes: A parallel distributed processing model of the Stroop effect. *Psychological Review*, **97(3)**, 332–361.

Cohen, J. D., & Servan-Schreiber, D. (1989). *A parallel distributed processing approach to behaviour and biology in schizophrenia*. Technical Report AIP-100. Department of Psychology, Carnegie Mellon University, Pittsburgh, Pennsylvania 15213.

Cohen, J. D., & Servan-Schreiber, D. (1992a). Context, cortex and dopamine: A connectionist approach to behavior and biology in schizophrenia. *Psychological Review*, **99**, 45–77.

Cohen, J. D., & Servan-Schreiber, D. (1992b). A theory of dopamine function and its role in cognitive deficits in schizophrenia. *Schizophrenia Bulletin* (in press).

Cohen, R. M., Semple, W. E., Gross, M., Holcomb, H. H., Dowling, M. S., & Nordahl, T. E. (1988). Functional localization of sustained attention: Comparison to sensory stimulation in the absence of instruction. *Neuropsychiatry, Neuropsychology, and Behavioral Neurology*, **1**, 2–20.

Cohen, R. M., Semple, W. E., Gross, M., Nordahl, T. E., DeLisi, L. E., Holcomb, H. H., King, A. C., Morihisa, J. M., & Pickar, D. (1987). Dysfunction in a prefrontal substrate of sustained attention in schizophrenia. *Life Sciences*, **40**, 2031–2039.

Cohn, J. R., & Tronick, E. Z. (1987). Mother-infant face to face interaction: The sequence of dyadic states at 3, 6 and 9 months. *Developmental Psychology*, **23**, 68–77.

Colby, K. M. (1974). *Artificial paranoia*. New York: Pergammon.

Colby, K. M., & Stoller, R. J. (1988). *Cognitive science and psychoanalysis*. Hillsdale, New Jersey: Analytic Press.

Coles, G. S. (1987). *The learning mystique: A critical look at "learning disabilities"*. New York: Pantheon Books.

Collins, A. M., & Loftus, E. (1975). A spreading-activation theory of semantic processing. *Psychological Review*, **82**, 407–428.

Collins, A. M., & Quillian, M. R. (1969). Retrieval time from semantic memory. *Journal of Verbal Learning and Verbal Behavior*, **8**, 240–247.

Conrad, R. (1971). The chronology of the development of covert speech in children. *Developmental Psychology*, **5**, 398–405.

Corkin, S. (1982). Some relationships between global amnesias and the memory impairments in Alzheimer's disease. In S. Corkin, K. L. Davis, J. H. Growdon, E. Usdin, &

R. J. Wurtman (Eds.). *Alzheimer's disease: A report of progress in research.* (pp. 149–164). New York: Raven Press.

Corkin, S., Growdon, J. H., Nissen, M. J., Huff, F. J., Freed, D. M., & Sagar, H. J. (1984). Recent advances in the neuropsychological study of Alzheimer's disease. In R. J. Wurtman, S. Corkin, & J. H. Growden (Eds.), *Alzheimer's disease: Advances in basic research and therapies.* Cambridge, Massachusetts: Center for Brain Sciences and Metabolism Trust.

Cornblatt, B., Lenzenweger, M. F., & Erlenmeyer-Kimling, L. (1989). A continuous performance test, identical pairs version. II. Contrasting attentional profiles in schizophrenic and depressed patients. *Psychiatry Research,* **29,** 65–85.

Cormier, W. H., & Cormier, S. L. (Eds.) (1985). *Interviewing strategies for helpers: Fundamental skills and cognitive-behavioral interventions.* Monterey, California: Brooks/Cole.

Corteen, R. S., & Wood, B. (1972). Autonomic responses to shock associated threat words. *Journal of Experimental Psychology,* **94,** 308–313.

Corwin, J. V., Kanter, S., Watson, R. T., Heilman, K. M., Valenstein, E., & Hashimoto, A. (1986). Apomorphine has a therapeutic effect on neglect produced by unilateral dorsomedial prefrontal cortex lesions in rats. *Experimental Neurology,* **94,** 683–698.

Cossa, F. M., Della Sala, S., & Spinnler, H. (1989). Selective visual attention in Alzheimer's and Parkinson's patients: Memory and data-driven control. *Neuropsychologia,* **27,** 887–892.

Cowdry, R. W., & Gardner, D. L. (1988). Pharmacotherapy of borderline personality disorder. *Archives of General Psychiatry,* **45,** 111–119.

Coyne, J. C., & Gotlib, I. H. (1983). The role of cognition in depression: A critical appraisal. *Psychological Bulletin,* **94,** 472–505.

Cozolino, L. J. (1983). The oral and written productions of schizophrenic patients. In B. A. Maher (Ed.), *Progress in experimental personality research* (Vol. 12, pp. 101–152). New York: Academic Press.

Craighead, W. E., Hickey, K. S., & DeMonbreun, B. G. (1979). Distortion of perception and recall of neutral feedback in depression. *Cognitive Therapy and Research,* **3,** 291–298.

Craik, F. I. M., & Lockhart, R. S. (1972). Levels of processing: A framework for memory research. *Journal of Verbal Learning and Verbal Behavior,* **11,** 671–684.

Craik, F. I. M., & Tulving, E. (1975). Depth of processing and the retention of words in episodic memory. *Journal of Experimental Psychology,* **104,** 268–294.

Crow, T. J. (1968). Cortical synapses and reinforcement: A hypothesis. *Nature,* **219,** 736–737.

Crow, T. J. (1985). Neurochemical aspects of the functional psychoses. In M. Swash & C. Kennard (Eds.), *Scientific bases of clinical neurology* (pp. 719–735). Edinburgh: Churchill Livingstone.

Crowder, R. G. (1982a). The demise of short-term memory. *Acta Psychologia,* **50,** 291–323.

Crowder, R. G. (1982b). *The psychology of reading.* New York: Oxford University Press.

Dahl, H., Kachele, H., & Thoma, H. (Eds.) (1988). *Psychoanalytic process research strategies.* Berlin: Springer-Verlag.

Dall'Ora, P., Della Sala, S., & Spinnler, H. (1989). Autobiographical memory. Its impairment in amnesic syndromes. *Cortex,* **25,** 197–217.

Daly, H. B., & Daly, J. T. (1982). A mathematical model of reward and aversive nonreward: Its application in over 30 appetitive learning situations. *Journal of Experimental Psychology: General,* **111,** 441–480.

Damasio, A. R. (1979). The frontal lobes. In K. M. Heilman & E. Valenstein (Eds.), *Clinical Neuropsychology* (pp. 3360–411). New York: Oxford University Press.

Damianopoulous, E. N. (1987). Conditioning, attention, and the CS–UCS interval. *Pavlovian Journal of Biological Science,* **22,** 16–30.

Danion, J. M., Willard-Schroeder, D., Zimmermann, M. A., Grange, D., Schlienger, J. L., & Singer, L. (1991). Explicit memory and repetition priming in depression. *Archives of General Psychiatry*, **48**, 707–711.

Danion, J. M., Zimmermann, M. A., Willard-Schroeder, D., Grange, D., Schlienger, J. L., & Singer, L. (1990). Diazepam induces a dissociation between explicit and implicit memory. *Psychopharmacology*, **99**, 238–243.

Davidson, T. M., & Bowers, K. S. (1991). Selective hypnotic amnesia: Is it a successful attempt to forget or an unsuccessful attempt to remember? *Journal of Abnormal Psychology*, **100**, 133–143.

Davis, H. (1979a). Self-reference and the encoding of personal information in depression. *Cognitive Therapy and Research*, **3**, 97–110.

Davis, H. (1979b). The self-schema and subjective organization of personal information in depression. *Cognitive Therapy and Research*, **3**, 415–425.

Davis, H. P., & Unruh, W. R. (1981). The development of the self-schema in adult depression. *Journal of Abnormal Psychology*, **90**, 125–133.

Davis, P. (1990). Repression and the inaccessibility of emotional memories. In J. L. Singer (Ed.), *Repression and dissociation.* Chicago: (pp. 387–403). University of Chicago Press.

Davis, P. E., & Mumford, S. J. (1984). Cued recall and the nature of the memory disorder in dementia. *British Journal of Psychiatry*, **144**, 383–386.

Day, J., French, L. A., & Hall, L. (1985). Social influences on cognitive development. In D. L. Forrest-Pressley, G. E. MacKinnon, & T. G. Waller (Eds.), *Metacognition, cognition and human performance* (Vol. 1, *Theoretical perspectives*, pp. 33–56). New York: Academic Press.

Ajuriaguerra, J., & Tissot, R. (1975). Some aspects of language in various forms of senile dementia (comparisons with language in childhood). In E. H. Lenneberg & E. Lenneberg (Eds.), *Foundations of language development* Vol. 1. New York: Academic Press.

de Leon, M. J., Potegal, M., & Gurland, B. (1984). Wandering and parietal signs in senile dementia of the Alzheimer's type. *Neuropsychobiology*, **11**, 155–157.

Dember, W. N. (1974). Motivation and the cognitive revolution. *American Psychologist*, **29**, 161–168.

Dembrowski, T. M., MacDougall, J. M., Shields, J. L., Pettito, J., & Lushene, R. (1978). Components of the Type A coronary-prone behavior pattern and cardiovascular responses to psychomotor performance challenge. *Journal of Behavioral Medicine*, **1**, 159–176.

DeMonbreun, B. G., & Craighead, W. E. (1977). Distortion of perception and recall of positive and neutral feedback in depression. *Cognitive Therapy and Research*, **1**, 311–329.

Depue, R. A., & Monroe, S. M. (1978). Learned helplessness in the perspective of the depressive disorders. *Journal of Abnormal Psychology*, **87**, 3–21.

Depue, R. A., Slater, J., Wolfstetter-Kausch, H., Klein, D., Goplerud, E., & Farr, D. (1981). A behavioral paradigm for identifying persons at risk for bipolar depressive disorder: A conceptual framework and five validation studies. *Journal of Abnormal Psychology*, **90**, 381–437.

Depue, R. A., & Spoont, M. R. (1987). Conceptualizing a serotonin trait: A behavioral dimension of constraint. In J. J. Mann & M. Stanley (Eds.), *Psychobiology of suicidal behavior.* (pp. 47–62). New York: New York Academy of Sciences.

De Renzi, E., Liotti, M., & Nichelli, P. (1987). Semantic amnesia with preservation of autobiographical memory. A case report. *Cortex*, **23**, 575–597.

Derry, P. A., & Kuiper, N. A. (1981). Schematic processing and self-reference in clinical depression. *Journal of Abnormal Psychology*, **90**, 286–297.

de Schonen, S., & Mathivet, H. (1989). First come, first served: A scenario about the development of hemispheric specialisation in face recognition during infancy. *European Bulletin of Cognitive Psychology*, **9**, 3–44.

De Sousa, R. (1987). *The rationality of emotions.* Cambridge: MIT Press.

Detterman, D. K. (1975). The von Restorff effect and induced amnesia: Production by manipulation of sound intensity. *Journal of Experimental Psychology: Human Learning and Memory,* **1**, 614–628.

Diamond, A. (1985). Developmental of the ability to use recall to guide action, as indicated by infants' performance on AB. *Child Development,* **56**, 868–883.

Diamond, A. (1990a). The development and neural bases of memory functions as indexed by the AB and delayed response tasks in human infants and infant monkeys. In A. Diamond (Ed.), *The development and neural bases of higher cognitive functions* (pp. 267–317). New York: New York Academy of Science Press.

Diamond, A. (1990b). Developmental time course in human infants and infant monkeys, and the neural bases of, inhibitory control in reaching. In A. Diamond (Ed.), *The development and neural bases of higher cognitive functions* (pp. 637–676). New York: New York Academy of Science Press.

Diamond, A., & Doar, B. (1989). The performance of human infants on a measure of frontal cortex function, the delayed response task. *Developmental Psychobiology,* **22(3)**, 271–294.

Diamond, A., & Goldman-Rakic, P. S. (1989). Comparison of human infants and rhesus monkeys on Piaget's AB task: Evidence for dependence on dorsolateral prefrontal cortex. *Experimental Brain Research,* **74**, 24–40.

Dick, M. B., Kean, M-L., & Sands, D. (1989a). Memory for action events in Alzheimer-like dementia: Further evidence of an encoding failure. *Brain and Cognition,* **9**, 71–87.

Dick, M. B., Kean, M-L., & Sands, D. (1989b). Memory for internally generated words in Alzheimer-type dementia: Breakdown in encoding and semantic memory. *Brain and Cognition,* **9**, 88–108.

Dick-Barnes, M., Nelson, R., & Aine, C. J. (1987). Behavioral measures of multiple personality: The case of Margaret. *Journal of Behavior Therapy and Experimental Psychiatry,* **18**, 229–239.

Dixon, N. F. (1981). *Preconscious processing.* New York: Wiley.

Dixon, N. F., & Henley, S. H. A. (1991). Unconscious perception: Possible implications of data from academic research for clinical practice. *Journal of Nervous and Mental Disease,* **179**, 243–252.

Dobson, K. S. (Ed.) (1988). *Handbook of cognitive-behavioral therapies.* New York: Guilford Press.

Dobson, K. S., & Shaw, B. F. (1987). Specificity and stability of self-referent encoding in clinical depression. *Journal of Abnormal Psychology,* **96**, 34–40.

Dohr, K. V., Rush, A. J., & Bernstein, I. H. (1989). Cognitive biases and depression. *Journal of Abnormal Psychology,* **98**, 263–267.

Dohrenwend, B. S., Krasnoff, L., Askenasy, A. R., & Dohrenwend, B. P. (1978). Exemplification of a method for scaling life events: The PERI life events scale. *Journal of Health and Social Behavior,* **19**, 205–229.

Dollard, J., Doob, L. W., Miller, N. W., Mowrer, O. H., & Sears, R. R. (1939). *Frustration and aggression.* New Haven, Connecticut: Yale University Press.

Dreyfus, H. L., & Dreyfus, S. E. (1988). *Mind over machine: The power of human intuition and expertise in the era of the computer.* New York: Free Press.

Dryden, W., & Ellis, A. (1988). Rational-emotive therapy. In K. Dobson (Ed.), *Handbook of cognitive-behavioral therapies* (pp. 214–272). New York: Guilford Press.

Dryden, W., & Golden, W. L. (Eds.) (1986). *Cognitive-behavioral approaches to psychotherapy.* London: Harper & Row.

Dulany, D. E., Carlson, R. A., & Dewey, G. I. (1984). A case of syntactical learning and judgment: How conscious and how abstract? *Journal of Experimental Psychology: General,* **113**, 541–555.

Dunbar, K., & MacLeod, C. M. (1984). A horse race of a different color: Stroop interference patterns with transformed words. *Journal of Experimental Psychology: Human Perception and Performance*, **10**, 622–639.

Dunn, J. C., & Kirsner, K. (1988). Discovering functionally independent mental processes: The principle of reversed association. *Psychological Review*, **95**, 91–101.

Dyck, D. G. (1983). Severity of depressed mood, perfectionism, and self-referent encoding. In L. B. Alloy (Ed.), *Depression and schemata*. Symposium presented at the meeting of the American Psychological Association, Anaheim, California.

Dykman, B. M., & Volpicelli, J. R. (1983). Depression and negative processing of evaluative feedback. *Cognitive Therapy and Research*, **7**, 485–498.

Eagle, M. N. (1987). The psychoanalytic and the cognitive unconscious. In R. Stern (Ed.), *Theories of the unconscious and theories of the self* (pp. 155–190). Hillsdale, New Jersey: Erlbaum.

Easterbrook, J. A. (1959). The effect of emotion on cue utilization and the organization of behavior. *Psychological Review*, **66**, 183–201.

Edelman, G. M. (1987). *Neural Darwinism: The theory of neuronal group selection*. New York: Basic Books.

Ehri, L. C. (1991). Learning to read and spell words. In L. Rieben and C. A. Perfetti (Eds.), *Learning to read: Basic research and its implications*. Hillsdale, New Jersey: Erlbaum.

Eich, E. (1984). Memory for unattended events: Remembering with and without awareness. *Memory and Cognition*, **12**, 105–111.

Einhorn, H. J., & Hogarth, R. M. (1978). Confidence in judgement: Persistence of the illusion of validity. *Psychological Review*, **85**, 395–416.

Einhorn, H. J., & Hogarth, R. M. (1981). Behavioral decision theory: Processes of judgement and choice. *Annual Review of Psychology*, **32**, 53–88.

Ellenberger, H. F. (1970). *The discovery of the unconscious: The history and evolution of dynamic psychiatry*. New York: Basic Books.

Ellis, A. (1962). *Reason and emotion in psychotherapy*. Secaucus, New Jersey: Lyle Stuart.

Ellis, A. (1979). The theory of rational-emotive therapy. In A. Ellis & J. M. Whiteley (Eds.), *Theoretical and empirical foundations of rational-emotive therapy* (pp. 33–60). Monterey, California: Brooks/Cole.

Ellis, A. (1980). Rational-emotive therapy and cognitive behavior therapy: Similarities and differences. *Cognitive Therapy and Research*, **4**, 325–340.

Ellis, A. (1984a). The essence of RET—1984. *Journal of Rational–Emotive Therapy*, **2**, 19–25.

Ellis, A. (1984b). Is the unified-interaction approach to cognitive behavior modification a reinvention of the wheel? *Clinical Psychology Review*, **4**, 215–218.

Ellis, A. (1987). Integrative developments in rational–emotive therapy (RET). *Journal of Integrative and Eclectic Psychotherapy*, **6**, 470–479.

Ellis, A. (1989). Rational–emotive therapy. In R. J. Corsini & D. Wedding (Eds.), *Current psychotherapies* (4th ed., pp. 197–238). Itasca, Illinois: Peacock.

Ellis, A., & Bernard, M. E. (1985). What is rational–emotive therapy (RET)? In A. Ellis & M. E. Bernard (Eds.), *Clinical applications of rational-emotive therapy* (pp. 1–30). New York: Plenum.

Ellis, A., & Dryden, W. (1987). *The practice of rational–emotive therapy*. New York: Springer.

Ellis, A., & Harper, R. A. (1975). *A new guide to rational living*. North Hollywood, California: Wilshire.

Emde, R. N. (1983). The prerepresentational self and its affective core. *Psychoanalytic Study of the Child*, **38**, 165–192.

Emmelkamp, P. M. G. (1987). Obsessive–compulsive disorders. In L. Michelson & L. M. Ascher (Eds.), *Anxiety and stress disorders*. New York: Guilford Press.

Emmelkamp, P. M. G., & Van der Heyden, H. (1980). The treatment of harming obsessions. *Behavioral Analysis and Modification*, **4**, 28–35.

Emmelkamp, P. M. G., Visser, S., & Hoekstra, R. (1988). Cognitive therapy vs. exposure treatment in the treatment of obsessive-compulsives. *Cognitive Therapy and Research*, **12**, 103–114.

Engelmann, S. (1969). *Preventing failure in the primary grades*. Chicago: Science Research Associates.

Erdelyi, M. H. (1974). A new look at the New Look: Perceptual defense and vigilance. *Psychological Review*, **81**, 1–25.

Erdelyi, M. H. (1985). *Psychoanalysis: Freud's cognitive psychology*. New York: W. H. Freeman.

Erdelyi, M. H., & Appelbaum, G. A. (1973). Cognitive masking: The disruptive effect of an emotional stimulus upon the perception of contiguous neutral items. *Bulletin of the Psychonomic Society*, **1**, 59–61.

Erdelyi, M. H., & Blumenthal, D. (1973). Cognitive masking in rapid sequential processing: The effect of an emotional picture on preceding and succeeding pictures. *Memory and Cognition*, **1**, 201–204.

Erdelyi, M. H., & Goldberg, B. (1979). Let's not sweep repression under the rug: Toward a cognitive psychology of repression. In J. F. Kihlstrom & F. J. Evans (Eds.), *Functional disorders of memory*. Hillsdale, New Jersey: Erlbaum.

Ericksen, C. W. (1960). Discrimination and learning without awareness: A methodological survey and evaluation. *Psychological Review*, **67**, 279–300.

Erlenmeyer-Kimling, L., & Cornblatt, B. (1978). Attentional measures in a study of children at high-risk for schizophrenia. *Journal of Psychiatric Research*, **14**, 93–98.

Eslinger, P. J., Damsio, A. R., Benton, A. L., & Van Allen, M. (1985). Neuropsychological detection of abnormal mental decline in older persons. *Journal of American Medical Association*, **253**, 670–674.

Esman, A. H. (1989). Psychoanalysis and general psychiatry: obsessive-compulsive disorder as paradigm. *Journal of the American Psychoanalytic Association*, **37**, 319–336.

Fagan, J. F. (1984). The intelligent infant: Theoretical implications. *Intelligence*, **8**, 1–9.

Fagan, J. F., & McGrath, S. (1981). Infant recognition memory and later intelligence. *Intelligence*, **5**, 121–130.

Fang, J. C., Hinrichs, J. V., & Ghoneim, M. M. (1987). Diazepam and memory: Evidence for spared memory function. *Pharmacological Biochemical Behavior*, **28**, 347–352.

*Federal Register* (1977). Thursday, December 29. (65082–65085) Washington, D.C.

Fennell, M. J. V., & Campbell, E. A. (1984). The Cognitions Questionnaire: Specific thinking errors in depression. *British Journal of Clinical Psychology*, **23**, 81–92.

Fikes, R. E., & Nilsson, N. J. (1971). STRIPS: A new approach to the application of theorem proving to problem solving. *Artificial Intelligence*, **2**, 189–208.

Finkel, C. B., Glass, C. R., Merluzzi, T. V. (1982). Differential discrimination of self-referent statements by depressives and nondepressives. *Cognitive Therapy and Research*, **6**, 173–183.

Finley, G. E., Sharp, T., & Agramonte, R. (1990). Recall and recognition memory for remotely acquired information in dementia patients. *Journal of Genetic Psychology*, **151**, 267–268.

Fischoff, B. (1973). Hindsight = Foresight: The effect of outcome knowledge on judgement under uncertainty. *Journal of Experimental Psychology: Human Perception and Performance*, **1**, 288–299.

Fiske, S. T. (1981). Schema-triggered affect: Application to social perception. In M. S. Clark & S. T. Fiske (Eds.), *Affect and cognition*. (pp. 55–78). Hillsdale, New Jersey: Erlbaum.

Flanagan, O. J. (1984). *The science of the mind*. Cambridge: MIT Press.

Flavell, J. H. (1979). Metacognition and cognitive monitoring: A new area of cognitive-developmental inquiry. *American Psychologist*, **34**, 906–911.

Flesch, R. (1955). *Why Johnny can't read*. New York: Harper & Brothers.

Flicker, C., Ferris, S., Crook, T., & Bartus, R. (1987a). A visual recognition memory test for the assessment of cognitive function in aging and dementia. *Experimental Aging Research*, **13**, 127–132.

Flicker, C., Ferris, S., Crook, T., & Bartus, R. (1987b). Implications of memory and language dysfunction in the naming deficit of senile dementia. *Brain and Language*, **31**, 187–200.

Flicker, C., Ferris, S., Crook, T., Reisberg, B., & Bartus, R. (1988). Equivalent spatial-rotation deficits in normal aging and Alzheimer's disease. *Journal of Clinical and Experimental Neuropsychology*, **10**, 387–399.

Foa, E. B., & Kozak, M. J. (1988). Emotional processing of fear: Exposure to corrective information. *Psychological Bulletin*, **99**, 20–35.

Foa, E. B., & McNally, R. J. (1986). Sensitivity to feared stimuli in obsessive-compulsives: A dichotic listening analysis. *Cognitive Therapy and Research*, **22**, 259–265.

Fodor, J. A. (1983). *The modularity of mind: An essay on faculty psychology.* Cambridge: MIT Press.

Fodor, J. A., & Pylyshyn, Z. W. (1988). Connectionism and Cognitive Architecture: A Critical Analysis. *Cognition*, **28**, 3–71.

Fogel, A., & Walker, H. (1989). *Development of mother–infant face to face interaction: Asynchronies predict both change and individual differences.* Unpublished manuscript.

Fonte, R. J., & Stevenson, J. M. (1985). The use of propranolol in the treatment of anxiety disorders. *Hillside Journal of Clinical Psychiatry*, **7**, 54–62.

Foote, S. L., Freedman, R., & Oliver, A. P. (1975). Effects of putative neurotransmitters on neuronal activity in monkey auditory cortex. *Brain Research*, **86**, 229–242.

Ford, D. H. (1987). *Humans as self-constructing living systems. A developmental perspective on behavior and personality.* Hillsdale, New Jersey: Erlbaum.

Forgus, R., & Shulman, B. (1979). *Personality: A cognitive view.* Englewood Cliffs, New Jersey: Prentice-Hall.

Foulkes, D. (1985). *Dreaming: A cognitive-psychological analysis.* Hillsdale, New Jersey: Erlbaum.

Frankenhaeuser, M. (1979). Psychoneuroendocrine approaches to the study of emotion as related to stress and coping. In H. E. Howe & R. A. Dienstbier (Eds.), *Nebraska symposium on motivation 1978.* (pp. 123–161). Lincoln: University of Nebraska Press.

Frankl, V. E. (1960). Paradoxical intention: A logotherapeutic technique. *American Journal of Psychotherapy*, **14**, 520–525.

Frederiks, J. A. M. (1969). Disorders of the body schema. In P. J. Vinken & G. W. Bruyn (Eds.), *Handbook of clinical neurology 4. Disorders of speech perception and symbolic behavior.* (pp. 373–394). Amsterdam: Elsevier Press.

Freed, D. M. (1984). *Rate of forgetting in Alzheimer's disease.* Paper presented at the Annual Meeting of the Eastern Psychological Association, Baltimore, Maryland.

Freeman, A., & Simon, K. M. (1989). Cognitive therapy of anxiety. In A. Freeman, K. M. Simon, L. E. Beutler, & H. Arkowitz (Eds.), *Comprehensive handbook of cognitive therapy* (pp. 347–365). New York: Plenum.

Freeman, A., Simon, K. M., Beutler, L. E., & Arkovitz, H. (Eds.) (1989). *Comprehensive handbook of cognitive therapy.* New York: Plenum.

Freeman, W. J. (1979). Nonlinear gain mediating cortical stimulus–response relations. *Biological Cybernetics*, **33**, 243–247.

Freud, S. (1894/1962). The neuro-psychoses of defense. In J. Strachey (Ed.), *The standard edition of the complete psychological works of Sigmund Freud* (Vol. 3, pp. 43–68). London: Hogarth Press.

Freud, S. (1900/1975). The interpretation of dreams. In J. Strachey (Ed.), *The standard edition of the complete psychological works of Sigmund Freud* (Vols. 4 and 5). London: Hogarth Press.

Freud, S. (1901/1960). The psychopathology of everyday life. In J. Strachey (Ed.), *The standard edition of the complete psychological works of Sigmund Freud* (Vol. 6). London: Hogarth Press.

Freud, S. (1905/1953). Fragment of an analysis of a case of hysteria ("Dora"). In J. Strachey (Ed.), *The standard edition of the complete psychological works of Sigmund Freud* (Vol. 7, pp. 1–122). London: Hogarth Press.

Freud, S. (1908/1959). Character and anal erotism. In J. Strachey (Ed.), *The standard edition of the complete psychological works of Sigmund Freud* (Vol. 9, pp. 167–176). London: Hogarth Press.

Freud, S. (1909/1955). Notes upon a case of obsessional neurosis. In J. Strachey (Ed.), *The standard edition of the complete psychological works of Sigmund Freud* (Vol. 10, pp. 153–320). London: Hogarth Press.

Freud, S. (1911/1975). The unconscious. In J. Strachey (Ed.), *The standard edition of the complete psychological works of Sigmund Freud* (Vol. 14). London: Hogarth Press.

Freud, S. (1913/1958). The disposition to obsessional neurosis. In J. Strachey (Ed.), *The standard edition of the complete psychological works of Sigmund Freud* (Vol. 12, 311–326). London: Hogarth Press.

Freud, S. (1915/1925). Instincts and their vicissitudes. In J. Strachey (Ed.), *The standard edition of the complete psychological works of Sigmund Freud* (Vol. 4). London: Hogarth Press.

Freud, S. (1915b/1963). Introductory lectures on psychoanalysis (Parts 1 and 2). In J. Strachey (Ed.), *The standard edition of the complete psychological works of Sigmund Freud* (Vol. 15). London: Hogarth Press.

Freud, S. (1925/1959). An autobiographical study. In J. Strachey (Ed.), *The standard edition of the complete psychological works of Sigmund Freud.* (Vol. 20). London: Hogarth Press.

Freud, S. (1926/1959). Inhibitions, symptoms and anxiety. In J. Strachey (Ed.), *The standard edition of the complete psychological works of Sigmund Freud* (Vol. 20, pp. 77–175). London: Hogarth Press.

Freud, S. (1937/1964). Analysis terminable and interminable. In J. Strachey (Ed.), *The standard edition of the complete psychological works of Sigmund Freud* (Vol. 23, pp. 209–254). London: Hogarth Press.

Freud, S. (1940/1964). Outline of psycho-analysis. In J. Strachey (Ed.), *The standard edition of the complete psychological works of Sigmund Freud* (Vol. 23, pp. 141–207). London: Hogarth Press.

Freud, S., & Breuer, J. (1895/1955). Studies on hysteria. In J. Strachey (Ed.), *The standard edition of the complete psychological works of Sigmund Freud* (Vol. 2). London: Hogarth Press.

Fried, R. (1987). Relaxation with biofeedback-assisted guided imagery: The importance of breathing rate as an index of hypoarousal. *Biofeedback and Self Regulation,* **12**, 273–279.

Fried, R. (1990). *The breath connection.* New York: Plenum.

Frith, U. (1989). *Autism: Explaining the enigma.* Oxford: Blackwell.

Frostig, M. (1967). Testing as a basis for educational therapy. *Journal of Special Education,* **2**, 15–34.

Fuster, J. M. (1980). *The prefrontal cortex.* New York: Raven Press.

Fyer, A. J., Mannuzza, S., Martin, L. Y., Gallops, M. S., Endicott, J., Schleyer, B., Gorman, J. M., Liebowitz, M. R., & Klein, D. F. (1989). Reliability and assessment. II. Symptom agreement. *Archives of General Psychiatry,* **46**, 1102–1110.

Gabriel, E. (1989). Panic attack: The present state of it's notion. Proceedings of the World Psychiatric Association on the Psychopathology of Panic Disorders: Many faces of panic disorder (1988, Espoo, Finland). *Psychiatria Fennica, Supplement,* 47–52.

Galaburda, A. M. (1986). Animal studies and the neurology of developmental dyslexia. In G. Pavlidis & D. F. Fisher (Eds.), *Dyslexia: Its neuropsychology and treatment.* New York: Wiley.

Galaburda, A. M., Sherman, G. F., Rosen, G. D., Aboitiz, F., & Geschwind, N. (1985). Developmental dyslexia: Four consecutive patients with cortical anomalies. *Annals of Neurology,* **18**, 222–233.

Galatzer-Levy, R. M. (1988). On working through: A model from artificial intelligence. *Journal of the American Psychoanalytic Association*, **36**, 125–151.

Gallistel, E. (1985). *Multisyllable word builder.* Hamden, Connecticut: Montage Press.

Gallistel, E., Fischer, P., & Blackburn, M. (1977). *Manual: GFB sequence of objectives for teaching and testing reading.* Hamden, Connecticut: Montage Press.

Gambrell, L. B. (1984). How much time do children spend reading during teacher-directed reading instruction? In J. A. Niles & L. A. Harris (Eds.), *Changing perspectives on research in reading/language processing and instruction.* Rochester, New York: National Reading Conference.

Gardner, H. (1985). *The mind's new science: A history of the cognitive revolution.* New York: Basic Books.

Gavish, M., & Snyder, S. H. (1980). Benzodiazepine recognition sites on GABA receptors. *Nature*, **287**, 651–652.

Geraud, G., Arne-Bes, M. C., Guell, A., & Bes, A. (1987). Reversibility of hemodynamic hypofrontality in schizophrenia. *Journal of Cerebral Blood Flow and Metabolism*, **7**, 9–12.

Gergen, K. J. (1982). *Toward transformation in social knowledge.* New York: Springer-Verlag.

Germer, C. K., Efran, J. S., & Overton, W. F. (1982, April). *The Organicism-Mechanism Paradigm Inventory: Toward the measurement of metaphysical assumptions.* Paper presented at the 53rd Annual Meeting of the Eastern Psychological Association, Baltimore, MD.

Gerrig, R. J., & Bower, G. H. (1982). Emotional influences on word recognition. *Bulletin of the Psychonomic Society*, **19**, 197–200.

Gerwith, L. R., Shindler, A. G., & Hier, D. B. (1984). Altered patterns of word associations in dementia and aphasia. *Brain and Language*, **21**, 307–317.

Gerz, H. O. (1966). Experience with the logotherapeutic technique of paradoxical intention in the treatment of phobia and obsessive–compulsive patients. *American Journal of Psychiatry*, **123**, 548–553.

Geschwind, N. (1965). Disconnexion syndromes in animals and men. *Brain*, **88**, 237–294.

Gill, M. M. (1977). Psychic energy reconsidered. *Journal of the American Psychoanalytic Association*, **25**, 581–597.

Gillingham, A., & Stillman, B. (1966). *Remedial training for children with specific difficulty in reading, spelling, and penmanship* (7th ed.). Cambridge, Massachusetts: Educators Publishing Service.

Glass, A. L., & Holyoak, K. J. (1975). Alternative conceptions of semantic theory. *Cognition*, **3**, 313–339.

Glass, C. R., & Merluzzi, F. V. (1981). Cognitive assessment of social-evaluative anxiety. In T. V. Merluzzi, C. R. Glass, & M. Genest (Eds.), *Cognitive assessment* (pp. 388–438). New York: Guilford.

Goldberg, H. L. (1984). Benzodiazepine and nonbenzodiazepine anxiolytics. *Psychopathology*, **17**, 45–55.

Goldberger, E., & Rapoport, J. L. (1991). Canine acral lick dermatitis: Response to the anti-obsessional drug clomipramine. *Journal of the American Animal Hospital Association*, **27**, 179–182.

Goldfried, M. R. (1988). Application of rational restructuring to anxiety disorders. *The Counseling Psychologist*, **16**, 69–90.

Goldfried, M. R., & Robbins, C. (1983). Self-schema, cognitive bias, and the processing of therapeutic experiences. In P. C. Kendall (Ed.), *Advances in cognitive-behavioral research and therapy* (Vol. 2, pp. 33–80). New York: Academic Press.

Goldman, P. S. (1971). Functional development of the prefrontal cortex in early life and the problem of neuronal plasticity. *Experimental Neurology*, **32**, 366–387.

Goldman-Rakic, P. S. (1987). Circuitry of primate prefrontal cortex and regulation of behavior by representational memory. *Handbook of Physiology—The Nervous System,* **5,** 373–417.

Goldstein, A. J. (1978). Case conference: The treatment of a case of agoraphobia by a multifaceted treatment program. *Journal of Behavior Therapy and Experimental Psychiatry,* **9,** 45–51.

Golin, S. (1989). Schema congruence and depression: Loss of objectivity in self- and other-inferences. *Journal of Abnormal Psychology,* **98,** 495–498.

Goodglass, H., & Kaplan, D. (1983). *The assessment of aphasia and related disorders* (2nd ed.). Philadelphia: Lea and Febiger.

Goodman, K. S. (1976). Reading: A psycholinguistic guessing game. In H. Singer & R. Ruddell (Eds.), *Theoretical models and processes of reading.* Newark, Delaware: International Reading Association.

Goodman, K. S. (1986). *What's whole in whole language: A parent–teacher guide.* Portsmouth, New Hampshire: Helnemann.

Goodman, W. K., McDougle, C. J., Price, L. H., Riddle, M. A., Pauls, D. L., & Leckman, J. F. (1990). Beyond the serotonin hypothesis: A role for dopamine in some forms of obsessive–compulsive disorder? *Journal of Clinical Psychiatry,* **51 (Suppl.),** 36–43.

Goodwin, A. M., & Williams, J. M. G. (1982). Mood induction research: Its implications for clinical depression. *Behaviour Research and Therapy,* **20,** 373–382.

Goodwin, D. W., & Guze, S. B. (1989). *Psychiatric diagnosis* (4th ed.). New York: Oxford University Press.

Goren, C. C., Sarty, M., & Wu, P. Y. K. (1975). Visual following and pattern discrimination of face-like stimuli by newborn infants. *Pediatrics,* **56,** 544–549.

Gorman, J. M., Cohen, B. D., Liebowitz, M. R., Fyer, A. J., Ross, D., Davies, S. D., & Klein, D. F. (1986). Blood gas changes and hypophosphatemia in lactate-induced panic. *Archives of General Psychiatry,* **43,** 1067–1071.

Gotlib, I. H. (1981). Self-reinforcement and recall: Differential deficits in depressed and non-depressed psychiatric inpatients. *Journal of Abnormal Psychology,* **90,** 521–530.

Gotlib, I. H. (1983). Perception and recall of interpersonal feedback: Negative bias in depression. *Cognitive Therapy and Research,* **7,** 399–412.

Gotlib, I. H., & McCann, C. D. (1984). Construct accessibility and depression: An examination of cognitive and affective factors. *Journal of Personality and Social Psychology,* **47,** 427–439.

Gough, P. B., & Juel, C. (1991). The first stages of word recognition. In L. Rieben & C. A. Perfetti (Eds.), *Learning to read: Basic research and its implications.* Hillsdale, New Jersey: Erlbaum.

Grady, C., Grimes, A., Patronas, N., Sunderland, T., Foster, N., & Rapoport, S. (1989). Divided attention, as measured by dichotic speech performance, in dementia of the Alzheimer type. *Archives of Neurology,* **46,** 317–320.

Grady, C., Haxby, J., Horwitz, B., Sundaram, M., Berg, G., Schapiro, M., Freidland, R., & Rapoport, S. (1988). Longitudinal study of the early neuropsychological and cerebral metabolic changes in dementia of the Alzheimer type. *Journal of Clinical and Experimental Neuropsychology,* **10,** 576–596.

Graf, P., & Mandler, G. (1984). Activation makes words more accessible, but not necessarily more retrievable. *Journal of Verbal Learning and Verbal Behaviour,* **23,** 553–568.

Graf, P., Shimamura, A. P., & Squire, L. R. (1985). Priming across modalities and priming across category levels: Extending the domain of preserved function in amnesia. *Journal of Experimental Psychology: Learning, Memory, and Cognition,* **11,** 385–395.

Graf, P., Squire, L. R., & Mandler, G. (1984). The information that amnesiac patients do not forget. *Journal of Experimental Psychology: Learning, Memory, and Cognition,* **10,** 164–178.

Granholm, E., Asarnow, R. F., & Marder, S. R. (1991). Controlled information processing resources and the development of automatic detection responses in schizophrenia. *Journal of Abnormal Psychology*, **100**, 22–30.

Gray, C. G., & Singer, W. (1989). Stimulus specific neuronal oscillations in orientation columns in cat visual cortex. *Proceedings of the National Academy of Science (U.S.A.)*, **86**, 1698–1702.

Gray, J. A. (1990). Brain systems that mediate both emotion and cognition. *Cognition and Emotion*, **4**, 269–288.

Gray, J. A. (1982). *The neuropsychology of anxiety*. New York: Oxford University Press.

Greenberg, L. S., & Safran, J. D. (1990). *Emotion in psychotherapy*. New York: Guilford.

Greenberg, L. S., Safran, J., & Rice, L. (1989). Experiential therapy: Its relation to cognitive therapy. In A. Freeman, K. M. Simon, L. E. Beutler, & H. Arkowitz (Eds.), *Comprehensive handbook of cognitive therapy* (pp. 169–187). New York: Plenum.

Greenberg, M. S., & Beck, A. T. (1989). Depression vs. anxiety: A test of the content-specificity hypothesis. *Journal of Abnormal Psychology*, **98**, 9–13.

Greenwald, A. F. (1980). The totalitarian ego: Fabrication and revision of personal history. *American Psychologist*, **35**, 603–618.

Grimes, A., Grady, C., Foster, N., Sunderland, T., & Patronas, N. J. (1985). Central auditory function in Alzheimer's disease. *Neurology*, **35**, 352–358.

Grober, E., Buschke, H., Kawas, C., & Fuld, P. (1985). Impaired ranking of semantic attributes in dementia. *Brain and Language*, **26**, 276–286.

Grossberg, S. (1982). *Studies of mind and brain: Neural principles of learning, perception, development, cognition and motor control*. Boston: Reidel Press.

Grossberg, S. (1987). *The adaptive brain* (Vol. I, *Cognition, learning, reinforcement, and rhythm*). Amsterdam: North-Holland.

Grosz, H. J., & Zimmerman, J. A. (1965). Experimental analysis of hysterical blindness: A follow-up report and new experimental data. *Archives of General Psychiatry*, **13**, 255–260.

Grosz, H. J., & Zimmerman, J. A. (1970). A second detailed case study of functional blindness: Further demonstration of the contribution of objective psychological laboratory data. *Behavior Therapy*, **1**, 115–123.

Groth-Marnat, G. (1990). *Handbook of psychological assessment* (2nd ed.). New York: John Wiley.

Gudjonsson, G. H. (1979). The use of electrodermal responses in a case of amnesia (A case report). *Medicine, Science, and the Law*, **19**, 138–140.

Gudjonsson, G. H., & Haward, L. R. C. (1982). Case report—Hysterical amnesia as an alternative to suicide. *Medicine, Science, and the Law*, **22**, 68–72.

Guidano, V. F. (1987). *Complexity of the self: A developmental approach to psychopathology and therapy*. New York: Guilford.

Guidano, V. F. (1988). A systems-process-oriented approach to cognitive therapy. In K. S. Dobson (Ed.), *Handbook of cognitive-behavioral therapies* (pp. 307–354). New York: Guilford.

Guidano, V. F. (1990). *The self in process: Toward a postrationalist cognitive therapy*. New York: Guilford.

Gurnani, P. D., & Wang, M. (1990). Some reservations concerning the current cognitive emphasis in therapy. *Counselling Psychology Quarterly*, **3**, 21–41.

Haith, M. M., Hazan, C., & Goodman, G. S. (1988). Expectation and anticipation of dynamic visual events by 3.5-month old babies. *Child Development*, **59**, 467–479.

Hall, N. S., & O'Grady, M. (1991). Psychosocial interventions and immune function. In R. Ader, D. L. Felten, & N. Cohen (Eds.), *Psychoneuroimmunology* (2nd ed., pp. 1067–1080). San Diego: Academic Press.

Hamilton, E. W., & Abramson, L. Y. (1983). Cognitive patterns and major depressive disorder: A longitudinal study in a hospital setting. *Journal of Abnormal Psychology*, **92**, 173–184.

Hammen, C. L. (1983a). Cognitive and social processes in bipolar affective disorders: A neglected topic. In C. L. Hammen (Ed.), *Research issues and opportunities in bipolar affective disorder.* Symposium presented at the meeting of the American Psychological Association, Anaheim, California.

Hammen, C. L. (1985). Predicting depression. In P. C. Kendall (Ed.), *Advances in cognitive-behavioral research and therapy* Vol. 4. New York: Academic Press.

Hammen, C. L., Marks, T., deMayo, R., & Mayol, A. (1985a). Self-schemas and risk for depression: A prospective study. *Journal of Personality and Social Psychology,* **49,** 1147–1159.

Hammen, C. L., Marks, T., Mayol, A., & deMayo, R. (1985b). Depressive self-schemas, life stress, and vulnerability to depression. *Journal of Abnormal Psychology,* **94,** 308–319.

Hammen, C. L., Miklowitz, D. J., & Dyck, D. (1986). Stability and severity parameters of depression self schema responding. *Journal of Social and Clinical Psychology.* **4,** 23–45.

Hammen, C. L., & Zupan, B. A. (1984). Self-schemas, depression, and the processing of personal information in children. *Journal of Experimental Child Psychology,* **37,** 598–608.

Hammill, D. D. (1972). Training visual perceptual processes. *Journal of Learning Disabilities,* **5,** 552–559.

Hampl, S., Scott, W., Carmin, C., & Fleming, B. (1990). *Phobia Practice and Research Journal,* **3,** 27–32.

Hanson, S. J., & Burr, D. J. (1990). What connectionist models learn: Learning and representation in connectionist networks. *Behavioural and Brain Sciences,* **13,** 471–518.

Hanson, V. L. (1989). Phonology and reading: Evidence from profoundly deaf readers. In D. Shankweiler & I. Y. Liberman (Eds.), *Phonology and reading disability: Solving the reading puzzle.* Ann Arbor: University of Michigan Press.

Harré, R. (1988). Wittgenstein and artificial intelligence. *Philosophical Psychology,* **1,** 105–115.

Harrold, R. M. (1988). *Object naming in Alzheimer's disease: What is the cognitive deficit?* Paper presented at the 96th annual meeting of the American Psychological Association, Atlanta, Georgia.

Hart, R. P., Kwentus, J. A., Taylor, J. R., & Harkins, S. W. (1987). Rate of forgetting in dementia and depression. *Journal of Consulting and Clinical Psychology,* **55,** 101–105.

Hartley, D. (1991). Assessing interpersonal behavior patterns using Structural Analysis of Social Behavior (SASB). In M. J. Horowitz (Ed.), *Person schemas and maladaptive interpersonal patterns* (pp. 221–260). Chicago: University of Chicago Press.

Harvey, P. D. (1983). Speech competence in manic and schizophrenic psychoses: The association between clinically rated thought disorder and cohesion and reference performance. *Journal of Abnormal Psychology,* **92(3),** 368–377.

Hashtroudi, S., Parker, E. S., Delisi, L. E., Wyatt, R. J., & Mutter, S. A. (1984). Intact retention in acute alcohol amnesia. *Journal of Experimental Psychology: Learning, Memory and Cognition,* **10,** 156–163.

Head, H., & Holmes, G. (1911). Sensory disturbances from cerebral lesions. *Brain,* **34,** 102–254.

Hebb, D. O. (1946). On the nature of fear. *Psychological Review,* **53,** 259–276.

Henley, S. H. A. (1986). Perceptual defense: A paradigm for investigating psychopathology. In U. Hentschel, G. Smith, & J. G. Draguns (Eds.), *The roots of perception.* Amsterdam: Elsevier.

Henley, S. H. A., & Dixon, N. F. (1976). Preconscious processing in schizophrenics: An exploratory investigation. *British Journal of Medical Psychology,* **49,** 161–166.

Hier, D. B., Hagenlocker, K., & Shindler, A. G. (1985). Language disintegration in dementia: Effects of etiology and severity. *Brain and Language,* **25,** 117–133.

Higgins, E. T. (1987). Self-discrepancy: A theory relating self and affect. *Psychological Review,* **94,** 319–340.

Higgins, E. T. (1990). Personality, social psychology, and person–situation relations: Standards and knowledge activation as a common language. In L. A. Pervin (Ed.), *Handbook of personality theory and research* (pp. 301–338). New York: Guilford.

Higgins, E. T., & Bargh, J. A. (1987). Social cognition and social perception. *Annual Review of Psychology*, **38**, 369–425.

Highlen, P. S., & Hill, C. E. (1984). Factors affecting client change in individual counseling: Current status and theoretical speculations. In S. D. Brown & R. W. Lent (Eds.), *Handbook of counseling psychology* (pp. 334–396). New York: Wiley.

Hilgard, E. R. (1977). *Divided consciousness: Multiple controls in human thought and action.* New York: Wiley-Interscience.

Hilgard, E. R., & Marquis, D. G. (1940). *Conditioning and learning.* New York: Appleton-Century-Crofts.

Hiller, W., Zaudig, M., von Bose, M., & Rummler, R. (1989). Anxiety disorders: A comparison of the ICD-9 and DSM-III-R classification systems. *Acta Psychiatrica Scandinavica*, **79**, 338–347.

Himle, J. A., Himle, D. P., & Thyer, B. A. (1989). Irrational beliefs and the anxiety disorders. *Journal of Rational Emotive and Cognitive Behavior Therapy*, **7**, 155–165.

Hinton, G. E., & Shallice, T. (1991). Lesioning an attractor network: Investigations of acquired dyslexia. *Psychological Review*, **98**, 74–95.

Hirsh-Pasek, K., Kemler Nelson, D. G., Jusczyk, P. W., Wright, K., Druss, B., & Kennedy, L. J. (1987). Clauses are perceptual units for young infants. *Cognition*, **26**, 269–286.

Hockey, G. R. J. (1970). Effect of loud noise on attentional selectivity. *Quarterly Journal of Experimental Psychology*, **22**, 28–36.

Hodgson, R. J., & Rachman, S. (1972). The effects of contamination and washing in obsessional patients. *Behaviour Research and Therapy*, **10**, 11–117.

Hoffman, R. E. (1987). Computer simulation of neural information processing and the schizophrenia-mania dichotomy. *Archives of General Psychiatry*, **44**, 178–188.

Hoffman, J. V., O'Neal, S. F., Kastler, L. A., Clements, R. O., Segel, K. W., & Nash, M. F. (1984). Guided oral reading and miscue focused verbal feedback in second-grade classrooms. *Reading Research Quarterly*, **19**, 367–384.

Holender, D. (1986). Semantic activation without conscious identification in dichotic listening, parafoveal vision, and visual masking: A survey and appraisal. *The Behavioral and Brain Sciences*, **9**, 1–66.

Hollander, E., DeCaria, C. M., & Liebowitz, M. R. (1989). Biological aspects of obsessive–compulsive disorder. *Psychiatric Annals*, **19**, 80–87.

Hollander, E., DeCaria, C. M., Gully, R., Nitesen, A., Suckow, R. F., Gorman, J. M., Klein, D. F., & Liebowitz, M. R. (1990). Effects of chronic fluoxetine treatment on behavioral and neurodendocrine responses to meta-chloro-phenylpiperazine in obsessive–compulsive disorder. *Psychiatry Research*, **36**, 1–17.

Hollander, E., DeCaria, C. M., Nitesen, A., Gully, R., Suckow, R. F., Cooper, T. B., Gorman, J. M., Klein, D. F., & Liebowitz, M. R. (1992). Serotonergic function in obsessive–compulsive disorder. *Archives of General Psychiatry*, **49**, 21–28.

Hollander, E., Fay, M., Cohen, B., Campeas, R., Gorman, J. M., & Liebowitz, M. R. (1988). Serotonergic and noradrenergic sensitivity in obsessive-compulsive disorder: Behavioral findings. *American Journal of Psychiatry*, **145**, 1015–1017.

Hollander, E., Liebowitz, M. R., & Rosen, W. G. (1991). Neuropsychiatric and neuropsychological studies in obsessive–compulsive disorder. In *The psychobiology of obsessive-compulsive disorder.* J. Zohar, T. Insel, and S. Rasmussen (Eds.) pp. 126–145. New York: Springer.

Hollander, E., Schiffman, E., Cohen, B., Rivera-Stein, M., Rosen, W., Gorman, J. M., Fyer, A., Papp, L., & Liebowitz, M. R. (1990). Signs of central nervous dysfunction in obsessive–compulsive disorder. *Archives of General Psychiatry*, **47**, 27–32.

Hollon, S. D., & Beck, A. T. (1979). Cognitive therapy for depression. In P. C. Kendall & S. D. Hollon (Eds.), *Cognitive-behavioral interventions: Theory, research, and procedures* (pp. 153–204). New York: Academic Press.

Hollon, S. D., Kendall, P. C., & Lumry, A. (1986). Specificity of depressotypic cognition in clinical depression. *Journal of Abnormal Psychology,* **95**, 52–59.

Hollon, S. D., & Kriss, M. R. (1984). Cognitive factors in clinical research and practice. *Clinical Psychology Review,* **4**, 35–76.

Holmes, D. S. (1974). Investigations of repression: Differential recall of material experimentally or naturally associated with ego threat. *Psychological Bulletin,* **81**, 632–653.

Holmes, T. H., & Rahe, R. H. (1967). The social readjustment rating scale. *Journal for Psychosomatic Research,* **11**, 213–219.

Holt, P. E., & Andrews, G. (1989). Three elements of the panic reaction in four anxiety disorders. *Behaviour Research and Therapy,* **27**, 253–261.

Holt, R. (1964). The emergence of cognitive psychology. *Journal of the American Psychoanalytic Association,* **12**, 650–665.

Hope, D. A., Rapee, R. M., Heimberg, R. G., & Dombeck, M. J. (1990). Representations of the self in social phobia: Vulnerability to social threat. *Cognitive Therapy and Research,* **14**, 177–189.

Horney, K. (1945). *Our inner conflicts: A constructive theory of neurosis.* New York: Norton.

Horowitz, M. J. (1988a). Psychodynamic phenomena and their explanation. In M. J. Horowitz (Ed.), *Psychodynamics and cognition.* (pp. 3–20). Chicago: University of Chicago Press.

Horowitz, M. J. (1988b). *Introduction to psychodynamics.* New York: Basic Books.

Horowitz, M. J. (1991). Person schemas. In M. J. Horowitz (Ed.) *Person schemas and maladaptive interpersonal patterns.* (pp. 13–32). Chicago: University of Chicago Press.

Horowitz, M. J., Merluzzi, T. V., Ewert, M., Ghannan, J. H., Hartley, D., & Stenson, C. H. (1991). Role–relationship models configuration (RRMC). In M. J. Horowitz (Ed.), *Person schemas and maladaptive interpersonal patterns* (pp. 115–154). Chicago: University of Chicago Press.

Horton, K. D., & Petruk, R. (1980). Set differentiation and depth of processing in the directed forgetting paradigm. *Journal of Experimental Psychology: Human Learning and Memory,* **6**, 599–610.

Howard, G. S. (1986). *Dare we develop a human science?* Notre Dame, Indiana: Academic Publications.

Howard, G. S. (1991). Culture tales: A narrative approach to thinking, cross-cultural psychology, and psychotherapy. *American Psychologist,* **46**, 187–197.

Huey, S. R., & Sechrest, L. (1983). Hyperventilation syndrome and pathology. *Psychological Documents,* **13**, 25–26.

Huff, F. J., Corkin, S., & Growdon, J. H. (1986). Semantic impairment and anomia in Alzheimer's disease. *Brain and Language,* **28**, 235–249.

Huff, F. J., Mack, L., Mahlmann, J., & Greenberg, S. (1988). A comparison of lexical-semantic impairments in left hemispheric stroke and Alzheimer's disease. *Brain and Language,* **34**, 262–278.

Huppert, F. A., & Piercy, M. (1979). Normal and abnormal forgetting in amnesia: Effect of locus of lesion. *Cortex,* **15**, 385–390.

Ingram, R. E. (1984a). Information processing and feedback: Effects of mood and information favorability on the cognitive processing of personally relevant information. *Cognitive Therapy and Research,* **8**, 371–386.

Ingram, R. E. (1984b). Toward an information precessing analysis of depression. *Cognitive Therapy and Research,* **8**, 443–478.

Ingram, R. E. (Ed.) (1986). *Information processing approaches to clinical psychology.* New York: Academic Press.

Ingram, R. E. (1991). *Cognitive constructs, information processing, and depression.* Paper presentation at the meeting of the American Psychological Association.

Ingram, R. E., & Hollon, S. D. (1986) Cognitive therapy of depression from an information processing perspective. In R. Ingram (Ed.), *Information processing approaches to clinical psychology.* (pp. 261–284). New York: Academic Press.

Ingram, R. E., & Kendall, P. C. (1986). Cognitive clinical psychology: Implications of an information processing perspective. In R. E. Ingram (Ed.), *Information processing approaches to clinical psychology.* (pp. 3–21). New York: Academic Press.

Ingram, R. E., & Kendall, D. C. (1987). The cognitive side of anxiety. *Cognitive Therapy and Research,* **11**(5), 523–536.

Ingram, R. E., Lumry, A. E., Cruet, D., & Sieber, W. (1987). Attentional processes in depressive disorders. *Cognitive Therapy and Research,* **11**, 351–360.

Ingram, R. E., Smith, T. W., & Brehm, S. S. (1983). Depression and information processing: Self-schemata and the encoding of self-referent information. *Journal of Personality and Social Psychology,* **45**, 412–420.

Ingram, R. E., & Wisnicki, K. (1991). Cognition in depression. In P. A. Magaro (Ed.), *Cognitive bases of mental disorders* (pp. 187–230). Newbury Park: Sage.

Ingvar, D. H., & Franzen, G. (1974). Abnormalities of cerebral flow distribution in patients with chronic schizophrenia. *Acta Psychiatlica Scandinavica,* **50**, 425–462.

Ivey, A. E. (1986). *Developmental therapy: Theory into practice.* San Francisco: Jossey-Bass.

Ivey, A. E., Ivey, M. B., & Simek-Downing, L. (1987). *Counseling and psychotherapy: Integrating skills, theory, and practice.* Englewood Cliffs, New Jersey: Prentice-Hall.

Jacobs, W. J. (1987). *An algebraic model of conditioning: The interaction between representation and motivation.* Invited paper presented to the Spring Conference on Behavior and Brain: Second Meeting, Banff, Alberta.

Jacobs, W. J., & Blackburn, J. R. (in press). A model for Pavlovian conditioning: Variations in representations of the unconditional stimulus. *Integrative Physiology and Behavioral Science.*

Jacobs, W. J., & Nadel, L. (1985). Stress-induced recovery of fears and phobias. *Psychological Review,* **92**, 512–531.

Jacobs, W. J., & Nadel, L. (in preparation). *The neurobiology of panic and agoraphobia: The role of development and experience.* Manuscript available on request.

Jacobson, E. (1938). *Progressive relaxation.* Chicago: University of Chicago Press.

Jacoby, L. L., & Dallas, M. (1981). On the relationship between autobiographical memory and perceptual learning. *Journal of Experimental Psychology: General,* **110**, 306–340.

Jacoby, L. L., & Witherspoon, D. (1982). Remembering without awareness. *Canadian Journal of Psychology,* **36**, 300–324.

James, W. (1890). *Principles of psychology.* New York: Holt.

Janet, P. (1889). [*Psychological automatisms.*] Paris: Alcan.

Janet, P. (1893). L'amnesie continue [Continuous amnesia]. *Revue Generale Des Sciences,* **4**, 167–179.

Janet, P. (1901). *The mental state of hystericals: A study of mental stigmata and mental accidents.* New York: Putnam.

Janet, P. (1907). *The major symptoms of hysteria.* New York: Macmillan.

Janet, P. (1930). Pierre Janet. In C. Murchison (Ed.), *A history of psychology in autobiography* (Vol. 1, pp. 123–133). Worcester, Massachusetts: Clark University Press.

Jeffress, L. A. (Ed) (1951). *Cerebral mechanisms in behavior. The Hixon symposium.* New York: John Wiley.

Johnson, E., & Tversky, A. (1983). Affect, generalisation and the perception of risk. *Journal of Personality and Social Psychology,* **45**, 181–186.

Johnson, J. A., Germer, C. K., Efran, J. S., & Overton, W. F. (1988). Personality as the basis for theoretical predilections. *Journal of Personality and Social Psychology,* **55**, 824–835.

Johnson, J. E., Petzel, T. P., Hartney, L. M., & Morgan, R. A. (1983). Recall of importance ratings of completed and uncompleted tasks as a function of depression. *Cognitive Therapy and Research,* **7,** 51–56.

Johnson, M. H. (1988). Memories of mother. *New Scientist,* **160,** 60–62.

Johnson, M. H. (1990a). Cortical maturation and the development of visual attention in early infancy. *Journal of Cognitive Neuroscience,* **2,** 81–95.

Johnson, M. H. (1990b). Cortical maturation and perceptual development. In H. Bloch & B. Bertenthal (Eds.), *Sensory motor organisation and development in infancy and early childhood.* Dordrecht: Kluwer Academic Press (NATO series).

Johnson, M. H. (1991) Information processing and storage during filial imprinting. In P. G. Hepper (Ed.), *Kin recognition.* Cambridge: Cambridge University Press.

Johnson, M. H. (in press). Dissociating components of visual attention: A neurodevelopmental approach. In M. Farah & G. Radcliffe (Eds.), *The neural basis of high-level vision.* Hillsdale, New Jersey: Erlbaum.

Johnson, M. H., Dziurawiec, S., Bartrip, J., & Morton, J. (1992). The effects of movement of internal features on infants' preferences for face-like stimuli. *Infant Behavior and Development,* **15.**

Johnson, M. H., Dziurawiec, S., Ellis, H. D., & Morton, J. (1991b). Newborns preferential tracking of face-like stimuli and its subsequent decline. *Cognition,* **40,** 1–19.

Johnson, M. H., & Leslie, A. M. (1992). *A neural circuit account of the ontogeny of "theory of mind".* Unpublished manuscript.

Johnson, M. H., & Morton, J. (1991). *Biology and cognitive development: The case of face recognition.* Oxford: Blackwell.

Johnson, M. H., Posner, M. I., & Rothbart, M. K. (1991a). Components of orientating in early infancy: Contingency learning, anticipatory looking, and disengaging. *Journal of Cognitive Neuroscience,* **3,** 335–344.

Johnson, M. H., Siddons, F., Frith, U., & Morton, J. (1992). Can autism be predicted on the basis of infant screening tests? *Developmental Medicine and Child Neurology.* **00,** 0–00.

Johnson, M. K., & Hasher, L. (1987). Human learning and memory. *Annual Review of Psychology,* **38,** 631–668.

Johnson, M. K., Kim, J. K., & Risse, G. (1985). Do alcoholic Korsakoff's syndrome patients acquire affective reactions? *Journal of Experimental Psychology: Learning, Memory, and Cognition,* **11,** 27–36.

Johnson-Laird, P. N. (1983). *Mental models: Towards a cognitive science of language, inference and consciousness.* Cambridge: Cambridge University Press.

Johnson-Laird, P. N. (1988). *The computer and the mind: An introduction to cognitive science.* Cambridge: Harvard University Press.

Johnson-Laird, P. N., & Wason, P. C. (1970). A theoretical analysis of insight into a reasoning task. *Cognitive Psychology,* **1,** 134–148.

Jordan, M. I., & Rosenbaum, D. A. (1962). Action. In M. I. Posner (Ed.), *The foundations of cognitive science.* (pp. 727–768). Cambridge: MIT Press.

Jorgensen, R. S., & Houston, B. K. (1981). The Type A behavior pattern, sex differences, and cardiovascular response to and recovery from stress. *Motivation and Emotion,* **5,** 201–214.

Jorm, A. F. (1986). Controlled and automatic information processing in senile dementia: A review. *Psychological Medicine,* **16,** 77–88.

Jusczyk, P. W., & Bertoncini, J. (1988). Viewing the development of speech perception as an innately guided learning process. *Language and Speech,* **31,** 217–238.

Kagan, J. (1989). Temperamental contributions to social behavior. *American Psychologist,* **44,** 668–674.

Kamin, L. J. (1969). Selective association and conditioning. In N. J. Mackintosh & W. K. Honig (Eds.), *Fundamental issues in associative learning* (pp. 42–64). Halifax: Dalhousie University Press.

Kanfer, F. H., & Hagerman, S. M. (1986). Behavior therapy and the information-processing paradigm. In S. Reiss & R. R. Bootzin (Eds.), *Theoretical issues in behavior therapy* (pp. 3–33). Orlando, Florida: Academic Press.

Kant, I. (1969). *Critique of pure reason.* New York: St. Martin's Press. (Originally published 1791).

Kaplan, E., Goodglass, H., & Weintraub, S. (1983). *The Boston naming test.* Philadelphia: Lea and Febiger.

Karmiloff-Smith, A. (1990). Innate constraints and developmental change. In S. Carey & R. Gelman (Eds.), *Epigenisis of mind: Essays in biology and knowledge.* Hillsdale, New Jersey: Erlbaum.

Karmiloff-Smith, A. (1992). *Beyond modularity. A developmental perspective on cognitive science.* Cambridge: MIT Press.

Kaszniak, A. W., Garron, D. C., & Fox, J. (1979). Differential aspects of age and cerebral atrophy upon span of immediate recall and paired associate learning in older patients with suspected dementia. *Cortex, 15,* 285–295.

Kaszniak, A. W., Nussbaum, P. D., Berren, M. R., & Santiago, J. (1988). Amnesia as a consequence of male rape: A case report. *Journal of Abnormal Psychology, 97,* 100–104.

Katz, J. (1962). The use of staggered spondaic words for assessing the integrity of the central auditory nervous system. *Journal of Auditory Research, 2,* 327–337.

Katz, J. J., & Fodor, J. A. (1963). The structure of semantic theory. *Language, 39,* 170–210.

Katz, R. B., Shankweiler, D., & Liberman, I. (1981). Memory for item order and phonetic recoding in the beginning reader. *Journal of Experimental Child Psychology, 32,* 474–484.

Kaye, K., & Fogel, A. (1980). The temporal structure of face to face communication between mothers and infants. *Developmental Psychology, 16,* 454–464.

Kegan, R. (1982). *The evolving self: Problem and process in human development.* Cambridge: Harvard University Press.

Kelly, G. (1955). *The psychology of personal constructs.* New York: Norton.

Kelly, M. S., Best, C. T., & Kirk, U. (1989). Cognitive processing deficits in reading disabilities: A prefrontal cortical hypothesis. *Brain and Cognition, 11,* 275–293.

Kempler, D., Curtiss, S., & Jackson, C. (1987). Syntactic preservation in Alzheimer's disease. *Aphasiology, 2,* 147–159.

Kenardy, J., Evans, L., & Oei, T. P. (1989). Cognitions and heart rate in panic disorders during everyday activity. *Journal of Anxiety Disorders, 3,* 33–43.

Kenardy, J., Evans, L., & Oei, T. P. (1990). Attributional style and panic disorder. *Journal of Behavior Therapy and Experimental Psychiatry, 21,* 9–13.

Kendall, P. C. (Ed.) (1983). *Advances in cognitive-behavioral research and therapy* (Vol. 2). New York: Academic Press.

Kendall, P. C., & Ingram, R. E. (1987). The future for cognitive assessment of anxiety: Let's get specific. In L. Michelson & M. Archer (Eds.), *Cognitive-behavioral assessment and treatment of anxiety disorders* (pp. 89–104). New York: Guilford.

Kennerley, H. (1990). *Managing anxiety: A training manual.* New York: Oxford University Press.

Kessen, W., & Mandler, G. (1961). Anxiety, pain, and the inhibition of distress. *Psychological Review, 68,* 396–404.

Kettl, P. A., & Marks, I. (1986). Neurological factors in obsessive compulsive disorder: Two case reports and a review of the literature. *British Journal of Psychiatry, 149,* 315–319.

Kihlstrom, J. F. (1984). Conscious, subconscious, unconscious: A cognitive perspective. In K. S. Bowers & D. Meichenbaum (Eds.), *The unconscious reconsidered* (pp. 149–211). New York: Wiley-Interscience.

Kihlstrom, J. F. (1987). The cognitive unconscious. *Science, 237,* 1445–1452.

Kihlstrom, J. F. (1990). The psychological unconscious. In L. Pervin (Ed.), *Handbook of personality: Theory and research* (pp. 445–464). New York: Guilford.

Kihlstrom, J. F. (1991). Dissociation and dissociations: A comment on consciousness and cognition. *Consciousness and Cognition, 1(1),* 47–53.

Kihlstrom, J. F., & Klein, S. B. (1992). The self as a knowledge structure. In R. S. Wyer & T. K. Srull (Eds.), *Handbook of social cognition* (in press). Hillsdale, New Jersey: Erlbaum.

Kihlstrom, J. F., Barnhardt, T. R., & Tataryn, D. J. (1991). Implicit perception. In R. Bornstein & T. S. Pittman (Eds.), *Perception without awareness* (in press). New York: Guilford.

Kihlstrom, J. F., & Cantor, N. (1984). Mental representations of self. In L. Berkowitz (Ed.), *Advances in experimental social psychology* (Vol. 17, pp. 1–47). New York: Academic Press.

Kihlstrom, J. F., Cantor, N., Albright, J. S., Chew, B. R., Klein, S. B., & Niedenthal, P. M. (1988). Information processing and the study of the self. In L. Berkowitz (Ed.), *Advances in experimental social psychology* (Vol. 21, pp. 145–177). San Diego: Academic Press.

Kihlstrom, J. F., & Cunningham, R. L. (1991). Mapping interpersonal space. In M. J. Horowitz (Ed.), *Person schemas and maladaptive interpersonal patterns* (pp. 331–338). Chicago: University of Chicago Press.

Kihlstrom, J. F., & Evans, F. J. (1979). *Functional disorders of memory.* Hillsdale, New Jersey: Erlbaum.

Kihlstrom, J. F., & McGlynn, S. M. (1991). Experimental research in clinical psychology. In M. Hersen, A. E. Kazdin, & A. S. Bellack (Eds.), *Clinical psychology handbook* (2nd ed, pp. 239–257). New York: Pergamon.

Kihlstrom, J. F., & Nasby, W. (1981). Cognitive tasks in clinical assessment: An exercise in applied psychology. In P. C. Kendall & S. D. Hollon (Eds.), *Assessment strategies for cognitive-behavioral interventions,* (pp. 287–317). New York: Academic Press.

Kihlstrom, J. F., Tataryn, D. J., & Hoyt, I. P. (1990). Dissociative disorders. In P. B. Sutker & H. E. Adams (Eds.), *Comprehensive handbook of psychopathology* 2nd ed. New York: Plenum.

Kiecolt-Glaser, J. K., & Glaser, R. (1991). Stress and immune function in humans. In R. Ader, D. L. Felten, & N. Cohen (Eds.), *Psychoneuroimmunology* (2nd ed., pp. 849–868). San Diego: Academic Press.

Kinton, G. E., & Shallice, T. (1991). Lesioning an attractor network: Investigations of acquired dyslexia. *Psychological Review, 98,* 74–95.

Kirsner, K., Milech, D., & Standen, P. (1983). Common and modality-specific processes in the mental lexicon. *Memory and Cognition, 11,* 621–630.

Klatzky, R. L., Pellegrino, J. W., McCloskey, B. P., & Doherty, S. (1989). Can you squeeze a tomato? The role of motor representations in semantic sensibility judgments. *Journal of Memory and Language, 28,* 56–77.

Klein, D. F., & Klein, H. M. (1989). The utility of the panic disorder concept. *European Archives of Psychiatry and Neurological Sciences, 238,* 268–279.

Kluft, R. P., Steinberg, M., & Spitzer, R. (1988). DSM-IIIR revisions in the dissociative disorders: An exploration of their derivation and rationale. *Dissociation, 1,* 39–46.

Knutsson, E., & Martensson, A. (1985). Isokinetic measurements of muscle strength in hysterical paresis. *Electroencephalography and Clinical Neurophysiology, 61,* 370–374.

Koch, S. (1981). The nature and limits of psychological knowledge. *American Psychologist, 36,* 257–269.

Kokmen, E., Chandra, V., & Schoenberg, B. (1988). Trends in incidence of dementing illness in Rochester, Minnesota, in three quinquennial periods, 1960–1974. *Neurology, 38,* 975–980.

Kolb, B., & Whishaw, I. Q. (1983). Performance of schizophrenic patients on tests sensitive to left or right frontal, temporal, or parietal function in neurologic patients. *Journal of Mental and Nervous Disease, 171,* 435–443.

Kolb, B., & Wishaw, I. Q. (1990). *Fundamentals of human neuropsychology* (3rd ed.). New York: Freeman.

Kolers, P. A. (1975). Memorial consequences of automatized encoding. *Journal of Experimental Psychology: Human Learning and Memory, 1,* 689–701.

Kolers, P. A. (1976). Reading a year later. *Journal of Experimental Psychology: Human Learning and Memory, 2*, 554–565.

Kopelman, M. D. (1985). Rates of forgetting in Alzheimer-type dementia and Korsakoff's syndrome. *Neuropsychologia, 23*, 623–638.

Kopelman, M. D. (1989). Remote and autobiographical memory, temporal context memory and frontal atrophy in Korsakoff and Alzheimer patients. *Neuropsychologia, 27*, 437–460.

Kopelman, M. D., Wilson, and Baddeley (in press).

Koriat, A., Lichtenstein, S., & Fischoff, B. (1980). Reasons for confidence. *Journal of Experimental Psychology: Human Learning and Memory, 6*, 107–118.

Kornetsky, C. (1972). The use of a simple test of attention as a measure of drug effects in schizophrenic patients. *Psychopharmacologia (Berlin), 8*, 99–106.

Kovacs, M., & Beck, A. T. (1988). Maladaptive cognitive structures in depression. *American Journal of Psychiatry, 135*, 525–523.

Krames, L., & MacDonald, M. R. (1985). Distraction and depressive cognitions. *Cognitive Therapy and Research, 9*, 561–573.

Kuiper, N. A., & Derry, P. A. (1982). Depressed and nondepressed content self-reference in mild depressive. *Journal of Personality, 50*, 67–79.

Kuiper, N. A., Derry, P. A., & MacDonald, M. R. (1982). Self-reference and person perception in depression. In G. Weary & H. Mirels (Eds.), *Integrations of clinical and social psychology*. London: Oxford University Press.

Kuiper, N. A., & Rogers, T. B. (1981). Convergent evidence for the self as a cognitive prototype: The "inverted-URT effect" for the self and other judgments. *Personality and Social Psychology Bulletin, 7*, 438–443.

Kunst-Wilson, W. R., & Zajonc, R. B. (1980). Affective discrimination of stimuli that cannot be recognized. *Science, 207*, 557–558.

Kuoppasalmi, K., Lonnqvist, J., Pylkkanen, K., & Huttunen, M. O. (1989). Classification of mental disorders in Finland: A comparison of the Finnish classification of mental disorders in 1987 with DSM-III-R. *Psychiatria Fennica, 20*, 65–81.

LaBerge, D., & Samuels, S. J. (1974). Toward a theory of automatic information processing in reading. *Cognitive Psychology, 6*, 293–323.

LaBerge, D. L., & Lawrence, D. H. (1957). Two methods for generating forms of graded similarity. *Journal of Psychology, 43*, 77–100.

Lachman, R., & Lachman, J. L. (1986). Information processing psychology: Origins and extensions. In R. Ingram (Ed.), *Information processing approaches to clinical psychology*. New York: Academic Press.

Lachman, R., Lachman, J. L., & Butterfield, E. C. (1979). *Cognitive psychology and information processing: An introduction*. Hillsdale, New Jersey: Erlbaum.

LaFleche, G., & Albert, M. S. (1991). Deficits on "frontal" tasks in early Alzheimer's disease. *Journal of Clinical and Experimental Neuropsychology, 13*, 50.

Lakoff, G. (1980). Whatever happened to deep structure? *The Behavioral and Brain Sciences, 3*, 22–23.

Lakoff, G. (1987). *Women, fire, and dangerous things: What categories reveal about the mind*. Chicago: University of Chicago Press.

Lang, P. J. (1970). Stimulus control, response control, and desensitization of fear. In D. Levis (Ed.), *Learning approaches to therapeutic behavior change*. Chicago: Aldine.

Lang, P. J. (1977). Imagery in therapy: An information processing analysis of fear. *Behavior Therapy, 8*, 862–886.

Lang, P. J. (1985). The cognitive psychophysiology of emotion: Fear and anxiety. In A. H. Tuma & J. D. Maser (Eds.), *Anxiety and the anxiety disorders*. Hillsdale, New Jersey: Erlbaum.

Laraia, M. T., Stuart, G. W., & Best, C. L. (1989). Behavioral treatment of panic-related disorders: A review. *Archives of Psychiatric Nursing, 3*, 125–133.

Larsen, S. F., & Fromholt, P. (1976). Mnemonic organization and free recall in schizophrenia. *Journal of Abnormal Psychology*, **85**, 61–65.

Lazarus, R. S. (1991). *Emotion and adaptation.* New York: Oxford University Press.

Lehky, S. R., & Sejnowski, T. J. (1988). Network model of shape-from-shading; Neural function arises from both receptive and projective fields. *Nature*, **333**, 452–454.

Leslie, A. M. (1987). Pretense and representation in infancy: The origins of 'theory of mind.' *Psychological Review*, **94**, 84–106.

Levin, S. (1984). Frontal lobe dysfunctions in schizophrenia—II. Impairments of psychological and brain functions. *Journal of Psychiatry Research*, **18(1)**, 57–72.

Levis, D. J. (1987). Treating anxiety and panic attacks: The conflict model of implosive therapy. *Journal of Integrative and Eclectic Psychotherapy*, **6**, 450–461.

Levy, R., & Behrman, J. (1970). Cortical evoked responses in hysterical hemianaesthesia. *Electroencephalography and Clinical Neurophysiology*, **29**, 400–402.

Levy, R., & Mushin, J. (1973). The somatosensory evoked response in patients with hysterical anaesthesia. *Journal of Psychosomatic Research*, **17**, 81–84.

Lewicki, P. (1986). Processing information about covariations that cannot be articulated. *Journal of Experimental Psychology: Learning, Memory, and Cognition*, **12**, 135–146.

Lewinsohn, P. M., Bergquist, W. H., & Brelje, T. (1972). The repression–sensitization dimension and emotional response to stimuli. *Psychological Reports*, **31**, 707–716.

Lewinsohn, P. M., Hoberman, H., Teri, L., & Hautzinger, M. (1985). An integrative theory of depression. In S. Reiss & R. Bootzin (Eds.), *Theoretical issues in behavior therapy.* New York: Academic Press.

Lewinsohn, P. M., Mischel, W., Chaplin, W., & Barton, R. (1980). Social competence and depression: The role of illusory self-perceptions? *Journal of Abnormal Psychology*, **89**, 203–212.

Lewinsohn, P. M., Steinmetz, J. L., Larson, D. W., & Franklin, J. (1981). Depression related cognition: Antecedents or consequence? *Journal of Abnormal Psychology*, **91**, 213–219.

Ley, R. (1988a). Panic attacks during sleep: A hyperventilation-probability model. *Journal of Behavior Therapy*, **19**, 181–192.

Ley, R. (1988b). Panic attacks during relaxation and relaxation-induced anxiety: A hyperventilation interpretation. *Journal of Behavior Therapy*, **19**, 253–259.

Ley, R. (1989). Dyspneic-fear and catastrophic cognitions in hyperventilatory panic attacks. *Behavior Research and Therapy*, **27**, 549–554.

Liberman, A. (1989). Reading is hard just because listening is easy. In C. von Euler (Ed.), *Wenner-Gren international symposium series: Brain and reading.* (pp. 197–205). Hampshire, England: Macmillan.

Liberman, I. Y. (1989). Phonology and beginning reading revisited. In C. von Euler (Ed.), *Wenner-Gren international symposium series: Brain and reading.* (pp. 207–220). Hampshire, England: Macmillan.

Liberman, I. Y., & Liberman, A. (1990). Whole language vs. code emphasis: Underlying assumptions and their implications for reading instruction. *Bulletin of the Orton Society*, **40**, 51–76.

Lick, J., & Bootzin, R. (1975). Expectancy factors in the treatment of fear: Methodological and theoretical issues. *Psychological Bulletin*, **82**, 917–931.

Lickey, M. E., & Gordon, B. (1983). *Drugs for mental illness.* San Francisco: Freeman.

Liebert, R. S. (1984). An exploration of concepts of character. *Bulletin of the Association for Psychoanalytic Medicine.* (pp. 97–103).

Liebowitz, M. R., & Fyer, A. J. (1988). Tricyclic therapy of the DSM-III anxiety disorders: A review with implications for further research. *Journal of Psychiatric Research*, **22**, 7–31.

Liebowitz, M. R., & Hollander, E. (1991). Obsessive–compulsive disorder: Psychobiological integration. In J. Zohar, T. Insel, & S. Rasmussen (Eds.), *The psychobiology of obsessive-compulsive disorder.* (pp. 227–256). New York: Springer.

Linehan, M. M. (1989). Cognitive and behavior therapy for borderline personality disorder. In A. Tasman, R. E. Hales, & A. J. Frances (Eds.), *American psychiatric press: Annual review of psychiatry*. Washington, D.C.: American Psychiatric Press.

Lipowski, Z. J. (1989). Psychiatry: Mindless, brainless, both or neither? *Canadian Journal of Psychiatry*, **34**, 249–254.

Litz, B. T., & Keane, T. M. (1989). Information processing in anxiety disorders: Application to the understanding of post-traumatic stress disorder. *Clinical Psychology Review*, **9**, 243–257.

Lloyd, G. G., & Lishman, W. A. (1975). Effect of depression on the speed of recall of pleasant and unpleasant experiences. *Psychological Medicine*, **5**, 173–180.

Loftus, E. F., & Burns, T. E. (1982). Mental shock can produce retrograde amnesia. *Memory and Cognition*, **10**, 318–323.

Loftus, E. F., Loftus, G. R., & Messo, J. (1987). Some facts about "weapon focus." *Law and Human Behavior*, **11**, 55–62.

LoLordo, V. M. (1969). Positive conditioned reinforcers from aversive situations. *Psychological Bulletin*, **72**, 193–203.

Lonnqvist, J., & Kuoppasalmi, K. (1989). Panic disorder and mortality. Proceedings of the World Psychiatric Association on the Psychopathology of Panic Disorders: Many faces of panic disorder (1988, Espoo, Finland). *Psychiatria Fennica, Supplement*, 18–23.

Lovass, O. I., Koegel, R. L., & Schreibman, L. (1979). Stimulus overselectivity in autism: A review of the research. *Psychological Bulletin*, **86**, 1236–1254.

Lovass, O. I., Schreibman, L., Koegel, R. L., & Rehm, R. (1971). Selective responding by autistic children to multiple sensory input. *Journal of Abnormal Psychology*, **77**, 211–222.

Luborsky, L., Crits-Cristoph, P., & Alexander, K. J. (1990). Repressive style and relationship patterns—Three samples inspected. In J. L. Singer (Ed.), *Repression and dissociation: Implications for personality theory, psychopathology and health*. Chicago: University of Chicago Press.

Ludwig, A. M., Brandsma, J. M., Wilbur, C. B., Bendfeldt, F., & Jameson, D. H. (1972). The objective study of a multiple personality: Or, Are four heads better than one? *Archives of General Psychiatry*, **26**, 298–310.

Lundberg, I., Olofsson, A., & Wall, S. (1980). Reading and spelling skills in the first school years predicted from phonemic awareness skills in kindergarten. *Scandinavian Journal of Psychology*, **21**, 159–173.

Luxenberg, J., Swedo, S., Flament, M., Friedland, R., Rapoport, J., & Rapoport, S. I. (1988). Neuroanatomical abnormalities in obsessive–compulsive disorder detected with quantitative x-ray computed tomography. *American Journal of Psychiatry*, **145**, 1089–1093.

Lyddon, W. J. (1988). Information-processing and constructivist models of cognitive therapy: A philosophical divergence. *Journal of Mind and Behavior*, **9**, 137–166.

Lyddon, W. J. (1989a). Root metaphor theory: A philosophical framework for counseling and psychotherapy. *Journal of Counseling and Development*, **67**, 442–448.

Lyddon, W. J. (1989b). Personal epistemology and preference for counseling. *Journal of Counseling Psychology*, **36**, 423–429.

Lyddon, W. J. (1990). First- and second-order change: Implications for rationalist and constructivist cognitive therapies. *Journal of Counseling and Development*, **69**, 122–127.

Lyddon, W. J. (1991a). Socially constituted knowledge: Philosophical, psychological, and feminist contributions. *Journal of Mind and Behavior*, **12**, 263–280.

Lyddon, W. J. (1991b). Epistemic style: Implications for cognitive psychotherapy. *Psychotherapy*, **28**, 588–597.

Lyddon, W. J. (1992). A rejoinder to Ellis: What is and is not RET? *Journal of Counseling and Development*, **70**, 452–454.

Lyddon, W. J., & Adamson, L. A. (in press). Worldview and counseling preference: An analogue study. *Journal of Counseling and Development*.

Lyddon, W. J., & Alford, D. J. (in press). Constructivist assessment: A developmental-epistemic perspective. In G. L. Neimeyer (Ed.), *Casebook in constructivist assessment*. New York: Sage.

Lydiard, R. B., & Ballenger, J. C. (1987). Antidepressants in panic disorder and agoraphobia. *Journal of Affective Disorders, 13*, 153–168.

Lydiard, R. B., & Roy-Byrne, P. P. (1988). Recent advances in the psychopharmacological treatment of anxiety disorders. *Hospital and Community Psychiatry, 39*, 1157–1165.

Lyon, L. S. (1985). Facilitating telephone number recall in a case of psychogenic amnesia. *Journal of Behavior Therapy and Experimental Psychiatry, 16*, 147–149.

MacDowell, K. A. (1991). *Autonomic (sympathetic) responses predict subjective intensity of experience.* Poster presented at American Psychological Society Convention, Washington, D.C.

MacDowell, K. A., & Mandler, G. (1989). Constructions of emotion: Discrepancy, arousal, and mood. *Motivation and Emotion, 13*, 105–124.

Mackintosh, N. J. (1974). *The psychology of animal learning.* London: Academic Press.

Mackintosh, N. J. (1975). A theory of attention: Variations in the associability of stimuli with reinforcements. *Psychological Review, 82*, 276–298.

Mackintosh, N. J. (1983). *Conditioning and associative learning.* New York: Oxford University Press.

Maclean, M., Bryant, P., & Bradley, L. (1987). Rhymes, nursery rhymes, and reading in early childhood. Special Issue: Children's reading and the development of phonological awareness. (pp. 255–281). *Merrill-Palmer Quarterly.*

MacLeod, C., Mathews, A., & Tata, P. (1968). Attentional bias in emotional disorders. *Journal of Abnormal Psychology, 95*, 15–20.

MacLeod, C. M. (1975). Long-term recognition and recall following directed forgetting. *Journal of Experimental Psychology: Human Learning and Memory, 1*, 271–279.

MacLeod, C. M. (1989). Directed forgetting affects both direct and indirect tests of memory. *Journal of Experimental Psychology: Learning, Memory, and Cognition, 15*, 13–21.

MacLeod, C. M., & Bassili, J. N. (1989). Are implicit and explicit tests differentially sensitive to item-specific vs. relational information? In S. Lewandowsky, J. Dunn, & K. Kirsner (Eds.), *Implicit memory: Theoretical issues* (pp. 159–173). Hillsdale, New Jersey: Erlbaum.

MacLeod, C. M., & Mathews, A. (1988). Anxiety and allocation of attention to threat. *The Quarterly Journal of Experimental Psychology, 40A*, 653–670.

MacLeod, L., Mathews, A., & Tata, P. (1986). Attentional bias in emotional disorders. *Journal of Abnormal Psychology, 95*, 15–20.

Macmillan, M. B. (1986). Souvenir de la Salpetriere: M. le Dr. Freud a Paris, 1885. *Australian Psychologist, 21*, 3–29.

Maher, B. A. (1972). The language of schizophrenia: A review and interpretation. *British Journal of Psychiatry, 120*, 3–17.

Mahoney, M. J. (1974). *Cognition and behavior modification.* Cambridge, Massachusetts: Ballinger.

Mahoney, M. J. (1977). Personal science: A cognitive learning theory. In A. Ellis & R. Grieger (Eds.), *Handbook of rational-emotive therapy* (pp. 352–356). New York: Springer.

Mahoney, M. J. (1988). Constructivist metatheory: I. Basic features and historical foundations. *International Journal of Personal Construct Psychology, 1*, 1–35.

Mahoney, M. J. (1990). Developmental cognitive therapy. In J. K. Zeig & W. M. Munion (Eds.), *What is psychotherapy?* (pp. 164–168). San Francisco: Jossey-Bass.

Mahoney, M. J. (1991). *Human change processes.* New York: Basic Books.

Mahoney, M. J., & Lyddon, W. J. (1988). Recent developments in cognitive approaches to counseling and psychotherapy. *The Counseling Psychologist, 16*, 190–234.

Mahoney, M. J., Lyddon, W. J., & Alford, D. J. (1989). An evaluation of the rational-emotive theory of psychotherapy. In M. E. Bernard & R. DiGuiseppe (Eds.), *Inside rational-emotive therapy: A critical appraisal of the theory and therapy of Albert Ellis* (pp. 69–94). New York: Academic Press.

Malmo, H. P. (1974). On frontal lobe functions: Psychiatric patient controls. *Cortex, 10*, 231–237.

Malmo, R. B., Davis, J. F., & Barza, S. (1952–1953). Total hysterical deafness: An experimental case study. *Journal of Personality*, **21**, 188–204.

Mandler, G. (1964). The interruption of behavior. In E. Levine (Ed.), *Nebraska symposium on motivation: 1964.* (pp. 163–219). Lincoln: University of Nebraska Press.

Mandler, G. (1972). Helplessness: Theory and research in anxiety. In C. D. Spielberger (Ed.), *Anxiety: Current trends in theory and research* (Vol. II, pp. 359–374). New York: Academic Press.

Mandler, G. (1975a). Consciousness: Respectable, useful, and probably necessary. In R. Solso (Ed.), *Information processing and cognition: The Loyola symposium* (pp. 229–254). Hillsdale, New Jersey: Erlbaum. (Also in: Technical Report No. 41, Center for Human Information Processing, University of California, San Diego. March, 1974.)

Mandler, G. (1975b). *Mind and emotion.* New York: Wiley.

Mandler, G. (1979). Thought processes, consciousness, and stress. In V. Hamilton & D. M. Warburton (Eds.), *Human stress and cognition: An information processing approach.* (pp. 179–201). London: Wiley.

Mandler, G. (1984). *Mind and body: Psychology of emotion and stress.* New York: Norton.

Mandler, G. (1985). *Cognitive psychology: An essay in cognitive science.* Hillsdale, New Jersey: Erlbaum.

Mandler, G. (1989). Affect and learning: Causes and consequences of emotional interactions. In D. B. McLeod & V. M. Adams (Eds.), *Affect and mathematical problem solving: A new perspective.* (pp. 3–19). New York: Springer Verlag.

Mandler, G. (1990). A constructivist theory of emotion. In N. S. Stein, B. L. Leventhal, & T. Trabasso (Eds.), *Psychological and biological approaches to emotion.* (pp. 21–43). Hillsdale, New Jersey: Erlbaum.

Mandler, G. (1992a). Toward a theory of consciousness. In H. G. Geissler, S. Link, & J. G. Townsend (Eds.), *Cognition, information processing and psychophysics: Basic issues* (pp. 43–65). Hillsdale, New Jersey: Erlbaum.

Mandler, G. (1992b). Emotions, evolution, and aggression: Myths and conjectures. In K. T. Strongman (Ed.), *International review of studies on emotion*, Vol. II. Chichester: John Wiley and Sons.

Mandler, G. (in press). Approaches to a psychology of value. In M. Hechter, L. Cooper & L. Nadel (Eds.), *Towards a scientific study of value.* Palo Alto, CA: Stanford University Press.

Mandler, G., & Sarason, S. B. (1952). A study of anxiety and learning. *Journal of Abnormal and Social Psychology*, **47**, 166–173.

Mann, V. A., & Liberman, I. Y. (1984). Phonological awareness and verbal short-term memory. *Journal of Learning Disabilities*, **17**, 592–599.

Mann, V. A., Tobin, P., & Wilson, R. (1987). Measuring phonological awareness through the invented spellings of kindergarten children. *Merrill-Palmer Quarterly*, **33**, 365–391.

Mannuzza, S., Fyer, A. J., Martin, L. Y., Gallops, M. S., Endicott, J., Gorman, J., Liebowitz, M. R., & Klein, D. F. (1989). Reliability of anxiety assessment. I. Diagnostic agreement. *Archives of General Psychiatry*, **46**, 1093–1101.

Maratos, O. (1982). Trends in the development of early imitation in infancy. In T. G. Bever (Ed.), *Regressions in development: Basic phenomena and theories.* Hillsdale, New Jersey: Erlbaum.

Marcel, A. J. (1983a). Conscious and unconscious perception: Experiments on visual masking and word recognition. *Cognitive Psychology*, **15**, 197–237.

Marcel, A. J. (1983b). Conscious and unconscious perception: An approach to the relations between phenomenal experience and perceptual processes. *Cognitive Psychology*, **15**, 238–300.

Marks, I. M. (1981). *Cure and care of neurosis.* New York: Wiley.

Marks, I. M. (1987). *Fears, phobias, and rituals: Panic, anxiety, and their disorders.* New York: Oxford University Press.

Markus, H. (1977). Self-schemata and processing information about the self. *Journal of Personality and Social Psychology*, **35**, 63–78.

Markus, H., & Wurf, E. (1987). The dynamic self-conscious: A social psychological perspective. *Annual Review of Psychology*, **38**, 299–337.

Martin, A., Brouwers, P., Cox, C., & Fedio, P. (1985). On the nature of the verbal memory deficit in Alzheimer's disease. *Brain and Language*, **25**, 323–341.

Martin, A., & Fedio, P. (1983). Word production and comprehension in Alzheimer's disease: The breakdown of semantic knowledge. *Brain and Language*, **19**, 124–141.

Martin, L. L., & Tesser, A. (1989). Toward a motivational and structural theory of ruminative thought. In J. S. Uleman & J. A. Bargh (Eds.), *Unintended thought.* (pp. 306–326). New York: Guilford.

Martuza, R. L., Chiocca, E. A., Jenike, M. A., Giriunas, I. E., & Ballantine, H. T. (1990). Stereotactic radiofrequency thermal cingulotomy for obsessive compulsive disorder. *Journal of Neuropsychiatry*, **2**, 331–336.

Masson, M. E. J. (1984). Memory for the surface structure of sentences: Remembering with and without awareness. *Journal of Verbal Learning and Verbal Behavior*, **23**, 579–592.

Mathews, A. (1990). Why worry? The cognitive function of anxiety. *Behaviour Research and Therapy*, **28**, 445–468.

Mathews, A. (1991). Anxiety and the processing of emotional information. In L. J. Chapman, J. P. Chapman, & D. Fowles (Eds.), *Models and method of psychopathology (Progress in experimental personality and psychopathology research)*. New York: Springer.

Mathews, A., May, J., Mogg, K., & Eysenck, M. (1990). Attentional bias in anxiety: Selective search or defective filtering? *Journal of Abnormal Psychology*, **99**, 166–173.

Mathews, A. M., & MacLeod, C. (1985). Selective processing of threat cues in anxiety states. *Behaviour Research and Therapy*, **23**, 563–569.

Mathews, A. M., & MacLeod, C. (1986). Discrimination of threat cues without awareness in anxiety states. *Journal of Abnormal Psychology*, **95**, 131–138.

Mathews, A. M., Gelder, M. G., & Johnston, D. W. (1981). *Agoraphobia: Nature and treatment.* New York: Guilford.

Maultsby, M. C. (1984). *Rational behavior therapy.* Englewood Cliffs, New Jersey: Prentice-Hall.

Maurer, D., & Barrera, M. (1981). Infants' perception of natural and distorted arrangements of a schematic face. *Child Development*, **47**, 523–527.

Maurer, D., & Young, R. E. (1983). Newborns' following of natural and distorted arrangements of facial features. *Infant Behavior and Development*, **6**, 127–131.

Mavissakalian, M. (1987). Trimodal assessment in agoraphobia research: Further observations on heart rate and synchrony/desynchrony. *Journal of Psychopathology and Behavioral Assessment*, **9**, 89–98.

Maxmen, J. S. (1986). *Essential psychopathology.* New York: Norton.

McCarthy, R. A., & Warrington, E. K. (1990). *Cognitive neuropsychology: A clinical introduction.* San Diego: Academic.

McClelland, D. C., & Jemmott, J. B., III. (1980). Power motivation, stress and physical illness. *Journal of Human Stress*, **6**, 6–15.

McClelland, J. L. (1988). Connectionist models and psychological evidence. *Journal of Memory and Language*, **27**, 107–123.

McClelland, J. L., & Rumelhart, D. E. (Eds.) (1986a). *Parallel distributed processing: Explorations in the microstructure of cognition* (Vol. 1, *Foundations*). Cambridge: MIT Press.

McClelland, J. L., & Rumelhart, D. E. (Eds.) (1986b). *Parallel distributed processing: Explorations in the microstructure of cognition* (Vol. 2, *Psychological and biological models*). Cambridge: MIT Press.

McClelland, J. L., & Rumelhart, D. E. (1986c). Amnesia and distributed memory. In J. L. McClelland & D. E. Rumelhart (Eds.), *Parallel distributed processing: Explorations in the microstructure of cognition* (Vol. 2, *Psychological and biological processes*, pp. 503–527). Cambridge: MIT Press.

McConkey, K. M., Bryant, R. A., Bibb, B. C., Kihlstrom, J. F., & Tataryn, D. J. (1990). Hypnotically suggested anaesthesia and the circle-touch test: A real-simulating comparison. *British Journal of Experimental and Clinical Hypnosis, 7,* 153–157.

McCormick, C., & Samuels, S. J. (1979). Word recognition by second graders: The unit of perception and interrelationships among accuracy, latency, and comprehension. *Journal of Reading Behavior, 11,* 107–118.

McCullough, W., & Pitts, W. (1943). A logical calculus of the ideas immanent in nervous activity. *Bulletin of Mathematical Biophysics, 5,* 115–133.

McDowall, J. (1984). Recall of pleasant and unpleasant words in depressed subjects. *Journal of Abnormal Psychology, 93,* 401–407.

McFall, M. E., & Wollersheim, J. P. (1979). Obsessive–compulsive neurosis: A cognitive-behavioral formulation and approach to treatment. *Cognitive Therapy and Research, 3,* 333–348.

McGinnies, E. (1949). Emotionality and perceptual defence. *Psychological Review, 56,* 244–251.

McKhann, G., Drachman, D., Folstein, M., Katzman, R., Price, D., & Stadlan, E. M. (1984). Clinical diagnosis of Alzheimer's disease: Report of the NINCDS-ADRDA work group under the auspices of Department of Health and Human Services Task Force on Alzheimer's disease. *Neurology, 34,* 939–944.

McNally, R. J., Foa, E. B., & Donnell, C. D. (1990). Memory bias for anxiety information in patients with panic disorder. *Cognition and Emotion, 3,* 27–44.

McNally, R. J., Kaspi, S. P., Reimann, B. C., & Zeitlin, S. B. (1990). Selective processing of threat cues in posttraumatic stress disorder. *Journal of Abnormal Psychology, 99,* 398–402.

McNaughton, M. (1989). *Biology and emotion.* Cambridge: Cambridge University Press.

Meichenbaum, D. (1979). *Cognitive-behavior modification: An integrative approach.* New York: Plenum.

Meichenbaum, D. (1985). *Stress inoculation training.* Elmsford, New York: Pergamon.

Meichenbaum, D., & Gilmore, J. B. (1984). The nature of unconscious processes: A cognitive-behavioral perspective. In K. S. Bowers & D. Meichenbaum (Eds.), *The unconscious reconsidered* (pp. 273–298). New York: John Wiley.

Meichenbaum, D., & Turk, D. C. (1987). *Facilitating treatment adherence.* New York: Plenum.

Meltzer, H. Y., & Stahl, S. M. (1976). The dopamine hypothesis of schizophrenia: A review. *Schizophrenia Bulletin, 2,* 19–76.

Melzoff, A. (1990). Towards a developmental cognitive science. In A. Diamond (Eds.), *The development and neural basis of higher cognitive functions.* New York: New York Academy of Sciences Press.

Merluzzi, T. V., & Boltwood, M. D. (1989). Cognitive assessment. In A. Freeman, K. M. Simon, L. E. Beutler, & H. Arkowitz (Eds.), *Comprehensive handbook of cognitive therapy* (pp. 249–266). New York: Plenum.

Merluzzi, T. V., & Boltwood, M. D. (1990). Cognitive assessment. In C. E. Watkins & V. L. Campbell (Eds.), *Testing in counseling practice* (pp. 135–176). Hillsdale, New Jersey: Erlbaum.

Merluzzi, T. V., Rudy, T. E., & Glass, C. R. (1981). The information processing paradigm: Implications for clinical science. In T. V. Merluzzi, C. R. Glass, & M. Genest (Eds.), *Cognitive assessment* (pp. 77–126). New York: Guilford Press.

Merluzzi, T. V., Rudy, T. E., & Krejci, M. J. (1986). Social skill and anxiety: Information processing perspectives. In R. E. Ingram (Ed.), *Information processing approaches to clinical psychology* (pp. 109–131). Orlando, Florida: Academic Press.

Meyer, D. E. (1970). On the representation and retrieval of stored semantic information. *Cognitive Psychology, 1,* 242–300.

Miller, E. (1971). On the nature of the memory disorder in presenile dementia. *Neuropsychologia*, **9**, 75–78.

Miller, E. (1973). Short- and long-term memory in presenile dementia (Alzheimer's disease). *Psychological Medicine*, **3**, 221–224.

Miller, E. (1975). Impaired recall and the memory disturbance in presenile dementia. *British Journal of Social and Clinical Psychology*, **14**, 73–79.

Miller, G. A. (1985). The constitutive problem of psychology. In S. Koch & D. E. Leary (Eds.), *A century of psychology as science.* (pp. 40–45). New York: McGraw Hill.

Miller, G. A., Galanter, E., & Pribram, K. H. (1960). *Plans and the structure of behavior.* New York: Holt, Rinehart & Winston.

Minsky, M., & Papert, S. (1969). *Perceptrons.* Cambridge: MIT Press.

Miranda, J. & Persons, J. B. (1988). Dysfunctional attitudes are mood-state dependent. *Journal of Abnormal Psychology*, **97**, 76–79.

Miranda, J., Persons, J. B., & Byers, C. N. (1990). Endorsement of dysfunctional beliefs depends on current mood state. *Journal of Abnormal Psychology*, **99**, 237–241.

Miranda, J. & Persons, J. B. (in press). Dysfunctional thinking is activated by stressful life events. *Cognitive Therapy and Research.*

Mischel, W. (1968). *Personality and assessment.* New York: Wiley.

Mishkin, M., & Pribram, K. H. (1955). Analysis of the effects of frontal lesions in monkey. I. Variations on delayed alternation. *Journal of Comparative Physiological Psychology*, **338**, 492–495.

Mitchell, D. B., Hunt, R. R., & Schmitt, F. A. (1986). The generation effect and reality monitoring. *Journal of Gerontology*, **41**, 79–84.

Mitchell, S. A. (1988). *Relational concepts in psychoanalysis: An integration.* Cambridge: Harvard University Press.

Mogg, K., Mathews, A., & Weinman, J. (1987). Memory bias in clinical anxiety. *Journal of Abnormal Psychology*, **96**, 94–98.

Mohr, E., Cox, C., Williams, J., Chase, T. N., & Fedio, P. (1990). Impairment of central auditory function in Alzheimer's disease. *Journal of Clinical and Experimental Neuropsychology*, **12**, 235–246.

Moldofsky, H., & England, R. S. (1975). Facilitation of somatosensory average evoked potentials in hysterical anesthesia and pain. *Archives of General Psychiatry*, **32**, 193–197.

Money, J., Alexander, D., & Walker, H. T. (1965). *A standardized road-map test of direction sense.* Baltimore: Johns Hopkins University Press.

Mook, D. G. (1987). *The organization of action.* New York: Norton.

Morris, L. W., Davis, M. A., & Hutchings, C. L. (1981). Cognitive and emotional components of anxiety: Literature review and a revised worry-emotionality scale. *Journal of Educational Psychology*, **72**, 541–555.

Morris, R. G. (1984). Dementia and the functioning of the articulatory loop system. *Cognitive Neuropsychology*, **1**, 143–157.

Morris, R. G. (1986). Short-term forgetting in senile dementia of the Alzheimer's type. *Cognitive Neuropsychology*, **3**, 77–97.

Morris, R. G., & Kopelman, M. D. (1986). The memory deficits in Alzheimer-type dementia: A review. *Quarterly Journal of Experimental Psychology*, **38A**, 755–602.

Morris, R. G., Wheatly, J., & Britton, P. (1983). Retrieval from long-term memory in senile dementia: Cued recall revisited. *British Journal of Clinical Psychology*, **22**, 141–142.

Morrison, F. J. (1991). Learning (and not learning) to read: A developmental framework. In L. Rieben & C. A. Perfetti (Eds.), *Learning to read: Basic research and its implications.* Hillsdale, New Jersey: Erlbaum.

Morrison, F. J., & Manis, F. R. (1982). Cognitive processes and reading disability: A critique and proposal. In C. J. Brainerd & M. I. Pressley (Eds.), *Progress in cognitive development research* Vol. 2. New York: Springer-Verlag.

Morton, J., & Johnson, M. H. (1991). Conspec and conlern: A two-process theory of infant face recognition. *Psychological Review*, **98**, 164–181.

Morton, J., Johnson, M. H., & Maurer, D. (1990). On the reasons for newborns' responses to faces. *Infant Behavior and Development*, **13**, 99–103.

Mowrer, O. H. (1950). *Learning theory and personality dynamics*. New York: Ronald Press.

Muir, D. W., Clifton, R. K., & Clarkson, M. G. (1989). The development of a human auditory localization response: a U-shaped function. *Canadian Journal of Psychology*, **43**, 199–216.

Munoz, R. F. (1977). A cognitive approach to the assessment and treatment of depression. (Ph.D. Thesis. University of Oregon, City). *Dissertation Abstracts International*, **38**, 2873b (University Microfilms No. 77-26, 505, 154).

Munoz, R. F. (1986). *Treating anxiety disorders*. London: Jossey-Bass.

Munro, P. W. (1986). State-dependent factors influencing neural plasticity: A partial account of the critical period. In J. L. McClelland & D. E. Rumelhart (Eds.), *Parallel distributed processing: Explorations in the microstructure of cognition* (Vol. 2, *Psychological and biological processes*, pp. 471–502). Cambridge: MIT Press.

Musen, G., & Treisman, A. (1990). Implicit and explicit memory for visual patterns. *Journal of Experimental Psychology: Learning, Memory and Cognition*, **16**, 127–137.

Nadel, L., & Willner, J. (1980). Context and conditioning: A place for space. *Physiological Psychology*, **8**, 218–228.

Nadel, L., & Willner, J. (1989). Some implications for postnatal maturation in the hippocampal formation. In V. Chan-Palay and C. Kohler (Eds.), *The hippocampus: New vistas*. New York: Liss.

Nasby, W., & Kihlstrom, J. F. (1986). Cognitive assessment of personality and psychopathology. In R. Ingram (Ed.), *Information processing approaches to clinical psychology* (pp. 217–239). New York: Academic Press.

Natale, M., & Hantas, M. (1982). Effect of temporary mood states on selective memory about the self. *Journal of Personality and Social Psychology*, **42**, 927–934.

Nauta, J. H. W., & Domesick, V. B. (1981). Ramifications of the limbic system. In S. Matthysse (Ed.), *Psychiatry and the biology of the human brain: A symposium dedicated to Seymour S. Kety* (pp. 165–188). New York: Elsevier/North-Holland.

Navon, D., & Margalit, B. (1983). Allocation of attention according to informativeness in visual recognition. *Quarterly Journal of Experimental Psychology*, **35(a)**, 497–512.

Nebes, R. D. (1989). Semantic memory in Alzheimer's disease. *Psychological Bulletin*, **106**, 377–394.

Nebes, R. D., Boller, F., & Holland, A. (1986). Use of semantic context by patients with Alzheimer's disease. *Psychology and Aging*, **1**, 261–269.

Nebes, R. D., & Brady, C. B. (1989). Focussed and divided attention in Alzheimer's disease. *Cortex*, **25**, 305–315.

Nebes, R. D., Martin, D. C., & Horn, L. C. (1984). Sparing of semantic memory in Alzheimer's disease. *Journal of Abnormal Psychology*, **93**, 321–330.

Neimeyer, G. J. (Ed.) (in press). *Constructivist assessment*. New York: Sage.

Neimeyer, R. A. (1990). Personal construct therapy. In J. K. Zeig & W. M. Munion (Eds.), *What is psychotherapy?* (pp. 159–164). San Francisco: Jossey-Bass.

Neimeyer, R. A., & Neimeyer, G. A. (1987). *Personal construct therapy casebook*. Lincoln: University of Nebraska Press.

Neimeyer, G. L., Prichard, S., Lyddon, W. J., & Sherrard, P. A. (in press). The role of epistemic style in counseling preference and orientation. *Journal of Counseling and Development*.

Neisser, U. (1967). *Cognitive psychology*, New York: Appleton-Century-Crofts.

Neisser, U. (1976). *Cognition and reality: Principles and implications of cognitive psychology*. San Francisco: Freeman.

Neisser, U., & Winograd, E. (Eds.) (1988). *Remembering reconsidered: Ecological and traditional approaches to the study of memory.* Cambridge: Cambridge University Press.

Nelson, D. L., Canas, J. J., Bajo, M. T., & Keelean, P. D. (1987). Comparing word fragment completion and cued recall with letter cues. *Journal of Experimental Psychology: Learning, Memory, and Cognition, 13,* 542–552.

Nelson, R. E., & Craighead, W. E. (1977). Selective recall of positive and negative feedback, self-control behaviors, and depression. *Journal of Abnormal Psychology, 86,* 379–388.

Nemiah, J. C. (1990). Dissociation, conversion, and somatization. In A. Tasman (Ed.), *Psychiatric update* Vol. 10, pp. 248–275. Washington, D.C.: American Psychiatric Association.

Nicholas, M., Obler, L. K., Albert, M. L., & Helm-Estabrooks, N. (1985). Empty speech in Alzheimer's disease and fluent aphasia. *Journal of Speech and Hearing Research, 28,* 405–410.

Ninan, P., Insel, T., Cohen, R. M., Cook, J. M., Skolnik, P., & Paul, S. (1982). Benzodiazepine receptor-mediated experimental anxiety in primates. *Science, 218,* 1332–1334.

Nisbett, R. E., & Ross, L. (1980). *Human inference: Strategies and shortcomings of social judgement.* Englewood Cliffs, New Jersey: Prentice-Hall.

Nisbett, R. E., & Wilson, T. D. (1977). Telling more than we can know: Verbal reports on mental processes. *Psychological Review, 84,* 231–259.

Nissen, M. J., Ross, J. L., Willingham, D. B., Mackenzie, T. B., & Schacter, D. L. (1988). Memory and awareness in a patient with multiple personality disorder. *Brain and Cognition, 8,* 117–134.

Norman, D. A. (1980). Twelve issues for cognitive science. *Cognitive Science, 4,* 1–32.

Norman, D. A., & Bobrow, D. G. (1975a). On the role of active memory processes in perception and cognition. In C. N. Cofer (Ed.), *The structure of human memory.* (pp. 114–132). San Francisco: Freeman.

Norman, D. A., & Bobrow, D. G. (1975b). On data-limited and resource-limited processes. *Cognitive Psychology, 7,* 44–67.

Norman, D. A., & Shallice, T. (1980). *Attention to action: Willed and automatic control of behavior.* University of California, CHIP Report 99.

Norton, G. R., Schaefer, E., Cox, B. J., Doward, J., & Wozney, K. (1988). Selective memory effects in nonclinical panickers. *Journal of Anxiety Disorders, 2,* 169–177.

Nuechterlein, K. H. (1983). Signal detection in vigilance tasks and behavioral attributes among offspring of schizophrenic mothers and among hyperactive children. *Journal of Abnormal Psychology, 92,* 4–28.

Nuechterlein, K. H. (1984). Information processing and attentional functioning in the developmental course of schizophrenic disorders. *Schizophrenia Bulletin, 10,* 160–203.

Oatley, K. (1990). Freud's psychology of intention: The case of Dora. *Mind and Language, 5,* 69–86.

Oatley, K., & Bolton, W. (1985). A social-cognitive theory of depression in reaction to life events. *Psychological Review, 92,* 372–388.

Oatley, K., & Johnson-Laird, P. N. (1987). Toward a cognitive theory of emotions. *Cognition and Emotion, 1,* 29–50.

Ober, B. A., Dronkers, N. F., Koss, E., Delis, D. C., & Freidland, R. P. (1986). Retrieval in semantic memory in Alzheimer-type dementia. *Journal of Clinical and Experimental Neuropsychology, 8,* 75–92.

Ober, B. A., Koss, E., Friedland, R. P., & Delis, D. C. (1985). Processes of verbal memory failure in Alzheimer-type dementia. *Brain and Cognition, 4,* 90–103.

O'Conner, N., & Hermelin, B. (1984). Idiot savant calendrical calculators: Maths or memory? *Psychological Medicine, 14,* 801–806.

Oei, T. P., Gross, P. R., & Evans, L. (1989). Phobic disorders and anxiety states: How do they differ? *Australian and New Zealand Journal of Psychiatry, 23,* 81–88.

O'Keefe, J., & Nadel, L. (1978). *The hippocampus as a cognitive map.* London: Oxford University Press.

Oltmanns, T. F., & Neale, J. M. (1975). Schizophrenic performance when distractors are present: Attentional deficit or differential task difficulty? *Journal of Abnormal Psychology, 84,* 205–209.

Orne, M. T. (1959). The nature of hypnosis: Artifact and essence. *Journal of Abnormal and social Psychology, 58,* 277–279.

Orne, M. T. (1980). *Task force report 19: Biofeedback.* Washington, D.C.: American Psychiatric Association.

Orr, S. P., Claiborn, J. M., Altman, B., Forgue, D. F., deJon, J. B., Pitman, R. K., & Herz, L. R. (1990). Psychometric profile of posttraumatic stress disorder, anxious, and healthy Vietnam veterans: Correlations with psychophysiologic responses. *Journal of Consulting and Clinical Psychology, 58,* 329–335.

Orton, S. T. (1937). *Reading, writing, and speech problems in children.* New York: Horton.

Ost, L.-G. (1987). Applied relaxation: Description of a coping technique and review of controlled studies. *Behavior Research and Therapy, 25,* 397–409.

Paller, K. A. (1990). Recall and stem-completion priming have different electrophysiological correlates and are modified differentially by directed forgetting. *Journal of Experimental Psychology: Learning, Memory, and Cognition, 16,* 1021–1032.

Parks, C. W., & Hollon, S. D. (1989). Cognitive assessment. In A. S. Bellack & M. Hersen (Eds.), *Behavioral assessment: A practical handbook* (3rd ed., pp. 161–212). New York: Pergamon.

Parrot, W. G., & Sabini, J. (1990). Mood and memory under natural conditions: Evidence for mood incongruent recall. *Journal of Personality and Social Psychology, 54,* 213–336.

Pasnau, R. O. (1984). *Diagnosis and treatment of anxiety disorders.* Washington, D.C.: American Psychiatric Press.

Pasnau, R. O., & Bystritsky, A. (1990). An overview of anxiety disorders. *Bulletin of the Menninger Clinic, 54,* 157–170.

Passingham, R. E. (1985). Memory of monkeys (*Macaca mulatta*) with lesions in prefrontal cortex. *Behavioral Neuroscience, 99,* 3–21.

Pavlov, I. P. (1927). *Conditioned reflexes.* Oxford: Oxford University Press.

Pavlov, I. P. (1928). *Lectures on conditioned reflexes: The higher nervous activity of animals* (Vol. 1). London: Lawrence and Whishart.

Pearce, J. M. (1987). A model for stimulus generalization in Pavlovian conditioning. *Psychological Review, 94,* 61–73.

Pearce, J. M., & Hall, G. (1980). A model for Pavlovian learning: Variations in the effectiveness of conditioned but not unconditioned stimuli. *Psychological Review, 87,* 532–552.

Perfetti, C. A. (1982). Discourse context, word identification and reading ability. In J. F. LeNy & W. Kintsch (Eds.), *Language and comprehension.* Amsterdam: North-Holland.

Perfetti, C. A. (1986). Continuities in reading acquisition, reading skill, and reading disability. *Remedial and Special Education, 7,* 11–21.

Perfetti, C. A., Beck, I., Bell, L., & Hughes, C. (1987). Phonemic knowledge and learning to read are reciprocal: A longitudinal study of first grade children. Children's reading and the development of phonological awareness. (pp. 283–320). *Merrill-Palmer Quarterly,* Special Issue.

Perfetti, C. A., Finger, E., & Hogaboam, T. (1978). Sources of vocalization latency differences between skilled and less-skilled readers. *Journal of Educational Psychology, 70,* 730–739.

Perfetti, C. A., & Lesgold, A. (1977). Discourse comprehension and sources of individual differences. In M. Just & P. Carpenter (Eds.), *Cognitive processes in comprehension.* (pp. 141–183). Hillsdale, New Jersey: Erlbaum.

Perner, J., Leekham, S., & Wimmer, J. (1987). Three year olds difficulty with false belief. *British Journal of Developmental Psychology*, **5**, 125–137.

Perrett, D. I., Harries, M. H., Bevan, R., Thomas, S., Benson, P. J., Mistlin, A. J., Chitty, A. J., Hietanen, J. K., & Ortega, J. E. (1989). Frameworks of analysis for the neural representation of animate objects and actions. *Journal of Experimental Biology*, **146**, 87–113.

Perrett, D. I., Rolls, E. T., & Caan, W. (1982). Visual neurones responsive to faces in the monkey temporal cortex. *Experimental Brain Research*, **47**, 229–238.

Perry, C., & Laurence, J. -R. (1984). Mental processing outside of awareness: The contributions of Freud and Janet. In K. S. Bowers & D. Meichenbaum (Eds.), *The unconscious reconsidered* (pp. 9–48). New York: Wiley-Interscience.

Persons, J. B., & Miranda, J. (in press). Cognitive theories of vulnerability to depression: Reconciling negative evidence. *Cognitive Therapy and Research*.

Persons, J. B., & Rao, P. A. (1985). Longitudinal study of cognition, life events, and depression in psychiatric inpatients. *Journal of Abnormal Psychology*, **94**, 51–63.

Peterfreund, E. (1980). On information and systems models for psychoanalysis. *International Review of Psychoanalysis*, **7**, 327–345.

Peterson, L. R., & Peterson, M. J. (1959). Short-term retention of individual items (or verbal items). *Journal of Experimental Psychology*, **58**, 193–198.

Pfeifer, R., & Leuzinger-Bohleber, M. (1986). Applications of cognitive science methods to psychoanalysis: a case study and some theory. *International Review of Psychoanalysis*, **7**, 327–345.

Phaf, R. H., van der Heijden, A. H. C., & Hudson, P. T. W. (1990). SLAM: A connectionist model of attention for visual selection tasks. *Cognitive Psychology*, **22**, 273–341.

Piaget, J. (1952). *The origins of intelligence in children*. New York: International Universities Press.

Piaget, J. (1954). *The construction of reality in the child*. New York: Basic Books.

Piaget, J. (1970). *Psychology and epistemology: Toward a theory of knowledge*. New York: Viking.

Piaget, J. (1971). *Biology and knowledge*. Edinburgh: Edinburgh University Press.

Piaget, J. (1972). *Insights and illusions of philosophy*. London: Routledge and Kegan Paul.

Pinel, J., & Symans, J. P. (1989). Development of defensive burying in *Rattus norvegicus*: Experience and defensive responses. *Journal of Comparative Psychology*, **103**, 359–365.

Pitman, R. (1987). A cybernetic model of obsessive–compulsive psychopathology. *Comprehensive Psychiatry*, **28**, 334–343.

Poetzl, O. (1960). The relationship between experimentally induced dream images and indirect vision. *Psychological Issues*, **2**, 41–120. (Original work published in 1917.)

Pohl, R., & Rainey, J. M. (1984). Changes in the drug treatment of anxiety disorders. *Psychopathology*, **17**, 6–14.

Polkinghorne, D. (1983). *Methodology for the human sciences: Systems of inquiry*. Albany: State University of New York Press.

Polkinghorne, D. (1986). *Narrative knowing and the human sciences*. Albany: State University of New York Press.

Popper, K. R. (1972). *Objective knowledge: An evolutionary approach*. London: Oxford University Press.

Posner, M. I. (1980). Orienting of attention. *Quarterly Journal of Experimental Psychology*, **32**, 3–25.

Posner, M. I. (Ed.) (1990). *Foundations of cognitive science*. Cambridge: MIT Press.

Posner, M. I., & Peterson, S. E. (1990). The attention system of the human brain. *Annual Review of Neuroscience*, **13**, 25–42.

Posner, M. I., & Rothbart, M. K. (1990). *Attentional mechanisms and conscious experience*. Institute of Cognitive and Decision Sciences. University of Oregon Technical Report No. 90-17.

Posner, M. J. (1986). *Chronometric exploration of the mind*. New York: Oxford University Press.

Posner, M. J., & Bois, S. J. (1971). Components of attention. *Psychological Review*, **78**, 1–52.

Powell, M., & Hemsley, D. R. (1984). Depression: A breakdown of perceptual defence? *British Journal of Psychiatry*, **145**, 358–362.

Premack, D. G., & Woodruff, G. (1978). Does the chimpanzee have a theory of mind? *Behavioral and Brain Sciences*, **1**, 515–526.

Prince, M. (1939). *Clinical and experimental studies in personality* (2nd ed.). Cambridge, Massachusetts: Sci-Art.

Pryor, J. B., & Merluzzi, T. V. (1985). The role of expertise in processing social interaction scripts. *Journal of Experimental Social Psychology*, **21**, 362–379.

Pylyshyn, Z. W. (1973). *Computation and cognition: Toward a foundation for cognitive science*. Cambridge: MIT Press.

Rabbitt, P. (1979). Some experiments and a model for changes in attentional selectivity with old age. In F. Hoffmeister & C. Muller (Eds.), *Brain function in old age*. (pp. 82–94). Berlin: Springer-Verlag.

Rachman, S., & Hodgson, R. J. (1980). *Obsessions and compulsions*. Englewood Cliffs, New Jersey: Prentice-Hall.

Rachman, S. J. (1978). *Fear and courage*. San Francisco: Freeman.

Radnitzky, G., & Bartley, W. W. (Eds.) (1987). *Evolutionary epistemology, rationality, and the sociology of knowledge*. LaSalle, Illinois: Open Court.

Rahe, R. H. (1979). Life change events and mental illness: An overview. *Journal of Human Stress*, **5(3)**, 2–10.

Rapala, M. M., & Brady, S. (1990). Reading ability and short-term memory: The role of phonological processing. *Reading and Writing: An Interdisciplinary Journal*, **2**, 1–25.

Rapoport, J., & Wise, S. (1988). Obsessive–compulsive disorder: A basal ganglia disease? In J. Rapoport (Ed.), *Obsessive–compulsive disorder in children and adolescents* (pp. 327–344). Washington, D.C.: APPI Press.

Read, C., Ahang, Y., Nie, H., & Ding, B. (1984). *The ability to manipulate speech sounds depends on knowing alphabetic spelling*. Paper presented at the International Congress of Psychology, Acapulco.

Reber, A. S. (1976). Implicit learning of synthetic languages: The role of instructional set. *Journal of Experimental Psychology: Human Learning and Memory*, **2**, 88–94.

Reber, A. S., Allen, A., & Regan, S. (1985). Syntactical learning and judgment, still unconscious and still abstract: Comment on Dulany, Carlson, and Dewey. *Journal of Experimental Psychology: General*, **114**, 17–24.

Rebok, G., Brandt, J., & Folstein, M. (1990). Longitudinal cognitive decline in patients with Alzheimer's disease. *Journal of Geriatric Psychiatry and Neurology*, **3**, 91–97.

Regier, D. A., Boyd, J. H., Burke, J. D., Rae, D. S., Myers, J. K., Kramer, M., Robins, L. N., George, L. K., Karno, M., & Locke, B. Z. (1988). One-month prevalence of mental disorders in the United States: Based on five Epidemiologic Catchment Area sites. *Archives of General Psychiatry*, **45**, 977–986.

Rehm, L. P. (1977). A self-control model of depression. *Behavior Therapy*, **8**, 787–804.

Rescorla, R. A., & Wagner, A. R. (1972). A theory of Pavlovian conditioning. Variations in the effectiveness of reinforcement and nonreinforcement. In A. H. Black & W. F. Prokasy (Eds.), *Classical conditioning II: Current research and theory* (pp. 64–99). New York: Appleton-Century-Crofts.

Richards, A., & Millwood, B. (1989). Color identification of differentially valenced words in anxiety. *Cognition and Emotion*, **3**, 171–176.

Richardson-Klavehn, A., & Bjork, R. A. (1988). Measures of memory. *Annual Review of Psychology*, **39**, 475–543.

Robins, L. N. (1966). *Deviant children grown up: A sociological and psychiatric study of sociopathic personality*. Baltimore: Williams and Wilkins.

Robinson, F. P. (1961). Study skills for superior students in the secondary schools. *The Reading Teacher*, 29–33.

Robinson, N. S., McCarty, M. E., & Haith, M. M. (1988). *Visual expectations in early infancy.* Paper presented at the International Conference on Infant Studies, Washington, D.C.

Rochester, S. R., & Martin, J. R. (1979). *Crazy talk: A study in the discourse of schizophrenic speakers.* New York: Plenum.

Roediger, H. L. (1990). Implicit memory: A commentary. *Bulletin of the Psychonomic Society*, **28**, 373–380.

Roediger, H. L., & Blaxton, T. A. (1987a). Effects of varying modality, surface features, and retention interval on priming in word fragment completion. *Memory and Cognition*, **15**, 379–388.

Roediger, H. L., & Blaxton, T. A. (1987b). Retrieval modes produce dissociations in memory for surface information. In D. Gorfein & R. R. Hoffman (Eds.), *Memory and cognitive processes: The Ebbinghaus centennial conference* (pp. 349–377). Hillsdale, New Jersey: Erlbaum.

Roediger, H. L., Weldon, M. S., & Challis, B. H. (1989). Explaining dissociations between implicit and explicit measures of retention: A processing account. In H. L. Roediger & F. I. M. Craik (Eds.), *Varieties of memory and consciousness: Essays in honour of Endel Tulving* (pp. 3–41). Hillsdale, New Jersey: Erlbaum.

Rogers, M. P., Dubey, D., & Reich, P. (1979). The influences of the psyche and the brain on immunity and susceptibility to disease: A critical review. *Psychosomatic Medicine*, **41**, 147–167.

Rogers, T. B. (1981). A model of the self as an aspect of the human information processing system. In N. Cantor & J. F. Kihlstrom (Eds.), *Personality, cognition, and social interaction.* (pp. 193–214). Hillsdale, New Jersey: Erlbaum.

Rogers, T. B., Kuiper, N. A., & Kirker, W. S. (1977). Self-reference and the encoding of personal information. *Journal of Personality and Social Psychology*, **35**, 677–688.

Rosen, W. G. (1983a). Clinical and neuropsychological assessment of Alzheimer disease. In R. Mayeux & W. G. Rosen (Eds.), *The dementias.* New York: Raven Press.

Rosen, W. G. (1983b). Neuropsychological investigation of memory, visuoconstructional, visuoperceptual, and language abilities in senile dementia of the Alzheimer type. In R. Mayeux & W. G. Rosen (Eds.), *The dementias.* New York: Raven Press.

Rosenbaum, R. L., Soule, C. E., & Drexler, M. L. (1988). PDD patient's use of semantic cueing to enhance recall of new material. *Journal of Clinical and Experimental Neuropsychology*, **10**, 78.

Rosenblatt, A. D., & Thickstun, J. T. (1977). Energy, information, and motivation: A revision of psychoanalytic theory. *Journal of the American Psychoanalytic Association*, **25**, 529–558.

Rosenblatt, F. (1962). *Principles of Neurodynamics.* New York: Spartan.

Rosendkilde, K. E. (1979). Functional heterogeneity of the prefrontal cortex in the monkey: A review. *Behavioral Neural Biology*, **25**, 301–345.

Rosenshine, B., & Stevens, R. (1984). Classroom instruction in reading. In P. D. Pearson (Ed.), *Handbook of reading research.* New York: Longman.

Rosner, J. (1975). *Helping children with learning difficulties.* New York: Walker Press.

Ross, C., Heber, S., Norton, G., & Anderson, G. (1989). Differences between multiple personality disorder and other diagnostic groups on structured interview. *Journal of Nervous and Mental Disease*, **177**, 487–491.

Rosvold, K. E., Mirsky, A. F., Sarason, I., Bransome, E. D., & Beck, L. H. (1956). A continuous performance test of brain damage. *Journal of Consulting Psychology*, **20(5)**, 343–350.

Rosvold, K. E., Szwarcbart, M. K., Mirsky, A. F., & Mishkin, M. (1961). The effect of frontal lobe damage on delayed response performance in chimpanzees. *Journal of Comparative Physiological Psychology*, **54**, 368–374.

Roth, D., & Ingram, R. E. (1985). Factors in the self-deception questionnaire: Associations with depression. *Journal of Personality and Social Psychology*, **48**, 243–251.

Roth, D., & Rehm, L. P. (1980). Relationships among self-monitoring precesses, memory, and depression. *Cognitive Therapy and Research*, **4**, 149–157.

Rothbart, M. K., & Derryberry, D. (1981). Development of individual differences in temperament. In M. E. Lamb & A. L. Brown (Eds.), *Advances in developmental psychology* (Vol. 1, pp. 37–86). Hillsdale, New Jersey: Erlbaum.

Roy-Byrne, P. P., & Katon, W. (1987). An update on treatment of the anxiety disorders. *Hospital and Community Psychiatry*, **38**, 835–843.

Royce, J. R., & Mos, L. P. (1980). *Psycho-epistemological profile manual*. Edmonton, Canada: University of Alberta Press.

Rudy, T. E., & Merluzzi, T. V. (1984). Recovering social cognitive schemata: Descriptions and applications of multidimensional scaling for clinical research. In P. C. Kendall (Ed.), *Advances in cognitive-behavioral research and therapy*. (Vol. 3, pp. 61–102). New York: Academic Press.

Ruesch, J., & Bateson, G. (1968). *Communication: The social matrix of psychiatry*. New York: Norton.

Rumelhart, D. E. (1975). Notes on a schema for stories. In D. G. Bobrow & A. M. Collins (Eds.), *Representation and understanding: Studies in cognitive science*. (pp. 211–236). New York: Academic Press.

Rumelhart, D. E., Hinton, G. E., & Williams, R. J. (1986a). Learning internal representations by backpropagating errors. *Nature*, **323**, 533–536.

Rumelhart, D. E., Hinton, G. E., & Williams, R. J. (1986b). Learning internal representations by error propogation. In D. E. Rumelhart & J. L. McClelland (Eds.), *Parallel distributed processing: Explorations in the microstructure of cognition* (Vol. 1, *Foundations*, pp. 318–362). Cambridge: MIT Press.

Rumelhart, D. E., & McClelland, J. L. (Eds.) (1986a). *Parallel distributed processing: Explorations in the microstructure of cognition* (Vol. 1, *Foundations*). Cambridge: MIT Press.

Rumelhart, D. E., & McClelland, J. L. (1986b). PDP models and general issues in cognitive science. In D. E. Rumelhart & J. L. McClelland (Eds.), *Parallel distributed processing: Explorations in the microstructure of cognition* (Vol. 1, *Foundations*, pp. 110–146). Cambridge: MIT Press.

Rumelhart, D. E., & McClelland, J. L. (1986c). On learning the past tense of English verbs. In J. L. McClelland & D. E. Rumelhart (Eds.), *Parallel distributed processing: Explorations in the microstructure of cognition* (Vol. 2, *Psychological and biological models*, pp. 216–271). Cambridge: MIT Press.

Rumelhart, D. E., Smolensky, P., McClelland, J. L., & Hinton, G. E. (1986c). Schemata and sequential thought processes in PDP models. In J. L. McClelland & D. E. Rumelhart (Eds.), *Parallel distributed processing: Explorations in the microstructure of cognition* (Vol. 2, *Psychological and biological processes*, pp. 7–57). Cambridge: MIT Press.

Russo, J., & Prinz, P. N. (1984). Memory, attention, and functional status in community-residing Alzheimer type dementia patients and optimally healthy aged individuals. *Journal of Gerontology*, **39**, 58–64.

Rutschmann, J., Cornblatt, B., & Erlenmeyer-Kimling L. (1977). Sustained attention in children at risk for schizophrenia. *Archives of General Psychiatry*, **34**, 571–575.

Rutter, D. R. (1979). The reconstruction of schizophrenic speech. *British Journal of Psychiatry*, **134**, 356–359.

Ryle, G. (1949). *The concept of mind*. London: Hutchinson.

Sacco, W. P. (1981). Invalid use of the Beck depression inventory to identify depressed college students: A methodological comment. *Cognitive Therapy and Research*, **5**, 143–147.

Sackeim, H. R. (1983). Self-deception, self-esteem, and depression: The adaptive value of lying to oneself. In J. Masling (Ed.), *Empirical studies of psychoanalytic theory*. Hillsdale, New Jersey: Erlbaum.

Sacks, O. (1971). *Migraine: The evolution of a common disorder*. London: Faber. (Reprinted and abridged, 1973.)

Sacks, O. (1976). *Awakenings* (rev. ed.). Harmondworth: Pelican.

Sacks, O. (1990). Neurology and the soul. *New York Review of Books, 22 Nov,* 44–50.

Safran, J. D., & Greenberg, L. S. (1987). Affect and the unconscious: A cognitive perspective. In R. Stern (Ed.), *Theories of the unconscious and theories of the self* (pp. 191–212). Hillsdale, New Jersey: Erlbaum.

Sagar, H. J., Cohen, N. J., Sullivan, E. V., Corkin, S. and Growdon, J. H. (1988). Remote memory function in Alzheimer's disease and Parkinson's disease. *Brain,* **111,** 185–206.

Sahakian, B., Morris, R., Evenden, J., Heald, A., Levy, R., Philpot, M., & Robbins, T. (1988). A comparative study of visuospatial memory and learning in Alzheimer-type dementia and Parkinson's disease. *Brain,* **111,** 695–718.

Salkovskis, P. M. (1987). Obsessive and intrusive thoughts: Clinical and non-clinical aspects. In P. M. G. Emmelkamp, F. W. Kraaimaat, W. T. A. M. Everaerd, & M. J. van Son (Eds.), *Fresh perspectives on anxiety disorders*. Amsterdam: Swets & Zeitlinger.

Salkovskis, P. M., & Clark, D. M. (1990). Affective responses to hyperventilation: A test of the cognitive model of panic. *Behavior Research and Therapy,* **28,** 51–61.

Salkovskis, P. M., & Warwick, H. M. C. (1988). Cognitive therapy of obsessive-compulsive disorder. In C. Perris, I. M. Blackburn, & H. Perris (Eds.), *The theory and practice of cognitive therapy*. Heidelberg: Springer.

Salmon, D. P., Shimamura, A. P., Butters, N., & Smith, S. (1988). Lexical and semantic priming deficits in patients with Alzheimer's disease. *Journal of Clinical and Experimental Neuropsychology,* **10,** 477–494.

Salzinger, K., Portnoy, S., & Feldman, R. S. (1964). Verbal behavior of schizophrenic and normal subjects. *Annals of the New York Academy of Sciences,* **105,** 845–860.

Salzinger, K., Portnoy, S., Pisoni, D. B., & Feldman, R. S. (1970). The immediacy hypothesis and response-produced stimuli in schizophrenic speech. *Journal of Abnormal Psychology,* **76(2),** 258–264.

Salzman, L. (1985). *Treatment of the obsessive personality*. New York: Aronson.

Sampson, E. E. (1978). Scientific paradigms and social values: Wanted—a scientific revolution. *Journal of Personality and Social Psychology,* **36,** 1332–1343.

Sanderson, W. C., & Barlow, D. H. (1990). A description of patients diagnosed with DSM-III-R generalized anxiety disorder. *Journal of Nervous and Mental Disease,* **178,** 588–591.

Sano, M. (1988). Using computers to understand attention in the elderly. *American Behavioral Scientist,* **31,** 588–594.

Sano, M., Rosen, W., & Mayeux, R. (1984). *Attention deficits in Alzheimer's disease*. Washington, D.C.: American Psychiatric Association.

Sarason, I. G. (1961). The effects of anxiety and threat on the solution of a difficult task. *Journal of Abnormal and Social Psychology,* **62,** 165–168.

Sarbin, T. R. (1964). Anxiety: The reification of a metaphor. *Archives of General Psychiatry,* **10,** 630–638.

Sarbin, T. R. (1968). Ontology recapitulates philology: The mythic nature of anxiety. *American Psychologist,* **23,** 411–418.

Sarbin, T. R., & Coe, W. C. (1979). Hypnosis and psychopathology: Replacing old myths with fresh metaphors. *Journal of Abnormal Psychology,* **88,** 506–528.

Sarbin, T. R., & Mancuso, J. C. (1980). *Schizophrenia: Medical diagnosis or verdict?* Elmsford, New York: Pergamon.

Sawaguchi, T., & Goldman-Rakic, P. S. (1991). D1 dopamine receptors in prefrontal cortex: Involvement in working memory. *Science*, **251**, 947–251.

Scarborough, D. L., Gerard, L., & Cortese, C. (1979). Accessing lexical memory: The transfer of word repetition effects across task and modality. *Memory and Cognition*, **7**, 3–12.

Schacht, T. E., & Black, D. A. (1985). Epistemological commitments of behavioral and psychoanalytic therapists. *Professional Psychology: Research and Practice*, **16**, 316–323.

Schacter, D. L. (1962). Memory. In M. I. Posner (Ed.), *The foundations of cognitive science*. (pp. 683–726). Cambridge: MIT Press.

Schacter, D. L. (1983). Amnesia observed: Remembering and forgetting in a natural environment. *Journal of Abnormal Psychology*, **92**, 236–242.

Schacter, D. L. (1987). Implicit memory: History and current status. *Journal of Experimental Psychology: Learning, Memory, and Cognition*, **13**, 501–518.

Schacter, D. L. (1990). Toward a cognitive neuropsychology of awareness: Implicit knowledge and anosognosia. *Journal of Clinical and Experimental Neuropsychology*, **12**, 155–178.

Schacter, D. L. (1990). Perceptual representation systems and implicit memory: Toward a resolution of the multiple memory systems debate. In A. Diamond (Ed.), *Development and neural bases of higher cognition*. (pp. 543–571). New York: New York Academy of Sciences Press.

Schacter, D. L., & Graf, P. (1986). Effects of elaborative processing on implicit and explicit memory for new associations. *Journal of Experimental Psychology: Learning, Memory, and Cognition*, **12**, 432–444.

Schacter, D. L., & Kihlstrom, J. F. (1989). Functional amnesia. In F. Boller & J. Grafman (Eds.), *Handbook of neuropsychology* (Vol. 3, pp. 209–231). Amsterdam: Elsevier Science.

Schacter, D. L., & Tulving, E. (1982). Amnesia and memory research. In L. S. Cermak (Ed.), *Human memory and amnesia*. (pp. 1–32). Hillsdale, New Jersey: Erlbaum.

Schacter, D. L., Wang, P. L., Tulving, E., & Friedman, M. (1982). Functional retrograde amnesia: A quantitative case study. *Neuropsychologia*, **20**, 523–532.

Schaeffer, B., & Wallace, R. (1970). The comparison of word meanings. *Journal of Experimental Psychology*, **86**, 144–152.

Schafer, R. (1976). *A new language for psychoanalysis*. New Haven, Connecticut: Yale University Press.

Schaffer, H. R. (1984). *The child's entry into a social world*. London: Academic Press.

Schank, R. C. (1982). *Dynamic memory*. New York: Cambridge University Press.

Schank, R. C., & Abelson, R. P. (1977). *Scripts, plans, goals and understanding*. Hillsdale, New Jersey: Erlbaum.

Scheider, J. S. (1984). Basal ganglia role in behavior: Importance of sensory gating and its relevance to psychiatry. *Biological Psychiatry*, **19**, 1693–1710.

Schiller, P. H. (1985). A model for the generation of visually guided saccadic eye movements. In D. Rose & V. G. Dobson (Eds.), *Models of the visual cortex*. Chicester: John Wiley & Sons.

Schneider, J. S., Levine, M. S., Hull, C. D., & Buchwald, N. A. (1984). Effects of amphetamine on intracellular responses of caudate neurons in the cat. *Journal of Neuroscience*, **4**, 930–938.

Schneider, W., & Shiffrin, R. M. (1977). Controlled and automatic human information processing: I. Detection, search, and attention. *Psychological Review*, **84**, 1–66.

Schneiderman, S. (1983). *Jacques Lacan: The death of an intellectual hero*. Cambridge: Harvard University Press.

Schwartz, S. (1982). Is there a schizophrenic language? *The Behavioral and Brain Sciences*, **5**, 579–626.

Searle, J. R. (1990). Consciousness, explanatory inversion, and cognitive science. *Behavioral and Brain Science*, **13**, 585–642.

Segal, Z. V. (1988). Appraisal of the self-schemata construct in cognitive models of depression. *Psychological Bulletin*, **103**, 147–162.

Segal, Z. V., Hood, J. E., Shaw, B. F., & Higgins, E. T. (1988). A structural analysis of the self-schema construct in major depression. *Cognitive Therapy and Research*, **12**, 471–485.

Segal, Z. V., & Shaw, B. F. (1986). Cognition in depression: A reappraisal of Coyne and Gotlib's critique. *Cognitive Therapy and Research*, **10**, 671–693.

Segal, Z. V., & Vella, D. D. (1990). Self-schema in major depression: Replication and extension of a priming methodology. *Cognitive Therapy and Research*, **14**, 161–176.

Seidenberg, M. S., & McClelland, J. L. (1989). A distributed, developmental model of word recognition and naming. *Psychological Review*, **96**, 523–568.

Seligman, M. E. P., Abramson, L. Y., Semmel, A., & von Baeyer, C. (1979). Depressive attributional style. *Journal of Abnormal Psychology*, **88**, 242–247.

Selye, H. (1982). History and present status of the stress concept. In L. Goldberger & S. Breznitz (Eds.), *Handbook of stress: Theoretical and clinical aspects*. New York: The Free Press.

Senf, G. (1986). LD research in sociological and scientific perspective. In J. K. Torgesen & B. Y. L. Wong (Eds.), *Psychological and educational perspectives on learning disabilities*, (pp. 27–53). New York: Academic Press.

Servan-Schreiber, D. (1990). *From physiology to behavior: Computational models of catecholamine modulation of information processing*. Ph.D. Thesis. Tech. Rep. CMU-CS-90-167. Pittsburgh, Pennsylvania: Carnegie Mellon University, School of Computer Science.

Servan-Schreiber, D., Cleeremans, A., & McClelland, J. L. (1991). Graded state machines: The representation of temporal contingencies in simple recurrent networks. *Machine Learning*, **7**, 161–193.

Servan-Schreiber, D., Printz, H. W., & Cohen, J. D. (1990). A network model of catecholamine effects: Gain, signal-to-noise ratio, and behaviour. *Science*, **249**, 892–895.

Shakespeare, W. (1981). Macbeth. In A. Harbage (Ed.), *Complete Pelican Shakespeare: The tragedies*. Harmondsworth: Penguin. (Original work published 1623.)

Shakow, D. (1962). Segmental set: A theory of the formal psychological deficit in schizophrenia. *Archives of General Psychiatry*, **6**, 1–17.

Shallice, T. (1988). *From neuropsychology to mental structure*. Cambridge: Cambridge University Press.

Shankweiler, D., & Crain, S. (1986). Language mechanisms and reading disorder: A modular approach. *Cognition*, **24**, 139–168.

Shannon, C. E. (1938). *A symbolic analysis of relay and switching circuits*. Master's thesis. Cambridge: MIT. *Transactions of the American Institute of Electrical Engineers*, **57**, 1–11.

Sheehan, D. V. (1984). Delineation of anxiety and phobic disorders responsive to monoamine oxidase inhibitors: Implications for classification. *Journal of Clinical Psychiatry* **45**, 29–36.

Sheperd, G. M. (1988). *Neurobiology*. Oxford: Oxford University Press.

Shevrin, H. (1988). Unconscious conflict: A convergent psychodynamic and electrophysiological approach. In M. J. Horowitz (Ed.), *Psychodynamics and cognition*. (pp. 117–168). Chicago: University of Chicago Press.

Shiffrin, R. M., & Schneider, W. (1977). Controlled and automatic human information processing: II. Perceptual learning, automatic attending and a general theory. *Psychological Review*, **84**, 127–190.

Shiffrin, R. M., & Schneider, W. (1984). Controlled and automatic processing revisited. *Psychological Review*, **91**, 269–276.

Shoham-Salomon, V., Avner, R., & Neeman, R. (1989). You're changed if you do and changed if you don't: Mechanisms underlying paradoxical interventions. *Journal of Consulting and Clinical Psychology*, **57**, 590–598.

Shoham-Salomon, V., & Bootzin, R. (1990). *Outcome and process analysis of therapeutic paradoxes.* Grant Submission # 1001MH47451-01.

Shoham-Salomon, V., & Rosenthal, R. (1987). Paradoxical interventions: A meta-analysis. *Journal of Consulting and Clinical Psychology,* **55**, 22–28.

Sidis, B. (1902). *Psychopathological researches: Studies in mental dissociation.* New York: Stechert.

Sidis, B., & Goodhart, S. P. (1904). *Multiple personality: An experimental investigation into the nature of human individuality.* New York: Appleton.

Siever, L. J., Klar, H., & Coccaro, E. F. (1985). Psychobiologic substrates of personality. In H. Klar & L. J. Siever (Eds.), *Biologic response styles: Clinical implications.* (pp. 37–66). Washington D.C.: American Psychiatric Press.

Silberman, E. K., Putnam, F. W., Weingartner, H., Braun, B. G., & Post, R. M. (1985). Dissociative states in multiple personality disorder: A quantitative study. *Psychiatry Research,* **15**, 253–260.

Silverman, L. H. (1983). The subliminal psychodynamic activation method: Overview and comprehensive listing of studies. In J. Masling (Ed.), *Empirical studies of psychoanalytic theories* Vol. 1. Hillsdale, New Jersey: Erlbaum.

Simon, H. A. (1967). Motivational and emotional controls of cognition. *Psychological Review,* **74**, 29–39.

Simon, H. A. (1983). *Reason in human affairs.* Stanford, California: Stanford University Press.

Ska, B., Poissant, A., & Joanette, Y. (1990). Line orientation judgment in normal elderly and subjects with dementia of the Alzheimer's type. *Journal of Clinical and Experimental Neuropsychology,* **12**, 695–702.

Skinner, B. F. (1957). *Verbal behavior.* New York: Appleton-Century-Crofts.

Skinner, B. F. (1974). *About behaviorism.* New York: Knopf.

Slap, J. W., & Saykin, A. J. (1983). The schema: Basic concept in a nonmetapsychological model of the mind. *Psychoanalysis and Contemporary Thought,* **6**, 305–325.

Slife, D. B., Miura, S., Thompson, L. W., Shapiro, J. L., & Gallagher, D. (1984). Differential recall as a function of mood disorder in clinically depressed patients: Between and within subject differences. *Journal of Abnormal Psychology,* **93**, 391–400.

Slingerland, B. (1976). *A multisensory approach to language arts.* Cambridge, Massachusetts: Educators Publishing Service.

Sloman, A. (1987). Motives, mechanisms and emotions. *Cognition and Emotion,* **1**, 217–233.

Smith, C. R. (1991). *Learning disabilities: The interaction of learner, task, and setting.* Boston: Allyn and Bacon.

Smith, E. E. (1962). Concepts and induction. In M. I. Posner (Ed.), *The foundations of cognitive science.* (pp. 501–526). Cambridge: MIT Press.

Smith, F. (1973). *Psycholinguistics and reading.* New York: Holt, Rinehart & Winston.

Smith, S. T., Macaruso, P., Shankweiler, D., & Crain, S. (1989). Syntactic comprehension in young poor readers. *Applied Psycholinguistics,* **10**, 429–454.

Snyder, M., & White, P. (1982). Moods and memories: Elation, depression, and the remembering of events of one's life. *Journal of Personality,* **50**, 149–167.

Sorrentino, R. M., & Higgins, E. T. (Eds.) (1986). *Handbook of motivation and cognition: Foundations of social behavior.* New York: Guilford Press.

Southworth, S., & Kirsch, I. (1988). The role of expectancy in exposure-generated fear reduction in agoraphobia. *Behavior Research and Therapy,* **26**, 113–120.

Spear, L. C., & Sternberg, R. J. (1987). An information-processing framework for understanding reading disability. In S. J. Ceci (Ed.), *Handbook of cognitive, social, and neuropsychological aspects of learning disabilities* (Vol. 2, pp. 3–31). Hillsdale, New Jersey: Erlbaum.

Spelke, E. (1988). On the origins of physical knowledge. In L. Weiskrantz (Ed.), *Thought without language.* Oxford: Oxford University Press.

Spence, D. P. (1982). *Narrative truth and historical truth: Meaning and interpretation in psychoanalysis.* New York: Norton.

Spiegel, D., & Cardena, E. (1991). Disintegrated experience: The dissociative disorders revisited. *Journal of Abnormal Psychology*, **100**, 366–378.

Spitzer, H., Desimone, R., & Moran, J. (1988). Increased attention enhances both behavioural and neuronal performance. *Science*, **240**, 338–340.

Spitzer, R. L., Endicott, J., & Robins, E. (1978). *Research diagnostic criteria (RDC) for a selected group of functional disorders* (3rd ed.). New York: New York State Psychiatric Institute.

Spohn, H. E., Lacoursiere, R. B., Thomson, K., & Coyne, L. (1977). Phenothiazine effects on psychological and psychophysiological dysfunction in chronic schizophrenics. *Archives of General Psychiatry*, **34**, 633–644.

Squire, L. R., & Zola-Morgan, S. (1991). The medial temporal lobe memory system. *Science*, **253**, 1380–1386.

Stam, H. J., Rogers, T. B., & Gergen, K. J. (Eds.) (1987). *The analysis of psychological theory: Metapsychological perspectives.* New York: Hemisphere.

Stampfl, T. G., & Levis, D. G. (1967). The essentials of implosive therapy: A learning-theory based psychodynamic behavioral theory. *Journal of Abnormal Psychology*, **72**, 496–503.

Stanovich, K. E. (1986a). Cognitive processes and the reading problems of learning disabled children: Evaluating the assumption of specificity. In J. K. Torgesen & B. Y. L. Wong (Eds.), *Psychological and educational perspectives on learning disabilities.* (pp. 87–131). New York: Academic Press.

Stanovich, K. E. (1986b). Matthew effects in reading: Some consequences of individual differences in the acquisition of literacy. *Reading Research Quarterly*, **XXI**, 360–406.

Stechler, G., & Latz, E. (1966). Some observations on attention and arousal in the human infant. *Journal of the American Academy of Child Psychiatry*, **5**, 517–525.

Stein, D. J. (1992a). *Psychoanalysis and cognitive science: Contrasting models of the mind. Journal of the American Academy of Psychoanalysis.* (in press).

Stein, D. J. (1992b). *Cognitive science and clinical knowledge.* Integrative Psychiatry (in press).

Stein, D. J. (1992). Schemas in the cognitive and clinical sciences: An integrative construct. *Journal of Psychotherapy Integration.*, **2**, 45–63.

Stein, D. J., Shoulberg, N., Helton, K., & Hollander, E. (1992). A neuroethological model of OCD: Acral lick dermatitis. *Comprehensive Psychiatry.* (in press).

Stein, M., Miller, A. H., & Trestman, R. L. (1991). Depression and the immune system. In R. Ader, D. L. Felten, & N. Cohen (Eds.), *Psychoneuroimmunology* (2nd ed., pp. 897–930). San Diego: Academic Press.

Steinberg, M. (1991). *Systematizing dissociation: Symptomatology and diagnostic assessment.* Unpublished manuscript. New Haven, Connecticut: Yale University.

Steinberg, M., Rounsaville, B., & Cicchetti, D. (1990). The structured clinical interview for DSM-IIIR dissociative disorders: Preliminary report on a new diagnostic instrument. *American Journal of Psychiatry*, **147**, 76–82.

Stern, D. (1985). *The interpersonal world of the infant.* New York: Basic Books.

Sternberg, R. J. (1985). *Beyond IQ: A triarchic theory of human intelligence.* New York: Cambridge University Press.

Sternberg, R. J. (1986). *Intelligence applied: Understanding and increasing your intellectual skills.* San Diego: Harcourt, Brace, Jovanovich.

Sternberg, R. J. (1988a). *The triarchic mind: A new theory of human intelligence.* New York: Viking.

Sternberg, R. J. (1988b). Mental self-government: A theory of intellectual styles and their development. *Human Development*, **31**, 197–224.

Sternberg, R. J., & Wagner, R. K. (1982). Automatization failure in learning disabilities. *Topics in Learning and Learning Disabilities*, **2**, 1–11.

Stillings, N. A., Feinstein, M. H., Garfield, J. L., Rissland, E. L., Rosenbaum, D. A., Weisler, S. E., & Baker-Ward, L. (1987). *Cognitive science: An introduction.* Cambridge: MIT Press.

Stinson, C. H., & Palmer, S. E. (1991). Parallel distributed processing models of person schemas and psychopathologies. In M. J. Horowitz (Ed.), *Person schemas and maladaptive interpersonal patterns* (pp. 339–378). Chicago: University of Chicago Press.

Strauss, A. A., & Lehtinen, L. (1947). *Psychopathology and education of the brain-injured child.* New York: Grune and Stratton.

Strauss, M. E. (1975). Strong meaning-response bias in schizophrenia. *Journal of Abnormal Psychology,* **84(3)**, 293–298.

Street, L. L., Craske, M. G., & Barlow, D. H. (1989). Sensation, cognitions and the perception of cues associated with expected and unexpected panic attacks. *Behaviour Research and Therapy,* **27**, 189–198.

Strongman, K. T. (1987). *The psychology of emotion.* Chichester: Wiley.

Stroop, J. R. (1935). Studies of interference in serial verbal reactions. *Journal of Experimental Psychology,* **18**, 643–662.

Stuss, D. T., & Benson, D. F. (1984). Neuropsychological studies of the frontal lobes. *Psychological Bulletin,* **95**, 3–28.

Sullivan, E. V., Corkin, S., & Growdon, J. H. (1986). Verbal and nonverbal short-term memory in patients with Alzheimer's disease and in healthy elderly subjects. *Developmental Neuropsychology,* **2**, 387–400.

Sunderland, T., Hill, J. L., Mellow, A. M., Lawlor, B. A., Gundersheimer, J., Newhouse, P., & Grafman, J. H. (1989). Clock drawing in Alzheimer's disease: A novel measure of dementia severity. *Journal of the American Geriatrics Society,* **37**, 725–729.

Sutton-Simon, K. (1980). Assessing belief systems: Concepts and strategies. In P. C. Kendall & S. D. Hollon (Eds.), *Assessment strategies for cognitive-behavioral interventions* (pp. 59–84). New York: Academic Press.

Swanson, D. R. (1977). A critique of psychic energy as an explanatory concept. *Journal of the American Psychoanalytic Association,* **25**, 603–633.

Szasz, T. (1961). *The myth of mental illness: Foundations of a theory of personal conduct.* New York: Hoeber & Harper.

Szasz, T. (1970). *The manufacture of madness: A comparative study of the Inquisition and the mental health movement.* New York: Harper & Row.

Tait, R., & Silver, R. C. (1989). Coming to terms with major negative life events. In J. S. Uleman & J. A. Bargh (Eds.), *Unintended thought.* (pp. 351–382). New York: Guilford.

Tasman, A. (1991). *Psychiatric update* (Vol. 10). Washington, D.C.: American Psychiatric Association.

Tataryn, D., Nadel, L., & Jacobs, W. J. (1989). Cognitive therapy and cognitive science. In A. Freeman, K. S. Simon, H. Arkowitz, & L. Beutler (Eds.), *A handbook of cognitive therapy* (pp. 83–98). Cambridge: MIT Press.

Taylor, E. (1982). *William James on exceptional mental states: The 1896 Lowell lectures.* New York: Scribner's.

Taylor, M. B., & Williams, J. P. (1983). Comprehension of learning disabled readers: Task and text variations. *Journal of Educational Psychology,* **75**, 584–601.

Taylor, S. E., & Brown, J. D. (1988). Illusion and well-being: A social psychological perspective on mental health. *Psychological Bulletin,* **103**, 193–210.

Taylor, S. E., & Crocker, J. (1981). Schematic bases of social information processing. In E. T. Higgins, C. P. Herman, & M. P. Zanna (Eds.), *Social cognition. The Ontario symposium on personality and social psychology.* Hillsdale, New Jersey: Erlbaum.

Teasdale, J. D. (1983a). Affect and accessibility. In D. E. Broadbent (Ed.), *Functional aspects of memory.* London: The Royal Society.

Teasdale, J. D. (1983b). Negative thinking in depression: Cause, effect or reciprocal relationship? *Advances in Behavior Research and Therapy,* **5**, 3–25.

Teasdale, J. D. (1985). Psychological treatments for depression: How do they work? *Behavioral Research and Therapy,* **23**, 157–165.

Teasdale, J. D., & Dent, J. (1987). Cognitive vulnerability to depression: An investigation of two hypotheses. *British Journal of Clinical Psychology*, **26**, 113–126.

Teasdale, J. D., & Fogarty, S. J. (1979). Differential effects of induced mood on retrieval of pleasant and unpleasant events from episodic memory. *Journal of Abnormal Psychology*, **88**, 248–257.

Teasdale, J. D., & Russell, M. L. (1983). Differential effects of induced mood on the recall of positive, negative, and neutral words. *British Journal of Clinical Psychology*, **22**, 163–171.

Teasdale, J. D., & Taylor, R. (1981). Induced mood and accessibility of memories: An effect of mood state or of induction procedure? *British Journal of Clinical Psychology*, **20**, 39–48.

Teasdale, J. D., Taylor, R., & Fogarty, S. (1980). Effects of induced elation–depression on the accessibility of happy and unhappy experiences. *Behavior Research and Therapy*, **18**, 339–346.

Tennes, K., Emde, R., Kisley, A., & Metcalf, D. (1972). The stimulus barrier in early infancy: An exploration of some formulations of John Benjamin. In R. R. Holt & E. Peterfreund (Eds.), *Psychoanalysis and contemporary science*. New York: MacMillan.

Theodor, L. H., & Mandelcorn, M. S. (1973). Hysterical blindness: A case report and study using a modern psychophysical technique. *Journal of Abnormal Psychology*, **82**, 552–553.

Thomas, A., & Chess, S. (1984). Genesis and evolution of behavioral disorders, from infancy to early adult life. *American Journal of Psychiatry*, **141**, 1–9.

Thoren, P., Asberg, M., Bertillson, L., Mellstrom, B., Pharm, M., Sjoqvist, F., & Traskman, L. (1980). Clomipramine treatment of obsessive–compulsive disorder. II. Biochemical aspects. *Archives of General Psychiatry*, **37**, 1289–1294.

Thorndyke, P. W., & Hayes-Roth, B. (1979). The use of schemata in the acquisition and transference of knowledge. *Cognitive Psychology*, **11**, 82–106.

Thyer, B. A. (1987). *Treating anxiety disorders: A guide for human service professionals*. Beverley Hills, California: Sage.

Tomkins, S. S., & Messick, S. (1963). *Computer simulation of personality: Frontier of psychological theory*. New York: Wiley.

Torgesen, J. K., & Goldman, T. (1977). Verbal rehearsal and short-term memory in reading-disabled children. *Child Development*, **48**, 56–60.

Tosi, D. J., & Eshbaugh, D. M. (1980). Rational stage-directed therapy and crisis intervention. In R. Herink (Ed.), *The psychotherapy handbook* (pp. 550–553). New York: New American Library.

Treiman, R. (1991). The role of intrasyllabic units in learning to read. In L. Rieben and C. A. Perfetti (Eds.), *Learning to read: Basic research and its implications*. (pp. 149–160). Hillsdale, New Jersey: Erlbaum.

Tulving, E. (1972). Episodic and semantic memory. In E. Tulving & W. Donaldson (Eds.), *Organization of memory*. (pp. 381–403). New York: Academic Press.

Tulving, E. (1979). Relation between encoding specificity and levels of processing. In L. S. Cermak & F. I. M. Craik (Eds.), *Levels of processing in human memory*. (pp. 405–428). Hillsdale, New Jersey: Erlbaum.

Tulving, E. (1983). *Elements of episodic memory*. New York: Oxford University Press.

Tulving, E., & Schachter, D. L. (1990). Priming and human memory systems. *Science*, **247**, 301–305.

Tulving, E., Shachter, D. L., & Stark, H. A. (1982). Priming effects in word-fragment completion are independent of recognition memory. *Journal of Experimental Psychology: Learning, Memory, and Cognition*, **8**, 336–342.

Tulving, E., & Thompson, D. M. (1973). Encoding specificity and retrieval processes in episodic memory. *Psychological Review*, **80**, 352–373.

Tunmer, W. E. (1991). Phonological awareness and literacy acquisition. In L. Rieben and C. A. Perfetti (Eds.), *Learning to read: Basic research and its implications*. (pp. 105–119). Hillsdale, New Jersey: Erlbaum.

Turing, A. M. (1936). On computable numbers, with an application to the Entscheidungs-Problem. *Proceedings of the London Mathematical Society*, **42**, 230–265.

Turing, A. M. (1950). Computing machinery and intelligence. *Mind*, **59**, 236.

Turk, D. C., & Salovey, P. (1985). Cognitive structures, cognitive processes, and cognitive-behavior modification. I. Client issues. *Cognitive Therapy and Research*, **9**, 1–17.

Turk, D. C., & Speers, M. A. (1983). Cognitive schemata and cognitive processes in cognitive-behavioral interventions: going beyond the information given. In P. C. Kendall (Ed.), *Advances in cognitive-behavioral research and therapy*. (Vol. 2, pp. 1–31). New York: Academic Press.

Turner, S. M. (1984). *Behavioral theories and treatment of anxiety*. New York: Plenum.

Turner, S. M., & Turkat, I. D. (1988). Behavior therapy and the personality disorders. *Journal of Personality Disorders*, **2**, 342–349.

Tversky, M. T., & Kahneman, D. (1974). Judgment under uncertainty: Heuristics and biases. *Science*, **185**, 1124–1131.

Tversky, M. T., & Kahneman, D. (1983). Extensional vs. intuitive reasoning: The conjunction fallacy in probability judgment. *Psychological Review*, **90**, 293–315.

Uleman, J. S., & Bargh, J. A. (Eds.) (1989). *Unintended thought*. New York: Guilford Press.

Vaihinger, H. (1924). *The philosophy of 'as if'*. London: Routledge & Kegan Paul. (Original work published 1911.)

Vallar, G., & Baddeley, A. D. (1982). Short-term forgetting and the articulatory loop. *Quarterly Journal of Experimental Psychology*, **34(A)**, 53–60.

Van den Bergh, O., Vrana, S., Eelen, P. (1990). Letters from the heart: Affective categorization of letter combinations in typists and nontypists. *Journal of Experimental Psychology: Learning, Memory and Cognition*, **16**, 1153–1161.

Van den Bout, J., Cohen, L., Groen, P., & Kramer, H. (1987). Depression and attributional cognitions for hypothetical and stressful events in mental health center patients. *Cognitive Therapy and Research*, **11**, 625–633.

VanLehn, K. (1962). Problem solving and cognitive skill acquisition. In M. I. Posner (Ed.), *The foundations of cognitive science*. (pp. 527–580). Cambridge: MIT Press.

Varela, F. J. (1986). *The science and technology of cognition: Emergent directions*. Florence: Hopeful Monster.

Veith, I. (1965). *Hysteria: The history of a disease*. Chicago: University of Chicago Press.

Vellutino, F. R. (1979). *Dyslexia: Theory and research*. Cambridge: MIT Press.

Vellutino, F. R., & Scanlon, D. M. (1987). Phonological coding, phonological awareness, and reading ability: Evidence from a longitudinal and experimental study. *Merrill-Palmer Quarterly*, **33**, 321–363.

Vellutino, F. R., & Scanlon, D. M. (1991). The effects of instructional bias on word identification. In L. Rieben and C. A. Perfetti (Eds.), *Learning to read: Basic research and its implications*. (pp. 189–203). Hillsdale, New Jersey: Erlbaum.

Velmans, M. (1991). Is human information processing conscious? *Behavioral and Brain Science*, **14**, 651–669.

Velten, E. (1968). A laboratory test for induction of mood states. *Behaviour Research and Therapy*, **6**, 473–482.

Vico, G. (1948). *The new science*. (Trans. by T. G. Bergin & M. H. Fisch). Ithaca, New York: Cornell University Press. (Original work published 1725.)

Vinter, A. (1986). The role of movement in eliciting early imitations. *Child Development*, **57**, 66–71.

Vitaliano, P. P., Breen, A. R., Albert, M. S., Watkins, M. J., Watkins, O. C., Craik, F. I. M., & Mazuryk, G. (1973). Effect of nonverbal distraction on short-term storage. *Journal of Experimental Psychology*, **101**, 296–300.

von Hartmann, E. (1869). *Philosophie des Unbewussten*. Berlin: Duncker.

Von Hofsten, C. (1984). Developmental changes in the organisation of prereaching movements. *Developmental Psychology*, **20**, 378–388.

Von Neumann, J. (1958). *The computer and the brain.* New Haven, Connecticut: Yale University Press.

Vredenberg, K., & Krames, L. (1983). *Memory scanning in depression: The disruptive effects of cognitive schemas.* Paper presented at the meeting of the American Psychological Association, Anaheim, California.

Wachtel, P. L. (1977). *Psychoanalysis and behavior therapy: Toward an integration.* New York, Basic Books.

Wagner, A. R. (1971). Elementary associations. In H. H. Kendler & J. T. Spence (Eds.), *Essays in neobehaviorism: A memorial volume to Kenneth W. Spence* (pp. 187–213). New York: Appleton-Century-Crofts.

Wagner, A. R., & Rescorla, R. A. (1972). Inhibition in Pavlovian conditioning: Applications of a theory. In M. S. Halliday & R. A. Boakes (Eds.), *Inhibition and learning* (pp. 301–336). London: Academic Press.

Wagner, R. K., & Torgesen, J. K. (1987). The nature of phonological processing and its causal role in the acquisition of reading skills. *Psychological Bulletin,* **2,** 1–21.

Wapner, S., & Krus, D. M. (1960). Effects of lysergic acid diethylamide, and differences between normals and schizophrenics on the Stroop color-word test. *Journal of Neuropsychiatry,* **2,** 76–81.

Warren, R., Zgourides, G., & Englert, M. (1990). Relationships between catastrophic cognitions and body sensations in anxiety disordered, mixed diagnosis, and normal subjects. *Behaviour Research and Therapy,* **28,** 355–357.

Warren, R., Zgourides, G., & Jons, A. (1989). Cognitive bias and irrational belief as predictors of avoidance. *Behaviour Research and Therapy,* **27,** 181–188.

Warrington, E. K., & Weiskrantz, L. (1982). Amnesia: A disconnection syndrome? *Neuropsychologia,* **20,** 233–248.

Watkins, P. L., Lidren, D. M., & Champion, J. (1991). Panic in medical settings: Suggestions for interventions. *The Health Psychologist,* **13,** 2.

Watson, J. B., & Raynor, R. (1920). Conditioned emotional reactions. *Journal of Experimental Psychology,* **3,** 1–14.

Watts, F. N., McKenna, F. P., Sharrock, R., & Trezise, L. (1986). Colour naming of phobia related words. *British Journal of Psychology,* **77,** 97–108.

Watts, F. N., & Sharrock, R. (1985). Description and measurement of concentration problems in depressed patients. *Psychological Medicine,* **15,** 317–326.

Wechsler, D. (1945). A standardized memory scale for clinical use. *Journal of Psychology,* **19,** 87–95.

Wechsler, D. (1974). *Wechsler intelligence scale for children* (rev.). New York: The Psychological Corporation.

Wechsler, D. (1981). *Wechsler adult intelligence scale-revised.* New York: Psychological Corporation.

Weeks, S. J., & Hobson, P. R. (1987). The salience of facial expression for autistic children. *Journal of Child Psychology and Psychiatry,* **28,** 137–152.

Wegman, C. (1985). *Psychoanalysis and cognitive psychology: A formulation of Freud's earliest theory.* London: Academic Press.

Weimer, W. B. (1977). A conceptual framework for cognitive psychology: Motor theories of the mind. In R. Shaw & J. Bransford (Ed.), *Perceiving, acting, and knowing* (pp. 267–311). Hillsdale, New Jersey: Erlbaum.

Weimer, W. B. (1979). *Notes on the methodology of scientific research.* Hillsdale, New Jersey: Erlbaum.

Weimer, W. B., & Palermo, D. S. (1973). Paradigms and normal science in psychology. *Science Studies,* **3,** 211–244.

Weinberger, D. A., Schwartz, G. E., & Davidson, R. J. (1979). Low-anxious, high-anxious, and repressive coping styles: Psychometric patterns and behavioral and psychological responses to stress. *Journal of Abnormal Psychology,* **88,** 369–380.

Weinberger, D. R., Berman, K. F., & Chase, T. N. (1988). Mesocortical dopaminergic function and human cognition. *Annals of the New York Academy of Science* **537,** 330–338.

Weinberger, D. R., Berman, K. F., & Zec, R. F. (1986). Physiological dysfunction of dorsolateral prefrontal cortex in schizophrenia: I. Regional cerebral blood flow evidence. *Archives of General Psychiatry*, **43**, 114–125.

Weinberger, D. R., Bigelow, L. B., Kleinman, J. E., Klein, S. T., Rosenblatt, J. E., & Wyatt, R. J. (1980). Cerebral ventricular enlargement in chronic schizophrenia. *Archives of General Psychiatry*, **37**, 11–13.

Weingartner, H., Kaye, W., Smallberg, S. A., Ebert, H., Gillin, J. C., & Sitaram, N. (1981). Memory failures in progressive idiopathic dementia. *Journal of Abnormal Psychology*, **90**, 187–196.

Weiskrantz, L. (1986). *Blindsight: A case study and implications*. Oxford: Oxford University Press.

Weissman, M. M., Klerman, G. L., Markowitz, J. S., & Ouellette, R. (1989). Suicidal ideation and suicide attempts in panic disorder and attacks. *New England Journal of Medicine*, **321**, 1209–1214.

Weizenbaum, J. (1966). ELIZA—A computer program for the study of natural language communication between man and machine. *Communications of the Association for Computing Machinery*, **9**, 36–45.

Weizenbaum, J. (1976). *Computer power and human reason*. San Francisco: Freeman.

Wellman, H. M. (1985). The origins of metacognition. In D. L. Forrest-Pressley, G. E. MacKinnon, & T. G. Waller (Eds.), *Metacognition, cognition and human performance* (Vol. 1, *Theoretical perspectives*, pp. 1–32). New York: Academic Press.

Wells, G. (1981). Some antecedents of early educational attainment. *British Journal of Sociology of Education*, **2**, 181–200.

Weltman, G., Smith, J. E., & Egstrom, G. H. (1971). Perceptual narrowing during simulated pressure-chamber exposure. *Human Factors*, **13**, 99–107.

Wener, A. E., & Rehm, L. P. (1975). Depressive affect: A test of behavioral hypotheses. *Journal of Abnormal Psychology*, **84**, 221–227.

Wertheimer, M. (1938). Untersuchung zur Lehre von der Gestalt. (Translated and condensed as *Laws of organization in perceptual form*) In W. D. Ellis (Ed.), *A source book of gestalt psychology*. New York: Harcourt, Brace, & World.

Wessler, R. L., & Hankin-Wessler, S. W. R. (1987). Cognitive appraisal therapy. In W. Dryden & W. Golden (Eds.), *Cognitive-behavioral approaches to psychotherapy*. (pp. 196–223). London: Harper & Row.

Westen, D. (1988). Transference and information-processing. *Clinical Psychology Review*, **8**, 161–179.

Wetzel, C. D. (1975). Effect of orienting tasks and cue timing on the free recall of remember-and forget-cued words. *Journal of Experimental Psychology: Human Learning and Memory*, **1**, 556–566.

Wienberger, J., & Hardaway, R. (1991). Separating science from myth in subliminal psychodynamic activation. *Clinical Psychology Review*, **10**, 727–756.

Wiener, N. (1948). *Cybernetics, or control and communication in the animal and the machine*. Cambridge: MIT Press.

Wiessman, M. M., Markowitz, P. H., Ouellette, R., Greenwald, S., & Kahn, J. P. (1990). Panic disorder and cardiovascular/cerebrovascular problems: Results from a community survey. *American Journal of Psychiatry*, **147**, 1504–1508.

Wilensky, R. (1983). *Planning and understanding: A computational approach to human reasoning*. Reading, Massachusetts: Addison Wesley.

Williams, J. M. G. (1984). *The psychological treatment of depression: A guide to the theory and practice of cognitive behaviour therapy*. Beckenham: Groom-Helm.

Williams, J. M. G. (1992). *The psychological treatment of depression: A guide to the theory and practice of cognitive behaviour therapy* (2nd ed.). London: Routledge.

Williams, J. M. G., Watts, F. N., MacLeod, C., & Mathews, A. (1988). *Cognitive psychology and emotional disorders*. Chichester: John Wiley and Sons.

Wilson, R. S., Bacon, L. D., Fox, J. H., & Kaszniak, A. W. (1983). Primary and secondary memory in dementia of the Alzheimer's type. *Journal of Clinical Neuropsychology*, **5**, 337–344.

Wilson, R. S., Kaszniak, A. W., & Fox, J. H. (1981). Remote memory in senile dementia. *Cortex*, **17**, 41–48.

Wilson, W. R. (1979). Feeling more than we can know: Exposure effects without learning. *Journal of Personality and Social Psychology*, **37**, 811–821.

Wine, J. D. (1980). Cognitive-attentional theory of test anxiety. In I. Sarason (Ed.), *Test anxiety: Theory, research, and application*. Hillsdale, New Jersey: Erlbaum.

Winfrey, L. P. L., & Goldfried, M. R. (1986). Information processing and the human change process. In R. E. Ingram (Ed.), *Information processing approaches to clinical psychology* (pp. 241–258). New York: Academic Press.

Wing, J. K., Cooper, J. E., & Sartorius, N. (1974). *The description and classification of psychiatric symptoms: An instruction manual for the PSE and CATEGO system*. Cambridge: Cambridge University Press.

Wittgenstein, L. (1953). *Philosophical investigations*. Oxford: Blackwell.

Wolford, G., & Fowler, C. A. (1983). The perception and use of information in good and poor readers. In T. Tighe & B. Shepp (Eds.), *Perception, cognition, and development*. Hillsdale, New Jersey: Erlbaum.

Wolpe, J. (1958). *Psychotherapy by reciprocal inhibition*. Stanford, California: Stanford University Press.

Wong, B. Y. L. (1982). Strategic behaviors in selecting retrieval cues in gifted, normal achieving and learning disabled children. *Journal of Learning Disabilities*, **15**, 33–37.

Woodcock, R. W. (1973). *Woodcock reading mastery tests*. Circle Pines, Minnesota: American Guidance Service.

Woodward, A. E., Jr., Bjork, R. A., & Jongeward, R. H. (1973). Recall and recognition as a function of primary rehearsal. *Journal of Verbal Learning and Verbal Behavior*, **12**, 608–617.

Wysocki, J. J., & Sweet, J. J. (1985). Identification of brain-damaged, schizophrenic, and normal medical patients using a brief neuropsychological screening battery. *International Journal of Clinical Neuropsychology*, **7**(1), 40–49.

Young, E. J. (1990). *Cognitive therapy for personality disorders: A schema-focused approach*. Sarasota: Professional Resource Exchange.

Yussen, S. R. (1985). The role of metacognition in contemporary theories of cognitive development. In D. L. Forrest-Pressley, G. E. MacKinnon, & T. G. Waller (Eds.), *Metacognition, cognition and human performance* (Vol. 1, *Theoretical Perspectives*, pp. 253–284). New York: Academic Press.

Zimbardo, P. G. (1985). *Psychology and life*. Glenview, Illinois: Scott-Foresman.

Zipser, D., & Andersen, R. A. (1988). A back-progapation programmed network that simulates response properites of a subset of posterior parietal neurons. *Nature*, **331**, 679–684.

Zohar, J., & Insel, T. (1987). Obsessive–compulsive disorder: Psychobiological approaches to diagnosis, treatment, and pathophysiology. *Biological Psychiatry*, **22**, 667–687.

Zohar, J., Insel, T., Zohar-Kadouch, R., Hill, J., & Murphy, D. (1988). Serotonergic responsivity in obsessive–compulsive disorder. *Archives of General Psychiatry*, **45**, 167–172.

Zohar, J., Mueller, E. A., Insel, T. R., Zohar-Kadouch, R. C., & Murphy, D. L. (1987). Serotonergic responsivity in obsessive–compulsive disorder: Comparison of patients and healthy controls. *Archives of General Psychiatry*, **44**, 946–951.

Zucker, D., Taylor, C. B., Brouillard, M., Ehlers, A., Margraf, J., Telch, M., Roth, W. T., & Agras, W. S. (1989). Cognitive aspects of panic attacks: Content, course and relationship to laboratory stressors. *British Journal of Psychiatry*, **155**, 86–91.

Zuckerman, M. (1991). *Psychobiology of personality*. Cambridge: Cambridge University Press.

# Index